1 MONTH OF
FREE
READING

at
www.ForgottenBooks.com

By purchasing this book you are eligible for one month membership to ForgottenBooks.com, giving you unlimited access to our entire collection of over 1,000,000 titles via our web site and mobile apps.

To claim your free month visit: www.forgottenbooks.com/free776984

ISBN 978-0-332-91965-2
PIBN 10776984

This book is a reproduction of an important historical work. Forgotten Books uses
state-of-the-art technology to digitally reconstruct the work, preserving the original format
whilst repairing imperfections present in the aged copy. In rare cases, an imperfection in
the original, such as a blemish or missing page, may be replicated in our edition. We do,
however, repair the vast majority of imperfections successfully; any imperfections that
remain are intentionally left to preserve the state of such historical works.

PROCEEDINGS

OF THE

GRAND LODGE OF COLORADO,

OF THE

MOST ANCIENT AND HONORABLE FRATERNITY

OF

FREE AND ACCEPTED MASONS,

AT ITS

SEVERAL COMMUNICATIONS,

FROM A. L. 5861 TO A. L. 5869, INCLUSIVE.

———◆———

DAVENPORT:
GRIGGS, WATSON & DAY.
1869.

Published by authority of the following :

Resolved, That the R. W. Grand Secretary be authorized to have reprinted 800 copies pf the past proceedings of this Grand Lodge, *providing*
the fraternity of this jurisdiction shall subscribe for 300 copies of the same,
at an advance of fifty cents per copy upon actual cost. The price per copy
not to exceed two dollars; 300 copies to be retained in Library of the
Grand ⊐, for future use.

Passed Sept., 1869.

MASONIC CONVENTION

TO ORGANIZE

THE GRAND LODGE

OF THE

TERRITORY OF COLORADO,

HELD IN GOLDEN CITY, AUGUST 2, A. L., 5861.

GOLDEN CITY, C. T., August 2, 1861.

In accordance with the previous agreement, and appointment of the Masters and Wardens of the several ▭ of Free and Accepted Masons, of the Territory of Colorado, viz Golden City ▭, of Golden City; Summit ▭ No. 7, of Parkville; Rocky Mountain ▭ No. 8, of Gold Hill; a Convention was held this day for the purpose of organizing a Grand ▭ for the Territory of Colorado.

On motion, Bro. Eli Carter, of Golden City ▭, was called to preside, and

Bro. O. A. Whittemore, of Summit ▭, was chosen Secretary.

On motion, it was

Resolved, That a committee of three be appointed to report to the Convention what action is necessary to carry out the design of this Convention, namely, the formation of a Grand ▭ for the Territory of Colorado.

Bros. C. F. Holly, of Rocky Mountain ▭, S. M. Robbins, of Summit ▭, I. E. Hardy, of Golden City ▭, were appointed said committee, who made the following

REPORT:

The committee appointed to report what action is necessary to carry out the design of this Convention, respectfully report the following resolution:

Resolved, That we deem it highly expedient to organize a Grand ☐ for this Territory, and that the following order of proceeding be observed, to that end :

1. That a ☐ of Master Masons be opened in due form, the Master of the the oldest ☐ present presiding.

2. That the charters of the ☐ represented, and the credentials of the representatives, be presented and acted upon.

3. The election of officers, and

4. The installation of the officers elect.

All of which is respectfully submitted.

C. F. HOLLY, }
S. M. ROBBINS, } *Committee.*
I. E. HARDY, }

The report of the committee was unanimously adopted.

Whereupon, a ☐ of Master Masons was then duly opened, —Bro. James Ewing, of Summit ☐, presiding, (Bro. Eli Carter, Master of Golden City ☐, waiving his right,) Bro. I. E. Hardy, of Golden City ☐, acting as Senior Warden, Bro. S. M. Robbins, of Summit ☐, as Junior Warden.

Prayer by Rev. Bro. J. M. Chivington.

On motion, a committee of three, consisting of Bros. Robbins, Carter and Holly, was appointed to examine charters of ☐ claiming to be represented in this Convention, and credentials of representatives, under the same, which committee made the following

REPORT:

The committee appointed to examine the charters of the ☐ claiming to be represented in this Convention, and the credentials of the representatives under the same, have had the same under advisement, and respectfully beg leave to report the following ☐ duly chartered, and represented as follows, to-wit:

Golden City ☐ No. —, at Golden City, C. T. Chartered by the, M.·. W.·. Grand ☐ of Kansas, October 17th, 1860; and represented as follows: Bro. Eli Carter, W.·. M.·.; Bro. I. E. Hardy, proxy for S.·. W.·.; Bro. J. A. Moore, J.·. W.·.

Rocky Mountain ☐ No. 8, Gold Hill, C. T. Chartered June 5th, 1861, by the M.·. W.·. Grand ☐ of Nebraska; and represented as follows: Bro. C. F. Holly, as proxy for W.·. M.·. and S.·. W.·., and Bro. J. Chivington, as proxy for J.·. W.·.

Summit ☐ No. 7, Parkville, C. T. Chartered June 5th, 1861, by the M.· W.·. Grand ☐ of Nebraska, and represented as follows: Bro. James Ewing

W∴ M∴ ; Bro. O. A. Whittemore, proxy for S∴ W∴, and Bro. S. M. Robbins, proxy for J∴ W∴.

Your committee therefore beg leave to report the following resolutions:

Resolved, That the brethren heretofore named, are entitled to seats in this Grand □, here to be formed.

Resolved, That Bro. L. L. Bowen, Past Deputy Grand Master of Nebraska, and Bros. W. T. Wade and L. M. Frary, Past Masters, be allowed seats in this Convention.

S. M. ROBBINS,)
ELI CARTER, } *Committee.*
C. F. HOLLY,)

Which report was unanimously adopted.

On motion, it was

Resolved, That the following grand officers be now elected by ballot, viz: M∴ W∴ Grand Master; R∴ W∴ Deputy Grand Master; R∴ W∴ Senior Grand Warden; R∴ W∴ Junior Grand Warden; R∴ W∴ Grand Treasurer, and R∴ W∴ Grand Secretary.

Bros. Chivington and Carter were appointed tellers, when the □ proceeded to ballot for Grand Officers with the following result:

J. M. CHIVINGTON, Gold Hill, Grand Master.

S. M. ROBBINS, Parkville, Deputy Grand Master.

JAS. EWING, Parkville, Senior Grand Warden.

J. M. HOLT, Gold Hill, Junior Grand Warden.

ELI CARTER, Golden City, Grand Treasurer.

O. A. WHITTEMORE, Parkville, Grand Secretary.

The Grand Officers were then regularly installed into their respective stations.

The following officers, appointed by the Grand Master, were then installed by him.

C. F. HOLLY, Gold Hill, Grand Orator.

I. E. HARDY, Golden City, Grand Lecturer.

J. M. FERRELL, Golden City, Grand Marshal.

JOSHUA MILLER, Parkville, Senior Grand Deacon.

C. W. SMITH, Gold Hill, Junior Grand Deacon.

D. T. ROBLEY, Parkville, Grand Tyler.

E. S. GLOTFELTER, Gold Hill, Grand Steward.

J. A. MOORE, Golden City, Grand Sword Bearer.

The Grand □ of Colorado was then declared regularly organized, and its officers installed in due form.

JAMES EWING, *W. M.*

O. A. WHITTEMORE, *Sec'y.*

The Grand □ of Colorado being now regularly constituted,

On motion; a committee of three, composed of Bros. J. A. Moore, C. F. Holly and S. M. Robbins, was appointed to report a Constitution, By-Laws and Rules of Order, for the government of this Grand □, and Rules and Regulations for the government of subordinate ⊡.

The Grand □ then called from labor until 8 o'clock Saturday morning, the 3d inst.

SATURDAY MORNING.

The Grand □ resumed labor at 8 o'clock, when the committee on Constitution, By-Laws and Rules of Order for the government of this Grand □, and Rules and Regulations for the government of subordinate ⊡, made their report, (see Appendix,) which was adopted.

On motion, it was

Resolved, That the several ⊏, under the jurisdiction of this Grand □, be numbered anew, according to the age of their charters, beginning with number one.

The several subordinate ⊡ were then declared to be as follows:

Golden City □ No. 1, at Golden City.
Summit □ No. 2, at Parkville.
Rocky Mountain □ No. 3, at Gold Hill.

On motion, Bros. Robbins, Holly and Carter were appointed a committee to draft and procure the passage of a suitable act of incorporation for this Grand □, at the ensuing session of the General Assembly of Colorado.

On motion, it was

Resolved, That the Grand Secretary be authorized to draw on each of the ⊏ under this jurisdiction for the sum of $25.00, to meet the expenses of this Grand □, if necessary.

It was also

Resolved, That the Grand Secretary be directed to procure the necessary printing for this Grand □,—such as the proceedings of this session, Con-

stitution, By-Laws, Rules and Regulations, blank charters and dispensa
tions; also a seal and seal press.

On motion, it was

Resolved, That a school of instruction be established by this Grand □,
and that at least one day, at each Grand Communication, be set apart for
the purpose of instruction by the M∴ W∴ Grand Master, in order that uniformity in the work may be obtained in this jurisdiction.

On motion, it was

Resolved, That the work in this jurisdiction be adopted as exemplified in
the present session of this Grand □.

On motion, it was

Resolved, That when this Grand □ adjourn, it be to meet at Denver City,
on the first Monday in December, 1861.

The Grand □ then called from labor until 1 o'clock this
afternoon.

AFTERNOON SESSION.

The Grand □ resumed labor at 1 o'clock.

After some deliberation, and no further business appearing,
the Grand □ then closed its session in peace and harmony.

J. M. CHIVINGTON, *Grand Master.*

O. A. WHITTEMORE, *Grand Secretary.*

CONSTITUTION

OF THE

GRAND LODGE OF COLORADO.

WHEREAS, Every Grand □ possesses the inherent power to form a Constitution, as the fundamental law of its Masonic action, and to enact such By-Laws from time to time as it may deem necessary for its own government, and to make such rules and prescribe such regulations for the administration of its subordinate □, as will insure the prosperity thereof, and promote the general good of Masonry; and, WHEREAS, Every Grand □ is the true representative of all the fraternity in communication therewith, and is, in that behalf, an absolute and independent body, with supreme legislative authority: *Provided always,* That the ancient Landmarks of the Order be held inviolate.

Therefore, Upon these principles, which have never been disputed, the Grand □ of Colorado does hereby ordain, establish and promulgate the following Constitution and By-Laws for its future government, and does make and prescribe the following rules and regulations for the government of the □ under its jurisdiction.

ARTICLE I.

This Grand □ shall forever hereafter be known by the name and style of the Most Ancient and Honorable Fraternity of Free and Accepted Masons of Colorado.

ARTICLE II.

The Grand □ shall consist of a Grand Master, Deputy Grand Master, Senior Grand Warden, Junior Grand Warden,

Grand Treasurer, Grand Secretary, Grand Chaplain, Grand Orator, Grand Lecturer, Grand Marshal, Senior Grand Deacon, Junior Grand Deacon and Grand Tyler, with such other officers as it may, from time to time, create; together with the Masters and Wardens, or their proxies, duly constituted, of the chartered ⌺ under its jurisdiction, and such Past Grand Masters and Past Deputy Grand Masters as shall be present, and are members of a subordinate ▭.

ARTICLE III.

The Grand ▭ shall hold a stated communication, at least once in every two years, at such time and in such place as may be designated in its By-Laws.

ARTICLE IV.

The Grand ▭ shall not be opened, nor shall any business be transacted therein, unless there be present a representative from at least three of the chartered ⌺; but a smaller number may meet and adjourn from day to day, until a constitutional quorum shall attend.

ARTICLE V.

The officers of the Grand ▭ shall be styled, and take rank, as follows:

The Most Worshipful Grand Master.
The Right Worshipful Deputy Grand Master.
The Right Worshipful Senior Grand Warden.
The Right Worshipful Junior Grand Warden.
The Right Worshipful Grand Treasurer.
The Right Worshipful Grand Secretary.
The Right Worshipful Grand Chaplain.
The Right Worshipful Grand Orator.
The Right Worshipful Grand Lecturer.
The Right Worshipful Grand Marshal.
The Worshipful Senior Grand Deacon.
The Worshipful Junior Grand Deacon.
The Grand Tyler.

ARTICLE VI.

No brother shall be eligible to the office of Grand Master,

2

Deputy Grand Master, or Grand Warden, who has not been duly elected, installed, and presided over a subordinate ▭.

ARTICLE VII.

At each stated communication of the Grand ▭, there shall be elected, by ballot, from among the brethren who are at the time constitutionally eligible to seats therein, a Grand Master, a Deputy Grand Master, a Grand Senior Warden, a Grand Junior Warden, a Grand Treasurer and a Grand Secretary; all other Grand Officers shall be appointed by the Grand Master, with the advice and consent of the Grand ▭.

ARTICLE VIII.

No Grand Officer shall officiate in the station to which he is elected, until he has been legally installed.

ARTICLE IX.

The Most Worshipful Grand Master has the right to convene the Grand ▭, in special Grand Communication, on any emergency which, in his judgment, may require it. He has the power at his discretion to assemble any subordinate ▭, and preside therein, inspect its work, and require a strict conformity to the constitutional rules and regulations of order. For good cause, he may suspend the functions of any such ▭, until the ensuing stated communication of the Grand ▭. It is his prerogative to make Masons at sight, and, for this purpose, may summon to his assistance such brethren as he may deem necessary. He has the command of every other Grand Officer, touching the duties and ministrations of their several offices, and may call on any and all of them, at any time, for advice and assistance on all business relative to the craft.

ARTICLE X.

In case of the death, absence, or inability of the Grand Master, the powers and duties of his station, for all regular and necessary purposes, shall, for the time being, devolve upon the Deputy Grand Master, Senior Grand Warden, or Junior Grand Warden, in the order here enumerated.

ARTICLE XI.

During the recess of the Grand ▭, the Grand Master, and

Deputy Grand Master, severally, have power to grant dispensations, under their private seals, for instituting new ⬚.

ARTICLE XII.

No dispensation shall be granted for constituting a new ⬚, except upon the petition of eight Master Masons, one of whom must be a Past Master, and the recommendation of the chartered ⬚ nearest the location of the new ⬚, vouching for the moral character and Masonic qualifications of the petitioners.

ARTICLE XIII.

No warrant or dispensations, for the institution of a new ⬚, shall be granted for a less sum than twenty-five dollars, and thirty dollars additional for the charter.

ARTICLE XIV.

No charter or dispensation, for constituting new ⬚, shall be granted to any person or persons whomsoever residing out of this Territory (or State), if within the jurisdiction of any other constitutional Grand ⬚.

ARTICLE XV.

The Grand ⬚ has original and exclusive jurisdiction over all subjects of Masonic legislation, and appellate jurisdiction from the decisions of the subordinate ⬚; and its enactments and decisions upon all questions shall be the supreme Masonic law of the Territory or State. It shall prescribe such rules and regulations for the government of the subordinate ⬚ as will, in its arbitrament, conduce to the welfare, prosperity and happiness of the craft ; and may require from them such dues and fees as will at all times discharge the engagements of the Grand ⬚.

ARTICLE XVI.

The Book of Constitutions hereunto attached, this Grand ⬚ does recognize and adopt as the fundamental Laws, Rules and Regulations for the government of Masons ; and declares that it should be frequently read and perused by Masters, and other craftsmen, as well within the subordinate ⬚ as thereout, to the end that none may be ignorant of the excellent principles and precepts it inculcates.

ARTICLE XVII.

This Constitution may be altered or amended, in the following manner only: The proposed alteration or amendment must be made in writing, at some stated communication. If seconded by a majority of votes, it shall be entered upon the minutes, and be then submitted to the several subordinate ⌷, for their approval or rejection. If two-thirds of the ⌷ approve thereof by certificate, over their respective seals, to the next succeeding Grand ▭, the Grand Master shall put the question upon its adoption; and if concurred in, by a vote of three-fourths of the members present, it shall, from thenceforth, be considered as a part and parcel of this Constitution.

BY-LAWS

OF THE

GRAND LODGE OF COLORADO.

SECTION I.

There shall be an Annual Communication of the Grand □, except, for good cause, the same be adjourned for a longer period; but in no event shall such adjournment extend beyond the period of two years.

SECTION II.

The stated meetings of the Grand □ shall be held at Denver, on the first Monday in December, annually.

SECTION III.

On the day appointed for the meeting of the Grand □, a Master Mason's □ shall be opened, in ample form, at 10 o'clock A. M., when the M∴ W∴ Grand Master shall appoint a committee to examine visiting brethren, and a committee to examine credentials, each to consist of three members.

So soon as a constitutional quorum of ▣ is ascertained to be present, the Grand □ of Colorado shall be declared open for the despatch of business, and the Grand Master shall then appoint the following standing committees, each to consist of not less than three nor more than five members, to wit: A committee on Accounts; a committee on Charters and Dispensations; a committee on Foreign Communications; a committee on Ways and Means; a committee on Charity; a committee on Grievances; a committee on Unfinished Business; a committee to prepare a Pay Roll; a committee on Masonic Jurisprudence; a committee on School Fund; and a committee on Returns of subordinate ⌺, whose duty it shall be to examine and correct such returns.

SECTION IV.

The standing committees of the Grand ▢ shall perform and discharge the following specific duties, to wit:

1. The committee to examine visiting brethren shall perform the duties of their appointment according to established Masonic usage.

2. The returns of the subordinate ⌺ and the credentials of representatives and proxies shall be referred to the committee appointed to examine credentials, who shall report the number of ⌺ that are represented, the names of representatives and proxies, with the number of votes to which each is entitled.

3. It shall be the duty of the committee on Accounts to examine the books and vouchers of the Treasurer and Grand Secretary, settle and balance the same, and report the actual state of the funds to the Grand ▢.

4. The committee on Charters and Dispensations shall particularly examine the work, records, and By-Laws, of all ⌺ under dispensation, and the proceedings of the Grand Officers granting the same; they shall examine the amended By-Laws of all chartered ⌺ submitted for the approval of the Grand ▢; they will note all matters that are improper or unconstitutional, in any of such work, records and By-Laws, and report to the Grand ▢ with such recommendations as they shall deem meet and proper in the premises.

5. The Foreign Correspondence of the Grand ▢, including all communications made by other Grand ⌺, shall be referred to the committee on Foreign Communications, whose duty it shall be to examine the same, and report all matters found therein which effect the general or local welfare of the craft, accompanied with such recommendations as they may deem expedient.

6. It shall be the duty of the committee on Ways and Means to take into consideration the condition of the funds

and estate of the Grand □, and all propositions and resolutions, affecting its revenue, which may be offered; they shall specifically report thereon, and may recommend any measures, which in their opinion, will operate financially for the benefit of the institution.

7. All applications for appropriations from the charity fund of the Grand □ shall be submitted to the committee on Charity, who shall consider the same, and make report thereon to the Grand □.

8. All matters of controversy and grievance brought before the Grand □, shall be referred to the committee on Grievances, whose duty it shall be to examine into the same, and report, for the action of the Grand □.

9. It shall be the duty of the committee on Unfinished Business, to examine and report from the journal of the previous session, all such matters as were then pending and undetermined.

10. It shall be the duty of the committee to prepare a pay roll, to ascertain and report the per diem and traveling compensation allowed to the representatives and members of the Grand □.

11. It shall be the duty of the committee on Masonic Jurisprudence, to investigate and report upon all questions that may be referred to them by the Grand □: *Provided*, That, with the consent of the Grand □, said committee may retain any question or paper referred to them, and report thereon at the next regular Grand Communication.

12. It shall be the duty of the committee on the School Fund, to report to the Grand □ on all matters referred to them in relation to the school fund. They shall also make a report annually to the Grand □, of the state and condition of the school fund; and they shall also make a separate report, upon the particulars required in the several resolutions of the Grand □ creating said school fund.

SECTION V.

It shall be considered the duty of the M∴ W∴ Grand Master, to communicate in writing, immediately after the appoint-

ment of the standing committees, a statement of his official
acts during the recess of the Grand ▢, with such other matters as he may deem advantageous to the craft. He shall
also give to the Grand ▢ information upon subjects of Masonic
interest, and recommend for its consideration any measures
he shall deem expedient; which communication shall be referred to such appropriate committees as its various details require. The Deputy Grand Master shall also report, in writing, any official acts performed by him during the recess of
the Grand ▢.

SECTION VI.

The M∴ W∴ Grand Master is not authorized to make or
second any motion ; but on all questions where there is an
equal division, he shall give the casting vote.

SECTION VII.

It is the duty of the M∴ W∴ Grand Master to install his
successor and his Deputy when present; but he may if he
see fit, authorize any worthy Past Master to install all the
other Grand Officers.

SECTION VIII.

The M∴ W∴ Grand Master shall appoint at each stated
communication of the Grand ▢, a Grand Steward, a Grand
Sword Bearer and two Grand Pursuivants.

SECTION IX.

In the event of the death, resignation, or removal of any
of the Grand Officers during the recess of the Grand ▢, the
M∴ W∴ Grand Master has authority to appoint any
suitable brother to fill the vacant station and to install into office.

SECTION X.

It is the duty of the M∴ W∴ Grand Master in office or *pro
tempore* to subscribe the journal of the Grand ▢ at every
Grand Communication, and no transcript or minutes therefrom shall at any time be printed or published until examined
by him and subscribed as aforesaid.

SECTION XI.

On all questions arising in the Grand ⊐, the Grand Officers together with such Past Grand Masters and Past Deputy Grand Masters as may be present and are members thereof, shall each be entitled to one vote, and the Master and Wardens of each subordinate ⊐, or their regularly constituted proxies, shall each be entitled to one vote; but in no case whatsoever shall a member by virtue of any proxy or authority cast more than three votes.

SECTION XII.

The Grand Tyler shall not, *ex officio*, be entitled to any vote in the Grand ⊐.

SECTION XIII.

It shall be competent for the Master and Wardens of any subordinate ⊐ to appoint a suitable brother, being a member of some ⊐ under this jurisdiction, his or their proxy to the Grand ⊐ certified under their official signature; and it shall, in like manner, be competent for any ⊐, the officers of which decline attending the meeting of the Grand ⊐, and to appoint their proxies as aforesaid, to designate and make choice by resolution of some brother having the qualifications aforesaid, the proxy of said ⊐, which resolution must be certified by the Secretary thereof, and shall entitle the brother appointed to three votes: *Provided, however*, that no representative or proxy from a subordinate ⊐ shall hold a seat in the Grand ⊐ until he shall produce evidence that the ⊐ he represents has discharged in full its Grand Dues.

SECTION XIV.

All decisions of the Grand ⊐ shall be determined by a majority of the votes given. The yeas and nays may be ordered upon any question at the request of three members, when the roll shall be called and every vote counted.

SECTION XV.

The Grand Treasurer shall have charge of all the funds, securities and vouchers of the Grand ⊐, and shall pay all orders

3

from the moneys on hand that may be directed by the Grand ▢, or otherwise constitutionally drawn. It shall be his duty to attend all the communications of the Grand ▢ with his books of account, vouchers for money paid out, and all necessary papers relating to his office, in order that the same may be inspected and his accounts settled; and he shall meet with any Grand Committee when required, whose general or special province it may be to act in relation to the fiscal concerns of the Grand ▢. Before entering upon any of the duties of his office, he shall give bond with security, as the Grand ▢ may direct, conditioned for the faithful discharge thereof.

SECTION XVI.

It shall be the duty of the Grand Secretary to record the transactions of the Grand ▢, and he shall attend, personally, each Grand Communication, with the necessary books and papers of his office; he shall keep the seal of the Grand ▢ and affix the same with his attestation to all instruments required to be so executed; he shall receive, receipt for, and immediately pay over to the Grand Treasurer, all Grand Dues, fees and other moneys handed in at any communication of the Grand ▢, taking a proper voucher therefor; he shall keep a faithful journal of all its proceedings, distribute the same when ordered to be printed for circulation, and conduct any correspondence required of him under the orders of the Grand ▢, and the directions of the Grand Master; he shall procure all necessary books and stationery, and shall have charge of all the records, papers, parchments, certificates and documents, other than those belonging to the Grand Treasurer; he shall do and perform any other duties customary to his office and the established usages of Masons; and for his services in full he shall receive a salary of fifty dollars per annum.

SECTION XVII.

It shall be the duty of the Grand Lecturer to attend the communications of the Grand ▢. He shall, under the advice and with the concurrence of the M∴ W∴ Grand Master, cause the work of the several ▢▢ to be uniform; and upon any question and difference of opinion arising in the discharge of his duty, the decision of the Grand ▢, when in session, and of the Grand Master, at all other times, shall be final. He shall visit the subordinate ⊞ when called upon for that purpose, and communicate the proper and uniform mode of work; and for his services he shall be paid by the ▢ requiring them.

SECTION XVIII.

Each subordinate ▢ is required to be represented at the stated communications of the Grand ▢, such representation shall be paid out of the funds of the Grand ▢, one dollar and fifty cents for every twenty-five miles going to, and returning therefrom, to be estimated by the most direct and traveled route, and one dollar and fifty cents for each day's attendance: *Provided*, that no brother shall receive compensation as the representative or proxy of more than one ▢, or more than one representative from one ▢: *And, Provided, also*, that no representative, delegate, or proxy, who leaves said Grand ▢ before it is closed shall receive any compensation for his travel or attendance, unless he be excused on account of sickness, or other providential causes arising after his leaving home to attend said Grand ▢.

SECTION XIX.

Every subordinate ▢ shall pay annually to the Grand ▢, at the stated meetings thereof, the following Grand Dues, to wit: For each initiation, the sum of five dollars, and for each member, the sum of one dollar and fifty cents, but no Grand ▢ dues shall be required for any member for whom an initiation fee is paid during the same year.

SECTION XX.

Every subordinate ▢ which shall not be represented for two successive Grand Communications, and neglect for two consecutive years to discharge its Grand Dues, shall be suspended from all its Masonic functions; and it shall be the duty of the Grand Secretary to give such delinquent ▢ immediate notice thereof, and, unless within one year from date of suspension, the said ▢ shall faithfully discharge all arrearages, and show good cause to the contrary, it shall forfeit its charter and be struck from the roll of 🏛; and in no case, and under no pretence, whatever, shall such ☐ be resuscitated until all Grand Dues be paid, together with a dispensation fee of twenty-five dollars.

SECTION XXI.

When a charter shall be surrendered or become forfeit, the whole of the property of the subordinate ☐ of every kind and description shall be vested in the Grand ☐ and subject to its disposal.

SECTION XXII.

The subordinate 🏛 shall have authority to assess such dues upon their members, from time to time, as they shall deem just and expedient; and the By-Laws of each ☐ shall designate the amount of dues so assessed, and the times for the payment thereof, which shall be considered sufficient notice to each member. And it is hereby made the imperative duty of the Master to cause the Secretary to enter "suspended" every member who shall be in arrears, and forthwith to notify him of the same; if, within a reasonable time thereafter, as the ☐ may determine, the member so suspended does not discharge his dues, he shall be expelled.

SECTION XXIII.

The Master of each ☐ shall cause the Secretary to give immediate notice to the Grand Secretary of every suspension or expulsion that is ordered in his ☐, whether for non-payment of dues, or otherwise; and it is hereby declared that suspension or expulsion for non-payment of dues, works an absolute forfeiture, for the time being, of all Masonic privileges.

SECTION XXIV.

It shall be the duty of the Grand Secretary, in making up the annual minutes of the Grand ☐ for publication, to embrace therein a list of the suspensions and expulsions from the several subordinate 🏛, setting forth the cause in each particular case.

SECTION XXV.

Whenever the Grand □ shall abrogate the decision of a subordinate □ suspending or expelling a brother, and thus restore him to the benefits and privileges of Masonry, he shall not thereby be reinstated to membership in the subordinate □ without its unanimous consent.

SECTION XXVI.

Every society of Masons applying for a dispensation shall, before the same be granted, deposit with the M∴ W∴ Grand Master or Deputy Grand Master issuing the same, the sum of twenty-five dollars for the use of the Grand □, which shall entitle the □ so constituted to a charter upon the additional payment of thirty dollars, provided its work is approved by the Grand □.

SECTION XXVII.

No dispensation shall authorize a □ to work beyond the period fixed for the next succeeding stated meeting of the Grand □; at which time the dispensation, together with a copy of its By-Laws and a record of its proceedings, shall be presented to the Grand □ for inspection; when the dispensation may be continued, a charter granted, or its labors interdicted, as the Grand □ may deem meet.

SECTION XXVIII.

No □ under dispensation shall be permitted to hold a public celebration on any Masonic occasion, whatever, unless the consent of the M∴ W∴ Grand Master, or in his absence, of the Deputy Grand Master, be first obtained.

SECTION XXIX.

No □ is authorized to commence work under its charter until the officers thereof have been regularly installed, and for this purpose, whenever a charter is granted, the M∴ W∴ Grand Master, or in his absence, the Deputy Grand Master, shall appoint a suitable and early day for constituting said □, and for the installation of its officers, and, when convenient, shall in person conduct such ceremony. They have the power, however, at their discretion, to appoint some worthy Past Master to act as their proxy on such occasions.

SECTION XXX.

Every resolution or motion contemplating an appropriation from the funds of the Grand ▢, shall be proposed by, or referred to, some standing committee of that body before it can be acted upon.

SECTION XXXI.

When an appeal from the decision of a subordinate ▢, on any matter of Masonic discipline, shall be perfected and entered in the Grand ▢, it shall be referred to the standing committee on Grievances, or decided without such reference if deemed most expedient; and in either case the subordinate, or the appellant brother, shall have the benefit of any additional testimony, providing the same has been taken agreeably to the notice prescribed in the Rules and Regulations of the Grand ▢ for the government of the ▣ under its jurisdiction.

SECTION XXXII.

No By-Law shall be altered or done away, or any new one adopted, until the proposed alteration, amendment, nullification, or addition be reduced to writing and seconded by five members; it shall then be entered upon the minutes, and lie over until the next succeeding stated meeting of the Grand ▢, when, if approved by two-thirds of the members present, the same shall be adopted : *Provided*, that by an unanimous vote, any proposition as aforesaid, may be acted upon instanter.

RULES AND REGULATIONS

OF THE

GRAND LODGE OF COLORADO,

FOR THE

GOVERNMENT OF SUBORDINATE LODGES.

---

1. A subordinate ▢ shall consist of at least a Master, a Senior and Junior Warden, a Treasurer, Secretary, Senior and Junior Deacon, a Tyler, and as many members as are convenient.

The officers above enumerated shall be elected by ballot by a majority of votes, at the stated meeting in November or December, annually, and be installed into office as near the festival of St. John the Evangelist as practicable.

2. No brother shall be eligible to the Mastership, unless he has been elected and served in the station of Warden, in some regular ▢. In the absence of the Master, the Senior and Junior Warden, according to rank, shall succeed to the duties of his station.

3. Each subordinate ▢ possesses the inherent right to enact By-Laws and ordinances for its own government, provided the same are not inconsistent with the Constitution, By-Laws, Rules and Regulations of the Grand ▢, and the fundamental principles of Masonry. And to the end that there shall be preserved always inviolate, it is hereby declared that no By-Law or ordinance of government of a subordinate ▢, shall be of any permanent validity until approved by the Grand ▢.

4. Each ▢ shall assemble for work at least once in every

calendar month; and if any ▢ under this jurisdiction shall cease to meet for twelve successive months it shall forfeit its charter, and be erased from the Grand ▢ book.

Previous to advancements, all candidates shall be examined in open ▢, in the degree which they have taken, and be found to possess at least a knowledge of that degree.

5. All the proceedings, ballotings and business of the ▢ shall be had in a ▢ of Master Masons, that of conferring the inferior degrees alone excepted.

6. No religious test shall ever be required of any applicant for the benefits of Masonry, other than a steadfast belief in the existence and perfections of Deity; and no ▢ under this jurisdiction shall receive any candidate without the acknowledgment of such belief.

7. No ▢ shall confer the first three degrees in Masonry for a less sum than thirty dollars.

A *unanimous* vote must be had in favor of the applicant for each degree, but in no case shall a ballot be taken until the money required for the fee shall be in actual deposit.

8. No ▢, in the absence of the Master and Wardens, shall initiate, craft, or raise, unless a Past Master be present and presiding.

9. All applications for initiation or for membership, shall be made at the regular stated meeting of the ▢, and lie over at least from one communication to another, unless, by a vote of three-fourths of the members present, it shall be regarded a case of emergency, when, by a unanimous vote, a ballot may be ordered.

10. After a petition is regularly received by a subordinate ▢, and entered upon its minutes, it shall not be drawn without the consent of the ▢,—at least three-fourths of the members present .concurring therein.

11. If any member of a subordinate ▢ shall, from trifling, captious, sinister or unworthy motives, attempt to arrest the legitimate work of the ▢, he shall thereby be rendered amenable to Masonic discipline. And it is made the duty of the ▢, in all such cases, to proceed to the investigation

thereof, and to reprimand, suspend or expel the offending member, as a majority present may deem best.

12. No ▭ shall initiate into the mysteries of the craft, any person whomsoever, without being first satisfied, by a test, or otherwise, that the candidate has not made application to some other ▭ and been rejected; and if it shall appear that he has been rejected, then the ▭ must be satisfactorily convinced that such rejection has not been on account of any circumstances that ought to preclude him from the benefits of Masonry; otherwise, the interdiction is positive and peremptory.

13. No ▭ shall receive into membership, a Mason from any other ▭, until he shall produce satisfactory evidence that he has paid all dues to the ▭ of which he was last a member.

14. No one can become a member of a subordinate ▭, or be entitled to a vote therein, until he has received the third degree in Masonry.

15. No candidate shall be received in any ▭ out of the county in which he resides, if there is a regular working ▭ in such county, unless with the unanimous recommendation thereof. If there are two or more ▭ in any county, then the candidate must apply to the ▭ nearest his residence. In a town, or city, any ▭ therein may receive an applicant, resident of such town or city.

16. It shall be unlawful for any ▭ under this jurisdiction to receive, as a visitor, a brother while known to be under sentence of suspension or expulsion from any constitutional Masonic body.

17. When the physical disabilities of a candidate are not such as to prevent him from being initiated into the several degrees and mysteries of Freemasonry, his admission shall not be construed an infringement upon the *ancient landmarks*, but, on the contrary, will be perfectly consistent with the spirit of the institution.

18. In no case, for non-payment of dues, shall a subordinate ▭ publish, in a newspaper, the suspension or expulsion of any

4

of its members, unless the consent of the Grand ▢, or of the
M.·. W.·. Grand Master be first obtained.

19. The subordinate ⬒ have the power, at their discretion,
to require of all Master Masons residing within their respective jurisdictions, to contribute pecuniary aid to purposes
strictly Masonic. But this power shall not be exercised except with proper caution and deliberation.

20. Each subordinate ▢ shall bury a deceased worthy member of its body with Masonic rites, if requested by decedent
in his lifetime, or by his near relations, after his death; and
in all other cases, such Masonic honors may be granted or
withheld, as the ▢ may consider best.

21. When convenient, the several subordinate ⬒ should be
supplied with libraries of useful and practical books; and it is
enjoined upon them, as often as it is feasible, to introduce into
their meetings, lectures and essays upon Masonic polity, and
the various arts and sciences connected therewith.

22. Subordinate ⬒ not only possess the power, but it shall
be their express duty, to take cognizance of brethren within
their vicinity, whether subordinate to the jurisdiction of this
Grand ▢, or otherwise, and to suspend or expel from the privileges of the order, any brother who shall be found guilty of
unmasonic conduct—subject, however, to an appeal to the
Grand ▢.

23. No Grand ▢ shall proceed to suspend a brother for unmasonic conduct of any description whatever, except for the
non-payment of dues, unless it be upon written charges and
specifications, made out and filed with the Secretary, whose
duty it shall be to furnish the accused brother with a copy
thereof, if of a nature to be reduced to writing, at least ten
days previous to the trial, with notice of the time and place of
trial. It is the privilege of the accused to take any proof or testimony to be heard in evidence, that he may desire, upon giving three days' notice to the Master of the ▢; and in all cases,
when the hearing comes on, the whole of the testimony shall
be reduced to writing, and be carefully preserved by the Secretary of the ▢: *Provided*, That when a brother, charged as

aforesaid, shall abscond, proceedings may be had in his absence without notice.

24. Any brother feeling himself aggrieved by the decision of the ▢, pronounced against him, may, at any time within one year thereafter, take an appeal to the Grand ▢, and on his application, it shall be the duty of the Secretary of such ▢ to make and forward to the Grand Secretary, a certified copy of the proceedings had in his case, with the original testimony, as far as the same shall have been reduced to writing.

25. These Rules and Regulations may be altered or amended in the same manner as prescribed for the alteration or amendment of the By-Laws of the Grand ▢.

RULES OF ORDER

FOR

Conducting the Business of the Grand Lodge.

————

1. The Most Worshipful Grand Master shall take the chair every day precisely at the hour to which the Grand ▭ shall have adjourned on the preceding day, when the journal shall be read, to the end that any mistake or improper entries may be corrected.

2. During the hours of business, the members are required to keep their seats and observe strict order and decorum ; and no member shall leave the hall without leave, or absent himself from the service of the Grand ▭, unless he have permission, or be sick and unable to attend.

3. When the M∴ W∴ Grand Master, or presiding officer, rises, all debate shall cease, and there shall be strict silence.

4. Every member shall stand when he speaks, and shall address himself, with respect and decorum, to the presiding officer for the time being. He shall not be permitted to say anything which will have a tendency wantonly to influence or irritate, as the sole objects of debate are to enlighten and expand the mind on the subject under consideration, to elicit truth, and to conscientiously endeavor to have everything done decently and in order.

5. The M∴ W∴ Grand Master, or the presiding officer, shall be the judge of order and debate. When his decision is fairly questionable, an appeal may be made to the Grand ▭; but such appeal must be neither captious, contemptuous, or

contumacious.   Truth, justice and candor must be the desiderata in such appeal.

6. No member shall be permitted to speak more than twice upon any subject, unless it is merely to explain, without permission from the Grand ▭.   If any member is twice called to order at any meeting, for transgressing these rules, and is guilty of a third offence of the same nature, the presiding officer shall peremptorily order him to leave the Grand ▭; and he may further be amenable to reprimand, suspension or expulsion, as the Grand ▭ shall deem proper.

7. When a question is put, it shall be the duty of every member present to vote, unless, for good cause, the Grand ▭ may excuse him; but no member shall vote upon any question, in the event of which he is personally interested.

8. No motion shall be entertained, until it is seconded; and there shall no debate be had thereon, until it is stated by the chair.

9. Every motion shall be reduced to writing, with the name of the mover indorsed thereon, if the chair or Grand Secretary desire it.

10. When a question is under debate, no motion shall be received but to adjourn, to lay on the table, to commit, to amend, or to postpone indefinitely; which several motions shall have precedence in the order in which they are here arranged, and the motion to adjourn shall always be in order, and be decided without debate.

11. Any member may call for the division of a question, which shall be divided if it comprehends questions so distinct, that one being taken away, the rest may stand entire for the decision of the Grand ▭.   A motion to strike out and insert shall be deemed indivisible.

12. When a motion has been once made and carried, in the affirmative or negative, it shall be in order for any member of the majority to move for a re-consideration thereof.

13. All questions shall be propounded in the order in which they were moved, except in filling up blanks, when the largest sum and longest time shall be put first.

14. No report shall be received from any of the committees of the Grand ▭, unless the same be reduced to writing and signed by at least a majority of the members thereof.

15. No committee shall sit, during the sitting of the Grand ▭, without special leave.

16. These Rules of Order may be altered, added to, or abrogated, at any meeting of the Grand ▭, two-thirds of the members present concurring therein.

PROCEEDINGS

OF THE

FIRST ANNUAL COMMUNICATION

OF THE

GRAND LODGE OF COLORADO,

HELD IN DENVER, DECEMBER 10, A. L. 5861.

———

The First Annual Communication of the Most Worshipful Grand □ of Ancient Free and Accepted Masons of the Territory of Colorado, was held at the city of Denver, commencing Tuesday, the 10th day of December, A. D. 1861, A. L. 5861, at 2 o'clock, P. M.

Officers present as follows:

M∴ W∴ J. M. CHIVINGTON, Grand Master.
R∴ W∴ S. M. ROBBINS, Deputy Grand Master.
M. C. WHITE, Senior Grand Warden, *pro tem.*
O. B. BROWN, Junior Grand Warden, *pro tem.*
WM. TRAIN MUIR, Grand Treasurer, *pro tem.*
R∴ W∴ O. A. WHITTEMORE, Grand Secretary.
J. E. DAWSON, Senior Grand Deacon, *pro tem.*
L. POLLARD, Junior Grand Deacon, *pro tem.*
WM. McCONNELL, Grand Tyler, *pro tem.*

The Most Worshipful Grand □ was then opened in ample form.

The Most Worshipful Grand Master then appointed the following committee on Credentials, viz: Bros. A. O. Whittemore, Wm. T. Muir and M. C. White.

The Most Worshipful Grand Master then appointed Bro. J. E. Dawson a committee to examine visiting brethren.

The □ was then called from labor to meet again at 7½ o'clock P. M.

7½ O'CLOCK P. M.

The M∴ W∴ Grand □ was called to labor, when the committee on Credentials reporting a quorum of ▭ not present, the □ was called from labor to meet again on Wednesday, the 11th inst., at 3 P. M.

WEDNESDAY, 11TH DEC., 3 O'CLOCK P. M.

The □ resumed labor, when the committee on Credentials made the following.

REPORT:

To the M∴ W∴ Grand □ of Colorado:

Your committee on Credentials would report the following ▭ represented as follows, to wit:

Golden City □ No. 1, J. E. Dawson, proxy for S∴ W∴.

Summit □ No. 2, M. C. White, W∴ M∴, O. B. Brown, S∴ W∴, J. Thatcher, J∴ W∴.

Rocky Mountain □ No. 3, Chas. F. Holly, proxy for W∴ M∴ and J∴ W∴

And find that the members above named are entitled to seats in this body.

Fraternally submitted,

O. A. WHITTEMORE, } *Committee.*
M. C. WHITE,

On motion, the report of the committee as submitted, was accepted.

The M∴ W∴ Grand Master then appointed the following committee on Charters and Dispensations: Bros. O. A. Whittemore, C. F. Holly and J. E. Dawson.

The committee on Charters and Dispensations made the following

REPORT:

To the M∴ W∴ Grand Lodge of Colorado:

The undersigned, committee on Charters and Dispensations, beg leave to report as follows, to wit:

That they have examined the return of Summit ▢ No. 2, and find it correct.

Rocky Mountain ▢ No. 3, and Golden City ▢ No. 1, make no returns.

The committee find that the M∴ W∴ Grand ▢ of Kansas has chartered a ▢ within this jurisdiction, of Nevada City, under the name of Nevada ▢ No. 36, which has been surrendered to us to be exchanged for one from this ▢. No work has been done under the Kansas.charter, issued, we presume, in ignorance of the existence of this Graud ▢.

We recommend that the application of the ▢ at Nevada City be accepted, and that a charter be granted to said ▢ upon such surrender, without charter fee.

We recommend further, that the ▢ making no returns to this body be allowed ninety days from our adjournment to file their returns with the Grand Secretary.

We recommend that, a charter be granted to Denver ▢, working under dispensation granted by the M∴ W∴ Grand Master, Oct. 24th, 1861, their work being found correct.

We also find the work of Chivington ▢ to be correct under dispensation granted by the M∴ W∴ Grand Master, Sept. 19th, 1861, and we therefore recommend that a charter be granted to said ▢.

Respectfully submitted,

O. A. WHITTEMORE, ⎫
CHAS. F. HOLLY,   ⎬ *Committee.*
JAS. E. DAWSON,   ⎭

On motion, the report of the committee was received and adopted.

On motion of Bro. C. F. Holly, it was

Resolved, That Nevada ▢ No. 36 be admitted to representation in this body, and that the officers therefrom present, be authorized to take their seats therein as such.

The committee on Credentials then made the following additional

REPORT:

The committee on Credentials beg leave to report Bros. Andrew Mason, Master, and L. W. Chase, Junior Warden, of Nevada ▢ No. 4, as present with correct credentials and in their seats by act of this Grand ▢.

The M∴ W∴ Grand Master then announced the following regular

COMMITTEES:

On Accounts—Bros. J. Thatcher, L. W. Chase and C. F. Holly.

On Foreign Correspondence—Bros. A. Mason, J. E. Dawson and M. C. White.

5

On Ways and Means—Bros. O. A. Whittemore, A. Mason and O. B. Brown.

Charity—Bros. S. M. Robbins, C. F. Holly and A. Mason.

Grievances—Bros. Holly, Mason and White.

Unfinished Business—Bros. Chase, Dawson and Thatcher.

Pay Roll—Bros. White, Chase and Whittemore.

Masonic Jurisprudence—Bros. Mason, Holly and Brown.

School Fund—Bros. Chase, Dawson and Thatcher.

The M∴ W∴ Grand Master then delivered the following, his

ANNUAL ADDRESS:

To the Most Worshipful, the Grand ▭ *of Ancient Free and Accepted Masons:*

BRETHREN:—But few things have occurred during our short existence which require to be noticed in my annual communication to you.

Two dispensations have been granted by me for new ▭, one to Bro. Allyn Weston and others, at Central City, whose petition came recommended by Golden City ▭ No. 1.

The other was from Bro. Blake, and the members of the old Auraria ▭, U. D. from the Grand ▭ of Kansas, who in the true spirit of fraternal brotherhood, surrendered their authority to the M∴ W∴ Grand Lodge of Kansas, and asked for a dispensation from your jurisdiction until your present meeting.

Both of the ▭, it is to be presumed, will be here with their work and By-Laws for your inspection, and asking for charters, which I recommend be granted to them.

I learn that there has been a ▭ chartered at Nevada City by our sister, the M∴ W∴ Grand ▭ of Kansas.

This would seem to be an anomaly in Masonry, but when it is known that the Grand ▭ of Kansas were not advised of our existence as a grand body, the matter is sufficiently explained.

I will here state, however, that at an early day after the adjournment of the Grand ▭ at Golden City, I wrote to Grand Master Fairchild at Atchison, Kansas.

I presume that he either did not receive my letter, or inadvertently neglected to lay the matter before the Grand ▭ of Kansas, for I cannot believe that the Most Worshipful Grand ▭ of Kansas, (or any other Grand ▭ of Masons,) would, knowing of our existence, interfere in our jurisdiction; such a course would be subversive of every principle held sacred by Masonry, and destructive of that "peace and harmony" which is the "strength and support of all institutions, especially this of ours."

The brethren of Nevada ▭ will, in all probability, be here to surrender their charter from the Grand ▭ of Kansas, and to take one from this Grand ▭.

If so, I would most cordially recommend that you grant their request.

I may add in this connection that brethren from Canon City have sent a petition, which is in my hands, praying for a dispensation to meet and work as a legal ☐, and your attention is respectfully called to their petition.

A liberal charter for our Grand ☐ was passed by the recent session of our Territorial Legislature, and all that we have to do is henceforth to be temperate, discreet, vigilant, aye, jealous and zealous for the honor and reputation of the craft, guarding well the door of admission to her sacred temples, to which, if we do, we have a future as bright in prospect as it will be glorious in reality.

Allow me to say, brethren, such are my engagements that I do not believe it best, if it were your choice, to re-elect me to the position I now hold.

Yet, in all time to come, I am with you in every good work, and I shall not, amid the vicissitudes of life, permit myself to forget the honor conferred upon me by being made the first Grand Master of the Grand ☐ of Colorado.

Brethren, accept my thanks for that uniform courtesy and kindness which I have received at the hands of all during my brief term of office, and to you I would say, look to the angel Masonry, its unerring finger will point you steadily to the path of brotherly love, relief and truth.

                                                J. M. CHIVINGTON.

On motion of Bro. Holly, it was

Resolved, That the address of the M∴ W∴ Grand Master be published with the proceedings.

R∴ W∴ Deputy Grand Master, S. M. Robbins, then submitted the following, his

ANNUAL REPORT:

To the Most Worshipful Grand ☐ of Colorado:

I have to report as my official acts during the term I have had the pleasure of acting as Deputy Grand Master of Masons of Colorado, that I have granted dispensations to pass and raise Bro. Nicholas Thede, August 3, 1861; to raise Bro. A. R. Peters, September 7, 1861; to raise Bro. A. K. Bleim, October 23, 1861, all of Summit ☐ No. 2. It was made to appear to the undersigned that each case was one of emergency.

Fraternally submitted,   S. M. ROBBINS,
                                    D∴ G∴ M∴ of Masons of Colorado.

Bro. Holly moved to amend Section 2 of the By-Laws, by striking out all after the word "at" and inserting the following words: "such time and place as shall be previously elected by the Grand ☐."

By unanimous consent, the ☐ took instant action, when, on vote, the amendment was carried.

The ☐ was then called from labor, to meet at 7½ o'clock P. M.

7½ O'CLOCK P. M.

The ☐ resumed labor when, on motion of Bro. Robbins, it was

Resolved, That the Master and Wardens of Denver ☐ No. 5 be admitted to seats as members of this Grand ☐, and to participate in its proceedings.

Bro. Holly offered the following resolution :

Resolved, That on application of Rocky Mountain ☐ No. 8, the M∴ W∴ Grand Master be requested to pass and raise Bro. B. L. Sanford, who has been initiated in that ☐, as requested by the representatives of that ☐.

Bro. Robbins moved to amend by striking out all after the word "resolved," which was carried.

Bro. Pfouts, of Denver ☐, moved that to-morrow, at 10 o'clock A. M., we proceed to election of officers for the ensuing year; carried.

The ☐ was then called from labor to meet again to-morrow, at 10 o'clock A. M.

THURSDAY, 12TH, 10 o'CLOCK A. M.

The ☐ resumed labor, the R∴ W∴ D∴ Grand Master presiding, when the ☐ proceeded to the election of officers with the following result:

M∴ W∴ J. M. CHIVINGTON, Grand Master.
ANDREW MASON, R∴ W∴ D∴ Grand Master.
P. S. PFOUTS, R∴ W∴ Senior Grand Warden.
M. C. WHITE, R∴ W∴ Junior Grand Warden.
O. B. BROWN, R∴ W∴ Grand Treasurer.
O. A. WHITTEMORE, R∴ W∴ Grand Secretary.

Bro. Pfouts moved that the next Regular Communication of the M∴ W∴ Grand ☐ of Colorado be held in Denver City, on the first Monday in October next.

Bro. Whittemore moved to amend, by inserting "Parkville" in place of "Denver," and the time, "first Monday in November."

Bro. Holly moved to amend the amendment by inserting "Gold Hill," and the time, "first Monday in December next," which was lost.

The amendment of Bro. Whittemore was lost. The question recurring on the original motion, it was lost.

Bro. Pfouts moved that the next Annual Communication of the Grand ▭ of Colorado be held in Denver, on the first Monday in November, A. D. 1862.

Bro. Hólly moved to amend by making the place Golden City.

Bro. Brown moved to amend the amendment by making the place Central City, which was carried.

The amendment, as amended, was lost.

The original motion was lost.

Bro. White moved that the next Annual Communication be held at Colorado City, on the first Monday in November next.

Bro. Holly moved to amend, by inserting Golden City; amendment lost.

Bro. Pfouts moved to lay on the table; carried.

On motion of Bro. Holly, it was

Resolved, That the next Annual Communication of this Grand ▭ be held at Central City, on the first Monday in November next.

Bro. Blake moved to amend rule 4 of the Rules and Regulations for the government of subordinate ▭, so as to read " and if any ▭ under this jurisdiction shall cease to meet for three successive months, it shall forfeit its charter."

Which motion was seconded by Bros. Mason, Pfouts, Chase, Holly and White.

The ▭ was then called from labor to meet this afternoon at 2 o'clock.

---

2 O'CLOCK P. M.

The ▭ resumed labor, the M∴ W∴ J. M. Chivington, Grand Master, presiding.

When, on motion of Bro. Pfouts, the officers elect were installed in due form.

The following officers were then appointed by the M∴ W∴ Grand Master :

W. A. KENNY, R∴ W∴ Grand Chaplain.
RICHARD SOPRIS, R∴ W∴ Grand Orator.
ALLYN WESTON, R∴ W∴ Grand Lecturer.
J. E. DAWSON, R∴ W∴ Grand Marshal.
C. H. BLAKE, W∴ Senior Grand Deacon.
L. W. CHASE, W∴ Junior Grand Deacon.
J. W. RATLIFF, Grand Tyler.
E. S. GLOTFELTER, Grand Steward.
C. W. SMITH, Grand Sword Bearer.
JOSEPH THATCHER, } Grand Pursuivants.
WM. McCONNELL, }

Who were then duly installed.

Bro. White moved to amend Section 19 of the By-Laws, as follows : Add after the words "and for each member the sum of one dollar and fifty cents," the words "unless the same shall be remitted by the ▢ for good cause shown."

The amendment was lost.

Bro. White also moved to amend section 22 by striking out "and it is hereby made the imperative duty of the Master," and insert in lieu thereof, "the Master has the authority with the consent of the ▢," which motion prevailed.

On motion of Bro. Pfouts, it was

Resolved, That Bros. Mason, White, Weston and Whittemore be appointed a committee to revise the By-Laws and Rules of Order of the Grand ▢ of Colorado, and make a report on the first day of the next Annual Communication of this Grand ▢.

On motion of Bro. Robbins, Bro. Pfouts was added to that committee.

The committee to prepare a pay roll, then made the following

REPORT:

To the M∴ W∴ Grand ▢ of Colorado Territory :

Your committee appointed to report the pay roll for delegates in attendance at the Annual Communication of the Grand ▢, held December, 1861, at Denver City, respectfully report :

GOLDEN CITY ▢ NO. 1.

Entitled to pay for one delegate as follows :

Mileage going to and returning from Grand ▢, 32 miles, at the rates allowed by the Grand ▢........ ....$ 1 93
Per diem 3 days... 4 50

ROCKY MOUNTAIN ☐ NO. 3.

Entitled to pay for one delegate:
Mileage 90 miles... 5 40
Per diem 2 days....... .... 3 00

NEVADA ☐ NO. 4.

Entitled to pay for two delegates:
Mileage 85 miles each....................................... 10 20
Per diem 2 days each.. 6 00

DENVER ☐ NO. 5.

Entitled to pay for two delegates:
Per diem 2 days each.. 6 00

SUMMIT ☐ NO. 2.

Entitled to pay for three delegates:
Mileage each 200 miles...................................... 36 00
Per diem each 3 days.. 13 50

All of which is respectfully submitted.

M. C. WHITE, *Chairman.*
L. W. CHASE.

The report of the committee was received and adopted.

The committee on Accounts submitted the following

REPORT:

To the M.˙. W.˙. Grand ☐ of Colorado :

Your committee on Accounts would respectfully report that they have examined the records of accounts of the M.˙. W.˙. Grand ☐ of Colorado, and find that there has been no return from any of the ☐ under its jurisdiction except Summit ☐ No. 2, and Chivington ☐ U. D.

Summit ☐, whose report is herewith submitted, reports that there is due and owing from them to the M.˙. W.˙. Grand ☐ of Nebraska, while working under its jurisdiction, the sum of forty-seven dollars, and ask that the same amount be remitted by this M.˙. W.˙. Grand ☐, in order that they may not be compelled to pay the amount twice.

There will then be due this M.˙. W.˙. Grand ☐, from Summit ☐ No. 2, the sum of $54.50.

Your committee would most respectfully recommend that the report of Summit ☐ be accepted, and the amount due the M.˙. W.˙. Grand ☐ of Nebraska, be remitted, in order that they may not have the amount to pay twice.

Your committee also recommend that the ☐ that have not made reports be allowed ninety days to make their returns to the Grand Secretary.

Your committee have examined the accounts of the Grand Secretary, and find that there has been received for the use of the ☐ from

Chivington ☐, for dispensation................................$25 00
Summit ☐ returns... 54 50
                                                            ———
                                                            79 50

For blank dispensations.................................$ 6 00
For printing proceedings of Grand □ .... 19 25 ·
For □ seal.. 18 00

                                                       43 25

Leaving still in the hands of the Secretary........................ 36 25
We also find still due for printing proceedings.................... 30 75
    No account has been rendered by the Treasurer, and we find from the accounts of the Secretary that no money has been paid to him.
            All of which is respectfully submitted.

                                  J. THATCHER, *Chairman.*

Report of the Secretary of Summit □ No. 2, of A. F. and A. M., Parkville, C. T. :

, *To the M∴ W∴ Grand □ of Colorado:*   ι   ·

    At a called meeting of Summit □ No. 2, A. F. and A. M., held at the hall of Summit □, in Parkville, Dec. 4th, A. L. 5861, A. D. 1861, it was

    Resolved, That the dues and Grand □ dues of all members of this □ who are paying dues and Grand □ dues to ▭ in the States be remitted.

    Sixteen members of Summit □ are paying □ and Grand □ dues to other ▭, whose dues are remitted in accordance with the above resolution.

    It was also

    Resolved, That as Summit □ was chartered by the M∴ W∴ Grand □ of Nebraska, and the charter members and those initiated while under the jurisdiction of the same are required to pay Grand □ dues and fees to said M∴ W∴ Grand □ of Nebraska: That our Secretary be required to report the names of the members paying dues to said □, and the initiations, while under such jurisdiction, to the M∴ W∴ Grand □ of Colorado Territory, and that our delegates request of the M∴ W∴ Grand □ of Colorado Territory, under whose jurisdiction we now are, to remit the dues for the work done while under the jurisdiction of the M∴ W∴ Grand □ of Nebraska, also the Grand □ dues of the charter members of Summit □ for the year 1861.

    The Secretary, therefore, would report that there were seven initiations while under the jurisdiction of the M∴ W∴ Grand □ of Nebraska, six of whom were passed, and five were raised and became members of Summit □, under the jurisdiction of the M∴ W∴ Grand □ of Colorado.

    Summit □ is indebted to the M∴ W∴ Grand □ of Nebraska for the fees of the five members initiated while under the jurisdiction of said M∴ W∴ Grand □, and also to the M∴ W∴ Grand □ of Colorado, for membership dues, unless the request of Summit □ be granted by the M∴ W∴ Grand □ of Colorado.

    The twenty-four original members of Summit □ are indebted to the M∴ W∴ Grand □ of Nebraska for Grand □ dues, and also to the M∴ W∴ Grand □ of Colorado, unless the request of Summit □ be granted as above.

    Trusting that the prayer of Summit □ will be granted, the Secretary returns as the Grand □ dues of Summit □, $54.50, being for ten initiations, and three admissions, while under the jurisdiction of the M∴ W∴ Grand □ of Colorado.

Fraternally submitted,

O. A. WHITTEMORE,
Secretary Summit □ No. 2.

On motion, it was

Resolved, That the Grand Tyler be paid one dollar and fifty cents per day for his services.

On motion of Bro. Holly, it was

Resolved, That the thanks of this Grand □ be tendered to Denver □ No. 5, for the free use of their commodious hall during the present session, together with the incidental conveniences attached thereto.

No further business appearing, the □ was closed in peace and harmony.

J. M. CHIVINGTON, *Grand Master.*

O. A. WHITTEMORE, *Grand Secretary.*

RETURNS

FROM

SUBORDINATE LODGES,

ENTERED DECEMBER 10, 1861.

GOLDEN CITY ▢, NO. 1, GOLDEN CITY.

OFFICERS.

Wm. Train Muir, W. M. Ira Quimby, J. W. John A. Moore, Sec'y.
L. W. Frary, S. W. John M. Ferrill, Treas. S. B. Williams, S. D.

MEMBERS.

Eli Carter, P. M. Reuben Borton, Daniel McCleery,
Isaac E. Hardy, P. M. John M. Saxton, Samuel F. Shaffer,
W. L. Rothrick, S. M. Breath, J. B. Hendry,
Fox Diefendorf, E. B. Smith, Hiram F. Ford.
James E. Dawson,

FELLOWCRAFT.
D. G. Dargin.

Initiated, 2; passed, 2; raised, 1; dimitted, 1; number of members, 18.

SUMMIT ▢ NO. 2, PARKVILLE.

OFFICERS.

James Ewing, W. M. George Oldham, Treas. L. Pollard, J D.
D. P. Sparks, S. W. O. A. Whittemore, Sec'y. H. E. Depp, Tyler.
M. C. White, J. W. Joshua Miller, S. D.

MEMBERS.

S. M. Robbins, D. G. M. Nelson Toncray, J. D. Thomas,
J. H. Depp, P. Asbury, Nicholas Thede,
D. T. Robley, Wm. Turner, Peter Valiton,
John L. Lewis, John Thompson, A. R. Peters,
F. E. Lewis, M. J. Walsh, W. M. Campbell,
Geo. Oswald, O. B. Brown, Frank Meyer,
G. W. Gillson, N. Berry, A. K. Blim,
C. C. Carpenter, J. N. Helstrom, John Coon,
George Reeder, R. S. Morris, J. Thatcher.

FELLOWCRAFTS.

Hans Walf, W. A. Williamson, H. B. Haskell,
Lewis Behm, Wm. Cox,

ENTERED APPRENTICES.

Harmon Duncan,   D. Stogsdall,   John Mentzer.
G. E. Kittle,

Number of admissions, 3; initiations, 10; passed, 13; raised, 8; dimitted, 4; suspended, 1; rejected, 4; number of members, 31.

ROCKY MOUNTAIN □ NO. 3, GOLD HILL.

OFFICERS.

J. M. Holt, W. M.   C. F. Holly, Treas.   A G. Raynor, J. D.
C. W. Smith, S. W.   S. S. Wemott, Sec'y.   H. A. Butler, Tyler.
E. S. Glotfelter, J. W.   H. J. Reuber, S. D.

MEMBERS.

J. M. Chivington, M. W. Henry Blake,   C. J. Goss,
  G. M.   M. G. Smith,   —— Barney.

ENTERED APPRENTICE.

B. N. Sanford.

Number of initiations, 1; died, 1; number of members, 13.

PROCEEDINGS

OF THE

SECOND ANNUAL COMMUNICATION

OF THE

GRAND LODGE OF COLORADO,

HELD AT CENTRAL CITY, NOVEMBER 3, A. L. 5862.

The second Annual Communication of the M∴ W∴ Grand ▢ of Ancient, Free and Accepted Masons of Colorado, was held at the hall of Chivington ▢ No. 6, in Central City, commencing on the first Monday of November, the 3d day, A. D. 1862, A. L. 5862.

Present—

R∴ W∴ ANDREW MASON, Deputy Grand Master.
R∴ W∴ P. S. PFOUTS, Senior Grand Warden.
R∴ W∴ M. C. WHITE, Junior Grand Warden.
R∴ W∴ O. B. BROWN, Grand Treasurer.
R∴ W∴ O. A. WHITTEMORE, Grand Secretary.
Bro. and Rev. W. H. FISHER, Grand Chaplain, *pro tem.*
R∴ W∴ ALLYN WESTON, Grand Lecturer.
Bro. A. J. VAN DEREN, Grand Senior Deacon, *pro tem.*
R∴ W∴ L. W. CHASE, Grand Junior Deacon.
W∴ J. W. RATLIFF, Grand Tyler.

A Master Masons' ▢ was opened.

R∴ W∴ Deputy Grand Master then appointed the following committee on Credentials:

Bros. Whittemore, Weston, and J. M. Van Deren,

Who reported as follows:

To the M∴ W∴ Grand Master:

The committee appointed on Credentials have attended to the duty assigned them, and respectfully report:

No returns have been received and no dues paid by Golden City ☐ No. 1.

Bro. Wm. T. Muir appeared before the committee, and stated that he was
Master of the ☐, and that the returns were not made and the dues not paid
because he was ignorant of the time of the meeting of the Grand ☐ till
Thursday last.

Bro. Muir wishes to represent the ☐ as Master, but your committee do
not consider that they have any official information to report him a member.

From the returns of ☐ and written proxies, we find the following named
brethren entitled to seats in this Grand body:

SUMMIT ☐ No. 2: M. C. White, W∴ M∴, O. B. Brown, S∴ W∴, H. B.
Haskell, proxy for J∴ W∴.

NEVADA ☐ No. 4: J. M. Van Deren, W∴ M∴, A. J. Van Deren, S∴
W∴, L. W. Chase, J∴ W∴.

DENVER ☐ No. 5: Richard E. Cooke, proxy for W∴ M∴, B. C. Hayman,
proxy for S∴ W∴, J. M. Broadwell, proxy for J∴ W∴.

CHIVINGTON ☐ No. 6: Wm. H. Fisher, proxy for W∴ M∴, H. M. Teller,
S∴ W∴, Geo. A. Pugh, proxy for J∴ W∴.

Your committee are informed by the Grand Secretary that all the above
named ☐, except Golden City No. 1, have paid their annual dues to this
Grand ☐.

Respectfully submitted,

O. A. WHITTEMORE, ⎫
ALLYN WESTON, ⎬ *Committee.*
J. M. VAN DEREN, ⎭

Report received and adopted.

A quorum of ☐ being found present, the R∴ W∴ Deputy
Grand Master declared the Grand ☐ opened in due form, and
a blessing was invoked by the Grand Chaplain.

On motion of Bro. Weston, the reading of the minutes of
the last Annual Communication was dispensed with, printed
copies being in the hands of members.

The R∴ W∴ Deputy Grand Master then appointed the following committees:

Visiting Brethren—Bros. A. J. Van Deren and B. C. Hayman.

On Accounts—Bros. O. B. Brown and H. M. Teller.

Foreign Correspondence—Bro. Weston.

Pay Roll—Bros. P. S. Pfouts and O. A. Whittemore.

Charters and Dispensations—Bros. O. B. Brown, A. J. Van Deren and B.
C. Hayman.

Bro. A. J. Van Deren moved that the first business on resuming labor in the afternoon, be the election of officers, which was carried.

The □ was then called from labor, to meet at 2 o'clock P. M.

MONDAY, NOV. 3, 2 o'clock P. M.

The Grand □ was called to labor by the R∴ W∴ Deputy Grand Master.

The committee on Credentials reported Bro. J. M. Broadwell as proxy for Junior Warden of Denver □ No. 5, as present and in his seat.

The election of officers being the special order of business, the R∴ W∴ Deputy Grand Master appointed Bros. J. M. Van Deren and J. M. Broadwell, tellers. R∴ W∴ Deputy Grand Master having declined an election, the Grand □ proceeded to the election of Grand Officers for the ensuing year, with the following result:

ALLYN WESTON, of Central City, Grand Master.
M. C. WHITE, of Parkville, Deputy Grand Master.
J. M. VAN DEREN, of Nevada, Senior Grand Warden.
RICHARD SOPRIS, of Denver, Junior Grand Warden.
O. B. BROWN, of Parkville, Grand Treasurer.
O. A. WHITTEMORE, of Colorado City, Grand Secretary.

The committee on Charters and Dispensations, submitted the following report:

To the M∴ W∴ Grand □ of Colorado:
The undersigned, committee on Charters and Dispensations, beg leave to report as follows, to wit:
We have examined the returns of Summit □ No. 2, and find that there is due the M∴ W∴ Grand □ of Colorado:

For 13 initiations..	$ 65 00
For 18 members..	27 00
Total...	$ 92 00

NEVADA □ NO. 4.

For 23 initiations..	$115 00
For 23 members..	34 00
Total...	$149 00

DENVER □ NO. 5.

For 18 initiations... $90 00
For 41 members.. 61 50

Total..$151 50

CHIVINGTON □ NO. 6.

For 24 initiations...$120 00
For 15 members............................... .... 22 50

Total........... ....$142 50

From Golden City □ No. 6, and Rocky Mountain □ No. 3, we have no returns.

Respectfully submitted,

O. B. BROWN,
A. J. VAN DEREN, } Committee.
B. C. HAYMAN,

Report adopted.

The R∴ W∴ Deputy Grand Master submitted the following

ANNUAL REPORT:

Brethren of the Grand □:

During nearly the whole of the past Masonic year, the M∴ W∴ Grand Master of the Territory has been absent upon pressing military duties, as you are all well aware.

I have not had the pleasure of receiving any communication from him since my election as Deputy Grand Master.

I have to report to you, brethren, that the only official act I have had occasion to perform during the past Masonic year has been as follows:

On May 3d, 1862, at the request of Denver □ No. 5, I granted dispensation to pass and raise Bro. H. Z. Salomon in a less time than required by the By-Laws, the case appearing to me to be one of emergency.

Trusting that the blessing of God may rest upon you and all regular Masons, in your labors for the good of our ancient and honorable craft,

I am your brother,
ANDREW MASON,
D∴ G∴ M∴ of Colorado.

The following communication, accompanied by a petition from the Secretary of Rocky Mountain □ No. 3, was referred to a special committee, consisting of Bros. White, Weston and J. M. Van Deren:

GOLD HILL, COLORADO TERRITORY, }
Oct. 31, A. L. 5862, A. D. 1862. }

To the M∴ W∴ Grand □ of Colorado:

There having been no meeting of Rocky Mountain □ No. 3, of A., F.

' and A. M., since the Annual Communication of the Grand ▭, held December, 1861, the Secretary has no report to make, farther than to state that the records of the ▭ remain the same as at that time. Delegates will be in attendance who will fully explain the reasons of such non-action; however, it may be well to state that nearly all the members of the ▭ left the district even before the meeting of the Grand ▭ the past year; and that at no time since has there been members enough here to hold regular or special communications.

~ The Secretary was in the States the past winter and summer, and upon his return found himself alone in the district, all other members having removed to different sections of the country, from which they could not well come here for Masonic labors.

Under the circumstances, it is necessary that some special action of the Grand ▭ be had in reference to the welfare of the ▭.

Application will be made for a removal of the ▭ from Gold Hill to Boulder City, where several members of the ▭ reside, and where many other brother Masons only wait the removal of the ▭ to join it.

The ▭ has necessarily slept the past year, and from so doing, by regulations of the Grand ▭, forfeits its charter. Trusting, however, that such unavoidable informality will be charitably treated, and that opportunity will be granted for more regular and efficient labor, by granting the removal of the ▭ to a more thickly settled portion of the country, the members await your action and decision.

Fraternally submitted,
S. S. WEMOTT,
Secretary Rocky Mountain ▭ No. 3.

Bro. Pfouts offered the following resolution :

Resolved, That the next Annual Communication of this Grand ▭ be held in the city of Denver, on the first Monday in November, 1863.

Bro. A. J. Van Deren moved as an amendment, that the time and place for the next meeting of the Grand ▭ be fixed by nomination and ballot.

On motion of Bro. Hayman, the matter was laid over until to-morrow morning.

The committee appointed at last stated communication to revise and report By-Laws, submitted the following report, which was received, and the By-Laws therein recommended were adopted :

To the M∴ W∴ Grand Master, Wardens and Brethren of the Grand ▭ of A., F. and A. M., of Colorado:

The undersigned, a committee appointed at the last Annual Communication to revise the By-Laws and Rules of Order of the Grand ▢, and report at the present Grand Communication, have attended to the duty assigned them, and respectfully recommend the following code (see appendix) for adoption.

ANDREW MASON, ⎫
ALLYN WESTON, ⎪
O. A. WHITTEMORE, ⎬ *Committee.*
M. C. WHITE, ⎭

The following communication from Chivington ▢ was read:

To the M∴ W∴ Grand Master, Wardens and Brethren of the Grand ▢ of Colorado:

At a Regular Communication of Chivington ▢ No. 6, of Ancient Free and Accepted Masons, held on the 22d day of October, A. L. 5862, it was resolved that the use of the Masonic hall, at Central City, be tendered free of charge, to the Grand ▢ during their session.

Central City, Nov. 1st, 1862.

WM. ROSENFIELD, *Sec'y,*
Chivington ▢ No. 6, A., F. and A. M.

On motion, it was

Resolved, That the thanks of the Grand ▢ be tendered to Chivington ▢ No. 6, for the free use of their hall.

On motion of Bro. Weston, it was

Resolved, That one-half of the amount of dues paid by any subordinate ▢ for the present year, to the Grand ▢ at this Annual Communication, be refunded to said ▢.

On motion of Bro. Weston, it was

Resolved, That the By-Laws heretofore in force in this Grand ▢ be rescinded.

The ▢ was then called from labor, to meet again at nine o'clock to-morrow morning.

TUESDAY, NOV. 4, 9 o'clock A. M.

The ▢ resumed labor.

Grand Officers at their several stations. Representatives present as yesterday.

Minutes of yesterday's meeting read and approved.

7

.Bro. White moved that one-half of the dues owing from Golden City ▭ No. 1, for the year 1861, be remitted to said ▭; motion lost.

The committee on By-Laws and Rules of Order, reported the following Rules of Order, (see appendix) and, on motion, they were adopted in place of those previously in force.

The special committee, to whom was referred the case of Rocky Mountain ▭ No. 3, made the following report, which was adopted:

To the M∴ W∴ Grand ▭ of Colorado:

Your committee to whom was referred the communication and petition from brethren of Rocky Mountain ▭ No. 3, beg leave to report that they have conversed with some of the petitioners and with the Secretary of said ▭, and find that it is their opinion, as well as that of your committee, that the charter of the ▭ be surrendered to the Grand ▭, together with such property as may remain to said ▭.

Respectfully submitted,

M. C. WHITE,
ALLYN WESTON, } *Committee.*
J. M. VAN DEREN,

The committee on Pay Roll submitted the following report, which was adopted:

To the M∴ W∴ Grand ▭ of Colorado:

Your committee appointed to report upon the Pay Roll of representatives in attendance on the Annual Communication of the Grand ▭, held November 3d, 1862, at Central City, respectfully report:

SUMMIT ▭ NO. 2.

Entitled to pay for three representatives:

Mileage each 200 miles...$36 00
Per diem each 2 days.. 9 00

NEVADA ▭ NO. 4.

Entitled to pay for three representatives:

Mileage each 2 miles... 37
Per diem each 2 days.. 9 00

DENVER ▭ NO. 5.

Entitled to pay for three representatives:

Mileage each 84 miles.. 15 00
Per diem each 2 days... 9 00

CHIVINGTON ▭ NO. 6.

Entitled to pay for three representatives:

Per diem each 2 days... 9 00

All of which is respectfully submitted,

P. S. PFOUTS,
O. A. WHITTEMORE, } *Committee.*

On motion of Bro. Teller, it was

Resolved, That the Annual Communication of the Grand □ shall be held on the first Monday of November in each year, alternately at the city of Denver, and Central City, the next Annual Communication to be held at Denver.

Which, on motion, was substituted for section 1 of the By-Laws.

On motion of Bro. Whittemore, it was

Resolved, That it shall be the duty of the Grand Lecturer, under the direction of the Grand Master, to visit the several ▱ in this jurisdiction, and instruct them in the work and lectures, and any □ requesting his services shall pay for the same.

On motion of Bro. Weston, it was

Resolved, That the Secretary is hereby required to have one hundred copies of the proceedings of the present Annual Communication printed, and that six copies of the same be sent to each subordinate □ in this jurisdiction.

The R∴ W∴ Deputy Grand Master then proceeded to install M∴ W∴ Allyn Weston, Grand Master.

The M∴ W∴ Grand Master then installed the following officers, P∴ D∴ G∴ M∴ A. Mason acting as Grand Marshal:

R∴ W∴ M. C. WHITE, Deputy Grand Master.
R∴ W∴ J. M. VAN DEREN, Senior Grand Warden.
R∴ W∴ RICHARD SOPRIS, Junior Grand Warden.
R∴ W∴ O. B. BROWN, Grand Treasurer.
R∴ W∴ O. A. WHITTEMORE, Grand Secretary.

The M∴ W∴ Grand Master then appointed, and subsequently installed, the following officers:

R∴ W∴ and Rev. W. H. FISHER, Grand Chaplain.
R∴ W∴ H. M. TELLER, Grand Orator.
R∴ W∴ A. J. VAN DEREN, Grand Lecturer.
R∴ W∴ R. E. COOKE, Grand Marshal.
W∴ L. W. CHASE, Senior Grand Deacon.
W∴ B. C. HAYMAN, Junior Grand Deacon.
Bro. J. W. RATLEFF, } Grand Stewards.
Bro. C. L. BARTLETT, }
Bro. L. W. FRARY, Grand Sword Bearer.
Bro. F. Z. SALOMON, Grand Pursuivant.
Bro. J. B. COFIELD, Grand Standard Bearer.
Bro. O. A. SEAMAN, Grand Tyler.

On motion of Bro. Grand Chaplain, a committee of three

was appointed to draft suitable resolutions commemorative of the death of our brother, R∴ W∴ W. A. Kenney, late Grand Chaplain, consisting of Bros. Fisher, Cook and Teller.

It was moved by Bro. D∴ G∴ Master, that article 12 of the Constitution be stricken out, which motion was seconded by eleven, which being a majority of all the members present, was ordered to be submitted to subordinate ⊡ for approval or rejection.

It was moved by Bro. D∴ G∴ Master, to amend article 17 of the Constitution, as follows :

Strike out " and be then submitted to the several subordinate ⊡ for their approval or rejection. If two-thirds of the ⊡ approve thereof, by certificate, over their respective seals, to the next succeeding Grand ☐," and insert in lieu thereof, " and if two-thirds of the members present consent."

Which, being seconded by eleven, a majority of the members present, was ordered to be submitted to the subordinate ⊡ for approval or rejection.

On motion of Bro. D∴ G∴ Master, it was

Resolved, That the Grand Secretary be allowed the sum of fifty dollars per year for his services, and that he be allowed his pay, at the above rates, for the last year.

On motion of Bro. Grand Lecturer, it was

Resolved, That the Grand Tyler be allowed the sum of three dollars per day for his services during the present Annual Communication of this Grand ☐.

The Grand Treasurer submitted his annual report, as follows, which was referred to the committee on Accounts :

To the M∴ W∴ Grand ☐ of Colorado:

The undersigned would respectfully report as follows :

That during the Masonic year, commencing on the 10th day of December, 1861, and ending on the 3d day of November, A. D. 1862, A. L. 5862, he has received from the R∴ W∴ Grand Secretary, $639.25 ; of which he has paid

Dec. 15, for printing proceedings of the formation of Grand ☐....	$ 30	75
" To representatives Summit ☐..........	31	25
Aug. 15, for printing proceedings 1st Annual...................	30	00
Total.....	92	00
Balance remaining on hand.............................	547	25

Respectfully submitted,

O. B. BROWN, *Grand Treasurer.*

The Grand Secretary submitted the following account, which was referred to the committee on Accounts :

O. A. WHITTEMORE, *Grand Secretary, in account with the Grand □ of Colorado:*

			DR.
Dec. 12,	to cash balance on hand		$ 36 25
"	"	Denver □ No. 5, charter	30 00
"	"	Chivington □ No. 6, charter	30 00
Aug. 4,	"	M∴ W∴ Grand Master, for dispensation King Solomon's □	10 00
Nov. 3,	"	Summit □ No. 2	92 00
"	"	Nevada □ No. 4	149 50
"	"	Denver □ No. 5	151 50
"	"	Chivington □ No. 6	142 50
			641 75

		CR.
By paid for stationery and postage		$ 2 50
" Grand Treasurer, as per receipts		639 25
		$641 75

The □ was then called from labor, to meet at 2 o'clock P. M.

TUESDAY, NOV. 4, 2 o'clock P. M.

The □ resumed labor.

The committee on Accounts submitted the following report, which was adopted :

To the M∴ W∴ Grand □ of Colorado:

Your committee on Accounts respectfully submit the following report, to-wit :

They have examined the accounts of the Secretary and Treasurer, also, the accounts of committee on Pay Roll, and accounts of Wm. McConnel for tyling the Grand □ of December, 1861, all of which we find correct.

O. B. BROWN, } *Committee.*
H. M. TELLER, }

The special committee who were appointed to report resolutions relative to the death of R∴ W∴ W. A. Kenney, Grand Chaplain, submitted the following, which were adopted :

WHEREAS, It has pleased the Supreme Ruler of the universe, in His wisdom, to call from labor to refreshment our highly esteemed and dearly beloved Bro., Rev. W. A. Kenney, Grand Chaplain of the Grand □ of Ancient Free and Accepted Masons of Colorado ; therefore,

Resolved, By this Grand □, that we bow submissively to this manifestation of God's, providence, ever praying that we may be duly prepared for the summons of the Grand Warden of Heaven, to enter into celestial rest.

Resolved, That in the demise of Bro. Kenney, the church has lost a faithful and efficient minister and pastor, his family a devoted husband and father, the community a worthy citizen, and the craft a just and upright brother.

Resolved, That we tender the friends of the deceased our condolence, in this, their hour of sorrow, hoping they may ever put their confidence in Him who doeth all things well.

Resolved, That the Grand Secretary be requested to forward a copy of these resolutions to the widow of our brother, and further, that they be embodied in the printed proceedings of this Grand □.

Respectfully submitted,

WM. H. FISHER, } *Committee.*
H. M. TELLER, }

On motion of Bro. D∴ G∴ Master, it was

Resolved, That the amount due Bro. Chas. F. Holly from the Grand □. for services as representative at the last Regular Communication, be applied on the dues of Rocky Mountain □ No. 3, for that year, and that the amount due J. E. Dawson, as representative at the last Regular Communication, be applied on the dues of Golden City □ No. 1, for that year, they having so desired.

On motion of Bro. Grand Treasurer, it was

Resolved, That if any subordinate □ under the jurisdiction of the M∴ W∴ Grand □ of Colorado, shall fail to meet for six successive months, their charter shall be declared forfeited.

On motion of Bro. Senior Grand Warden, a committee of three was appointed to prepare a suitable installation ceremony, consisting of Bros. S∴ G∴ W∴ J. M. Van Deren, D∴ G∴ M∴ M. C. White, and J∴ G∴ D∴ B. C. Hayman.

The M∴ W∴ Grand Master appointed the following committees :

Foreign Correspondence—Bros. Grand Secretary, S∴ G∴ Warden J. M. Van Deren, and J∴ G∴ Warden, R. Sopris.

Masonic Jurisprudence—Bros. Grand Orator, H. M. Teller, P∴ D∴ G∴ Master, A. Mason, and Grand Treasurer, O. B. Brown.

On motion, it was

Resolved, That the Grand Secretary be authorized to exchange parchment charters with subordinate □, for the paper charters now held by them; which said parchment charters shall set forth the names of the members and officers named in the old charter, the Grand Communication at which it was granted, the names of the Grand Officers attached thereto, the reason for the change, and shall be signed by the Grand Master, and attested by the Grand Secretary, under his hand and the seal of the Grand □.

On motion of Bro. Grand Lecturer, it was unanimously

Resolved, That the thanks of this Grand □ be and are hereby tendered Bro. Mason, P∴ D∴ G∴ M∴, for the able, Masonic and impartial manner in which he has presided over its labors at this Grand Communication.

There appearing no further business, after prayer by Rev. Bro. Grand Chaplain, the Grand □ of Colorado was closed in ample form.

ALLYN WESTON, *Grand Master.*

Attest:

O. A. WHITTEMORE, *Grand Secretary.*

CONSTITUTION

OF THE

GRAND LODGE OF COLORADO.

———

Whereas, Every Grand □ possesses the inherent power to form a Constitution, as the fundamental law of its Masonic action, and to enact such By-Laws from time to time as it may deem necessary for its own government, and to make such rules and prescribe such regulations for the administration of its subordinate ▣, as will insure the prosperity thereof, and promote the general good of Masonry; and, Whereas, Every Grand □ is the true representative of all the fraternity in communication therewith, and is, in that behalf, an absolute and independent body, with supreme legislative authority: *Provided always*, That the ancient Landmarks of the Order be held inviolate.

Therefore, ·Upon these principles, which have never been disputed, the Grand □ of Colorado does hereby ordain, establish and promulgate the following Constitution and By-Laws for its future government, and does make and prescribe the following rules and regulations for the government of the ▣ under its jurisdiction.

ARTICLE I.

This Grand □ shall forever hereafter be known by the name and style of the Most Ancient and Honorable Fraternity of Free and Accepted Masons of Colorado.

ARTICLE II.

The Grand □ shall consist of a Grand Master, Deputy Grand Master, Senior Grand Warden, Junior Grand Warden,

Grand Treasurer, Grand Secretary, Grand Chaplain, Grand Orator, Grand Lecturer, Grand Marshal, Senior Grand Deacon, Junior Grand Deacon and Grand Tyler, with such other officers as it may, from time to time, create; together with the Masters and Wardens, or their proxies, duly constituted, of the chartered ▣ under its jurisdiction, and such Past Grand Masters and Past Deputy Grand Masters as shall be present, and are members of a subordinate ▢.

ARTICLE III.

The Grand ▢ shall hold a stated communication, at least once in every two years, at such time and in such place as may be designated in its By-Laws.

ARTICLE IV.

The Grand ▢ shall not be opened, nor shall any business be transacted therein, unless there be present a representative from at least three of the chartered ▣; but a smaller number may meet and adjourn from day to day, until a constitutional quorum shall attend.

ARTICLE V.

The officers of the Grand ▢ shall be styled, and take rank, as follows:

The Most Worshipful Grand Master.
The Right Worshipful Deputy Grand Master.
The Right Worshipful Senior Grand Warden.
The Right Worshipful Junior Grand Warden.
The Right Worshipful Grand Treasurer.
The Right Worshipful Grand Secretary.
The Right Worshipful Grand Chaplain.
The Right Worshipful Grand Orator.
The Right Worshipful Grand Lecturer.
The Right Worshipful Grand Marshal.
The Worshipful Senior Grand Deacon.
The Worshipful Junior Grand Deacon.
The Grand Tyler.

ARTICLE VI.

No brother shall be eligible to the office of Grand Master,

8

Deputy Grand Master, or Grand Warden, who has not been duly elected, installed, and presided over a subordinate ▢.

ARTICLE VII.

At each stated communication of the Grand ▢, there shall be elected, by ballot, from among the brethren who are at the time constitutionally eligible to seats therein, a Grand Master, a Deputy Grand Master, a Grand Senior Warden, a Grand Junior Warden, a Grand Treasurer and a Grand Secretary ; all other Grand Officers shall be appointed by the Grand Master, with the advice and consent of the Grand ▢.

ARTICLE VIII.

No Grand Officer shall officiate in the station to which he is elected, until he has been legally installed.

ARTICLE IX.

The Most Worshipful Grand Master has the right to convene the Grand ▢, in special Grand Communication, on any emergency which, in his judgment, may require it. He has the power at his discretion to assemble any subordinate ▢, and preside therein, inspect its work, and require a strict conformity to the constitutional rules and regulations of order. For good cause, he may suspend the functions of any such ▢, until the ensuing stated communication of the Grand ▢. It is his prerogative to make Masons at sight, and, for this purpose, may summon to his assistance such brethren as he may deem necessary. He has the command of every other Grand Officer, touching the duties and ministrations of their several offices, and may call on any and all of them, at any time, for advice and assistance on all business relative to the craft.

ARTICLE X.

In case of the death, absence, or inability of the Grand Master, the powers and duties of his station, for all regular and necessary purposes, shall, for the time being, devolve upon the Deputy Grand Master, Senior Grand Warden, or Junior Grand Warden, in the order here enumerated.

ARTICLE XI.

During the recess of the Grand ▢, the Grand Master, and

Deputy Grand Master, severally, have power to grant dispensations, under their private seals, for instituting new ⌸.

ARTICLE XII.

No dispensation shall be granted for constituting a new ▢, except upon the petition of eight Master Masons, one of whom must be a Past Master, and the recommendation of the chartered ▢ nearest the location of the new ▢, vouching for the moral character and Masonic qualifications of the petitioners.

ARTICLE XIII.

No warrant or dispensations, for the institution of a new ▢, shall be granted for a less sum than twenty-five dollars, and thirty dollars additional for the charter.

ARTICLE XIV.

No charter or dispensation, for constituting new ⌸, shall be granted to any person or persons whomsoever residing out of this Territory (or State), if within the jurisdiction of any other constitutional Grand ▢.

ARTICLE XV.

The Grand ▢ has original and exclusive jurisdiction over all subjects of Masonic legislation, and appellate jurisdiction from the decisions of the subordinate ⌸; and its enactments and decisions upon all questions shall be the supreme Masonic law of the Territory or State. It shall prescribe such rules and regulations for the government of the subordinate ⌸ as will, in its arbitrament, conduce to the welfare, prosperity and happiness of the craft ; and may require from them such dues and fees as will at all times discharge the engagements of the Grand ▢.

ARTICLE XVI.

The Book of Constitutions hereunto attached, this Grand ▢ does recognize and adopt as the fundamental Laws, Rules and Regulations for the government of Masons ; and declares that it should be frequently read and perused by Masters, and other craftsmen, as well within the subordinate ⌸ as thereout, to the end that none may be ignorant of the excellent principles and precepts it inculcates.

ARTICLE XVII.

This Constitution may be altered or amended, in the following manner only: The proposed alteration or amendment must be made in writing, at some stated communication. If seconded by a majority of votes, it shall be entered upon the minutes, and be then submitted to the several subordinate ⌸, for their approval or rejection. If two-thirds of the ⌸ approve thereof by certificate, over their respective seals, to the next succeeding Grand ☐, the Grand Master shall put the question upon its adoption; and if concurred in, by a vote of three-fourths of the members present, it shall, from thenceforth, be considered as a part and parcel of this Constitution.

BY-LAWS.

SECTION 1. The Annual Communications of the Grand □ shall be held on the first Monday of November in each year, alternately at the city of Denver and Central City, the next Annual Communication to be held at Denver.

ELIGIBILITY.

SEC. 2. No brother shall be eligible to either of the offices of Grand or Deputy Grand Master, Senior or Junior Grand Warden, unless he shall have passed the chair in some regular □.

SEC. 3. No member shall be eligible to any office in this Grand □, who is not a member of a subordinate □ in this jurisdiction.

PROXIES.

SEC. 4. Whenever the Master or Wardens of a □ cannot attend in person, either of them may depute any Master Mason to act for him: *Provided,* That such person, so deputed, shall be a member of the □ from which the proxy is given.

ANNUAL RETURNS.

SEC. 5. Every □, subordinate to this Grand □, shall, on or before the first day of each Annual Grand Communication, pay to the Grand Secretary, for the use of the Grand □, the sum of one dollar and fifty cents for each Master Mason belonging to their □ at the time of making the annual return. And no representative of any □ shall be entitled to a seat in the Grand □, until the dues of this □ are paid, and the Grand Secretary's receipt therefor produced. And in case of the neglect or refusal of any □ to pay its annual dues, at the time herein specified, or on or before the next Annual Communication of the Grand □, such □ may be stricken from the books of the Grand □, and their warrant or charter considered null and void; but on proper application to the Grand □, making full returns, and paying of all dues, such □ may be restored to its former rank and privileges.

SEC. 7. No □ shall be required to pay dues for members who shall have permanently removed without the jurisdiction of this Grand □.

LEAVE OF ABSENCE.

SEC. 8. No brother, after having taken his seat as a member, shall be permitted to leave without obtaining permission of the Grand Master.

COMMITTEES—THEIR DUTIES.

SEC. 9. At each Annual Communication of the Grand □, as soon as practicable after its organization, the Grand Master shall appoint the following committees:

First. A committee on Credentials, to consist of three members, whose duty it shall be to examine the credentials of all Masons claiming the right of membership, and report their names and Masonic connection to the Grand □.

Second, A committee to examine visiting brethren, to consist of three members, whose duty it shall be to examine all visitors not properly vouched for, and report their respective names, address, and Masonic connection to the Grand □.

Third. A committee on Returns and Work of ⬚ U. D., on Chartered ⬚ and on Petitions, consisting of three members, whose duty it shall be to examine the By-Laws, records of work and the returns of ⬚ under dispensation, and to make report to the Grand □, if, or not, in their opinion, charters should be granted to such ⬚; to examine the returns of proceedings and work of chartered ⬚, to examine all petitions for the new ⬚ U. D., for changes of location, or for change of name, and report on the same to the Grand □.

Fourth. A committee on Appeals and Grievances, consisting of three members, whose duty it shall be to examine and report upon all appeals, memorials and petitions in relation to any matter of complaint or grievance within this jurisdiction which shall come before the Grand □.

Fifth. A committee on Finance, Mileage and Per Diem, consisting of three members, whose duty it shall be to examine and report on all accounts and financial matters to them referred, and to make a full report, before the close of each Annual Grand Communication, of the financial condition of the Grand □, also to ascertain the distance necessarily traveled by each officer and representative entitled to mileage and per diem, and report the same to the Grand □.

SEC. 10. Before the close of each Annual Communication of the Grand □, the Grand Master shall appoint three standing committees for the ensuing Masonic year, as follows, viz:

First. On Masonic Correspondence, to consist of three members, whose duty it shall be to examine the correspondence and documents from other Grand □, in correspondence with this Grand □, and report at each Annual Communication, whatever may seem of sufficient importance and interest to demand its attention or action.

Second. On Masonic Jurisprudence, to consist of three members, whose duty it shall be to examine and report upon all questions, documents and papers requiring investigation and decision upon points of Masonic law, and to make report upon the same.

SEC. 11. The Grand Officers, members of the committees on Masonic Correspondence and Masonic Jurisprudence, and the representative highest in rank from each □ under this jurisdiction, shall be allowed twelve and one-half cents per mile, going and returning, for every mile traveled from his place of residence, computed by the necessarily traveled route, and two dollars per day for each day's actual attendance at the Grand □; *Provided,* No one shall draw mileage both as a Grand Officer and representative.

LODGES UNDER DISPENSATION.

SEC. 12. No dispensation shall be granted by the Grand

Master or by the Grand ▢ for the formation of a new ▢, but upon the petition of seven known and approved Master Masons, in which their first Master and Wardens shall be nominated; said petition shall set forth the name of the county and place, also that the petitioners have procured a suitable room, with convenient ante rooms, for the practice of Masonic rites, and that the material in their town and neighborhood is sufficient to sustain a healthy and reputable ▢, which shall be accompanied by a recommendation from the ▢ nearest the place in which the new ▢ is to be holden, certifying to the truth of the statements contained in said petition, and that the brother named for Master is qualified to open and close a ▢, and to confer the three degrees.

SEC. 13. There shall be paid for every dispensation for a new ▢, the sum of forty dollars; for every charter, the sum of twenty dollars; and the further sum, in addition, of two dollars, to be paid to the Grand Secretary; which said sums, respectively, shall be paid before the delivery of the dispensation or charter.   The seal of the Grand ▢ shall be affixed to every charter without additional charge.   •

SEC. 14. No charter shall issue to a ▢ under dispensation, until it shall have conferred the degrees of Entered Apprentice, Fellowcraft and Master Mason, in manner and form as prescribed by the rules and regulations of the Grand ▢.

SPECIAL DISPENSATIONS.

SEC. 15. There shall be paid into the hands of the Grand Master the sum of five dollars for every dispensation granted to confer any degree or degrees in less than the usual time specified in the By-Laws or Regulations of this Grand ▢, to be paid in all cases before the dispensation is issued; also the sum of two dollars for every special dispensation for any other purpose.

NON-AFFILIATED MASONS.

SEC. 16. Jurisdiction and discipline shall be exercised over non-affiliated Masons by the oldest ▢ only, in cities or places where two or more ▣ may be situate.

EXPULSIONS, SUSPENSIONS, RESTORATIONS AND REJECTIONS.

SEC. 17. Notices of expulsions, suspensions and rejections, shall be given in the following manner: When any brother shall be suspended or expelled, or any candidate for initiation shall be rejected by any ▭, immediate notice thereof shall be sent to each ▭ in this jurisdiction. All expulsions and suspensions shall also be published with the proceedings of the Grand ▭. No member shall be permitted to make any expulsion or suspension public, or to communicate the same to any person not a Mason, except by a resolution to make public by the ▭ from which the brother has been suspended or expelled, and which shall also be reported to the Grand Secretary.

SEC. 18. All appeals from any subordinate ▭ shall be in writing, and left with the Grand Secretary, and the appellant shall give the other party reasonable notice thereof; and in case the decision of any ▭ suspending or expelling a brother shall be reversed by the Grand ▭, such brother shall be restored to all his rights and privileges as a member of the order.

SEC. 19. In all cases of the suspension or expulsion of a member, two-thirds of the members present shall be required; and in all cases of the restoration of a Mason suspended by any ▭ under the jurisdiction of this Grand ▭, the same majority shall be required. No expelled Mason shall be restored to the privileges of Masonry except by a vote of the Grand ▭, and such restoration shall not re-instate him in membership in the ▭ from which he was expelled, without the unanimous consent of the members thereof.

SEC. 20. No ▭ acting under the jurisdiction of this Grand ▭ shall, knowingly, receive any candidate in any of the degrees in Masonry who has been rejected by any other ▭, within twelve months after such rejection, without first receiving the unanimous consent of the ▭ that rejected him.

GRAND TREASURER—HIS DUTIES.

SEC. 21. The Grand Treasurer shall have charge of all the

9

funds, property, securities and vouchers of the Grand ▢; and it shall be his duty to attend at all Grand Communications, and report the condition of the finances of the Grand ▢; and finally, to pay or deliver over to his successor in office, or such other person or persons as the Grand ▢ may appoint, all the funds, property, securities, vouchers, records and books belonging to the Grand ▢.

GRAND SECRETARY—HIS DUTIES.

SEC. 22. The Grand Secretary shall attend at all regular and special communications of the Grand ▢, and duly record its proceedings, and shall receive, and accurately account for, and promptly pay or deliver over to the Grand Treasurer all the funds and property of the Grand ▢, from whatever source taking his receipt for the same. He shall keep a record of the returns made by subordinate ▢; receive and preserve all petitions, applications, appeals and other documents; sign, certify to, and duly seal all instruments of writing emanating from the Grand ▢; conduct the correspondence of the Grand ▢, under the direction of the Grand Master, and report annually to the several Grand ▢ in correspondence with this Grand ▢, the names of Grand Officers elected.

He shall, at each Annual Grand Communication, make a report to the Grand ▢, of moneys received and paid over to the Grand Treasurer; of failure or want of punctuality on the part of subordinate ▢ in paying dues, and making proper returns, and of such other matters, as in his judgment, may require the action of the Grand ▢.

He shall, in due time, previous to each Annual Grand Communication, furnish each subordinate ▢ with blank returns, with such instructions in regard to them as the Rules and Regulations of the Grand ▢ may require.

He shall cause the Constitution, By-Laws, Regulations and binding resolutions of this Grand ▢ to be published annually, with the proceedings of the Grand ▢.

OTHER OFFICERS—THEIR DUTIES.

SEC. 23. The Grand Chaplain shall attend the Communications of the Grand ▢, and perform religious services.

The Grand Marshal shall proclaim the Grand Officers at their installation, introduce the representatives of foreign Grand ▭ and distinguished visiting brethren, and conduct processions of the Grand ▢.

The Grand Standard Bearer shall take charge of the Grand Standard of the order in processions and public ceremonies.

The Grand Sword Bearer shall carry the sword in procession, and perform such other duties as by ancient usage pertain to his office.

The Grand Stewards shall have immediate superintendence, under the direction of the Junior Grand Warden, in the provisions to be made on all festive occasions.

The Grand Pursuivant shall communicate with the Grand Tyler, announce all applicants for admission by their Masonic address, names and connection, and take charge of the jewels and clothing.

The Grand Deacons shall perform the duties incident to their respective offices.

The Grand Tyler shall guard the door of the Grand ▢, on the outside, report all persons claiming admission, and see that none enter but such as are duly authorized and properly clothed.

The Grand Tyler shall have all the rights, and be entitled to all the honors of other Grand Officers, except the right to vote.

UNLAWFUL LECTURES.

SEC. 24. The delivery or teaching of any Masonic lectures not authorized, or which have not received the sanction of the Grand ▢, or of its lawful authority, is forbidden.

SEC. 25. On all questions arising in the Grand ▢, the elected Grand Officers, together with such Past Grand Masters and Past Deputy Grand Masters as may be present, and are members thereof, shall each be entitled to one vote, and the Master and Wardens of each subordinate ▢, or their regularly constituted proxies, shall each be entitled to one vote; but in no case whatsoever, shall a member, by virtue of any proxy or authority, cast more than three votes.

BY-LAWS PERTAINING TO ⌺.

INDIVIDUAL ▭—THEIR DUTIES.

SEC. 26. All ⌺ subordinate to this Grand ▭ shall, immediately after each annual election by such ▭, report to the Grand Secretary the names of the Master, Wardens, and Secretary elect.

SEC. 27. Upon the demise of any ▭ within the jurisdiction of this Grand ▭, the last Secretary and Treasurer of the ▭ shall, within three months thereafter, transmit to the Grand Secretary all the books, papers, jewels, furniture, funds, and other property, or evidence thereof, of the ▭ so demised.

SEC. 28. No elections for officers shall take place in a ▭ U. D., but all vacancies shall be filled by appointment by the W. Master.

PETITIONS FOR INITIATION OR MEMBERSHIP.

SEC. 29. Subordinate ⌺ are instructed not to act upon any petition, either for initiation or membership, unless the same shall have lain over one lunar month.

SEC. 30. Subordinate ⌺ shall not receive a petition for initiation from an applicant who lives nearer to another ▭ than the one he petitions, without first obtaining the unanimous consent of the other ▭, at a regular meeting.

SEC. 31. After a petition is regularly received by a subordinate ▭ and entered upon its minutes, it shall not be withdrawn without the unanimous consent of the ▭.

SEC. 32. The subordinate ⌺ under the jurisdiction of this Grand ▭ are instructed not to initiate any candidate who has not resided in the Territory of Colorado six calendar months before such application be made.

CONFERRING DEGREES.

SEC. 33. No subordinate ▭ in this jurisdiction shall confer the degrees upon any candidate unless he be a perfect man, having no maim or defect in his body that may render him incapable of learning the art and becoming perfect in the degrees.

SEC. 34. No subordinate ▭ in this jurisdiction shall confer

any of the degrees on non-resident citizens without the consent of the proper jurisdiction first had and obtained.

SEC. 35. No ▢, working under the jurisdiction of this Grand ▢, shall be allowed to do any work irregularly, unless it be by dispensation from the Grand Master; and any ▢ working under such dispensation shall return the same to the Grand Master.

SEC. 36. A petition from a ▢ to the M∴ W∴ Grand Master, praying for a special dispensation to confer degrees, shall set forth fully, and clearly, the emergency.

SEC. 37. Advancement to the degrees may be stayed at any time, for good reasons, by the ▢ or the Master.

SEC. 38. No candidate shall receive more than one degree on the same day without dispensation from the Grand Master, nor unless he has passed a satisfactory examination, in open ▢, on that degree; nor shall any ▢ confer the first section of the first, second or third degree on more than one candidate at the same time.

BALLOTING.

SEC. 39. No ballot shall be spread, except at a Regular Communication, unless by special dispensation.

SEC. 40. In balloting for candidates, all members of the ▢ present shall vote: for, according to an old regulation, "no man can be entered a brother in any particular ▢, or admitted to be a member thereof, without the unanimous consent of all the members of that ▢ then present when the candidate is proposed." No Mason shall be required, by the Master or ▢, to give his reasons for the vote he has deposited, for the very secrecy of the ballot is intended to secure the independence and irresponsibility to the ▢, of the voter.

SEC. 41. The ballot shall be spread for each degree, and shall be unanimous. A unanimous ballot for each of the three degrees should be understood literally, and should be the same in each, and unanimous in all, upon the moral, intellectual and Masonic qualifications of the applicant.

SEC. 42. After the ballot has been taken and duly examined,

first, by the Wardens, and finally by the Master, the result shall be declared by the Master, unless only one negative vote appears, in which case the Master may order the second trial of the ballot, which shall, in all cases, be final, nor can it be set aside by the ▭, Master, Grand Master, or even the Grand ▭.

FEES.

SEC. 43. No ▭ shall confer the three degrees for a less sum than thirty dollars, to be paid in advance.

RIGHTS OF WARDENS.

SEC. 44. The ▭ shall not open or call to labor unless the Master or one of the Wardens be present.

SEC. 45. Wardens may preside and confer degrees in the absence of the Master.

DIMITS.

SEC. 46. It is contrary to, and inconsistent with, the ancient usages and precepts of our order, to withdraw from a subordinate ▭, or to reside in the neighborhood of a subordinate ▭, without becoming a member thereof.

SEC. 47. A Masonic dimit dates from the ▭ record, when the same was granted, and membership ceases with said date.

CHARTERS.

SEC. 48. It is not in the power of a majority of the members of a subordinate ▭ to surrender the charter of said ▭, so long as seven Master Masons, members thereof, continue to work under said charter, and according to the ancient landmarks of Masonry.

SEC. 49. Whenever the charter of a ▭ shall be destroyed by fire, or any other manner, or shall be stolen, or surreptitiously taken and detained, or become so defaced as to be unfit for use, without the fault of the ▭ or Master, it shall be lawful for the Grand Master to order another charter to be issued to such ▭; which charter shall set forth the names of the members and officers named in the charter so lost, detained or destroyed, the Grand Communication at which it was granted, the names of the Grand Officers attached thereto, and the circumstances of its loss, destruction or detention, and shall be signed by the Grand Master, and attested by the Grand Secretary under his hand and the seal of the Grand □, without fee.

TRIALS.

SEC. 50. All trials for Masonic offences in Lodges under the jurisdiction of this Grand □, shall be as follows:

A regular charge in writing, specifying the nature of the offence, and signed by the accuser, shall be delivered to the Secretary, who shall read it at the next Regular Communication. And it shall be the duty of the Secretary to give due and timely notice to the accused, of the time, place and manner of the trial, who shall be entitled to a copy of the charges and to ample time and opportunity to prepare his defence.

SEC. 51. All Masonic trials shall be in the □ of the highest degree to which the accused has attained, in which the examination of witnesses shall take place in the presence of both the accused and the accuser, who shall have the right to be present at all examinations of witnesses in or out of the □, and to propose such relevant questions as they may desire.

SEC. 52. After the trial is concluded, the accused and accuser shall be requested to retire, and, in case the trial has been in a □ of Entered Apprentices or Fellowcrafts, the □ shall then be opened on the third degree, for no decision shall be made for or against a brother after regular trial, except in a Master Masons' □, in which the question of guilty or not guilty shall be put by the Master, in which all the members present shall be required to vote, and of which two-thirds shall be in the affirmative, or the accused shall be declared not guilty.

SEC. 53. If the verdict is guilty, the Master or presiding officer shall put the question as to the amount of punishment, beginning with the highest and ending with the lowest Masonic punishment herein provided. The vote on the nature of the punishment may be taken by show of hands, and decided by a two-thirds vote of the members present.

SEC. 54. If the residence of the accused is not known, or if, upon due summons, he refuses or neglects to attend, a ▢ may proceed to a trial without his presence.

SEC. 55. The witnesses, in all Masonic trials, whether Masons or not, shall be persons who have the use of their reason, and such religious belief as to feel the obligations of an oath, and who have not been convicted of any infamous crime.

SEC. 56. The testimony of Masons shall be taken in ▢ or in committee; that of competent persons, not Masons, by a committee, on oath administered by a competent legal officer, and may be by affidavit.

SEC. 57. A subordinate ▢ should not suspend a member for non-payment of dues, without written notice and fair trial.

PUNISHMENTS.

SEC. 58. The Masonic punishment which may and shall be inflicted by the Grand ▢ and its subordinates for unmasonic conduct shall be, either reprimand, definite or indefinite suspension, or expulsion from all the rights and privileges of Masonry.

SEC. 59. A reprimand may be either private or public, but shall not be given except by a majority vote of the members present, nor until the offender has had due notice and an opportunity for explanation or excuse, nor by any one but the acting Master, in the manner and form he may deem proper, to the offender in private, or in open ▢ from his appropriate station.

SEC. 60. When a Mason is expelled from a ▢, he is thereby expelled from all the rights and privileges of Masonry.

APPEALS—RESTORATIONS.

SEC. 61. All Masons have the right to appeal from the decisions of subordinate ▣ to the Grand ▢, in which case the ▢ shall furnish the Grand ▢, and the appellant, with an attested copy of its proceedings on the trial, and such testimony, in its possession, as he may require for his defense.

SEC. 62. An application to re-instate an expelled Mason, must, in all cases, be accompanied with a recommendation from the ▢ by which the brother was expelled: *Provided*, such ▢ be still in existence.

SEC. 63. Restoration, after definite suspension by a ▢, shall take place at the expiration of the time specified in the sentence.

SEC. 64. Restoration, after indefinite suspension by a ▢, shall be by the action of such ▢, at a regular meeting, after due notice, and by a two-thirds vote of the members present.

SUMMONS.

SEC. 65. A summons, issued by a subordinate ▢, or the Worshipful Master thereof, must be written or printed, and under the seal of the ▢.

SEC. 66. Any summons issued as aforesaid, need not contain any other matter, except the requisition to attend the ▢ issuing the same, or the Master thereof, when required.

SEC. 67. Every Master Mason is bound to attend before the ▢, at the meeting of the ▢ so requiring him, on being summoned or notified.

SEC. 68. Any member of a subordinate ▢ is subject to the discipline thereof, excepting only the Worshipful Master.

AMENDMENTS.

SEC. 69. No alteration or amendment shall take place in these By-Laws, except by two-thirds vote of the members present.

RULES OF ORDER

---

1. The Most Worshipful Grand Master shall take the chair every day precisely at the hour to which the Grand ▭ shall have adjourned on the preceding day, when the journal shall be read, to the end that any mistake or improper entries may be corrected.

2. During the hours of business, the members are required to keep their seats and observe strict order and decorum ; and no member shall leave the hall without leave, or absent himself from the service of the Grand ▭ unless he have permission, or be sick and unable to attend.

3. No member shall be permitted to speak more than twice upon any subject, unless it is merely to explain, without permission from the Grand ▭. If any member is twice called to order at any meeting for transgressing these rules, and is guilty of a third offence of the same nature, the presiding officer shall peremptorily order him to leave the Grand ▭; and he may further be amenable to reprimand, suspension or expulsion, as the Grand ▭ shall deem proper.

4. When a question is put, it shall be the duty of every member present to vote, unless, for good cause, the Grand ▭ may excuse him; but no member shall vote upon any question in the event of which he is personally interested.

5. No motion shall be entertained until it is seconded, and there shall no debate be had thereon, until it is stated by the chair.

6. Every motion shall be reduced to writing, with the name of the mover indorsed thereon, if the chair or Grand Secretary desire it.

7. When a question is under debate, no motion shall be received but to adjourn, to lay on the table, to commit, to amend, or to postpone indefinitely; which several motions shall have precedence in the order in which they are here arranged, and the motion to adjourn shall always be in order, and be decided without debate.

8. Any member may call for the division of a question, which shall be divided if it comprehends questions so distinct, that, one being taken away, the rest may stand entire for the decision of the Grand ▢. A motion to strike out and insert shall be deemed indivisible.

9. When a motion has been once made, and carried, in the affirmative or negative, it shall be in order for any member of the majority to move for a reconsideration thereof.

10. All questions shall be propounded in the order in which they were moved, except in filling up blanks, when the largest sum and the longest time shall be put first.

11. No report shall be received from any of the committees of the Grand ▢, unless the same be reduced to writing and signed by at least a majority of the members thereof.

12. No committee shall sit during the sitting of the Grand ▢, without special leave.

13. These Rules of Order may be altered, added to, or abrogated, at any meeting of the Grand ▢, two-thirds of the members present concurring therein.

RETURNS OF LODGES.

SUMMIT □ NO. 2, PARKVILLE.

OFFICERS.

Time of meeting: Saturday on or before each full ☾.

M. C. White, W. M.   O. A. Whittemore, Treas.   Martin J. Walsh, J. D.
O. B. Brown, S. W.   D. T. Robley, Sec'y.   Wm. Turner, Tyler.
Jos. E. Thatcher, J. W.   D. P. Sparks, S. D.

MEMBERS.

George Oldham,	N. Beery,	J. E. Sawyer,
L. Pollard,	John D. Thomas,	L. F. Valiton,
John S. Lewis,	A. K. Blinn,	C. H. Blair,
F. E. Lewis,	John Coon,	S. S. Woodbury,
Geo. Oswald,	Wm. Cox,	E. Bidle,
Geo. Rader,	H. B. Haskell,	G. Krack,
Nelson Toncray,	D. Stogsdall,	W. D. Smith,
P. Asbury,	John G. Gill,	

ADMITTED.

C. H. Williams,   C. H. Blair,   W. D. Smith.

ENTERED APPRENTICES.

Harmon Duncan,   H. L. Pearson,   N. B. Hale.
G. E. Kettle,   Samuel Burk,

FELLOWCRAFT.

W. A. Williamson.

DIMITTED.

Wm. Turner,	S. M. Robbins, P. D. G. M.	O. Flinn,
James Ewing, P. M.	C. C. Carpenter,	C. H. Williams.
Joshua Miller,	Nicholas Thede,	D. G. W. Whiting,
H. E. Depp,	Peter Valiton,	H. B. Keene.
J. H. Depp,	F. F. Fries,	

SUSPENDED.

John Thompson.

DEATHS.

John Mentzer, E. A.

Initiated, 13; passed, 11; raised, 13; rejected, 3; number of members, 31; dues paid, $92.

NEVADA □ NO. 4, NEVADA CITY.

OFFICERS.

J. M. Van Deren, W. M.   John C. Russell, Treas.   J. W. Ratliff, J. D.
A. J. Van Deren, S. W.   Chase Withrow, Sec'y.   Robt. Russell, Tyler.
L. W. Chase, J. W.   W. T. Potter, S. D.

MEMBERS.

Andrew Mason, P. M.
Wm. L. Sawtell,
Wm. D. Perkins,
J. H. Gest,
E. W. Henderson,
D. L. Fairchild,
Jos. W. Bowles,
Preston Scott,
Leopold Weil,
Jas. C. Bradley,
Thos. Newlen,
Preston Anderson,
J. H. Haines,

B. W. Eussen,
E. Shelden,
W. H. Grafton,
J. K. Rutledge,
J. F. Philips,
Wm. H. Belcher,
Silas G. Brown,
T. D. Randall,
J. E. Gregg,
H. A. Haskin,
Wm. H. James,
Wm. F. Avery,

David Lees,
Wm. P. Grace,
A. C. Megeath,
C. P. McGarr,
Addi Vincent,
Wm. H. Jester,
James Lees,
E. B. Newman,
O. North,
Jno. Allen,
J. A. Burdick,
H. A. Johnson.

ADMITTED.

J. K. Rutledge.

DIMITTED.

David Dick.

ENTERED APPRENTICES.

Charles Alber,
Chas W. Cassell,

Ashel Cassell,

B. F. Shaffer.

DEATHS.

Robert Russell.

Initiated, 28; passed, 19; raised, 19; rejected, 4; number of members, 42; dues paid, $149.50.

DENVER ☐ NO. 5, DENVER.

Time of meetings; first and third Saturday in each month.

OFFICERS.

P. S. Pfouts, W. M.
Chas. H. Blake, S. W.
John H. Gerrish, J. W.

Fred. Z. Salomon, Treas.
Geo. W. Kassler, Sec'y.
Andrew Sagendorf, S. D.

E. S. Wilhite, J. D.
E. W. Cobb, S. S.
C. L. Bartlett, J. S.

MEMBERS.

A. H. Barker,
Joseph Ehle,
John C. Spencer,
Gus. Newman,
Wm. M. Slaughter,
John Wanless,
Wm. Porter,
Wm. Dunn,
Wm. N. Byers,
Matthew Teed,
Charles Porter,
Alfred S. Cobb,
John T. Henderson,
Nahum H. Rice,
Daniel Moyn,
A. Hanæur,
F. M. Durkee,

Richard E. Cooke,
J. M. Fox,
M. J. Dougherty,
Joseph Faivre,
Henry Mittnacht,
E. W. Kingsbury,
Chas. A. Cook,
H. Z. Salomon,
J. M. Broadwell,
A. J. Snider,
George Tritch,
Benj. C. Hayman,
James McNasser,
Oscar A. Sedman,
Richard Sopris,
William Gray,
Sam. H. Cook,

W. R. Ford,
H. F. Ford,
Chas. Massard,
C. E. Cooke,
E. H. Jewett,
Jeremiah Kershow,
A. P. Allen,
Louis Behm,
J. Lloyd Smith,
A. McCune,
Noah Hill,
J. J. Saville,
John B. Lamber,
George W. Clayton,
Thos. W. Lavin,
Nicholas Thede,
George W. Hertel.

ENTERED APPRENTICES.

Samuel McLellen,	Chas. A. Brassler,	DeWitt C. Waugh,
John Upton,	J. B. Doyle.	

FELLOWCRAFT.

Wm. M. Keith.

DIMITTED.

Mathew Teed,   A. Jacobs.

Initiated, 18; passed, 17; raised, 19; rejected, 1; number of members, 51; dues, $151.50.

CHIVINGTON □ NO. 6, CENTRAL CITY.

Time of meetings: first and third Wednesday in each month.

OFFICERS.

Allyn Weston, W. M.	James Clark, Treasurer,	Robt. Frazer, J. D.
H. M. Teller, S. W.	William Rosenfield, Sec.	George Schram, Tyler,
E. L. Gardner, J. W.	J. L. Pritchard, S. D.	

MEMBERS.

T. J. Brower,	David Loeb,	Galen G. Norton,
A. Jacobs,	H. A. Johnson,	B. Greene,
D. H. Warren,	Job C. McClellan,	C. W. Johnson,
S. F. Tappan,	Henry A. Woods,	Joseph B. Cofield,
E. H. Brown,	James Harby,	Luther G. H. Greene,
E. H. Beals,	George A. Pugh,	A. G. Raynor,
H. S. Robinson,	J. Nelson Smith,	Wm. H. Fisher.
Jacob Mack,	William Watson,	

ENTERED APPRENTICES.

Lawrence Kennedy,	Leonard Merchant,	U. B. Holloway,
A. J. Culbertson,	D. S. Greene,	Dubois Tooker.

FELLOWCRAFTS.

Adriel B. Davis,	Thos. Barnes,	James T. White.

DIMITTED.

James Harby.

Initiated, 24; passed, 18; raised, 15; rejected, 14; number of members 30; dues, $142.50.

PROCEEDINGS

OF THE

SPECIAL COMMUNICATION

OF THE

GRAND LODGE OF COLORADO,

HELD AT CENTRAL CITY, MAY 6, A. L. 5863.

The M∴ W∴ Grand ☐ of Ancient, Free and Accepted Masons of the Territory of Colorado, met in Special Communication at the hall of Chivington ☐ No. 6, at Central City, on Wednesday, the 6th day of May, A. D. 1863, A. L. 5863.

Present—

M∴ W∴ ALLYN WESTON, Grand Master.
Bro. CHASE WITHROW, *as* Senior Grand Warden.
Bro. GEO. A. PUGH, *as* Junior Grand Warden.
R∴ W∴ O. B. BROWN, Grand Treasurer.
R∴ W∴ O. A. WHITTEMORE, Grand Secretary.
R∴ W∴ and Rev. W. H. FISHER, Grand Chaplain.
R∴ W∴ H. M. TELLER, Grand Orator.
R∴ W∴ A. J. VAN DEREN, Grand Lecturer.
W∴ L. W. CHASE, Senior Grand Deacon.
W∴ B. C. HAYMAN, Junior Grand Deacon.
Bro. L. W. FRARY, Grand Sword Bearer.
Bro. F. Z. SALOMON, Grand Pursuivant.
Bro. J. W. RATLIFF, *as* Grand Tyler.

PERMANENT MEMBERS.

M∴ W∴ J. M. CHIVINGTON, Past Grand Master.
R∴ W∴ ANDREW MASON, Past Deputy Grand Master.

There being representatives from a constitutional number of ☐☐ present, the M∴ W∴ Grand ☐ was opened in ample form, with prayer by the Grand Chaplain.

The M∴ W∴ Grand Master appointed a committee on Credentials, consisting of Bros. Whittemore, Van Deren and Blair, who, in a short time, made the following

REPORT:

To the M∴ W∴ Grand □ of Colorado:

The undersigned, your committee on Credentials, respectfully report the following named officers of the Grand □, and representatives of subordianate ▱, as present, and entitled to seats and votes in this Grand □:

M∴ W∴ ALLYN WESTON, Grand Master.
R∴ W∴ O. B. BROWN, Grand Treasurer.
R∴ W∴ O. A. WHITTEMORE, Grand Secretary.
M∴ W∴ J. M. CHIVINGTON, Past Grand Master.
R∴ W∴ ANDREW MASON, Past Deputy Grand Master.

REPRESENTATIVES.

GOLDEN CITY □ No. 1. L. W. Frary, S∴ W∴, S. B. Williams, J∴ W∴.

SUMMIT □ No. 2. O. B. Brown, W∴ M∴, H. B. Haskell, proxy for S∴ W∴, C. H. Blair, J∴ W∴.

NEVADA ▱ No. 4. A. J. Van Deren, W∴ M∴, Chase Withrow, S∴ W∴, W. T. Potter, J∴ W∴.

DENVER □ No. 5. A. Sagendorf, S∴ W∴, T. P. Ames, proxy for J∴ W∴.

CHIVINGTON □ No. 6. H. M. Teller, W∴ M∴, H. S. Robinson, S∴ W∴, Geo. A. Pugh, J∴ W∴.

Respectfully submitted,

O. A. WHITTEMORE, ⎫
A. J. VAN DEREN, ⎬ *Committee.*
C. H. BLAIR, ⎭

Report concurred in.

The M∴ W∴ Grand Master then delivered the following address:

Brethren of the Grand □:

While we have abundant cause to offer to the Supreme Architect of the Universe heartfelt thanks for the manifold blessings which we have enjoyed since the last Annual Grand Communication, it is a fact painful alike to all of us, that the harmony of our jurisdiction has been disturbed.

In performance of my official duties, I have found it necessary to suspend the Masters of two ▱ for malfeasance in office. It was with reluctance and not without due deliberation, that I took such a step.

Had our subordinates been numerous, and several of them located in distant parts of the Territory, I should not have called you together at this time; but as two ▱ comprise nearly half the Masonic bodies in the jurisdiction, and the next Annual Grand Communication is six months in the future, and as the expense and inconvenience of assembling are comparatively small, I deemed it expedient to convene the Grand body for the purpose of permanently settling the grievances complained of, and restoring that peace and harmony which should prevail among the craft.

On the sixteenth day of April last, the following charges were presented to me :

To the Most Worshipful Allyn Weston, Grand Master of Masons in the Territory of Colorado:

The undersigned, a member of Denver ▭ No. 5, of A., F. and A. M., respectfully represents that P. S. Pfouts, W. Master of said ▭, has been derelict in the discharge of his official duties, as follows :

First. In permitting the ballot to be reconsidered, contrary to the By-Laws of the Grand ▭. Said ballot was reconsidered on petition of Bro. Kimball and others.

Second. In subsequently initiating said Kimball and others who were elected when the ballot was reconsidered, as aforesaid.

Third. By entertaining a motion to reconsider the ballot, at a meeting two weeks subsequent to the meeting to which the first charge refers.

Said first meeting was about six weeks ago.

The said proceedings being contrary to Masonic law, and the By-Laws of the Grand ▭, the undersigned respectfully asks that said Bro. Pfouts may be dealt with as in your judgment the interests of the fraternity may require.   A. A. NEWMAN.

April 18th, 1863.

There were present at the hearing of the charges, besides myself, the accuser and the accused, R.∴ W.∴ O. A. Whittemore, Grand Secretary ; Bro. A. J. Sagendorf, Senior Warden of the ▭, and Bros. F. Z. Salomon and J. E. Dalliba. Bro. Pfouts admitted that all the charges were correct, and that he had violated a By-Law of the Grand ▭, in permitting the ballot to be reconsidered.

As to the facts charged there could be no dispute, for they all appeared on the records of the ▭.

On the seventh day of March last, at a regular communication of Denver ▭, the ballot was taken on the petition of George K. Kimball, for initiation, and was found dark. But one black ball appearing, the ballot was immediately spread again, and one or more black balls still appearing, the candidate was declared by Bro. Pfouts, the Master, duly rejected.

At the same meeting, the ballot on the petition of Wm. Nowlan for initiation, was spread by the same process, and with the same result, and he was also declared duly rejected.

In like manner the ballot on the petition of Bro. F. E. W. Patton for affiliation, was taken, and he was declared duly rejected.

The petition of Mr. H. Zulauf was also acted on, and there appearing several black balls when the ballot was taken, he was decided duly rejected.

After the ballots were had and the results declared as described, the Master informed those present that if the brother who cast the black ball would disclose the fact to the ▭ before any one who had participated in the ballot should leave the room, and would further say that he had made a mistake in depositing the black ball, or was influenced by unworthy mo-

11

tives, it would be in the power of the Master to have the ballot reconsidered. No one making such a declaration as was suggested by Bro. Pfouts, he then stated that if some member would make a motion that the ballot be reconsidered, and the motion should be unanimously carried, another ballot could be had on the petitions of the candidates who had been declared rejected. Such a motion was made with regard to the petition of one of the candidates, and entertained by the Master.

Bro. John Wanless, a member of the ⬠, made some remarks opposing the entertaining of the motion, and the design of reconsidering the ballot as contrary to Masonic law and usage.

The motion was, however, taken, and no one voting against it, was declared unanimously carried. In the same manner, motions to reconsider the ballots on the petitions of all the other rejected candidates, excepting Mr. Zulauf, were made, entertained, and declared unanimously carried.

A motion was made to reconsider the ballot on the petition of Mr. Zulauf, but the Master refused to entertain it, on the ground that there were five or six black balls on the ballot taken.

The ballot was again successively spread on the petitions of Kimball, Nowlan and Patton, found clear, and they were. severally declared duly elected—the first two for initiation, and the last for affiliation.

The next day, at a called meeting, the Master initiated Kimball, and about three weeks after, he conferred the first degree on Nowlan.

At a Regular Communication, two weeks subsequent to the one already alluded to, the ballot was taken on the petition of S. M. Irwin, for initiation, found dark, and he was declared duly rejected. A motion was then made and entertained by the Master, to reconsider the ballot, but was not carried.

The law of the Grand ⬠ prescribes that the ballot shall be taken for each degree, and that "no ballot shall be spread except at a Regular Communication, unless by special dispensation." The regulation to which the charges allude, is Section 42, on page 34, of the last printed proceedings of this body, and is as follows:

"SEC. 42. After the ballot has been taken and duly examined, first by the Wardens, and finally by the Master, the result shall be declared by the Master, unless only one negative vote appears, in which case the Master may order the second trial of the ballot, which shall, in all cases, be final, nor can it be set aside by the ⬠, Master, Grand Master, or even the Grand ⬠."

It will be seen by this, that the action of Bro. Pfouts was in direct opposition to a plain and specific requirement of the Grand ⬠. As to the construction of the By-Law there can be no dispute; and the accused admitted that his action in reconsidering the ballot was a violation of the clause quoted. In explanation, he said that he did not, at the time, know there was such a regulation, and that a member informed him immediately after the ballot was taken, that he had cast the negative ballot because some of his friends had been unjustly rejected.

He did not, however, give any excuse for his ignorance of the law. The accused further stated, that on the evening of the balloting, but after the ▭ was closed, he read the By-Law referred to, and discovered that he had violated it. I sought to ascertain why it was, that after he had knowledge of his error, and knew that Kimball and Nowlan were illegally elected, he initiated them—the first, one day after the Regular Communication, and the latter, some three weeks subsequently. His only excuse was, that he had never given the matter any particular consideration.

I endeavored to obtain from Bro. Pfouts an explanation of his conduct, two weeks subsequent to the regular meeting designated, and after he knew he had violated a By-Law of the Grand ▭, in again entertaining a motion to reconsider the ballot, when such a reconsideration could have been founded only on a violation of the same By-Law.

He answered that he entertained the motion merely out of courtesy to the brother who made it ; that had no one else voted against it, he should have done so, and thus defeated it. I further inquired if he, at the time of the meeting last referred to, thought it in accordance with Masonic law, to entertain a motion to reconsider the ballot, in any case.

He replied that he did not, and in explanation again said that he entertained the motion merely out of courtesy to the brother who made it.

In answer to the interrogatory, if he thought it right or excusable for a Master to violate Masonic law, and to entertain a motion founded on a violation of a plain requirement of the Grand ▭, he replied that he did not consider it wrong for a Master to violate the letter of the law, if he did it in a Masonic spirit.

I ought to add, in connection with the subject of the reconsideration of the ballot, that Bro. Pfouts admitted he had told R∴ W∴ A. J. Van Deren, Grand Lecturer, that he " did not think he had done wrong, and that under the same circumstances he should do the same thing again." The accused also altered the minutes of the Regular Communication at which the ballot was reconsidered, after the same had been approved, and thereby placed on record a fact which did not appear to the ▭. This act was reprehensible.

I could not but regard the action of Bro. Pfouts as grossly culpable. No authority has yet come under my notice, sustaining his conduct in entertaining a motion to reconsider the ballot. " Mackey's Masonic Jurisprudence," to which the accused had access, and to which he was in the habit of referring as authority, expressly condemns the course which he pursued.

According to the distinguished author's idea of the law of Masonry, the ballot whenever reconsidered, can only be so on the sole authority of the Master. He says :

" But in the particular case of a reconsideration of the ballot, there is another and more strictly Masonic rule, which would make such a motion out of order. To understand the operation of this second rule, it is necessary to make a preliminary explanation. The proceedings of a ▭ are of two kinds—that relating to business, and that relating to Masonic labor. Now in all matters purely of a business character, in which the ▭ assumes the nature of a mere voluntary association of men, such for instance, as the appropriation of the funds, every member is entitled to a voice in the deliberation, and may make any motion relative to the business in hand, which would not be a violation of the parliamentary rules of order which prevail in all deliberative societies, and of those other few rules of order which particularly distinguish the Masonic from any other association or society. But all matters relating to Masonic labor are under the exclusive control of the Master. He alone is responsible to the Grand ☐ for the justice and excellence of his work, and he alone should therefore be permitted to direct it. If the time when and the manner how labor is to be conducted, be left to the decision of a majority of a ☐, then the Master can no longer be held responsible for results, in producing which he had, in common with the other members, only one voice. It is wisely, therefore, provided that the labor of the ☐ shall be wholly and solely controlled and directed by the Master."

This I consider to be sound reasoning, and the general law of our institution.

That Bro. Pfouts was culpably negligent in not knowing an important law of the Grand ☐, which was plain and unmistakable in its meaning, and related to that " great landmark" of our order, the *ballot*, I entertained not the least doubt.

Like all of us, he was bound by the most sacred obligations to maintain the Constitution, laws and edicts of the Grand ☐, under which his ☐ was held, and at his installation he had solemnly assented to the ancient charge, which is in these words:

"You promise to pay homage to the Grand Master for the time being, and to his officers when duly installed, and strictly to conform to every edict of the Grand ☐ or General Assembly of Masons, that is not subversive of the principles and ground work of Masonry."

The present By-Laws of this Grand body were adopted by sections, at the last Annual Communication, when Bro. Pfouts was present and acting as Senior Grand Warden.

During the past five months, printed copies of the same have been in his possession.

Bound by the most sacred obligation, and his solemn assent to the ancient charges, it was his especial and imperative duty, as Master, to use every possible means to gain a knowledge of the laws of the Grand ☐, and not only not to see them infringed or violated, but to require that they be strictly obeyed and conformed to in his ☐.

Under these, ignorance of the law could not be justifiably pleaded.

If it be otherwise, then are the ties which bind us as frail as gossamer webs, and the duties and obligations which should be held as sacred, are but mockeries in the sight of Heaven, and a lasting disgrace to us.

It was not simply in negligently violating the regulations of the Grand ☐ that Bro. Pfouts' conduct presents itself in the worst light. According to his own admission, he examined the By-Law on the same evening the ballots were reconsidered, and at once understood its meaning, and knew that he had violated it.

What was then the condition of the case, which any one at all interested in the matter must have perceived?

The act of reconsideration was illegal—*wholly null and void*—for the ballot in the first instance, agreeably to the requisitions of the By-Laws, was "*final,*" and could "not be set aside by the ▢, Master, Grand Master, or even the Grand ▢." The candidates were legally rejected, and the subsequent action was without any force and effect—*a complete nullity.* There was but one course for the Master to pursue, and that was plain, and free from doubt. He should have stated to his ▢ the mistake which he had made, declared the reconsideration of the ballot void, the candidates rejected, and should have refused to initiate them.

In this way he would have practically relieved his error, shown a desire and determination to obey, and conform to the laws of the Grand ▢, and would have manifested a true Masonic spirit. As it was, he proceeded, deliberately, to practically consummate the illegal acts, and make the violation of the law complete.

As late as four weeks after the reconsideration of the ballots, when he had had time for mature reflection, he initiated Nowlan, one of the candidates who had been illegally elected.

If there was any valid excuse for ignorance of the law, there certainly seemed to me to be none for thus deliberately perfecting its violation.

The explanation given by the accused, that he did not think particularly about the matter, injured, rather than benefitted his case.

To the acts enumerated was added his conduct in entertaining a motion at the second meeting, to reconsider the ballot, which, of course, was founded only on the assumed right to reconsider, in violation of a law of which he then had full knowledge, and which conduct he could not excuse, save on the ground of showing courtesy to a brother.

This, in my judgment, could not only be construed, in connection with the preceding acts, as .evidence of an utter disregard of the legal enactments of this body, and when considered with his admitted declarations to R∴ W∴ A. J. Van Deren, that he would, under the same circumstances, do the same thing again, removed from my mind every doubt as to the course which I ought to pursue.

I suspended Bro. Pfouts from his office, until this Grand ▢ should act upon the charges, and ordered Bro. Sagendorf, Senior Warden, to take charge of the ▢ and perform the duties of Master.

Another case in which I have been called to act, is that of Bro. William Train Muir, Worshipful Master of Golden City ▢.

The following charges were preferred:

To the Most Worshipful Grand Master of Masons of the Territory of Colorado:

The undersigned, members of Golden City ▢ No. 1, of A., F. & A. M., respectfully represent and show, that Wm. Train Muir, W∴ M∴ of said ▢, has been guilty of gross unmasonic conduct in the performance of his official duties, as follows:

CHARGE 1.—By balloting at special meetings on the application of candidates for advancement to the second and third degrees.

Specification 1.—At a Special Communication, held Thursday, April 7th, 1863, the application of Bro. John Keane and A. J. Butler, Fellowcrafts, for the third degree, were balloted for as charged.

Specification 2.—At a Special Communication of said □, held February 14th, 1863, the application of Bros. John F. Kirby, G. M. Wilson and D. E. Harrison, Entered Apprentices, were balloted for for the second degree, as charged, and at various other times.

CHARGE 2.—In opening said □, and raising candidates to the third degree, when only three Master Masons were present.

Specification 1.—At a Special Communication of said □, held April 7th, 1863, Bros. John Keane and A. J. Butler were raised to the third degree, when the only persons present were the W∴ M∴ Muir, Bros. D. E. Harrison and S. B. Williams—and they being the only persons present when said □ was opened and the said degrees conferred.

CHARGE 3.—In defrauding the □ out of twenty-five dollars or upwards.

Specification 1.—On or about the 22d day of February, A. D. 1863, said □ held a festival in honor of Washington's birthday, for its own benefit. The said Wm. Train Muir, as editor of the Colorado *Democrat*, furnished and printed some supper tickets and programmes, of the value of ten dollars; the said Muir sold the tickets on the evening of said festival, and out of the proceeds of such sales, appropriated forty dollars to his own use for said services, without a vote of the said □ or the consent thereof.

Specification 2.—At a special meeting of said □, held April 7th, 1863, the said Muir rendered a bill against said □, of five dollars, for advertising meetings of the □ for six weeks, and in favor of Colorado *Democrat;* that at the same meeting, out of money by him received from candidates raised, the said Muir reserved the said five dollars in liquidation of said bill, the said money never having been paid to the Secretary or having been in the hands of the Treasurer, and the said advertisement never having been authorized by the □, or the said bill allowed by the □, and at the same time drew his warrant on the Treasurer for the said bill, and placed the same among the papers of the □.

CHARGE 4.—That said Muir has refused to sit as Master and conduct the □ as long as certain persons, members, *attended* the meetings.

Wherefore, and in consideration of the causes herein mentioned and charged, we, your petitioners, respectfully request that the said Muir be suspended from his office as Worshipful Master. And, as in duty bound, : will ever pray.

L. W. FRARY, S∴ W∴
E. B. SMITH, Treasurer.
JOHN F. KIRBY, Sec.
D. E. HARRISON.

GOLDEN CITY, April 17th, 1863.

On the hearing, Bro. Muir admitted the charges of balloting at special meetings, and conferring the third degree, as charged, to be true.

He denied the allegations of fraud, but admitted that he received the five dollars as charged, and drew his warrant for the same, but he asserted that in doing so he was not actuated by intent to defraud.

To the charge of refusing to sit as Master, he said he could not plead definitely, as the specification was vague and uncertain, but he presumed it might be true.

In justice to Bro. Muir, I will here say that the charge of defrauding the □ was not sustained before me, and that my action was not in the least founded upon it.

I will relate the facts in this case as briefly as possible. In violation of the By-Law of the Grand □, which says that "no ballot shall be spread except at a Regular Communication, unless by Special Dispensation," the accused allowed the ballot to be taken, as charged, and in excuse pleaded ignorance of law.

On the 7th day of April last, Bro. Muir pretended to open his □ and hold a Special Communication, when no one was present but himself, Bro. Williams, (who is Junior Warden,) and Bro. Harrison. The ballot was taken on the applications of Bros. Keane and Butler, Fellowcrafts, for advancement to the third degree, and the Master declared them elected. Neither of the applicants passed the requisite examination as to his proficiency, as required by the laws of this body. Keane and Butler were then severally prepared, introduced, and the accused conferred upon them the third degree. At the same meeting he presented a bill of five dollars in favor of a newspaper, of which he was the editor, for advertising meetings of the □. The same being allowed, he drew his official warrant for the amount, and retained five dollars from the fees received from the candidates. From the beginning of the opening, to the end of the closing, there was no one present except Bro. Muir, Bro. Williams, Bro. Harrison, and the two candidates, Keane and Butler. The □ was not at any time tiled. The publication of the advertisement for which the bill was rendered, was made voluntarily by Bro. Muir, and without authority from the subordinate body over which he presided. He explained by asserting that he believed he had the right to do so, as he had done, in advertising and in conferring the third degree.

He admitted that he did not know of any precedent for his action in raising Keane and Butler.

The whole proceeding was such a palpable violation of law, and of the established usages and customs of the fraternity, and gave evidence of so great a disregard of the interests of the craft, that I could not but consider it as unjustifiable, and a heinous dereliction of official duty.

I accordingly suspended Bro. Muir from office, and placed the □ in charge of the Senior Warden, Bro. Frary.

The custom of tiling a □ when it convenes, is so old and universal, that it is enumerated as one of the most ancient landmarks.

"The necessity that every □, when congregated," says Bro. Mackay, "should be duly tiled, is an important landmark of the institution, which is never neglected. The necessity of this law arises from the esoteric character of Masonry. As a secret institution, it portals must of course be guarded from the intrusion of the profane, and such a law must therefore always have been in force from the very beginning of the order. It is therefore properly classed among the most ancient landmarks. The office of Tiler is wholly independent of any special enactment of Grand or subordinate □, although these may and do prescribe for him additional duties, which vary in different jurisdictions. But the duty of guarding the door, and keeping off cowans and eaves-droppers, is an ancient one, which constitutes a landmark for his government."

The tiling of the □ is not only one of the most ancient, but one of the most important usages of the fraternity, and I doubt not that it has the force of a landmark.

This custom, founded on obvious necessity, and dating far back in the ages of the past, centuries before warranted □ and Grand □ had any existence, universally acknowledge and observed by the craft, admitted by all intelligent Masons to be an imperative law—this custom thus rendered sacred by the practice of years that can be numbered only by thousands, recognized and approved by the fraternity, wheresoever dispersed on the globe, and having the force and effect of a landmark, was wholly disregarded and set at nought by Bro. Muir. He not only failed to preserve, but deliberately violated it.

The opening of a Master Masons' □ and conferring the third degree, when only three persons are present, was somethidg entirely new to me. So long and so universal has been the custom of requiring seven (the number constituting a perfect □) to be present at the opening of a □, that I regarded it as an established usage in this country, which cannot be discreetly, if legally, departed from. □ should be virtually opened in the first and second degrees, before opening on the third. Respecting this, as well as other subjects, I find but few Masonic books in our Territory, to refer to. I am, however, convinced that a □ must, in each degree, be ruled by three officers—the Master and Wardens—actually present in the room when the □ is at labor, and that if a □ can be opened with less than seven, there must be at least *five* Master Masons to legally do the work in the third degree. I again quote from Mackey's Jurisprudence:

"The government of the craft, when so congregated in a □ by a Master and two Wardens, is also a landmark. To show the influence of this ancient law, it may be observed by the way, that a congregation of Masons meeting together under any other government, as that, for instance, of a president and vice-president, or a chairman or sub-chairman, would not be recognized as a □. The presence of a Master and two Wardens is as essential to the valid organization of a □, as a warrant of constitution is at the present day. The names, of course, vary in different languages, the Master, for instance, being called 'Venerable' in French Masonry, and the Wardens, 'Surveillants,' but the officers, their number, prerogatives and duties, are everywhere identical."

Again he says:

"It is a landmark of the order, that every □ should be governed by a Master and two Wardens, and that the secrecy of its labors should be secured by a Tiler."

In this Masonic Lexicon, the same author says:

"*Our* unwritten laws say that *three must* rule a □, five *may* hold a □, but only seven can make a □ perfect."

It may be safely asserted that work cannot be legally done in the third degree with less than *five*. As a matter of necessity, three (the Master and Wardens) must rule the □, and, consequently, remain in the room; and there must be two others—one to tile, and one to prepare the candidate.

In the case under consideration, Bros. Williams and Harrison retired from the □ room and prepared the candidates, leaving the Master alone, and he performed the reception ceremony.

In the absence of Bros. Williams and Harrison, what became of the □ ? It was composed solely and exclusively of Bro. Muir.

Who ever before heard of a Master holding a □ when no one was present but himself, and he had not a single Mason to preside over?

⚜ Can it be admitted, for an instant, that such a course was in accordance with the established usage and custom with the well settled law of the craft?

There are some things so plain, both in the civil law and Masonic, that no authority is needed to elucidate them. Such is the present case. The youngest Master Mason must see the absurdity and illegality of such a proceeding. The act was something worse than a violation of Masonic law; it was an outrage on the fraternity, and a fraud on the candidates. The degree—solemn, beautiful and impressive, when properly conferred—must have been converted into a farce, which brought disgrace upon the craft. The candidates could not have appreciated it, and could not have experienced the deep and lasting effects which it is designed to produce; and these illegally made, were clandestine Master Masons. Bro. Harrison had been raised but a few months, was uninstructed in the work, and was prompted in almost all that he said in the work.

What renders the case more aggravating, is the fact that several members were almost within a stone's throw of the □ room, and would have attended if they had been notified of the meeting.

The innocent Fellowcrafts who were clandestinely raised, I subsequently healed at a called communication of the □.

The action of Bro. Muir, in taking the five dollars on the bill rendered, was opposed to the well established usage that all moneys must pass through the hands of the Secretary, into the possession of the Treasurer, and can only be drawn out by a warrant of the Master, authorized by a vote of the □.

I found Golden City □ in a very bad condition.

It did not meet for eight months immediately preceding the last Annual Communication of this Grand body. During four months from December last, no minutes of proceedings have been entered on the record book, but were temporarily kept on small slips of paper.

In many instances they failed to show material facts. Such as who opened the □, how many and who were present, the date of the meeting, etc. The □ room had no stations, and no furniture but cheap pine tables and benches. The brethren are dull in the work and lectures, and but few candidates have been properly instructed. I consider it my duty to add, in justice to the members, that they have manifested a commendable zeal to improve their condition and the state of the □. They have recently procured a new room, spacious and convenient, and have furnished it in a manner which reflects upon them much credit. With proper instructions they will maintain a creditable □, and by our next Annual Communication, give a satisfactory account of their stewardship.

As to the power of a Grand Master to suspend a Master, and place the

12

▢ in charge of the Senior Warden, there is not in my mind the shadow of a doubt, although there was a spirit manifested by certain brethren to resist my authority. It is now too well settled by the law of Masonry to admit of successful contradiction, that in the recess of the Grand ▢, the Grand Master possesses all its executive functions. The decisions of Grand bodies to this effect are numerous, and practical instances of the exercise of such a power by Grand Masters, have several times come under my personal observation. In the absence of reports of Grand ▢, I can cite but a few authorities from the many that exist. I will again quote from Bro. Mackay's Jurisprudence:

"In the exercise of its executive functions, the Grand ▢ carries its laws into effect, and sees that they are duly enforced. But as a Grand ▢ is in session only during a few days of the year, it is necessary that these functions should be exercised for it, by some one acting as its agent; and hence, to use the language of the Grand ▢ of New York, 'all the executive powers of a Grand ▢, when not in session, are reposed in its Grand Master.'"

Again Bro. Mackay says:

"But it will sometimes happen that the offences of the Master are of such a nature as to require immediate action, to protect the character of the institution, and to preserve the harmony of the ▢. The Grand ▢ may not be in session, and will not be for some months, and in the meantime, the order is to be protected from the evil effects that would arise from the continuance of a bad Master in office.

The remedy provided by the usages of the institution for such an evil are of a summary nature. The Grand Master is, in an extraordinary case like this, invested with extraordinary powers, and may suspend the Master from office until the next communication of the Grand ▢, when he will be subjected to a trial. In the meantime, the Senior Warden will assume the office and discharge the functions of the Master."

I will cite one other authority on this point; but that will carry weight with every intelligent Mason. The name of Philip C. Tucker takes rank among those of the most distinguished Masonic jurists.

After a long experience in performing arduous official duties pertaining to the highest office of our order, he has been summoned to a brighter world. In his address to the Grand ▢ of Vermont, in 1860, as Grand Master, he said:

"I have had to meet the extraordinary spectacle of finding an *expelled mason* filling the chair of one of our subordinate ▢, as its regularly chosen Master. At first, I was wholly incredulous that such a circumstance could be possible,—and yet, investigation proved it to be true. I had before me, previous to taking any action in the case, a copy of the record of his expulsion from the ▢ of another State; the fact that he took no appeal; the proof of his personal identity; evidence of his return within this Masonic jurisdiction, (from which he originally went out,) of his secreting the fact of his expulsion; of his obtaining membership improperly in the old ▢ to which he at first belonged; of his election to and service in the chair one year as Master, and of his re-election, and some months service under it, in his second year.

This was the state of facts before me, and upon them I acted thus: I ordered the Senior Warden to take possession of the charter of the ▢ and the key of the ▢ room; to direct the ▢ door to be shut against the Master, and to take the East himself and go on with the business of the ▢ as if the Master were dead. I directed him also, as soon as he should possess himself of the charter, and before the next Regular Communication of the □, to place in the Master's hands an order from me as Grand Master, suspending him from office, and citing him to appear before the Grand □ on the first day of the present communication, to show cause why that suspension should not be made perpetual, and to abide such order as this Grand body should make in the case.

So far as I am informed, no case of precisely this character has before occurred in our order—certainly none in this Masonic jurisdiction. Neither the constitution or By-Laws of this Grand □ have, in direct terms, provided for the suspension or arrest of the action of the Master of a □, nor is such a case, in terms, provided for by the old regulations; and it is well settled that a subordinate □ can neither try or discipline its Master. In the constitutions of several of the Grand □ of the United States, this power of suspension or 'arrest' is directly placed in the hands of the Grand Master, and has been several times exercised, on good and sufficient cause being shown.

The second section of the By-Laws of our own Grand □ declares, that 'the Grand Master enjoys all the powers and prerogatives conferred by the ancient constitutions, and the usages and landmarks of the craft. He shall exercise a general superintendence over the □ in this jurisdiction, inspect the proceedings, and require a strict compliance with the constitution and laws of the Grand □. He may preside in any □ with the W∴ M∴ at his left hand, and shall do all other acts and deeds as are warranted or required of him by the constitution, custom and usages of the fraternity.'

I had no difficulty in finding in this section authority enough for the action which I have taken; and if I had *not* found it there, should still have thought it clearly within the *prerogative* of a Grand Master, to arrest the farther official action of any expelled Mason, and to forbid his presence within the walls of a □ room, until the Grand □ should have an opportunity of considering and acting on the subject."

This maintains the principles on which I have acted in its broadest extent.

I caused notices to be served by the R∴ W∴ Grand Secretary, on Bros. Pfouts and Muir, to appear before the Grand □ at this meeting, and answer to the charges which were prepared against them, and on which they were suspended.

It is the province of this body to take such action on the future condition of the accused and their relations to their respective □, as it may deem proper.

It can re-instate the brothers who have been suspended from office; it can permanently suspend them, or deal out any other punishment it may consider just. Although the Grand □ is not called upon to pass judgment directly on my official action as such, yet the course which you will adopt, may virtually approve or disapprove of that action.

Brethren of the Grand □: I have full confidence to believe that you will act wisely, dealing out justice tempered with mercy; and in whatever you may do, that you will be influenced only by a sincere desire to promote the best interests of the fraternity.

On motion of Bro. Grand Orator, the address of the M∴ W∴ Grand Master was referred as follows:

That portion of the address referring to Bro. Pfouts, to a committee of three, consisting of Bros. H. M. Teller, A. J. Van Deren and O. B. Brown.

That referring to Bro. Muir, to a committee of three, consisting of P.·. G.·. M.·. J. M. Chivington, Bros. Potter and Haskell.

On motion of Bro. Grand Lecturer, the committees were allowed time until one o'clock P. M. to make their reports.

On motion of Bro. Grand Treasurer, a committee of three was appointed on Finance, Mileage and Per Diem, consisting of Bros. Chase Withrow, H. S. Robinson and C. H. Blair.

The M.·. W.·. Grand □ was then called from labor, to meet at one o'clock P. M.

---

1 O'CLOCK P. M.

The M.·. W.·. Grand □ resumed labor, officers and members present as before, when the committee on that portion of the M.·. W.·. Grand Master's address referring to Bro. Pfouts, made the following

REPORT:

To the Most Worshipful Grand □ of Colorado:

Your committee to whom was referred that portion of the address of the M.·. W.·. Grand Master referring to Bro. Pfouts, W.·. M.·. of Denver □, respectfully report:

That Bro. Pfouts appeared before your committee and acknowledged that the records of Denver □, which were produced to your committee, were correct, and that he did, as charged, spread the ballot the third time for G. K. Kimball and others, as stated in the Grand Master's address, and as charged by Bro. Newman, and that he conferred the E. A. degree on the said Kimball, on the 8th day of March, and about three weeks afterwards conferred the E. A. degree on the said Nowlan, and that afterwards, as stated in the Grand Master's address, entertained a motion to reconsider the ballot in the case of ――, which motion was lost.

Bro. Pfouts claimed that he acted in ignorance of the law when he spread the ballot the third time, and that he had been informed by a brother that he had cast the black ball against G. K. Kimball, though inadvertently, and produced to your committee a letter from Henry Mittnacht, stating that he had so cast the black ball against G. K. Kimball, and so informed Bro. Pfouts on that evening.

Bro. Pfouts did not claim to the committee that he received any such information in reference to the other candidates.

Bro. Pfouts further claimed, that if the motion to reconsider had been carried at the meeting two weeks subsequent, he should not have spread the ballot.

Your committee, therefore, report that that they find this action of M∴ W∴ Grand Master Allyn Weston, was fully justifiable in suspending Bro. Pfouts, and placing the □ in the hands of the S∴ W∴, and we do therefore recommend that the matter be left with our Grand Master, and that he re-instate Bro. Pfouts whenever he shall deem it for the good of Masonry. And your committee are of the opinion that if our M∴ W∴ Grand Master had failed to take notice of the violation of our laws, that he would have failed to do justice to the fraternity within this jurisdiction.

> H. M. TELLER, }
> A. J. VAN DEREN, } *Committee.*
> O. B. BROWN, }

The report was received and committee discharged.

Bro. Whittemore moved the adoption of the report.

P∴ G∴ M∴ J. M. Chivington moved to amend, by striking out on second page of report, all after the words "your committee therefore report," and insert the following resolutions:

1. *Resolved*, That this Grand □ fully sustain the action of the Most Worshipful Grand Master, in his action in this case.

2. *Resolved*, That, believing the evil charged fully cured, Bro. Pfouts be restored to the Mastership of his □.

Amendment lost.

Original motion carried and report adopted.

The committee on that portion of the M∴ W∴ Grand Master's address referring to Bro. Muir, then made the following

REPORT:

To the M∴ W∴ Grand □ of the Territory of Colorado:

Your committee, to whom was referred that part of Most Worshipful Allyn Weston's communication to the Grand □ referring to the case of Bro. Wm. Train Muir, W∴ M∴ of Golden City □ No. 1, beg leave to report that we find the facts in the case as stated in your communication.

We submit for your action the following:

1. *Resolved*, That the conduct of the M∴ W∴ Grand Master in suspending Bro. Muir from the Mastership of Golden City □ No. 1, was eminently fitting and wise.

2. *Resolved*, That Bro. Wm. Train Muir is hereby suspended from all the rights and benefits of Masonry.

> J. M. CHIVINGTON, }
> H. B. HASKELL, } *Committee.*
> W. T. POTTER, }

Report received and committee discharged.

Bro. Pugh moved the adoption of the report.

Bro. Grand Treasurer moved to amend the report by striking out the second resolution, and inserting in lieu thereof, the following:

Resolved, That Bro. Wm. Train Muir be indefinitely suspended as Master of Golden City ▢ No. 1, to be reinstated at the option of the M∴ W∴ Grand Master.

Which amendment was adopted.

Rport as amended adopted.

The committee on Finance, Mileage and Per Diem, made the following

REPORT:

To the M∴ W∴ Grand ▢ of the Territory of Colorado:

Your committee appointed to report upon the per diem and mileage of members in attendance at the Special Communication of the M∴ W∴ Grand ▢, held May 6th, 1863, at Central City, respectfully report members present entitled to mileage and per diem, as follows:

	Miles.	Mileage.	Per diem.	Amount.
M∴ W∴ Grand Master Allyn Weston			$2 00	$2 00
R∴ W∴ Grand Treasurer O. B. Brown	200	$25 00	2 00	27 00
R∴ W∴ Grand Secretary O. A. Whittemore	80	10 00	2 00	12 00
R∴ W∴ Grand Chaplain W. H. Fisher			2 00	2 00
R∴ W∴ Grand Orator H. M. Teller			2 00	2 00
R∴ W∴ Grand Lecturer A. J. Van Deren	2	25	2 00	2 25
W∴ S∴ Grand Deacon L. W. Chase			2 00	2 00
W∴ J∴ Grand Deacon B. C. Hugman	80	10 00	2 00	12 00
Grand Steward J. W. Ratliff	2	25	2 00	2 25
Grand Sword Bearer L. W Frary	50	6 25	2 00	8 25
Grand Pursuivant F. Z. Salomon	80	10 00	2 00	12 00
P∴ G∴ M∴ J. M. Chivington	80	10 00	2 00	12 00
P∴ D∴ G∴ M∴ Andrew Mason	30	3 75	2 00	5 75
Golden City ▢ No. 1, S. B. Williams, J∴ W∴		6 25	2	8
Summit ▢ No. 2, H. B. Haskell, proxy S∴ W∴	2	25 00	2	27
Nevada ▢ No. 4, Chase Withrew, S∴ W∴	50	25	2	2
Denver ▢ No. 5, A. Sagendorf, S∴ W∴	80	10 00	2 00	12 25
Chivington ▢ No. 6, H. S. Robinson, S∴ W∴			2 00	2 00
				153 00

Respectfully submitted,

CHASE WITHROW, ⎫
H. S. ROBINSON,   ⎬ *Committee.*
CHAS. H. BLAIR.   ⎭

Report received.

Bro. Grand Orator moved to amend by substituting the names of Bro. L. W. Frary, S∴ W∴, Golden City ▢ No. 1, in place of Bro. S. B. Williams, J∴ W∴; Bro. O. B. Brown, W∴ M∴, of Summit ▢ No. 5, in place of Bro. H. B. Haskell, proxy for S∴ W∴; A. J. Van Deren, W∴ M∴ Nevada ▢ No. 4, in place of Chase Withrow, S∴ W∴; and H. M. Teller, W∴ M∴,

Chivington ▢ No. 6, in place of H. S. Robinson, S.∴W.∴; and the names so substituted to be stricken from the report where they appear as Grand Officers.

P.∴ G.∴ M.∴ Chivington moved to amend by striking out all after the word "report."

Amendment of P.∴ G.∴ M.∴ Chivington lost.

Motion of Bro. Teller prevailed, and amendment adopted.

P.∴ G.∴ M.∴ Chivington, P.∴ D.∴ G.∴ M.∴ A. Mason, M.∴ W.∴ G.∴ M.∴ Allyn Weston, Bros. H. M. Teller, F. Z. Salomon, A. Sagendorf, J. W. Ratliff and A. J. Van Deren, donated to the Grand ▢, their mileage and per diem.

The M.∴ W.∴ Grand Master stated that he had received two petitions for the formation of new ▢▢; one for the formation of a new ▢ at Denver, and one to form a new ▢ at Empire City, which he referred to the Grand ▢.

On motion of Bro. H. M. Teller, they were referred back to the M.∴ W.∴ Grand Master for such action as he might deem for the best interests of Masonry.

The M.∴ W.∴ Grand ▢ was then closed in ample form, with prayer by the Grand Chaplain.

ATTEST: ALLYN WESTON, *Grand Master.*
O. A. WHITTEMORE, *Grand Secretary.*

PROCEEDINGS-

THIRD GRAND ANNUAL COMMUNICATION

OF THE

GRAND LODGE OF COLORADO,

HELD AT DENVER, NOV. 2, A. L. 5863.

The Most Worshipful Grand ▢ of Ancient, Free and Accepted Masons, of the Territory of Colorado, met in Annual Communication, at the hall of Denver ▢ No. 5, in Denver, on Monday, the 2d day of November, A. D. 1863, A. L. 5863, at 10 o'clock A. M.

Present—

R∴ W∴ M. C. WHITE, D∴ G∴ M∴, *as* Grand Master.

R∴ W∴ H. M. TELLER, *as* Grand Senior Warden.

Bro. GEO. E. PUGH, *as* Grand Junior Warden.

R∴ W∴ O. B. BROWN, Grand Treasurer.

R∴ W∴ O. A. WHITTEMORE, Grand Secretary.

R∴ W∴ A. J. VAN DEREN, Grand Lecturer.

Bro. J. W. RATLIFF, *as* Grand Senior Deacon.

Bro. C. H. BLAIR, *as* Grand Junior Deacon.

Bro. CHASE WITHROW, *as* Grand Tyler.

Permanent Member—P∴ G∴ M∴ J. M. CHIVINGTON.

A ▢ of Master Masons was opened, when, there appearing a quorum of chartered ▢, the M∴ W∴ Grand ▢ of Colorado was opened in due form, with prayer by P∴ G∴ M∴ Chivington.

The M∴ W∴ Grand Master appointed as committee on

13

Credentials, Bro. Grand Secretary, R∴ W∴, A. J. Van Deren, and Bro. Charles H. Blair.

On motion of R∴ W∴ A. J. Van Deren, the election of officers was made the special order of business for the afternoon, after hearing the report of the committee on Credentials.

The M∴ W∴ Grand □ was then called from labor, to meet at 2 o'clock P. M.

MONDAY, 2 o'clock P. M.

The M∴ W∴ Grand □ resumed labor. Officers and members present as at morning session.

The committee on Credentials presented the following

REPORT:

To the M∴ W∴ Grand □ of Colorado:

Your committee on Credentials have attended to the duty assigned them, and respectfully report that we find in attendance:

R∴ W∴ M. C. WHITE, Deputy Grand Master.
R∴ W∴ O. B. BROWN, Grand Treasurer.
R∴ W∴ O. A. WHITTEMORE, Grand Secretary.
R∴ W∴ A. J. VAN DEREN, Grand Lecturer.
R∴ W∴ H. M. TELLER, Grand Orator.
Bro. J. W. RATLIFF, Grand Steward.
Bro. L. W. FRARY, Grand Sword Bearer.
M∴ W∴ J. M. CHIVINGTON, Past Grand Master.

And representatives from the following named chartered □:

GOLDEN CITY □ No 1. L. W. Frary Senior Warden.

SUMMIT □ No. 2. O. B. Brown, Master, Charles H. Blair, Junior Warden.

NEVADA □ No. 4. A. J. Van Deren, Master, Chase Withrow, Senior Warden.

DENVER □ No. 5. T. P. Ames, proxy for Senior Warden, Wm. Porter, Junior Warden.

CHIVINGTON □ No. 6. H. M. Teller, Master and proxy for Senior Warden, George A. Pugh, Junior Warden.

Fraternally submitted,

O. A. WHITTEMORE, ⎫
A. J. VAN DEREN, ⎬ *Committee.*
CHAS. H. BLAIR, ⎭

Which report was concurred in, and the brethren therein named admitted to seats.

The time having arrived for the election of officers, the M∴ W∴ Grand Master appointed Bros. Van Deren and Frary, tellers, and the Grand □ proceeded to an election, and the following named brothers were duly elected Grand Officers for the ensuing year:

H. M. TELLER, of Chivington □ No. 6, Grand Master.
A. J. VAN DEREN, of Nevada □ No. 4, Deputy Grand Master.
O. B. BROWN, of Summit □ No. 2, Grand Senior Warden.
J. H. GEST, of Nevada □ No. 4, Grand Junior Warden.
L. W. FRARY, of Golden City □ No. 1, Grand Treasurer.
O. A. WHITTEMORE, of Summit □ No. 2, Grand Secretary.

The Grand Master elect was then duly installed by P∴ G∴ M∴ J. M. Chivington, Bro. Van Deren acting as Grand Marshal.

The following officers were then duly installed by the M∴ W∴ Grand Master.

R∴ W∴ A. J. VAN DEREN, Deputy Grand Master.
R∴ W∴ O. B. BROWN, Grand Senior Warden.
R∴ W∴ J. H. GEST, Grand Junior Warden.
R∴ W∴ L. W. FRARY, Grand Treasurer.
R∴ W∴ O. A. WHITTEMORE, Grand Secretary.

The M∴ W∴ Grand Master then appointed, and subsequently installed, the following named officers:

R∴ W∴ B. C. Dennis, Grand Chaplain.
R∴ W∴ CHASE WITHROW, Nevada □ No. 4, Grand Lecturer.
R∴ W∴ J. R. GILBERT, Golden City □ No. 1, Grand Marshal.
R∴ W∴ T. P. AMES, Denver □ No. 5, Grand Orator.
W∴ JAMES T. WHITE, Chivington □ No. 6, Grand Senior Deacon.
W∴ CHARLES H. BLAIR, Summit □ No. 2, Grand Junior Deacon.
Bro. H. B. HASKELL, Summit □ No. 2, } Grand Stewards.
Bro. JOHN WANLESS, Denver □ No. 5, }
Bro. C. A. COOK, Denver □ No. 5, Grand Sword Bearer.
Bro. D. E. HARRISON, Golden City □ No. 1, Grand Standard Bearer.
Bro. A. L. MILLER, Nevada □ No. 4, Grand Tyler.

The minutes of the Special Communication were then read and approved; the reading of the minutes of the last Annual Communication having been dispensed with, printed copies being in the hands of the members.

The M∴ W∴ Grand Master then appointed the following committees:

On Accounts.—Bros. D∴ G∴ M∴ A. J. Van Deren and Geo. A. Pugh.

Finance, Mileage and Per Diem.—Bros. G∴ S∴ W∴ O. B. Brown, G∴ S∴ O. A. Whittemore, and G∴ L∴ Chase Withrow.

Charters and Dispensations.—Bros. D∴ G∴ M∴ A. J. Van Deren, P∴ G∴ M∴ J. M. Chivington, and G∴ O∴ T. P. Ames.

Visiting Brethren.—Bros. G∴ T∴ L. W. Frary, G∴ J∴ D∴ C. H. Blair, and Wm. Porter.

The M∴ W∴ Grand □ was then called from labor, to meet to-morrow at 10 o'clock A. M.

TUESDAY, 10 o'clock A. M.

M∴ W∴ Grand □ resumed labor.

Present—

M∴ W∴ H. M. Teller, Grand Master.

R∴ W∴ A. J. Van Deren, Deputy Grand Master.

R∴ W∴ O. B. Brown, Grand Senior Warden.

Bro. George A. Pugh, *as* Grand Junior Warden.

R∴ W∴ L. W. Frary, Grand Treasurer.

R∴ W∴ O. A. Whittemore, Grand Secretary.

R∴ W∴ Chase Withrow, Grand Lecturer.

R∴ W∴ T. P. Ames, Grand Orator.

Bro. J. W. Ratliff, *as* Grand Senior Deacon.

W∴ Chas. H. Blair, Grand Junior Deacon.

Bro. John Wanless, Grand Steward.

Permanent Members—P∴ G∴ M∴ J. M. Chivington, P∴ D∴ G∴ M∴ M. C. White, and representatives as yesterday.

Minutes of yesterday's meeting read and approved.

The following address of Deputy Grand Master M. C. White was read, and ordered to be published with the proceedings:

To the M∴ W∴ Grand □ of Colorado:

Brethren: I have to report to the M∴ W∴ Grand □ of Colorado Territory, that during the past Masonic year I have, in the absence of the M∴ W∴ Grand Master, granted two special dispensations, as follows, to-wit: August 13th, 1863, A. L. 5863, I granted dispensation to Summit □ No. 2, A., F. & A. M., to raise Bro. David McShane, and to pass and raise Bros. J. M. Carpenter and R. W. Beery; and on the 12th of September, 1863, A. L. 5863, I granted dispensation to pass and raise Bro. J. F. Turner—all in less time than required by the By-Laws, they appearing to me to be cases of emergency.

Trusting that the blessing of God may rest upon you and all regular Masons, and that when called from earth we may meet in the Grand □ above, where the Supreme Architect of the Universe presides.

I am your brother,
M. C. WHITE,
D∴ G∴ M∴ of Colorado.

The Grand Secretary presented account of moneys received and paid, as follows :

O. A. Whittemore, Secretary, in account with Grand □:

DR.

Nov. 4, 1862, to Golden City □ No. 1, dues 1862.................$ 21 00
Jan. 5, 1863, to J. M. Chivington, P∴ G∴ M∴, on dispensation
    King Solomon's □ 15 00
Feb. 9, 1863, to Golden City □ No. 1, dues 1861.................. 30 58
April 18, 1863, to M∴ W∴ Allyn Weston, G∴ M∴, dispensation
    Montana □... 40 00

Nov. 2, 1863, to Golden City □ No. 1, dues...................... 45 00
  " " " " Summit   " " 2, " 43 50
  " " " " Nevada   " " 4, " 61 50
  " " " " Denver   " " 5, " 63 00
  " " " " Chivington " " 6, " 69 00

$388 58
CR.

Nov. 4, 1862, R∴ W∴ O. B. Brown, Grand Treasurer......$ 21 00
March 1, 1863, "   "   "   " 45 58
May 1,   "   "   "   "   " 40 00
Nov. 3,   "   " L. W. Frary   "   " 282 00

$388 58

Fraternally submitted,

O. A. WHITTEMORE, *Grand Secretary.*

Bro. O. B. Brown, Grand Treasurer, presented accounts and vouchers, according to report, as follows:

O. B. Brown, Grand Treasurer, in account with Grand □:

DR.

Nov. 3, 1862, to amount on hand as per report...................$547 25
  " 4,   " " amount received for Grand Secretary............. 21 00
March 1, 1863, to "   "   " " " " 45 58
May 1,   "   " "   "   "   " " 40 00

$653 83
DR.

Nov. 4, 1862, by order No. 1, W. T. Muir refunded to Golden
    City □...$ 2 50
Nov. 4, 1862, by order No. 2, dues refunded Nevada □.... 74 75
  " 4, " " " " 3, "   " Chivington □. 71 25
  " 4, " " " " 4, "   " Denver □.... 75 75
  " 4, " " " " 5, per diem and mileage; Rep.

Nevada ▢... 9 37
Nov. 4, 1862, by order No. 6, per diem and mileage, Rep.
   Chivington ▢........ .... 9 00
Nov. 4, 1862, by order No. 7, per diem and mileage, Rep.
   Denver ▢... 24 00
Nov. 4, 1862, by order No. 8, dues refunded Summit ▢..... 46 00
   " 4, " " " " 9, per diem Rep. Summit ▢.... 45 00
   " 4, " " " " 10, Grand Tyler, 1862............ 6 00
   " 4, " " " " 11, "   " 1861............ 4 00
   " 4, " " " " 12, salary Grand Sec'y 1861–62.. 100 00
   " 4, " " " " 13, bal. due Summit ▢ Rep. 1861. 17 25
Dec. 15, " " " " 14, printing proceedings......... 71 50
Oct. 1, " " " " 15, printing charters and returns. 50 00
   " 1, " " " " 16, Gr. Sec. postage and stationery 7 25

$613 62
      Balance.................... .... 40 21

$653 83

Fraternally submitted,

         O. B. BROWN, *Grand Treasurer.*

The committee on Charters and Dispensations made the following report, which was received and report adopted:

To the M∴ W∴ Grand ▢ of A., F. and A. M. of Colorado Territory:

The undersigned committee beg leave to make the following report:

That they find that the W∴ M∴ of Montana ▢, U. D., has moved out of the Territory, and the members of the ▢ are desirous of surrendering their dispensation.

We find from their returns that they have conferred the E. A., F. C. and M. M. degrees on one Vans F. Inskeep, in due and ancient form, and that they have conferred the E. A. degree on one Madora Cushman.

The dispensation books, papers, and eight dollars, have been returned to the Grand ▢.

Your committee also have under consideration a petition from Bros. M. S. Beach, Jno. C. Anderson, Eli M. Ashley, Louden Mullin, J. G. Vawter, J. F. Hamilton, E. H. Collins, Chas. Ruter, J. R. Boyce, Jay J. Johnson, Jno. Evans, S. H. Elbert, H. B. Hitchings, Francis R. Bill, J. M. Chivington, M. C. White and O. A. Whittemore, for a new ▢, to be established in Denver, and to be chartered at once by this Grand ▢; and we recommend that the prayer of the petitioners be granted.

         A. J. VAN DEREN, } *Committee.*
         J. M. CHIVINGTON, }

The committee on Finance, Mileage and Per Diem, presented the following

REPORT:

To the M∴ W∴ Grand ▢ of A., F. and A. M. of the Territory of Colorado:

Your committee appointed to report upon the Finance, Mileage and Per

Diem, respectfully report that we find the following Grand Officers and representatives present and entitled to the following pay:

	Miles Traveled	Mileage	Per Diem.	Total.
P∴ G∴ M∴, J. M. Chivington..	....	$......	$ 4 00	$ 4 00
R∴ W∴ D∴ G∴ M∴, M. C. White......................................	....	....	4 00	4 00
R∴ W∴ O. A. Whittemore, Grand Secretary.......................	....	....	4 00	4 00
Golden City ▭ No. 1, Bro. L. W. Frary, S∴ W∴...................	80	3 75	4 00	7 75
Summit ▭ No. 2, Bro. O. B. Brown, W∴ M∴......................	200	25 00	4 00	29 00
Nevada ▭ No. 4, Bro. A. J, Van Deren, W∴ M∴..................	80	10 00	4 00	14 00
Denver ▭ No. 5, Bro. T. P. Ames, proxy for S∴ W∴............	....	....	4 00	4 00
Chivington ▭ No. 6, Bro. H. M. Teller, W∴ M∴...................	80	10 00	4 00	14 00
				$80 75

O. B. BROWN,
O. A. WHITTEMORE, } *Committee.*
CHASE WITHROW,

Bro. P∴ G∴ M∴ Chivington donated to the M∴ W∴ Grand ▭ his per diem.

The report of the committee on Foreign Correspondence was presented by Bro. O. A. Whittemore, chairman.

To the M∴ W∴ Grand ▭ of Colorado:

Your committee on Foreign Correspondence respectfully present the following brief report:

At this, their Annual Communication, your committee are able to report but seventeen Grand ▭ in correspondence with this Grand ▭.

The proceedings of the organization, and of the First and Second Annual Communications, have been sent to all Grand ▭ in America with which we have communication by mail, and in return we have copies of the proceedings of the following Grand ▭, to-wit:

California,
District of Columbia,
Indiana,
Illinois,
Iowa,
Kansas,
Louisiana,
Maine,
Massachusetts,
Michigan,
Missouri,
New York,
New Jersey,
Oregon,
Vermont,
Wisconsin,
Washington Territory.

All of which send fraternal greetings to this, the youngest among the sisterhood of Grand ▭.

To plead want of time, is usually but another way to acknowledge neglect, but at the risk of the plea being so received, we must, in the present instance, offer it as an apology for the brevity of our report. Most of the proceedings received have come to hand within the past few weeks, when the pressure of business has prevented us from giving them that careful perusal necessary for a proper report.

The war that is desolating portions of our country, has had its blighting effect upon Masonry in those States where it has held high carnival, but in most jurisdictions the order has steadily increased in numbers and usefulness. We notice that applications to confer degrees in less than the usual time have been numerous, and, in some jurisdictions, granted to all that so apply. In Massachusetts alone, dispensations being granted for *initiating, passing and raising one hundred and thirteen men, all within five consecutive hours.* But we are glad to find that this wholesale manufacture of Masons does not meet the approval of the fraternity generally.

We think there is much danger in the exercise of the prerogative of making Masons at sight, this *putting through* of those who are suddenly called to some new sphere of action, or are about to remove to some other locality, and all of a sudden discover that they may be in some way benefitted by Masonry. The necessity of caution with regard to the material for our temple, is well expressed in the following extract from the address of M∴ W∴ Josiah H. Drummond, Grand Master of Maine. He says:

"Our institution is now popular. Candidates are rushing to our doors, and, instead of *asking*, are almost *demanding* admission. Here lies our greatest danger. In the time of our prosperity, designing men may endeavor to use Masonry to extend their business, or as a stepping-stone to influence in the community. Candidates influenced by such motives as these, would be cancers that would eat out our vitals. Another class of candidates make *negative* Masons. They are to Masonry what drones are to the hive. They add nothing to our strength. We need large hearted, disinterested, live men. We should not hesitate to reject those who are not worthy. Fix your standard high, and if the candidate does not come up to it, reject him.

And if a candidate—your friend—is rejected, do not break up the harmony of your ☐ by foolishly resenting it. It is unpleasant to have one's friend rejected. But we should consider whether we will quietly submit, or prefer to endeavor to vindicate our friend at the expense of the harmony of the ☐. The true Mason cannot hesitate which course to take. He will place the good of the order above every other consideration. He will apply to it the words of the Psalmist:

'If I forget thee, O Jerusalem, let my right hand forget her cunning.'

'If I do not remember thee, let my tongue cleave to the roof of my mouth; if I prefer not Jerusalem to my chief joy!'"

Fraternally submitted,

O. A. WHITTEMORE, *Chairman.*

Bro. D∴ G∴ M∴ A. J. Van Deren, presented the following resolutions:

WHEREAS, Attempts are being made to force upon sister Grand ☐, the institution known as the "Conservator's Association," contrary to, and in violation of, the ancient and cardinal principles and regulations of our beloved order; therefore, be it

Resolved, 1. That the M∴ W∴ Grand ☐ of Colorado, solemnly declare the said association a corrupt organization, treasonable to the institution of

Masonry, and subversive of its sacred interests, honor and perpetuation.

2. That the M∴ W∴ Grand ▭ of Colorado peremptorily interdict and forbid the introduction of the above mentioned work or organization, in any Masonic body in this Grand jurisdiction.

8. That no Mason, subject or adhering to said association, shall be allowed to sit in, or visit this Grand ▭, or any subordinate ▭ thereunder, or hold affiliation with, or be recognized by, any Mason in this jurisdiction.

4. That hereafter no Grand Officer of this Grand ▭, and no officer of any subordinate ▭, shall be installed until he shall have made a solemn pledge in open ▭, that on his honor as a Mason, he repudiates and condemns the said association.

5. That the Grand ▭ under which Robert Morris, the "Chief Conservator," holds, or pretends to hold membership, be respectfully and fraternally requested by this Grand ▭, to bring him to condign and merited punishment, for the high crimes with which he stands self-convicted; and that all our sister Grand ▭ be requested to join us in this, our solemn demand, and to co-operate with us in the total suppression of the criminal innovations of said association.

6. That printed copies of these resolutions, attested by the R∴ W∴ Grand Secretary, be forwarded immediately to all our sister Grand ▭ of the United States, and to the subordinate ▭ of this jurisdiction.

Which, on motion of Bro. G∴ S∴ Warden, were made the special order for this afternoon at 2 o'clock P. M.

The M∴ W∴ Grand ▭ was then called from labor until 2 o'clock P. M.

TUESDAY, 2 o'clock P. M.

The M∴ W∴ Grand ▭ resumed labor.   Officers and members present as at the morning session.

R∴ W∴ G∴ S∴ Warden offered the following substitute for the resolutions presented at the morning session.

Resolved, That this Grand ▭ forbids the introduction of the work known as the Webb-Preston work, and promulgated by what is known as the "Conservator's Association," into any of the subordinate ▭ in this jurisdiction.

P∴ G∴ M∴ Chivington moved to amend by striking out the words "known as the Webb-Preston work and." Which amendment was accepted.

After discussion by P∴ G∴ M∴ Chivington, M∴ W∴

14

Grand Master H. M. Teller and others, the amendment of Bro. G∴ S∴ Warden was lost.

Bro. Blair moved that the resolutions be adopted *seriatim*. Motion lost.

Motion to adopt resolutions as presented by D∴ G∴ M∴ Van Deren, carried by a vote of 12 ayes to 5 noes.

Bro. Whittemore offered the following resolution, which was adopted :

Resolved, That no ☐ under the jurisdiction of this Grand ☐, shall admit to membership any brother who shall be exempt from any of the Masonic duties, obligations and privileges required by the Constitution, regulations and landmarks of the order.

Bro. Grand Senior Warden offered the following resolution, which was adopted :

Resolved, That non-affiliated Masons shall be required to pay Grand ☐ dues, or not be permitted to visit any of the subordinate ☐ in this jurisdiction, more than twice.

Bro. Grand Senior Warden also offered the following, which was adopted:

Resolved, That Summit ☐ No. 2 be authorized to suspend work until the Regular Communication in June next, as most of the members have removed from the jurisdiction for the winter ; also, that the Grand Master issue a dispensation to said Summit ☐, to elect officers at said communication in June, if, in his opinion, the interests of the craft so demand. And that the charter of said ☐ be left in the hands of the Grand Secretary, until the Grand Master orders it returned to Summit ☐.

Bro. Whittemore offered the following resolution, which was adopted :

Resolved, That from and after this communication of the Grand ☐ of Colorado, it shall not be lawful for the ☐ under its jurisdiction to hold communications on the Sabbath day for any purpose whatever, except to attend the funeral of a member thereof, or of a brother Master Mason.

The committee on Accounts presented the following

REPORT:

To the M∴ W∴ Grand ☐ of A., F. and A. M. of the Territory of Colorado:

Your committee on Accounts beg leave to report the following :

That we have examined the accounts of the Secretary and Treasurer, and find them to be correct.

                 A. J. VAN DEREN, } *Committee.*
                 GEO. A. PUGH,   }

R∴ W∴ D∴ Grand Master offered the following resolution, which was adopted:

Resolved, That the Grand Tyler be allowed the sum of three dollars per day for his services.

The following resolution was offered by P∴ D∴ Grand Master M. C. White, and, on motion, adopted:

Resolved, That the Grand Secretary be authorized to print such number of proceeding as, in his estimation, shall seem necessary.

The M∴ W∴ Grand Master then appointed the following committees:

Foreign Correspondence.—P∴ G∴ M∴ Allyn Weston, P∴ D∴ G∴ M∴ M. C. White, and Grand Secretary O. A. Whittemore.

Masonic Jurisprudence.—P∴ G∴ M∴ J. M. Chivington, P∴ G∴ M∴ Allyn Weston and D∴ G∴ M∴ A. J. Van Deren.

D∴ G∴ M∴ Van Deren offered the following motion, which was seconded by a majority of the members present, and ordered to be referred to the subordinate ▱, as provided in the constitution:

Resolved, That article 17 of the Constitution be amended as follows: strike out all from the word "votes" in the fourth line, to the word "▱" in the eighth line, including the word "▱."

On motion of P∴ G∴ M∴ Chivington, it was

Resolved, That the thanks of this M∴ W∴ Grand ▱ be tendered to Denver ▱ No. 5, for the free use of their hall during this Annual Grand Communication.

The M∴ W∴ Grand ▱ of Colorado was then closed in ample form, with prayer by P∴ G∴ M∴ Chivington, peace and harmony prevailing.

H. M. TELLER, *Grand Master.*

ATTEST: O. A. WHITTEMORE, *Grand Secretary.*

AMENDMENT PROPOSED TO THE CONSTITUTION.

Resolved, That Article XVII of the Constitution be amended as follows: Strike out all from the word "votes," in the fourth line, to the word "□," in the eighth line, including the word "□."

RETURNS OF LODGES.

GOLDEN CITY ☐ NO. 1, GOLDEN CITY.
Time of meetings: first and third Saturdays of each month.

OFFICERS.

—————, W. M.   E. B. Smith, Treasurer.   G. M. Wilson, J. D.
L. W. Frary, S. W.   W. A. H. Loveland, Sec.   —————, Tyler.
S. B. Williams, J. W.   Duncan E. Harrison, S. D.

MEMBERS.

S. M. Breath,	A. J. Butler,	G. Bailey,
Reuben Borton,	John Kean,	John Gilmore,
Eli Carter,	Joseph Casto,	Henry Shea,
J. B. Hendry,	John F. Kirby,	C. R. Huntsman,
Joseph W. Maynard,	John H. Gilbert,	Wm. Nelson,
Ira Quimby,	George Morrison,	David G. Dargin,
John A. Moore,	Jonathan C. Bowles,	Fox Dieffendorff,
W. L. Rothrock,	Henry Stevens,	J. M. Sexton,
J. C. Remington,	James Kelly,	Daniel McCleary,
Samuel F. Shaffer,	Lewis Davis,	J. M. Ferrell.

DIMITTED.
W. T. Muir.

FELLOWCRAFTS.
Perry Pollock,   Theodore Cummins.

ENTERED APPRENTICES.

W. D. Annis.	W. D. Rippey,	James Stevens,
Joseph Parrott,	C. S. Birdsell,	Felix Crocker.
J. B. Langdon,	Washington Jones,	Joseph Bartholomew
	Bruce Woodward,	

Members living out of the Territory, 6.

SUMMIT ☐ NO. 2, PARKVILLE.
Time of meetings: Saturday on or before each ☉.

OFFICERS.

O. B. Brown, W. M.   J. L. Lewis, Treasurer.   —————, J. D.
—————, S. W.   N. D. Haskell, Sec'y,   —————, Tyler
C. H. Blair, J. W.   H. B. Haskell, S. D.

MEMBERS.

M. C. White, P. D. G. M.,	O. A. Whittemore,	P. Asbury,
J. E. Thatcher,	Wm. D. Smith,	D. Stogsdall,
S. S. Woodbury,	Geo. Rader,	Geo. Oswald,
John Coon,	John L. Dyer,	Nelson Toncray
John Thompson,	J. E. Sawyer,	L. F. Valiton,
D. W. Willey,	D. C. Twibell,	Milton Pulver,

L. Peabody,
Calvin Pulver,
Wm. Moore,
William McCartney,

G. Krack,
Frederick Baer,
B. F. Turner,
John McCaskill,

Hobart Murray,
D. W. Johnson,
E. Carter.

DIMITTED.

M. J. Walsh,
J. D. Thomas,
William Cox,
S. Burk,

A. K. Blinn,
J. G. Gill,
David McShane,
J. M. Carpenter,

R. W. Berry,
F. E. Lewis,
N. Beery,
D. Sparks.

DIED.
E. Bidle.

FELLOWCRAFT.
D. S. Hinkle.

ENTERED APPRENTICES.

S. J. Pratt,   R. V. Fairbanks,   A. Heath.

Members living out of the Territory, 9.

NEVADA □ NO. 4, NEVADA.

Time of meetings: second and fourth Saturdays in each month.

OFFICERS.

A. J. Van Deren, W. M.
Chase Withrow, S. W.
W. T. Potter, J. W.

John W. Ratliff, Treas.
J. F. Phillips, Sec'y.
O. North, S. D.

Addi Vincent, J. D.
Thos. Newland. Tyler.

MEMBERS.

Andrew Mason. P. M.
J. M. Van Deren, P. M.
Chas. S. Abbott,
J. C. Russell,
J. H. Haines,
John E. Gregg,
W. H. Belcher,
Wm. F. Avery,
J. K. Rutledge,
James Lees,
Jas. A. Burdick,
George Marshall,
D. J. Ball,
Wm. T. Carrothers,
Joshua Jennings,
R. M. Foster,
Lyman W. Chase,

W. L. Sawtell,
E. W. Henderson,
D. L. Fairchild,
David Lees,
A. C. Megath,
Edward B. Newman,
Charles W. Cassell,
J. W. Martin,
B. F. Pease,
John Jackson,
Andrew Nichols,
J. M. Smith,
A. L. Miller,
Isaac B. Brunell,
J. H. Gest,
J. W. Bowles,

Preston Anderson,
F. D. Randall,
W. H. James,
Wm. H. Jester,
John Allen,
T. H. Clewell,
A. M. Jones,
Preston Scott,
James C. Beverly,
B. W. Eussen,
Silas G. Brown,
H. A. Haskin,
Edward Crockett,
D. T. Sparks,
J. W. Stanton,
W. D. Perkins.

DIMITTED.

W. H. Grafton,   D. Dick,   J. L. Buck.
                   L. B. Weil,

EXPELLED.
Wm. P. Grace.

DIED.
C. P. McGarr.

FELLOWCRAFTS.
Charles Alber,   D. A. Hamar.

Wm. McFeeters,   A. W. Cassell,   Benail Walls,
George W. Brock,   James Huff,   B. C. Waterman,
Wm. L. Ireland,   F. R. Waggoner,   G. W. Hall.
M. Symonds,   B. F. Shaffer,

 Living out of the Territory, 16.

DENVER ☐ NO. 5, DENVER.

Time of meetings: first and third Saturdays in each month.

OFFICERS.

———————, W. M.   ———————, Sec'y.   Geo. Tritch, ⎬ Stewards.
A Sagendorf, S. W.   B. C. Hayman, S. D.   ———————, ⎭
Wm. Porter, J. W.   Daniel Moyn, J. D.   Thos. W. Lavin, Tyler.
R. E. Cooke, Treas.

MEMBERS.

C. H. Blake,   A. P. Allen,   Geo. T. Clark,
Geo. W. Kassler,   H. F. Ford,   M. B. Sherwood,
E. W. Cobb,   Wm. M. Keith,   W. H. Grafton,
Chas A. Cook,   Geo. W. Hertel,   Wm. N. Byers,
James McNassar,   W. S. Cheesman,   A. Hanauer,
Sam. H. Cook,   Geo. Lyman Moody,   Joseph Faivre,
J. H. Gerrish,   T. P. Ames,   J. M. Broadwell,
A. H. Barker,   Geo. K. Kimball,   W. R. Ford,
Gus. Newman,   M. E. Hall,   Richard Sopris, P. M.,
Fred. Z. Salomon,   John Wanless,   E. H. Jewett,
Joseph Ehle,   Nahum H. Rice,   Geo. W. Clayton,
Charles L. Bartlett,   M. J. Dougherty,   J. Lloyd Smith,
William M. Slaughter,   J. Kershow,   De Witt C. Waugh,
John T. Henderson,   Louis Behm,   J. S. Howell,
F. M. Durkee,   John B. Lamber,   John E. Tappan,
William Gray,   Nicholas Thede,   J. Richardson,
Ed. W. Kingsbury,   J. C. Davidson,   Wm. M. Dailey,
Andy J. Snyder,   John L. Dailey,   Wm. Stepp.

DIMITTED.

Paris S. Pfouts,   E. S. Wilhite,   John C. Spencer,
Charles Porter,   Alfred S. Cobb,   J. M. Fox,
Henry Mittnacht,   Oscar A. Sedman,   F. E. W. Patten,
John M. Clark,   J. C. Guy,   C. Massard.

DIED.

Wm. Dunn,   C. E. Cooke.

FELLOWCRAFTS.

Edwin Scudder,   H. Hitchins,   W. H. Garvin.
F. H. Page,   A. McCune,

ENTERED APPRENTICES.

John W. Kerr,   Wm. Nowlan,   G. W. Lowe.
 Living out of the Territory, 12.

CHIVINGTON ☐ NO. 6, CENTRAL CITY.

Time of meetings: second and fourth Wednesdays in each month.

OFFICERS.

H. M. Teller, W. M.   Thos. Barnes, Treasurer, A. B. Davis, J. D.

Henry S. Robinson, S. W. Wm. Rosenfield, Sec'y.   A. G. Raynor, Tyler.
Geo. A. Pugh, J. W.   Jas. T. White, S. D.

MEMBERS.

Allyn Weston,M.W.G.M.T.	J. Brower,	A. E. Buckmiller,
J. L. Pritchard,	S. F. Tappan,	J. M. Chivington, P.G.M.
D. H. Warren,	Jas. Clark,	A. Jacobs,
E. L. Gardner,	E. H. Beals,	Geo. Schram,
E. H. Brown,	H. A. Johnson,	R. Frazier,
D. Loeb,	H. J. Kruse,	J. Mack,
H. A. Woods,	D. Kline,	J. C. McClellan,
A. J. Culbertson,	J. W. Smith,	William Watson,
B. Greene,	L. Merchant,	G. G. Norton,
J. B. Cofield,	D. S. Greene,	C. W. Johnson,
U. B. Holloway,	L. G. H. Green,	W. H. Fisher,
B. W. Wisebart,	D. Tooker,	J. N. Adams,
D. C. Collier,	J. Clarkson,	Ed. C. Parmelee,
L. Weil,	F. Poznanski,	D. W. Tilton.
J. Coleman,	E. Crosier,	

DIMITTED.
H. Kline.

FELLOWCRAFTS.
J. J. Dunnegan,   C. L. Hill.

ENTERED APPRENTICES.

Lawrence Kennedy,	J. C. Bruce,	D. T. Beals,
Wm. Humphrey,	N. L. Sibley,	J. A. Tidland,
W. C. M. Jones,	Jacob Weidman,	Wm. B. Squires,
	A. Schonecker,	

Living out of the Territory, 6.

MONTANA ▭, U. D., CENTRAL CITY.
Time of meetings : fiirst and third Tuesdays in each month.

OFFICERS.
J. M. Van Deren, W. M. Wm. Jones, Treas.   B. W. Wisebart, J. D.
Lyman W. Chase, S. W. —————, Sec'y.   John C. Spencer, Tyler.
Wm. Z. Cozens, J. W.   E. A. Brown, S. D.

MEMBERS.
O. E. Colony,   Ed. C. Parmelee,   Vans F. Inskeep.

ENTERED APPRENTICE.
Madora Cushman.

Dispensation surrendered.

PROCEEDINGS

OF THE

GRAND LODGE OF COLORADO,

· HELD AT CENTRAL CITY, NOV. 7, A. L. 5864.

FOURTH ANNUAL COMMUNICATION.

———

The Most Worshipful Grand ▢ of Ancient, Free and Accepted Masons of the Territory of Colorado met in Annual Communication at the hall of Chivington ▢ No. 6, in Central City, on Monday, the 7th day of November, A. D. 1864, A. L. 5864, at 10 o'clock A. M.

Present—

M∴ W∴ HENRY M. TELLER, Grand Master.
R∴ W∴ A. J. VAN DEREN, Deputy Grand Master.
R∴ W∴ O. B. BROWN, Senior Grand Warden.
R∴ W∴ J. H. GEST, Junior Grand Warden.
Bro. GEO. A. PUGH, *as* Grand Treasurer.
R∴ W∴ O. A. WHITTEMORE, Grand Secretary.
Bro. ALMOND BARRELLE, *as* Grand Chaplain.
R∴ W∴ CHASE WITHROW, *as* Senior Grand Deacon.
Bro. SAM. H. ELBERT, *as* Junior Grand Deacon.
Bro. A. M. JONES, *as* Grand Tyler:

Past Grand Officers present—

ANDREW MASON, P∴ D∴ G∴ M∴.
M. C. WHITE, P∴ D∴ G∴ M∴.

The Grand ▢ was opened in ample form, with prayer by the Grand Chaplain.

The Grand Master appointed as committee on Credentials, Bros. D∴ G∴ Master Van Deren, S∴ G∴ Warden O. B. Brown, and Sam. H. Elbert.

The M∴ W∴ Grand ▢ was then called from labor until 2 o'clock P. M.

AFTERNOON SESSION.

The M∴ W∴ Grand ☐ resumed labor at 2 o'clock P. M.
Present—

M∴ W∴ HENRY M. TELLER, Grand Master.
R∴ W∴ A. J. VAN DEREN, Deputy Grand Master.
R∴ W∴ O. B. BROWN, Senior Grand Warden.
R∴ W∴ J. H. GEST, Junior Grand Warden.
Bro. Geo. A. PUGH, *as* Grand Treasurer.
R∴ W∴ O. A. WHITTEMORE, Grand Secretary.
Bro. ALMOND BARRELLE, *as* Grand Chaplain.
R∴ W∴ CHASE WITHROW, Grand Lecturer.
W∴ JAMES T. WHITE, Senior Grand Deacon.
Bro. L. W. CHASE, *as* Junior Grand Deacon.
Bro. W. P. CALDWELL, *as* Grand Tyler.

Members and others as at morning session.

The committee on Credentials presented the following report:

To the M∴ W∴ Grand ☐ of Colorado:

Your committee on Credential beg leave to report that the following persons are present, and entitled to seats and votes in the Most Worshipful Grand ☐ of Colorado, to be holden in Central City, Nov. 7, 1864:

M∴ W∴ Henry M. Teller, Grand Master, 2 votes; R∴ W∴ A. J. Van Deren, D∴ G∴ Master, 1 vote; R∴ W∴ Andrew Mason, P∴ D∴ G∴ M∴, 1 vote; R∴ W∴ M. C. White, P∴ D∴ G∴ M∴, 1 vote; R∴ W∴ O. B. Brown, S∴ G∴ W∴, 1 vote; R∴ W∴ J. H. Gest, J∴ G∴ W∴, 1 vote; R∴ W∴ O. A. Whittemore, Grand Secretary, 1 vote.

Summit ☐ No. 2: S. S. Woodbury, proxy for W∴ M∴, 1 vote; D. T. Twibell, proxy for J∴ W∴, 1 vote.

Rocky Mountain ☐ No. 3: No representative present.

Nevada ☐ No. 4: Chase Withrow, W∴ M∴, 1 vote; A. M. Jones, S∴ W∴, 1 vote; J. W. Ratliff, J∴ W∴, 1 vote.

Chivington ☐ No. 6: L. W. Chase, W∴ M∴, 1 vote; Geo. A. Pugh, S∴ W∴, 1 vote; James T. White, J∴ W∴, 1 vote.

Union ☐ No. 7: S. H. Elbert, W∴ M∴, 1 vote; M. C. White, proxy for S∴ W∴, 1 vote.

A. J. VAN DEREN,
O. B. BROWN,
SAM. H. ELBERT.

A majority of your committee find three proxies. One from D. E. Harrison, J∴ W∴, of Golden City ☐ No. 1, to J. C. Bowles; also one from Thos. P. Ames, S∴ W∴ of Denver ☐ No. 5, to John Wanless; also one from E. M. Ashley, J∴ W∴ of Union ☐ No. 7, to Mark C. White, all of which proxies were given in blank, and the above names inserted by persons unknown to your committee. Upon the propriety of the recognition of these proxies your committee are disagreed, and report them back for the action of the ▢.

A. J. VAN DEREN,
O. B. BROWN,
SAM. H. ELBERT.

On motion of Bro. Junior Grand Warden, the report was received and adopted, so far as the committee unanimously agree.

On motion of Bro. Junior Grand Warden, Bro. M. C. White was admitted as proxy for Junior Warden of Union ▢ No. 7.

On motion of Bro. White, further consideration of the report was postponed until 7 o'clock P. M.

On motion of P.·. D.·. G.·. M.·. Mason, the election of Grand Officers for the ensuing Masonic year was made the special order for to-morrow morning at 9 o'clock.

The M.·. W.·. Grand ▢ was then called from labor until 7 o'clock P. M.

EVENING SESSION.

The M.·. W.·. Grand ▢ resumed labor, officers and members present as at afternoon session.

On motion of Bro. Junior Grand Warden, it was

Resolved, By the Grand ▢ of Colorado, That no proxies issued in blank by the W.·. M.·. or Wardens of any subordinate ▢ in this jurisdiction shall be received or entitle the holders thereof to a vote in this Grand body.

The M.·. W.·. Grand Master then appointed the following committees :

To Examine Visiting Brethren.—Bros. M. C. White, Pugh and Ratliff.
On Returns and Work of ▢.—Bros. Van Deren, Elbert and Brown.
On Appeals and Grievances.—Bros. Mason, M. C. White and Withrow.
On Finance, Mileage and Per Diem.—Bros. Gest, Woodbury and Chase.

On motion of Bro. M. C. White, the reading of the minutes of the last Annual Communication was dispensed with, printed copies of proceedings being in the hands of members.

The M.·. W.·. Grand ▢ was then called from labor until 9 o'clock, Tuesday.

TUESDAY, NOV. 8, A. D. 1864, A. L. 5864.

The M∴ W∴ Grand ⊐ was called to labor at 9 o'clock A. M.
Officers and members present as yesterday.

Minutes of yesterday read and approved.

The election of officers being the special order, Bros. M. C.
White and Chase Withrow were appointed tellers, when the
Grand ▢ proceeded to an election of officers for the ensuing
Masonic year, with the following result:

M∴ W∴ A. J. VAN DEREN, Central City, Grand Master.
R∴ W∴ O. B. BROWN, Denver, Deputy Grand Master.
R∴ W∴ ANDREW SAGENDORF, Denver, Senior Grand Warden.
R∴ W∴ CHASE WITHROW, Nevada, Junior Grand Warden.
R∴ W∴ L. W. CHASE, Central City, Grand Treasurer.
R∴ W∴ O. A. WHITTEMORE, Denver, Grand Secretary.

The Grand Secretary's account was read and referred to
Finance comittee.

O. A. WHITTEMORE, *Grand Secretary, In account with Grand ▢ of A., F.
and A. M. of Colorado:*

```
1863. Nov. 3, Received of Montana ▢ U. D......................$ 8 00
  "     "  21,      "       "  Union ▢ No. 7, for charter............. 60 00
1864. Jan'y 27,     "       of M∴ W∴ G∴ Master for spec'l dispensation 10 00
  "   Feb'y 26,     "       "       "       "       "       "       " 10 00
  "   March 8,      "       "       "       "       "       " 5 00
  "   June 12,      "       "       "       "       " 5 00
  "   Nov. 5, Received of Golden City ▢ No. 1, dues.............. 40 50
  "    "  5,      "       " Union ▢ No. 7, dues.................... 48 00
  "    "  7,      "       " Chivington ▢ No. 6, dues............... 97 50
  "    "  7,      "       " Nevada No. 4, dues...................... 54 00
  "    "  7,      "       " M∴ W∴ Grand Master's Dispensations... 10 00
  "    "  7,      "       " Summit ▢ No. 2, dues.................. 28 50
                                                              _____
                                                              $376 50
1864. March 1, Paid postage............................... 5 00
  "     "    "    " L. W. Frary, Grand Treasurer...........63 00
                                                          _____ 68 00
                                                                _____
        Balance in hands of Grand Secretary.....................$308 50
```

The Grand Secretary also presented the following statement
of warrants drawn and moneys paid to the Grand Treasurer,
which was read and referred to Finance committee:

STATEMENT *of Warrants drawn on* R∴ W∴ L. W. FRARY, *Grand Treasurer:*

1863. Nov. 3,	No. 17,	Favor of	M. C. White.....................	4 00
"	"	"	"	18,	"	" D. W. Frary.....................	7 75
"	"	"	"	19,	"	" O. B. Brown.....................	29 00
"	"	"	"	20,	"	" A. J. Van Deren.................	14 00
"	"	"	"	21,	"	" H. M. Teller.............	14 00
"	"	"	"	22,	"	" O. B. Brown.....................	27 00
"	"	"	"	23,	"	" O. A. Whittemore...............	12 00
"	"	"	"	24,	"	" L. W. Frary.....................	8 25
"	"	"	"	25,	"	" O. A. Whittemore...............	4 00
"	"	"	"	26,	"	" O. A. Whittemore...............	100 00
" Dec. 3,	"	27,	"	" Jay J. Johnson..................	3 00
1864. Feb. 13,	"	28,	"	" A. L. Miller...................	8 00
" March 1,	"	29,	"	" Byers & Dailey.................	194 16

$420 16

Money paid to Grand Treasurer:

By R∴ W∴ O. B. Brown, Gr. Treas., bal. as per last report,$ 40 21
By O. A. Whittemore, Grand Secretary, per receipts...... 345 00
                                              ———— 385 21

Amount overdrawn, probably due Byers & Dailey............$34 95

The Grand Secretary reported that four ▭ had approved the proposed amendment to Article XVII of Constitution of Grand ▭, when the Grand Master put the question upon its adoption, which was unanimously concurred in.

The committee on returns of ▭ presented the following report:

To the M∴ W∴ *Grand Master, Wardens and Brethren of the Grand ▭ of Colorado:*

Your committee to whom was referred the returns of the several ▭ in your jurisdiction, beg leave to submit the following:

That we have examined the returns of Golden City ▭ No. 1, and find them correct, with the exception that they are not signed by the Master, neither is the ▭ seal attached.

Summit ▭ No. 2, correct; Rocky Mountain ▭ No. 3, no returns; Nevada ▭ No. 4, correct; Denver ▭ No. 5, no returns; Chivington ▭ No. 6, correct; Union ▭ No. 7, correct, except the omission of ▭ seal.

A. J. VAN DEREN, ⎫
SAM. H. ELBERT. ⎬ *Committee.*
O. B. BROWN, ⎭

On motion, the report was received.

Bro. Withrow moved the following amendment to By-Laws:

Strike out all after the word "person," in the second line, and insert instead, "The ▭ shall appoint some member or members of said ▭ to act in his or their stead at the last regular communication preceding such annual session of the Grand ▢."

Motion concurred in by a vote of 17 ayes to 2 nays.

The M∴ W∴ Grand Master then delivered the following

ADDRESS:

Through the favor of Divine Providence we are again assembled to review our past actions, and to consult upon, and adopt for the future, such a course as may serve to promote the interests of the craft in this jurisdiction, as well as to strengthen the bonds of brotherly love among the fraternity at large, and let us therefore render our sincere thanks to the Supreme Architect of the Universe, for the manifold blessings and comforts we have enjoyed during the past Masonic year, and let us invoke His benign influence upon us, and the fraternity at large, during the year to come.

My official acts have been few and unimportant during the past year. I granted a dispensation to the brethren of Summit ▢ No. 2, to elect their officers in accordance with the resolution of the Grand ▢ at its last Grand Communication. The charter was not returned until after the time mentioned in the resolution. I had considerable doubt as to the propriety of returning the charter at all, and was finally induced to do so by the urgent request of the brothers of Summit ▢ No. 2, as well as that of brethren not connected with that ▢, but more particularly at the request of P∴ D∴ G∴ M∴ White, who recommended me so to do. The brethren of Summit ▢ No. 2, elected their officers and are now represented in the Grand ▢. I am not informed as to the desire of the brethren of that ▢, or what action it be best to take in reference to their meetings during the coming winter. I have, also, in several cases, appearing to me to be cases of emergency, granted dispensations to the various ▭ to ballot at special communications, in which case I have required the ▢ asking for such dispensation to pay to the R∴ W∴ Treasurer the fee for granting such dispensation as is prescribed by Section 15 of the Grand ▢ By-Laws, shall be paid to the Grand Master. This fund was intended to pay the expenses of the Grand Master, but in so small a jurisdiction as this, the Grand Master's labors are not arduous, and I would therefore recommend that the money now in the hands of the Treasurer from that source, as well as sums hereafter received for dispensation, be used for the purpose of creating a library fund for the Grand ▢.

During the past year several persons, residents of this jurisdiction, while temporarily in New York City, have received in ▭ of that city the several degrees of Masonry. Such persons, on returning to this jurisdiction, have claimed the right to visit our ▭. As the persons desirous of exercising the right of visit were able to afford satisfactory evidence that they had been regularly made, and no objection being raised to their moral character, I directed, in all such cases, they should be admitted. Considerable feeling has been created among the fraternity by what they deem an infringement of our rights, by the making Masons of citizens of Colorado while in New York. I have not had sufficient data to justify me in laying the matter before the Grand Master of New York, until since the obstruction of the mail. If the ☐ of New York persist in making Masons of the citizens of Colorado, who may happen in New York for a few days or weeks, it will greatly disturb the good feeling which we are anxious to cultivate with sister Grand ☐. I would therefore recommend that this matter be referred to a committee of three, to lay the matter before the Grand Master and Grand ☐ of New York, with a request that a stop be put to the practice of making Masons of citizens of Colorado in the ☐ of New York. Article Eleventh of the Constitution provides, "That during the recess of the Grand ☐, the Grand Master and D∴ G∴ Master have power to issue dispensations for constituting new ☐." I cannot find the authority, either in the ancient usages or in the Constitution, authorizing the Deputy Grand Master to issue dispensations while the Grand Master is within the jurisdiction. The granting of dispensations is the inherent prerogative of the Grand Master, and the authorizing the use of the dispensing power by any other persons while the Grand Master is within the jurisdiction and able to exercise the power himself, is clearly, in my opinion, inexpedient and unconstitutional. I would therefore recommend a change, accordingly, in Article Eleventh of the Constitution.

The past Masonic year has been one of prosperity to the fraternity of this jurisdiction. Peace and harmony have prevailed among the brethren, and our membership has been largely increased by the admission of very worthy men. The only danger to be apprehended at this time is, that the increasing popularity of our institution may induce unworthy men to apply for admission from mercenary motives. It is the quality, and not the quantity, that should govern us in the selection of material for our building, and it behooves us to look well to the character of those who present themselves for the rights and benefits of Masonry. Let no one be admitted without suitable inquiry into his character, and do not leave this matter to the committees alone; let every member make careful inquiry into the character of the applicant, and if he is not found to be of sound mind and morals reject him. Admit no one because you can find nothing bad in him; make it a rule that no man shall be admitted who does not possess some trait of character which recommends him for admission. Do not fill our ☐ with men against whom nothing can be said good or bad, but rather fill our ☐ with men of an affirmative character, men in whose favor something may be said, men noted for integrity and moral worth, who, should the storms of adversity sweep over us in the future as in the past, will be true to their trust. The interest of the fraternity requires the frequent judicious use of the black ball.

I am happy to say that, during the past year, the work of the various ☐ has become quite uniform, under the supervision of our R∴ W∴ Grand Lecturer. The work and lectures, as taught by the R∴ W∴ Grand Lecturer, under the direction of the Grand Master, is usually known as the Baltimore, or National Work. I shall not detain you, either with the history or a defense of the work as taught in this jurisdiction. An accurate knowledge of the lectures, as taught by the R.·. W.·. Grand Lecturer, will insure you admission in all regular and well organized Masonic ⌂, and it is hoped that the Worshipful Masters and Wardens will see that all the members of their respective ⌂ are duly instructed in the work.

I wish to call your attention to the great lack of Masonic reading among the fraternity. Very few Masons read any books or papers written expressly for the order. This should not be. We have now several Masonic publications worthy of a place in any library in the land. Masonic periodicals are now published by well informed brethren devoted to the interest of the craft. The expense is trifling, the knowledge gained of incalculable value. Let the Masters and Wardens of ⌂ see to this, that the brethren become regular subscribers to one or more standard Masonic papers, and if any ⌂ has a member too poor to subscribe, let the ⌂ take a certain number of copies for gratuitous distribution among the members.

In conclusion, allow me to return to the officers of the Grand ⌂ my heartfelt thanks for their kindness during the past year. I am under lasting obligations to the officers of the Grand and subordinate ⌂, for their hearty co-operation with me in all my efforts to promote harmony among the fraternity, and it is with great pleasure that I am enabled to say at this time, that our united efforts have been crowned with success. I pledge to you, my brethren, my hearty co-operation with whomsoever you may see proper to elect as my successor, and I ask for him at your hands the same kindness that you have extended to me, and may the blessing of Heaven be upon you and yours, while here below, and when we shall have finished the course, may we all meet in that upper and better ⌂ where the Supreme Architect of the Universe presides.

H. M. TELLER,

G.·. M.·. of Masons in Colorado.

On motion of Bro. Whittemore, the Grand Master's address was referred to committees, as follows:

That portion recommending a change of By-Laws—To Bros. P.·. D.·. G.·. M.·. Mason, Sam. H. Elbert, S.·. G.·. W.·. Brown.

That referring to actions of N. Y. ⌂—To Bros. J.·. G.·. W.·. J. H. Gest, S. S. Woodbury, Jas. T. White.

To Masonic Library—Bros. Chase Withrow, Geo. A. Pugh, D. C. Twibell.

The Grand Secretary stated that he had in his possession the sum of $105, received from a comrade of Bro. John G. Brandley, a soldier of Co. C, 1st cavalry of Colorado, who was killed in a battle with the Indians, in May or June last, who, previous to his death, had expressed a wish that the money should be given to the Masonic fraternity.

On motion of P.·. D.·. G.·. M.·. White, a committee of three was appointed to report to the Grand □ what action was necessary, and what disposition should be made of the money.

Bro. White being compelled to be absent, the Grand Master appointed Bros. Sam. H. Elbert, A. J. Van Deren and O. B. Brown, said committee.

On motion' of Bro. Ratliff, the installation of officers was made the special order for this afternoon at 2 o'clock.

The Grand □ was called from labor until 2 o'clock P. M.

AFTERNOON SESSION.

The M∴ W∴ Grand □ resumed labor at 2 o'clock P. M.

The committee on Returns and Work presented the following report :

To the Grand □ of Colorado:

Your committee on Returns of □ beg leave to make a further report.

We have received the returns of Denver □ No. 5, and find them imperfect, not having the signature of the Worshipful Master or the seal of the □, but recommend that the Grand □ receive the returns and have them corrected as soon as practicable.

Respectfully submitted,

A. J. VAN DEREN, ⎫
SAM. H. ELBERT, ⎬ *Committee.*
O. B. BROWN, ⎭

On motion of Bro. J∴ G∴ Warden, the report was received and committee discharged.

On motion of D∴ G∴ M∴ Van Deren, Bro. John Wanless was admitted as proxy for S∴ W∴ of Denver □ No. 5.

INSTALLATION OF OFFICERS.

By the special order of Grand Master Teller, assisted by R∴ W∴ Bro. Andrew Mason, P∴ D∴ G∴ M∴, as Grand Marshal, installed and conducted M∴ W∴ A. J. Van Deren, as Grand Master, to his seat in the East.

The Grand Master them made the following appointments:

Rev. B. T. VINCENT, Chivington □ No. 6, Grand Chaplain.

Rev. O. A. WILLARD, Union □ No. 7, Grand Orator.

JOHN WANLESS, Denver □ No. 5, Grand Lecturer.

W. A. H. LOVELAND, Golden City □ No. 1, Grand Marshal.

GEO. W. KASSLER, Denver □ No. 5, Senior Grand Deacon.

E. H. COLLINS, Union ☐ No. 7, Junior Grand Deacon.

NOAH D. HASKELL, Summit ☐ No. 2, Grand Sword Bearer.

D: C. TWIBELL, Summit ☐ No. 2, Grand Steward.

A. HANAUER, Denver ☐ No. 5, Grand Steward.

A. DAVIDSON, Denver ☐ No. 5, Grand Tyler.

The Grand Master then installed the other Grand Officers.

The committee on that portion of the Grand Master's address relating to a Masonic library, made the following report :

To the M∴ W∴ Grand ☐ of Colorado:

Your committee to whom was referred that portion of the Grand Master's address relatiug to the establishment of a Masonic library, respectfully report :

That we recommend the establishment of a Masonic library for the use of the several ☐ in this Territory, to be located in some place to be determined after we collect a sufficient number of books to warrant, as nearly central as can be, so as to accommodate all ☐.

And that Section 15 of the By-Laws be amended as follows : Strike out the word " Master," in the second line, and insert the word " Treasurer," and add the words, " and all such sums as shall have accrued during the past year, and all that may accrue in future from such special dispensations, be set apart for the purpose of adding to and improving said library."

And that the money donated to the Grand ☐ by Bro. John G. Brandley be set apart for same object.

CHASE WITHROW, }
GEO. A. PUGH,   }   *Committee.*
D. C. TWIBELL, }

Report received and adopted.

The committee to whom was referred that portion relating to the granting of dispensations, made the following report :

To the M∴ W∴ Grand Master, Wardens and Brethren of the Grand ☐ of Colerado:

Your committee to whom was referred that portion of M∴ W∴ Grand Master's address, in regard to the powers of the R∴ W∴ Deputy Grand Master, beg leave to submit the following :

That they fully concur and approve the suggestions of the M∴ W∴ Grand Master, and recommend that the Constitution be so amended as to give power of granting dispensations by the R∴ W∴ Deputy Grand Master, only in the absence of the M∴ W∴ Grand Master from this Grand ☐ jurisdiction.

We therefore recommend that article XI of the Constitution be repealed.

ANDREW MASON, }
SAM. H. ELBERT, }   *Committee.*
O. B. BROWN, }

Report received and adopted.

P∴ G∴ M∴ Teller moved that article XI of the Constitution be repealed, which being seconded by a majority of votes, was put upon its adoption, and was unanimously concurred in.

The committee to whom was referred that portion of the address relating to the action of the New York 🔲, reported as follows:

To the M∴ W∴ Grand ☐ of Colorado:

Your committee to whom was referred that portion of the Grand Master's address, in relation to the action of the subordinate ☐ in the jurisdiction of the Grand ☐ of New York, or other jurisdictions, infringing upon our rights in conferring the degrees upon citizens of this Territory, approve of the suggestions therein made, and would recommend that a committee of three be appointed by this Grand body to remonstrate with the Grand ☐ and Grand Master of New York, upon the unmasonic action of their subordinates.

All of which is respectfully submitted,

J. H. GEST,
S. S. WOODBURY, } *Committee.*
JAS. T. WHITE,

Report received and adopted, and the following committee appointed, as recommended, to report:

P∴ G∴ M∴ Henry M. Teller, Sam. H. Elbert, D∴ G∴ M∴ O. B. Brown.

P∴ G∴ M∴ Teller offered the following

Resolved, That Article XVII of the Constitution be amended, by striking out the words "If seconded by a majority of votes."

The resolution being seconded by a majority, was put upon its adoption and unanimously concurred in.

On motion of P∴ G∴ M∴ Teller, Section 10 of By-Laws was amended by striking out the word "three" in second line, and inserting "two" in lieu thereof.

The committee to whom was referred the subject of the donation of Bro. John G. Brandley, made the following report:

To the M∴ W∴ Grand ☐ of Colorado:

Your committee to whom was referred the matter of the donation of one hundred and five dollars to the Masons of this jurisdiction, by Bro. John G. Brandley, deceased, beg leave to report that they have had the same under consideration, and recommend the passage of the following

PREAMBLE AND RESOLUTIONS:

WHEREAS, Bro. John G. Brandley, of Company "C," 1st Colorado Cavalry, was mortally wounded during the last summer in a fight with the

Indians; and, whereas, it was his dying wish, expressed to a comrade in arms, that the sum of one hundred and five dollars, which he then had with him, should be given to the Masons of this jurisdiction; and, whereas, the deceased is not known to have any living relations or representative, therefore,

Resolved, That the said donation belongs properly to the Grand ☐ of Colorado as a body, representing the entire fraternity of this jurisdiction.

Resolved, That the expenditure of the said donation in the purchase of books of Masonic law and literature, to go into the library of the Grand ☐, would be an appropriate use of said money, and must fully meet the dying wish of the gallant soldier and brother who gave it.

Resolved, That the name, date and manner of death of the deceased brother, and fact of this donation, be inscribed in the books so purchased, as a fitting testimonial of our regret for his death, and our respect for the memory of one, who, in obedience to the first teachings of our order, "Fidelity to the government under which we live," has given his life to his country.

Resolved, That in the death and last wish of this brother, we find additional reason for an attachment to an order, to the mystic ties and beautiful relations of which, the dying soldier, unblessed by dearer ties of blood, turns his last thoughts and sends his last greeting.

Respectfully submitted,

SAM. H. ELBERT, ⎫
A. J. VAN DEREN, ⎬ *Committee.*
O. B. BROWN, ⎭

Report received and unanimously adopted.

Committee on Finance, Mileage and Per diem presented the following report, which was received and adopted:

To the M∴ W∴ Grand ☐ of Colorado:

Your committee on Mileage and Per Diem would respectfully report that they find the following named officers and members in attendance and entitled to pay, as follows:

M∴ W∴ H. M. Teller, Grand Master			2 days,	$4 00
R∴ W∴ A. J. Van Deren, D∴ G∴ M∴		2 "		4 00
R∴ W∴ Andrew Mason, P∴ D∴ G∴ M∴	24 miles,	2 "		7 00
R∴ W∴ M. C. White, P∴ D∴ G∴ M∴	200 "	2 "		29 00
R∴ W∴ O. B. Brown, G∴ S∴ W∴	80 "	2 "		14 00
R∴ W∴ J. H. Gest, G∴ J∴ W∴	4 "	2 "		4 50
R∴ W∴ O. A. Whittemore, Grand Secretary	80 "	2 "		14 00
Bro. S. S. Woodbury, proxy for W∴ M∴, Summit ☐ No. 2	200 "	2 "		29 00
Bro. Chase Withrow, W∴ M∴ No. 4	4 "	2 "		4 00
Bro. L. W. Chase, W∴ M∴ No. 6		2 "		4 00
Bro. Sam. H. Elbert, W∴ M∴ No. 7	80 "	2 "		14 00
Bro. John Wanless, proxy for S∴ W∴ No. 5	80 "	2 "		14 00

All of which is respectfully submitted.

J. H. GEST, ⎫
S. S. WOODBURY, ⎬ *Committee.*
L. W. CHASE, ⎭

The same committee also submitted the following report:

To the M∴ W∴ Grand ▢ of Colorado:

Your committee on Finance, &c., would most respectfully report that they have examined the accounts of the Grand Secretary, and find them correct; and from statement furnished them by the Grand Secretary, in absence of report from Grand Treasurer, they find that there was paid over to Grand Treasurer, L. W. Frary, a balance of $40.21, in hands of Past Grand Treasurer O. B. Brown, and by Grand Secretary O. A Whittemore, the sum of $345, making a total of $385.21, and that warrants have been drawn on Grand Treasurer to the amount of $420.16, leaving a deficit in treasury of $34.95.

J. H. GEST,
S. S. WOODBURY, } *Committee.*
L. W. CHASE,

On motion of D∴ G∴ M∴ Brown, it was

Resolved, That a page of the proceedings be set apart to the memory of Bro. Brandley.

The following communication from Chivington ▢ No. 6, was read and ordered placed on file:

MASONIC HALL,
Nov. 8, A. D. 1864, A. L. 5864. }

At a Regular Communication of Chivington ▢ No. 6. A., F. and A. M., held Wednesday, Oct. 26th, it was voted that the use of this hall be tendered the M∴ W∴ Grand ▢ of Colorado, for the purpose of holding their Annual Communication.

Attest: L. W. CHASE, W∴ M∴.

ED. C. PARMELEE, *Secretary.*

The M∴ W∴ Grand Master then appointed the following committees :

Foreign Correspondence—P∴ G∴ M∴ Henry M. Teller, Bro. Sam. II. Elbert, Bro. O. A. Whittemore.

Masonic Jurisprudence—P∴ D∴ G∴ M∴ Andrew Mason, P∴ G∴ M∴ H. M. Teller, P∴ G∴ M∴ J. M. Chivington.

Bros. Teller, Van Deren, Mason and Withrow donated to library fund their per diem and mileage.

P∴ D∴ G∴ M∴ Mason offered the following, which was unanimously adopted :

Resolved, That the thanks of this M∴ W∴ Grand ▢ be tendered to Chivington ▢ No. 6, for the free use of their hall during this Annual Grand Communication.

On motion of Bro. Ratliff, it was voted that the Tyler be paid four dollars per day for his services during this session of the Grand ▢.

On motion of Bro. Gest, the Grand Secretary was authorized to procure a suitable desk or case, for keeping the records of the Grand ▢, as may in his judgment be necessary.

Bro. D∴ G∴ Master moved the adoption of the following resolution:

Resolved, That Summit ▢ No. 2 be authorized to suspend work until the regular communication in June next, as most of the members have removed from the jurisdiction for the winter. Also, that the Grand Master issue a dispensation to said Summit ▢, to elect officers at said communication, in June, if, in his opinion, the interests of the craft so demand. And that the charter of said ▢ be left in the hands of the Grand Secretary, until the Grand Master orders it returned to Summit ▢.

After some discussion, the motion was lost.

On motion of Bro. Gest, it was

Resolved, By the Grand ▢ of Colorado, that the sum of one hundred dollars be allowed our Grand Secretary, O. A. Whittemore, for his services during the past year.

Minutes of this day's proceedings read and approved.

The M∴ W∴ Grand ▢ of Colorado was then closed in ample form, with prayer by the Grand Chaplain, peace and harmony prevailing.

Attest: A. J. VAN DEREN, *Grand Master.*

O. A. WHITTEMORE, *Grand Secretary.*

IN
MEMORY
OF

Brother
John G. Brandley.

17

RETURNS OF LODGES.

GOLDEN CITY □ NO. 1, GOLDEN CITY,

Time of meetings: first and third Saturdays of each month.

OFFICERS.

L. W. Frary, W. M.	W. A. H. Loveland, Tr.	——————, S. D.
E. Fellows, S. W.	John R. Gilbert,	W. H. Shea, J. D.
D. E. Harrison, J. W.		Wm. Mack, Tyler.

MEMBERS.

Wm. P. Pollock,	J. H. Durham,	D. G. Dargin,
J. S. Scott,	Eli Carter,	J. S. Maynard,
Wm. Fredericks,	W. L. Rothrock,	Charles Remington,
Wm. Newton,	Fox Diefendorf,	John F. Kirby,
J. B. Langdon,	Reuben Borton,	A. J. Butler,
M. H. Floyd,	S. M. Breath,	John Kean,
T. P. Boyd,	John A. Moore,	G. M. Wilson,
G. M. Chilcott,	John M. Ferrill,	Joseph Casto,
Wm. D. Rippy,	E. B. Smith,	J. C. Bowles,
W. D. Annis,	Daniel McCleery,	Henry Stevens,
Felix Crocker,	Samuel F. Shaffer,	John Gilmore,
Abraham Slater,	J. B. Hendry,	George Morrison,
Martin Opal,	Ira Quinby,	S. Bailey,
J. D. Carnes,	S. B. Williams,	James Kelley,
G. N. Belcher,	John Sexton,	Lewis Davis,
Jno. Strouse,		W. R. Nelson,

DIMITTED.

B. C. Dennis,	Thomas M. Pope,	T. Cummigs.
	C. R. Huntsman,	

FELLOWCRAFT.

L. L. Rene.

ENTERED APPRENTICES.

Leon Mellet,	Milo Smith,	P. L. Smith,
A. M. Wallingford,	J. W. Bartholomew,	James Stevens,
Bruce Woodward,	Joseph Parrot,	C. S. Birdsall,

Number of members, 54; members living out of the Territory, 24.

SUMMIT □ NO. 2, PARKVILLE.

Time of meetings: Saturday on or before ☾.

OFFICERS.

C. H. Blair, W. M.	L. Peabody, Treas.	D. W. Willey, S. D.
Milton Pulver, S. W.	S. S. Woodbury, Sec'y.	H. Murray, J. D.
D. C. Twibell, J. W.		D. W. Johnson, Tyler.

MEMBERS.

O. B. Brown, S. G. W.
Noah D. Haskell,
H. B. Haskell,
John S. Lewis,
John Coon,
John Thompson,

Calvin Pulver,
William Moore,
William McCartney,
J. E. Sawyer,
John L. Dyer,
Frederick Barr,

John McCaskill,
Edwin Carter,
P. Asbury,
D. Stogsdall,
George Oswald,
L. F. Valiton.

DIMITTED.

J. E. Thatcher,
G. Krack,

William D. Smith,
B. F. Turner,

George Rader,
Nelson Toncray.

ENTERED APPRENTICES.

S. J. Pratt,   A. Heath.

Number of members, 20; members living out of the Territory, 7.

NEVADA □ NO. 4.

Time of meetings: second and fourth Saturdays in each month.

OFFICERS.

Chase Withrow, W. M.
A. M. Jones, S. W.
John W. Ratliff, J. W.

John C. Russell, Treas.
J. F. Phillips, Sec'y.

Ed. B. Newman, S. D.
W. T. Carothers, J. D.
William H. Jester, Tyler.

MEMBERS.

A. Mason, P. D. G. M.
J. M. Van Deren, P. M.
A. J. Van Deren, D.G.M.
Asa L. Miller,
W. L. Sawtell,
Chas. S. Abbott,
E. W. Henderson,
J. H. Gest,
D. L. Fairchild,
J. W. Bowles,
Preston Scott,
James C. Bradley,
Thomas Newlan,
Preston Anderson,
B. W. Eussen,
W. N. Belcher,
Silas G. Brown,

John E. Gregg,
H. A. Haskin,
William H. James,
W. H. Avery,
David Lees,
A. C. Megeath,
T. H. Clewell,
Addi Vincent,
Orlando North,
James A. Burdick,
J. W. Martin,
D. J. Ball,
B. F. Pease,
Edward Crockett,
O. F. Sparks,
Joshua Jennings,
Andrew Nichols,

R. M. Foster,
D. A. Hamer,
J. W. Stanton,
J. M. Smith,
W. D. Perkins,
B. C. Waterman,
W. R. Uren,
John H. Mitchell,
John E. Craine,
C. E. Forgy,
Robert Milliken,
Chas. E. Clarke,
George Craine,
Theodore Haswell,
Asahel Cassell,
W. T. Potter,
George Marshall,

DIMITTED.

Lyman W. Chase,
J. K. Rutledge,

I. B. Brunell,
James Lees,
L. D. Randall.

J. H. Haines,
John Allen,

DIED.

Chas. W. Cassell,   John Jackson.

FELLOWCRAFTS.

Chas. Alber,   C. H. Merrill.

ENTERED APPRENTICES.

Wm. McFeeters,
Mavine Symonds,
F. R. Wagoner,
Andrew J. Biggs,

Geo. W. Brock,
B. F. Shaffer,
Benair Walls,

F. T. Sherman,
W. L. Ireland,
James Huff,
G. W. Hall.

Number of members, 59; members living out of the Territory, 23.

DENVER ▭ NO. 5.

Time of meetings: first and third Saturdays in each month.

OFFICERS.

A. Sagendorf, W. M.
Thos. James, S. W.
Geo. W. Kassler, J. W.

A. J. Snider, Treasurer,
A. McCune, Secretary,
J. H. Vorhies, S. D.
A. Davidson, Tyler,

J. L. Dailey, J. D.
J. C. Davidson, S. S.
J. M. Broadwell, J. S.

MEMBERS.

A. P. Allen,
Wm. N. Byers,
Chas. H. Blake,
A. H. Barker,
Chas. L. Bartlett,
Geo. H. Bryant,
Gardner G. Brewer,
E. W. Cobb,
George W. Clayton,
W. H. Garvin,
A. Goldsmith,
L. N. Greenleaf,
Wm. H. Grafton,
J. E. Gates,
H. H. Gillett,
C. J. Goss,
A. Hanauer,
J. S. Howell,
B. C. Hayman,
Noah Hill,
Geo. W. Hertell,
Henry Hitchins,
Wm. E. Hall,
Jas. H. Hodges,
E. H. Jewett,
Wm. M. Keith,

Richard E. Cooke,
Sam. H. Cook,
Chas. H. Cook,
Geo. T. Clark,
Fred A. Clark,
W. S. Cheesman,
M. J. Dougherty,
Wm. M. Dailey,
F. M. Durkee,
Ed. W. Kingsbury,
Jerry Kershow,
Geo. K. Kimball,
Henry Kline,
John B. Lamber,
Thos. W. Lavin,
Geo. Lyman Moody,
F. Meserve,
Jas. McNasser,
Wm. Porter,
Frank H. Page,
Thos. C. Porter,
Nahum H. Rice,
Jarius Richards,
E. E. Ropes,
J. D. Ramage,

Henry J. Rogers,
J. R. Devor,
J. H. Dudley,
Joseph Ehle,
Joseph Faivre,
Wm. R. Ford,
Hi. F. Ford,
Henry Feuerstein,
John H. Gerrish,
William Gray,
Richard Sopris, P. M.
Wm. M. Slaughter,
Fred. Z. Salomon,
H. Z. Salomon,
J. J. Saville,
J. Lloyd Smith,
Edwin Scudder,
M. B. Sherwood,
William Stepp,
C. W. Smith,
Geo. L. Shoup,
John E. Tappan,
George Tritch,
Nicholas Thede,
John Wanless,
DeWitt C. Waugh.

FELLOWCRAFT.

F. R. Wagoner.

ENTERED APPRENTICES.

Chas. L. Brassler,
Augustus Bartlett,
John C. Carter,
John Good,

Moses Hallett,
John W. Kerr,
Geo. W. Lowe,

Samuel McClellan,
Wm. Nowlan,
Chas. F. Parkhurst,
John Upton,

DIMITTED.

Louis Behm,

John T. Henderson,

Gus. Newman.

DIED.

Daniel Moyn,   J. B. Doyle.

Number of members, 86; members living out of the Territory, 24.

CHIVINGTON ▭ NO. 6.

Time of meetings: second and fourth Wednesdays of each month.

OFFICERS.

Lyman W. Chase, W. M.
George A. Pugh, S. W.
James T. White, J. W.

William Jones, Treas.
Ed. C. Parmelee, Sec'y.
Benj. F. Wisebart, S. D.
Basil Green, Tyler.

Leopold Well, J. D.
David C. Collier, S. S.
H. J. Kruse, J. S.

MEMBERS.

H. M. Teller, M. W. G. M.
Allyn Weston, P. G. M.
Jesse L. Pritchard,
Thomas J. Brower,
A. Jacobs,
D. H. Warren,
S. F. Tappan,
George Schram,
William Rosenfield,
E. L. Gardner,
James Clark,
Robert Frazier,
E. H. Brown,
E. H. Beals,
H. S. Robinson,
Jacob Mack,
David Loeb,
H. A. Johnson,
Job C. McClellan,
Henry A. Woods,
Phillip McGran,
William B. Squires,

William Watson,
A. B. Davis,
L. Merchant,
G. G. Norton,
David S. Green,
C. W. Johnson,
J. B. Cofield,
L. G. H. Greene,
Thomas Barnes,
A. G. Raynor,
U. B. Holloway,
Dubois Tooker,
J. N. Adams,
J. E. Plummer,
J. J. Dunnegan,
Felix Poznansky,
David Kline,
Charles L. Hill,
W. C. M. Jones,
Jos. Coleman,
H. R. Eldred,

O. H. Harker,
A. E. Buckmiller,
D. W. Tilton,
Jacob Weidman,
W. P. Caldwell,
M. C. Wythe,
P. H. Dunnegan,
G. B. Cornell,
Aug. H. Whitehead,
Wm. T. Ellis,
Isaac B. Brunell,
David J. Martin,
Hal. Sayr,
John M. Rank,
O. E. Colony,
Rev. B. T. Vincent,
H. M. Orahood,
Rev. A. Barrelle,
J. K. Rutledge,
H. J. Hammond,
George W. Buchanan,
R. Hutchins.

DIMITTED.

J. M. Chivington, P. G. M.
A. J. Culbertson,

Rev. William H. Fisher,
E. R. Crosier,

James Clarkson,
Isaac Louis.

DIED.

J. Nelson Smith.

FELLOWCRAFTS.

J. W. Watson,
B. S. Buell,

Frank Hall,
J. G. Mahany,

John Kip,
John Y. Glendinen.

ENTERED APPRENTICES.

L. Kennedy,
A. Schonecker,
S. I. Lorah,
A. McNamee,
George W. Jacobs,

John C. Bruce,
N. L. Sibley,
J. W. Wilson,
W. H. Nichols,

Benj. Lake,
William Humphrey,
D. T. Beals,
G. B. Reed,
George E. Wilson.

Number of members, 75; members living out of the Territory, 10.

UNION ▭ NO. 7, DENVER.

Time of meetings: second and fourth Saturdays of each month.

OFFICERS.

Sam. H. Elbert, W. M.
John C. Anderson, S. W.
E. M. Ashley, J. W.

J. R. Boyce, Treasurer,
O. A. Whittemore, Sec.
M. C. White, S. D.
E. H. Collins, J. D.

H. B. Hitchings, Chap.
Loudon Mullin, S. S.
Jay J. Johnson, J. S.

MEMBERS.

J. M. Chivington, P.G.M.
Francis R. Bill,
Charles Donnelly,
R. V. Fairbanks,
Norton W. Welton,
W. D. Pease,
Langdon Clark,

John Evans,
Richard Leach,
Elisha Millerson,
John Pierce,
Jonas Deitch,
Clarence J. Clarke,
John Charmard,
Henry Henson,

Charles Ruter,
Simeon Whitley,
Jacob Downing,
O. A. Willard,
D. C. Corbin,
Luther Kountze,
John D. Simpson.

DIMITTED.

George C. Betts.

FELLOWCRAFTS.

John S. Fillmore,   Chauncy Barbour.

ENTERED APPRENTICES.

Daniel Witter,   O. M. Whittier,   Isaac Chandler,
John E. Stewart,   Redwood Fisher,   David A. Chever,
W. D. Anthony,   Luther Wilson,   Joseph Finley,
Henry C. Leach,   George E. Crater,   Thomas Barnum.
                      J. L. Bailey,

Number of members, 32.

PROCEEDINGS

OF THE

GRAND LODGE OF COLORADO,

HELD AT DENVER, NOV. 6, A. L. 5865.

FIFTH ANNUAL COMMUNICATION.

———

The Most Worshipful Grand ☐ of Ancient, Free and Accepted Masons of Colorado met in Annual Communication at the Masonic Hall, in Denver, on the first Monday, it being the 6th day of November, A. D. 1865, A. L. 5865, at 10 o'clock A. M.

Present—

M∴ W∴ A. J. VAN DEREN, Grand Master.
R∴ W∴ O. B. BROWN, Deputy Grand Master.
R∴ W∴ ANDREW SAGENDORF, Senior Grand Warden.
R∴ W∴ CHASE WITHROW, Junior Grand Warden.
Bro. R. SOPRIS, *as* Grand Treasurer.
R∴ W∴ B. T. VINCENT, Grand Chaplain.
R∴ W∴ O. A. WHITTEMORE, Grand Secretary.
W∴ GEO. W. KASSLER, Senior Grand Deacon.
Bro. B. W. WISEBART, *as* Junior Grand Deacon.
Bro. A. DAVIDSON, Grand Tyler.

PAST GRAND OFFICERS.

J. M. CHIVINGTON, P∴ G∴ Master.
H. M. TELLER, P∴ G∴ Master.
ANDREW MASON, P∴ D∴ G∴ Master, and representatives from subordinate ☐.

18

A Master Masons' ☐ was opened, when it appearing that a constitutional number of ⬓ was represented, the M∴ W∴ Grand ☐ of Colorado was opened in ample form, with prayer by the Grand Chaplain.

The Grand Master appointed as committee on Credentials:

D∴ G∴ M∴ O. B. Brown, J∴ G∴ W∴ Chase Withrow, Bro. L. N. Greenleaf.

The M∴ W∴ Grand ☐ was then called from labor until 2 o'clock P. M.

----

2 O'CLOCK P. M.

The M∴ W∴ Grand ☐ resumed labor, officers and members present as at morning session, when the committee on Credentials made the following report, which was adopted:

To the M∴ W∴ Grand ☐ of Colorado, A., F. and A. M.:

Your committee on Credentials respectfully report that the following named persons are present, and entitled to seats and votes in this Grand ☐.

Bro. A. J. Van Deren, M∴ W∴ G∴ M∴, 2 votes; Rro. O. B. Brown, R∴ W∴ D∴ G∴ M∴, 1 vote; Bro. A. Sagendorf, R∴ W∴ S∴ G∴ W∴, 1 vote; Bro. Chase Withrow, R∴ W∴ J∴ G∴ W∴, 1 vote; Bro. O. A. Whittemore, R∴ W∴ Grand Secretary, 1 vote; Bro. J. M. Chivington, P∴ G∴ M∴, 1 vote; Bro. H. M. Teller, P∴ G∴ M∴, 1 vote; Bro. Andrew Mason, P∴ D∴ G∴ M∴, 1 vote.

Nevada ☐ No. 4: Bro. J. F. Phillips, proxy for W∴ M∴, 1 vote; Bro. O. North, S∴ W∴, 1 vote; Bro. J. W. Ratliff, J∴ W∴, 1 vote.

Denver ☐ No. 5: Bro. L. N. Greenleaf, S∴ W∴, 1 vote; Bro. A. McCune, J∴ W∴, 1 vote.

Chivington ☐ No. 6: Bro. James F. White, W∴ M∴, 1 vote; Bro. B. W. Wisebart, S∴ W∴, 1 vote; Bro. Nelson Z. Cozens, proxy for J∴ W∴, 1 vote.

Union ☐ No. 7: Bro. E. M. Ashley, W∴ M∴, 1 vote; Bro. O. A. Whittemore, S∴ W∴, 1 vote; E. H. Collins, J∴ W∴, 1 vote.

Golden City ☐ No. 1: Bro. James Kelly, S∴ W∴, 1 vote.

O. B. BROWN,
CHASE WITHROW, } *Committee.*
L. N. GREENLEAF,

* The reading of the minutes of the last Annual Communication was dispensed with, printed copies being in the hands of members.

The M∴ W∴ Grand Master, A. J. Van Deren, then delivered the following

ADDRESS:

Another year with its duties, sorrows and joys has been added to those that have gone before; and while standing on the threshhold of the new year, let us review our past actions and see if we have faithfully performed the duties assigned us.

The Grand Architect of the Universe has spared our lives, until we are again permitted to assemble in Grand Communication to hold fraternal intercourse, that, by an interchange of views, we may adopt for the future such a course as will best promote the harmony, welfare and usefulness of the order, and strengthen the fraternal bonds throughout our young and growing jurisdiction. For this, and the numerous other blessings of the past year, let us return devout thanks to our Supreme Grand Master, and invoke His divine blessing upon us and the fraternity at large for the year to come.

During the Masonic year just closing, my official acts have been few. Soon after our last Grand Communication I issued dispensations to the required number of brethren to open ▭. One at Empire City, Clear Creek County, in this Territory, and another at Helena, Adgerton County, Montana Territory, which will probably be returned to this Grand body with a request for a perpetual charter. I have, also, at the request of different ▭, issued special dispensations, allowing them to ballot upon the application of candidates for the second and third degrees in less than the usual time, they appearing to be cases of emergency.

I have no knowledge of the action of your committee, appointed last year to correspond with the officers of the Grand ▭ of New York and other eastern States, with reference to their subordinate ▭ conferring the degrees upon persons residing within our jurisdiction, neither have I heard of any recent recurrence of that infringement, and hope that they will, in the future, give us no further cause of complaint in that respect.

The Grand Lecturer appointed last year, having been absent from the country, I have nothing to report as to his services, but am happy to report that there has been much improvement, and an earnest desire on the part of most of the ▭, to become more perfect and uniform in the work and lectures adopted by this Grand ▭.

I congratulate you on the harmony that has prevailed throughout the ju‚ risdiction, and the unusual prosperity that has attended the different ⌷ during the past year. Our noble institution still continues to grow in pop- ular favor. The doors of our ⌷ are thronged by persons anxious to be admitted to our mysteries. Permit me here, my brethren, to remind you that we cannot be too vigilant in guarding the doors of our ⌷, or too care- ful in the use of the ballot. In this lies our safety. Allow *none to pass the threshold* except they be worthy. Advance none that have not sufficient zeal to learn the lectures of the several degrees. Make proficiency in these respects a requisite to advancement, and you will avoid the blighting effect of filling your ⌷ with inefficient and inactive members, to become drones in the hive of Masonry, consuming its vitals.

I also congratulate you that since our last Grand Communication, peace has been restored to our beloved country, and that it is fast resuming its former happy and prosperous condition. Let us exercise due Masonic charity towards those who have been separated from us by the recent na- tional difficulties, and promptly stretch forth the hand of fellowship, and give them every facility and offer them every inducement to return to their former relations of friendship, fraternity and union, and enjoy with us the prosperity and blessings of our Ancient Order, and of a free and united people.

On account of the usual inclement weather at this season of the year, rendering it often difficult for the officers and members of the Grand ⌷ to get to the place of meeting, I would recommend that the time of meeting be changed to an earlier date.

That our order may continue to be blessed with peace, harmony and prosperity, and increase in intelligence and usefulness, until we shall be- come a bright and shining light in this western land, is my earnest wish and prayer.

On motion of P.·. G.·. M.·. Teller, that portion of the ad- dress recommending a change of time for holding the annual meeting of the Grand ⌷, was referred to the following named committee:

P.·. G.·. M.·. H. M. Teller, D.·. G.·. M.·. O. B. Brown, J.·. G.·. W.·. Chase Withrow.

The M.·. W.·. Grand Master then appointed the following committees, viz:

Visiting Brethren—Bros. L. N. Greenleaf, N. Z. Cozens, and J. F. Phillips.

Charters and Dispensations—P.·. G.·. M.·. H. M. Teller, Bros. E. M. Ashley and O. North.

Appeals and Grievances—Bro. E. H. Collins, P∴ D∴ G∴ M∴ A. Mason, Bro. J. Kelly.

Finance, Mileage and Per Diem—Bro. Chase Withrow, D∴ G∴ M∴ O. B. Brown, Bro. Geo. W. Kassler.

P∴ G∴ M∴ J. M. Chivington moved that the election of officers for the ensuing Masonic year, be the special order for to-morrow, at 9 A. M., which motion was concurred in.

Grand ▢ was called from labor for half an hour.

––––––––––

Grand ▢ resumed labor, when the committee on Charters and Dispensations made the following report, which was received and adopted :

To the M∴ W∴ Grand ▢ of the Most Ancient and Honorable Fraternity of Free and Accepted Masons:

Your committee appointed on ▢ under dispensation, respectfully report that they have examined the returns of Empire ▢ U. D., and find them correct. They also find that said ▢ has conferred the first, second and third degrees, and that the Worshipful Master and Wardens of said ▢ are now present, and desire that a charter be granted and the officers installed by the M∴ W∴ Grand ▢. Your committee do therefore recommend that a charter and number be given to said Empire ▢ under dispensation, and that the officers be installed by the Grand ▢. Your committee have not had time to examine the other cases presented for charters, and therefore respectfully ask for further time to make an additional report.

H. M. TELLER,
E. M. ASHLEY, } *Committee.*
ORLANDO NORTH,

D∴ G∴ M∴ O. B. Brown presented his report for the past Masonic year, as follows :

To the M∴ W∴ Grand Master, Wardens and Brethren, of the Grand ▢ of Colorado:

I have the honor to report that, during the last Masonic year, and in the absence from the jurisdiction of the M∴ W∴ Grand Master, I have granted the following dispensations, viz:

December 17, 5864, Golden City ▢ No. 1, to open and elect officers from the floor; December 14, 5864, Nevada ▢ No. 4, to pass Bro. Andrew J. Briggs; December 14, 5864, Denver ▢ No. 5, to raise Bro. Augustus Bartlett; January 7, 5865, Union □ No. 7, to raise Bro. Merrick A. Rogers; January 12, 5865, to raise Bro. John E. Stewart; May 1, 5865, to raise Bro. Redwood Fisher; February 23, 5865, to ballot upon the petition of Mr. W. R. Irwin.

Each of the above dispensations were granted upon the petition of Master and Wardens of the several □, and represented as being cases of emergency to a sufficient extent to justify the issuing of said dispensations. On the 4th day of April, 1865, I granted a dispensation to a number of brethren at Virginia City, Montana Territory, for the formation of a new □ at that place, to be called Montana □, appointing H. L. Hosmer to be their first Master, L. W. Frary to be their first Senior Warden, and William Gray to be their first Junior Warden. The petition of the said brethren was recommended by Virginia City □ No. 43, and also by Union □ No. 7.

Wishing that harmony, which should ever characterize true Masons, either in their public capacity or in the private walks of life, may exist during our present assembly, and with the □ of the jurisdiction during the Masonic year upon which we are just entering,

I am, brethren, fraternally yours,

O. B. BROWN,
D∴ G∴ M∴ of Colorado.

The Grand Secretary presented his report and accounts as follows:

To the M∴ W∴ Grand □ of Colorado :

I have the honor respectfully to submit the accompanying account for the current year, showing received as dues from □ and other sources, five hundred and fifty-seven dollars and fifty cents, to account of general fund, and from special dispensations the sum of forty-two dollars on account of library fund.

Returns have been received from all chartered □ now working under the jurisdiction of this Grand □.

Summit □ No. 2 has surrendered its charter and returned the records of the □, no work having been done or meetings held since the last Annual Grand Communication. Empire □ U. D., Montana □ U. D., and Helena City □ U. D., have returned their dispensations and records of work, and pray for charters.

Very respectfully,

O. A. WHITTEMORE, *Grand Secretary.*

O. A. Whittemore, Grand Secretary, in account with Grand ▢ of Colorado:

DR.

Nov. 17, 1864, to Empire ▢, U. D., dispensation..................	$ 40 00
April 4, 1865, to Montana ▢, U. D., dispensation................	40 00
July 10, 1865, to Helena City ▢, U. D., dispensation...	40 00
Oct. 15, 1865, to Montana ▢, U. D., with petition for charter.....	20 00
Oct. 25, 1865, to Helena City ▢, U. D., with petition for charter..	20 00
Nov. 6, 1865, to Golden City ▢ No. 1, dues.....................	46 50
" " " " Denver ▢ No. 5, dues.........................	90 00
" " " " Nevada ▢ No. 4, dues.........................	70 50
" " " " Chivington ▢ No. 6, dues.....................	133 50
" " " " Union ▢ No. 7, dues..........................	57 00

$557 50

CR.

Nov. 12, by postage circulars..........................	$ 3 00	
April 1, " " reports received...................	4 65	
" 1. " " " sent......................	8 64	
July 1, " " " received...................	7 59	
Oct. 1, " " "	2 60	
" 1, stationery......................................	2 00	
" 31, ruling blanks..................................	2 10	
Nov. 6, Grand Treasurer's receipt.....................	526 92	$557 50

O. A. Whittemore, Grand Secretary, in account with Grand ▢ of Colorado:

LIBRARY FUND.   DR.

Nov. 30, 1864, M.·. W.·. A. J. Van Deren, G.·. M.·., special dispensation..	$ 5 00
Dec. 14, 1864, R.·. W.·. O. B. Brown, D.·. G.·. M.·., special dispensation..	5 00
Dec. 17, 1864, to R.·. W.·. O. B. Brown, D.·. G.·. M.·., special dispensation..	2 00
Jan. 13, 1865, to R.·. W.·. O. B. Brown, D.·. G.·. M.·. special dispensation..	5 00
Feb. 23, 1865, to R.·. W.·. O. B. Brown, D.·. G.·. M.·., special dispensation..	15 00
May 1, 1865, to R.·. W.·. O. B. Brown, D.·. G.·. M.·., special dispensation..	5 00
July 8, 1865, to R.·. W.·. O. B. Brown, D.·. G.·. M.·., special dispensation..	5 00

$42 00

CR.

Nov. 6, 1865, by Grand Treasurer's receipt...............$ 42 00

Report and account referred to committee on Finance, Mileage and Per Diem.

The following report, presented by the Grand Treasurer, was referred to same committee.

L. W. CHASE, *Grand Treasurer, in account with M∴ W∴ Grand □ of Colorado:* DR.

	LIBRARY FUND.	GENERAL FUND.
Nov. 8, 1864, to cash from Grand Secretary, library fund.	$145 00	
Nov. 8, 1864, to cash from Grand Secretary, general fund.		$361 50
1865, to cash from M∴ W∴ A. J. Van Deren, special dispensation.	10 00	
Nov. 6, 1865, to cash from Grand Secretary.		526 92
Nov. 6, 1865, to cash from Grand Secretary.	42 00	
	$197 00	$888 42

CR.

Nov. 8, 1864, by paid warrant No. 30, S. S. Woodbury....	$ 29 00
" " " " " 31, W. P. Caldwell.....	8 00
" " " " " 32, S. H. Elbert........	14 00
" " " " " 33, O. B. Brown...,....	14 00
" " " " " 34, J. H. Gest..........	4 50
" " " " " 35, John Wanless......	14 00
" " " " " 36, M. C. White.......	29 00
" " " " " 37, O. A. Whittemore..	14 00
" " " " " 38, O. A. Whittemore..	100 00
" " " " " 39, L. W. Chase........	4 00
" " " " " 40, Collier & Wells.....	235 00
	$465 50

Balance in treasury, general fund,		$422 93
Balance in treasury, library fund	$197 00	

All of which is respectfully submitted,

L. W. CHASE, *Grand Treasurer.*

On motion of S∴ G∴ W∴ Andrew Sagendorf, a charter was granted to Empire □, to be numbered eight.

The officers elect of Empire □ No. 8, Bros. Andrew Mason, W∴ M∴, H. A. Haskins, Senior Warden and John S. Jones, as proxy for J. Mullen, being present, they were duly installed by P∴ G∴ M∴ Teller, Bro. Richard Sopris acting as Grand Marshal.

On motion of P∴ G∴ M∴ Andrew Mason, Section 7 of Rules of Order was amended, by striking out the words "to adjourn" where they occur in the section.

Bro. Whittemore moved to strike out the entire section as amended.

Bro. Teller moved to amend the motion, by striking out all after the word "arranged," in fourth line, which motion was concurred in.

On motion of P∴ G∴ M∴ Chivington, it was

Resolved, That it is the sense of the Grand □ of Colorado, that the non-payment of dues cannot work a forfeiture of Masonic standing.

The Grand □ was then called from labor, to meet to-morrow morning, at 9 o'clock.

TUESDAY, NOV. 7, A. D. 1865, A. L. 5865.

Grand □ resumed labor at 9 A. M. Officers and members present as yesterday. Minutes of yesterday read and approved.

It being the hour named for the election of officers, the Grand □ proceeded to an election with the following result, Bros. Eli M. Ashley and James T. White acting as tellers:

Bro. ANDREW MASON, Empire □ No. 8, Grand Master.

Bro. O. B. BROWN, Union □ No. 7, Deputy Grand Master.

Bro. CHASE WITHROW, Nevada □ No. 4, Senior Grand Warden.

Bro. JAS. T. WHITE, Chivington □ No. 6, Junior Grand Warden.

Bro. RICHARD SOPRIS, Denver □ No. 5, Grand Treasurer.

Bro. O. A. WHITTEMORE, Union □ No. 7, Grand Secretary.

The committee on Returns of ⊡ U. D. made an additional report, as follows:

To the M∴ W∴ Grand □ of Colorado:

Your committee on ⊡ U. D. would respectfully further report: That they have examined the returns of Montana □ U. D., and find the same correct. They also find that the brethren of Montana □ have conferred the first, second and third degrees, and are desirous of receiving from this Grand □ a charter. Your committee would therefore respectfully recommend that a charter be granted to said brethren, and such □ be known as Montana □ No. 9. Your committee also further report, that they have examined the returns of Helena City □, U. D., and find the same correct. We find that the brethren of Helena City □ have conferred the first and second degrees, but for want of time have not conferred the third. Your committee are satisfied that the brethren of Helena City □ are competent to confer the third degree in due form, and as the brethren are very desirous of receiving a charter, your committee would therefore recommend that Article 14 of our By-Laws be suspended, and that a charter be granted to said brethren, and such □ be known as Helena City □ No. 10.

H. M. TELLER,
ORLANDO NORTH, } *Committee.*
E. M. ASHLEY,

Report received, and, on motion of S∴ G∴ W∴ A. Sagendorf, was adopted.

On motion of P∴ G∴ M∴ Teller, Article 14 of By-Laws was suspended, when, on motion of J∴ G∴ W∴ Chase Withrow, charters were granted to Montana ☐ to be numbered nine, and Helena City ☐ to be numbered ten.

P∴ G∴ M∴ Teller, chairman of committee on Foreign Correspondence, submitted the following report:

To the M∴ W∴ Grand Master and Brethren of the Grand ☐ of Colorado:

The committee on Foreign Correspondence respectfully report that they have no report to make on the condition of the fraternity, for the following reasons:

During the past year, your committee have been unable to obtain the proceedings of but a few of our sister Grand ☐. The Grand ☐ with which we are in communication have, undoubtedly, mailed a copy of their proceedings as usual, but owing to the fact that, by an Act of Congres, all printed matter coming west of the west line of the State of Kansas must pay letter postage, pre-paid, we do not receive them. If the R∴ W∴ Grand Secretaries of sister Grand ☐ expect us to receive copies of their proceedings, it will be necessary for them to pay letter postage on such matter at the office where deposited.

H. M. TELLER, Chairman.

The ☐ was then called from labor until 2 o'clock P. M.

AFTERNOON SESSION—2 o'clock P. M.

The Grand ☐ resumed labor, when the committee on Charters and Dispensations submitted the following report:

To the M∴ W∴ Grand Master, Wardens and Brethren of the Grand ☐ of Colorado:

Your committee to whom was referred the returns of chartered ☐, beg leave to report that we have examined the returns of Golden City ☐ No. 1, Nevada ☐ No. 4, Chivington ☐ No. 6, and Union ☐ No. 7, and find them correct. We have also examined the returns of Denver ☐ No. 5, and find that the names of members residing out of Territory are not given—in all other respects correct.

E. M. ASHLEY,
ORLANDO NORTH, } Committee.

Report received and adopted.

The committee on Finance, Mileage and Per Diem presented the following report:

To the M∴ W∴ Grand ☐ of A., F. and A. M. of Colorado:

Your committee have examined the reports of the Grand Treasurer and Grand Secretary and find them correct; and we also find that there is a balance in the treasury of six hundred and nineteen dollars and ninety-two cents, including library fund.

Respectfully submitted,

CHASE WITHROW,
O. B. BROWN.

The committee on Recommendations contained in the address of the M∴ W∴ Grand Master, concerning time for holding Annual Communications, submitted the following report and resolution, which was received and resolution adopted :

To the M∴ W∴ Grand ☐ A., F. and A. M. of Colorado:

Your committee to whom was referred that portion of the Grand Master's address relating to the change of time of holding Annual Communications, respectfully report the following resolution, and recommend its adoption :

Resolved; That the word " November," in the second line of section 1 of the By-Laws be stricken out, and the word " October" inserted in its stead.

H. M. TELLER,
CHASE WITHROW,
O. B. BROWN.

On motion of J∴ G∴ W∴ Chase Withrow, it was

Resolved, That when a petition has been rejected for initiation in any ☐ in its jurisdiction, the applicant shall not be allowed to petition the same ☐ in a less time than six months, nor any other ☐ in this jurisdiction in a less time than one year.

Bro. Ashley presented the following resolution, and moved its adoption :

Resolved, by the Grand ☐ of Colorado, That after this Grand Communication, it shall be unlawful for any subordinate ☐ in this jurisdiction to bury with Masonic honors any brother who may have been an habitual drunkard.

Resolution lost.

On motion of Bro. Collins, the fourth of the resolutions concerning the Conservator's Association, adopted November, 1863, was stricken out.

The committee on Finance, Mileage and Per Diem submitted the following report, which was received and adopted :

To the M∴ W∴ Grand ☐ of A., F. and A. M. of Colorado:

Your committee on Mileage and Per Diem find the following named officers and members in attendance and entitled to pay, as follows:

NAMES.	Miles traveled.	Attendance Days.	Amount.
M∴ W∴ A. J. Van Deren, Grand Master	80	2	$14 00
R∴ W∴ O. B. Brown, D∴ G∴ M∴		2	4 00
R∴ W∴ A. Sagendorf, S∴ G∴ W∴		2	4 00
R∴ W∴ Chase Withrow, J∴ G∴ W∴	80	2	14 00
R∴ W∴ O. A. Whittemore, Grand Secretary		2	4 00
Bro. J. M. Chivington, P∴ G∴ M∴		2	4 00
Bro. H. M. Teller, P∴ G∴ M∴	80	2	14 00
Bro. S. H. Elbert, Com. Foreign Correspondence		2	4 00
Bro. James Kelly, Golden City ☐ No. 1	24	2	7 00
J. F. Phillips, Nevada ☐ No. 4	80	2	14 00
J. T. White, Chivington ☐ No. 5	80	2	14 00
L. N. Greenleaf. Denver ☐ No. 6		2	4 00
E. M. Ashley, Union ☐ No. 7		2	4 00
Andrew Mason, Empire ☐ No. 8	104	2	17 00

Respectfully submitted,

CHASE WITHROW,
O. B. BROWN.

On motion of D∴ G∴ M∴ Brown, it was

Resolved, That it shall be and is hereby made the imperative duty of the subordinate ☐ in this jurisdiction to restrain, as far as possible, the Masonic crime of intemperance by trial and suspension, or expulsion, as the case may require, and for the faithful performance of that duty, the said subordinate ☐ will be held accountable to this Grand ☐.

On motion of D∴ G∴ M∴ Brown, it was

Resolved, That a warrant be drawn on the Treasurer for one hundred dollars, in favor of R∴ W∴ O. A. Whittemore, for services as Grand Secretary during the past Masonic year; also, a warrant for ten dollars in favor of Bro J. W. Webster, for services as Tyler during the present session of this Grand ☐.

On motion of Bro. S∴ G∴ Warden, the installation of officers was made the special order, when M∴ W∴ Grand Master Van Deren, assisted by R∴ W∴ A. Sagendorf, S∴ G∴ Warden *as* Grand Marshal, installed and conducted M∴ W∴ Andrew Mason, as Grand Master, to his seat in the east.

The M∴ W∴ Grand Master then made the following appointments:

Rev. Bro. B. T. VINCENT, Chivington □ No. 6, Grand Chaplain.

P∴ G∴ M∴ H. M. TELLER, Chivington □ No. 6, Grand Orator.

J∴ G∴ W∴ JAMES T. WHITE, Chivington □ No. 6, Grand Marshal.

P∴ G∴ M∴ J. M. CHIVINGTON, Union □ No. 7, Grand Marshal.

Bro. GEORGE W. KASSLER, Denver □ No. 5, Senior Grand Deacon.

Bro. JAMES KELLY, Golden City □ No. 1, Junior Grand Deacon.

Bro. S. G. BROWN, Grand Tyler.

The officers elect and appointed were then duly installed by the M∴ W∴ Grand Master.

On motion of P∴ G∴ M∴ Van Deren, it was

Resolved, That the thanks of this Grand □ be tendered to Denver □ No. 5, and Union □ No. 7, for the free use of their hall during this Annual Grand Communication.

The Grand Master announced the following committees for the Masonic year:

Foreign Correspondence.—P∴ G∴ M∴ Henry M. Teller, P∴ G∴ M∴ J. M. Chivington, Bro. O. A. Whittemore.

Masonic Jurisprudence.—P∴ G∴ M∴ A. J. Van Deren, P∴ S∴ G∴ W∴ Andrew Sagendorf, S∴ G∴ W∴ Chase Withrow.

The minutes were then read and approved, when this Annual Communication of the M∴ W∴ Grand □ of Ancient, Free and Accepted Masons of the Territory of Colorado was closed in ample form, and with prayer, by R∴ W∴ and Rev. B. F. Vincent, Grand Chaplain.

O. A. WHITTEMORE, *Grand Secretary.*

RETURNS OF LODGES.

GOLDEN CITY □ NO. 1, GOLDEN CITY.

Time of meetings: first and third Saturdays of each month.

OFFICERS.

James S. Scott, W. M. W. A. H. Loveland, Treas. G. N. Belcher, S. D.
James Kelly, S. W. Stephen Bailey, Sec. W. D. Amos, J. D.
Lewis Davis, J. W. Martin Opal, Tyler.

MEMBERS.

L. W. Frary,	S. C. Clinton,	J. Sexton,
E. Fellows,	L. L. Reno,	D. G. Durgin,
D. E. Harrison,	J. H. Durham,	J. S. Maynard,
J. R. Gilbert,	Eli Carter,	Charles Remington,
W. P. Pollock,	W. L. Rothrock,	John F. Kirby,
Wm. Fredrick,	Fox Diefendorf,	A. J. Butler,
Wm. Newton,	Reuben Borton,	John Keane,
J. B. Longdon,	S. M. Breath,	G. M. Wilson,
T. P. Boyd,	John A. Moore,	Joseph Casto,
G. M. Chilcott,	John M. Ferrill,	J. C. Bowles,
W. D. Rippy,	E. B. Smith,	Henry Stevens,
Felix Crocker,	Daniel McCleery.	Geo. Morrison,
A. Slater,	S. F. Shaffer,	W. R. Nelson,
J. D. Carnes,	J. B. Hendry,	H. M. Bussell,
Milo Smith,	S. B. Williams,	Owen Williams,
John Strouse,		Wm. Ashley.

DIMITTED.

M. H. Floyd, Ira Quimby, John Gilmore.

FELLOWCRAFTS.

P. L. Smith, Wesley Teter.

ENTERED APPRENTICES.

Lewis Mallett,	Bruce Woodward,	Barney Pratt,
A. M. Wallinford,	Joseph Parrott,	M. H. Knapp,
J. W. Bartholomew,	C. S. Burdsall,	Thos. Sheridan,
James Stevens,	Allen Lewis,	C. L. Eggers.

Initiated, 9; passed, 6; raised, 5; rejected, 2; number of members, 56; living out of Territory, 25; Grand □ dues, $46.50.

NEVADA □ NO. 4.

Time of meetings: second and fourth Saturdays of each month.

OFFICERS.

A. M. Jones, W. M. W. H. Jester, Treasurer, W. T. Carothers, S. D.
Orlando North, S. W. J. F. Phillips, Secretary, W. R. Uren, J. D.
John W. Ratliff, J. W. Silas G. Brown, Tyler.

MEMBERS.

A. J. Van Deren,	J. H. Mitchell,	Andrew Nichols,
Andrew Mason,	E. B. Newnum,	Theo. Haswell,
C. Withrow, P. M.	A. J. Biggs,	Geo. Marshall,
Asa L. Miller,	J. H. Gest,	F. T. Sherman,
W. L. Sawtell,	D. L. Fairchild,	J. E. Gregg,
Chas. S. Abbott,	J. W. Bowles,	H. A. Haskin,
E. W. Henderson,	Preston Scott,	Wm. H. James,
A. C. McGeath,	Jas. C. Bradley,	Wm. F. Avery,
T. H. Clewell,	Thomas Newlun,	David Lees,
Addi Vincent,	J. E. Craine,	H. K. Pearson,
Jas. A. Burdick,	C. E. Forgy,	O. H. Henry,
J. W. Martin,	Robert Milliken,	James Jones,
D. J. Ball,	George Craine,	Thos. Woodward,
B. F. Pease,	Pres. Anderson,	J. C. Donnelly,
R. M. Foster,	B. W. Eussen,	Jos. Standley,
D. A. Hamer,	W. H. Belcher,	Robert Huges,
J. W. Stanton,	Edward Crockett,	James Baxter,
J. M. Smith,	O. T. Sparks,	T. H. Craven,
W. D. Perkins,	Joshua Jennings,	J. W. Lester,
B. C. Waterman,		B. F. Shaffer.

DIMITTED.

J. M. Van Deren,	W. T. Potter,	A. Cassell,
	C. E. Clark.	

FELLOWCRAFTS.

Chas. Alber,	C. H. Merrill,	T. J. Johns.

ENTERED APPRENTICES.

Wm. McFeeters,	Benair Walls,	James Huff,
Marine Symonds,	W. L. Ireland,	Abraham Stafford,
Geo. W. Brock,		Geo. W. Miller.

Geo. W. Hall, permit to pass and raise by Empire □, U. D.

Admitted, 1; initiated, 12; passed, 13; raised, 12; rejected, 13; number of members, 68; living out of Territory, 21; Grand □ dues, $70.50.

DENVER □ NO. 5, DENVER.

Time of meetings: first and third Saturdays of each month.

OFFICERS.

—————, W. M.	Geo. Tritch, Treasurer,	O. A. Ashley, S. S.
L. N. Greenleaf, S. W.	J. E. Gates, Secretary,	Jos. Kline, J. S.
Alvin McCune, J. W.	F. A. Clark, S. D.	Alex. Davidson, Tyler.
	W. M. Keith, J. D.	

MEMBERS.

A. P. Allen,
W. D. Arnett,
Wm. Antes,
Wm. N. Byers,
C. H. Blake,
A. H. Barker,
C. L. Bartlett,
Augustus Bartlett,
G. H. Bryant,
G. G. Brewer,
Bernard Berry,
E. W. Cobb,
G. W. Clayton,
S. H. Cook,
G. T. Clark,
C. A. Cook,
W. S. Cheesman,
Robert Cleveland,
W. M. Dailey,
F. A. McDonald,
Frank H. Page,
N. H. Rice,
E. E. Ropes,
H. J. Rogers,
W. D. Robinson,
A. T. Randall,
Richard Sopris,

F. M. Durkee,
J. R. Devor,
J. H. Dudley,
M. W. Edson,
W. R. Ford,
H. F. Ford,
Henry Feurstein,
J. H. Gerrish,
William Gray,
W. H. Garvin,
A. Goldsmith,
W. H. Grafton,
H. H. Gillett,
C. J. Goss,
G. H. Greenslit,
A. Hanauer,
J. S. Howell,
B. C. Hayman,
Noah Hill,
W. M. Slaughter,
J. J. Saville,
H. Z. Solomon,
Edwin Scudder,
M. B. Sherwood,
William Stepp,
C. W. Smith,
G. L. Shoup,
John L. Dailey,

G. W. Hutel,
Henry Hitchings,
J. H. Hodges,
J. W. Huntington,
S. L. Ireland,
E. H. Jewett,
E. W. Kingsbury,
Jerry Kershaw,
G. K. Kimball,
Henry Kline,
I. H. Kastor,
J. B. Lamber,
T. W. Lavin,
Isaac Louis,
G. L. Moody,
F. Maserve,
Jas. McNassar,
Julius Mitchell,
L. B. McLain,
Samuel Schwaub,
W. W. Slaughter,
J. E. Tappan,
Nicholas Thede.
Thomas Thompson,
John Wanless,
F. R. Wagoner,
J. T. Yonkers.

DIMITTED.

R. E. Cook,
A. J. M. Crook,
Joseph Ehle,
Joseph Faiver,

M. E. Hall,
J. M. Morgan,
T. C. Porter,

William Porter,
J. D. Ramadge,
J. L. Smith,
A. J. Snyder.

FELLOWCRAFTS

J. C. Casler,

J. W. Douglass,

H. P. Herbert.

ENTERED APPRENTICES.

B. F. Bennett,
C. L. Bresler,
H. B. Chamberlain,
B. F. Downer,
W. N. Evans,

John Good,
Moses Hallet,
Warren Hussey,
J. W. Kerr,
G. W. Lowe,

S. McClelland,
Wm. Nowlan,
C. F. Parkhurst,
Geo. Richardson,
G. W. Webster.

DIED.

M. J. Dougherty,   Jared Richardson,

Admitted, 5; initiated, 26; passed, 21; raised, 19; dimitted, 11; died, 2; rejected, 19; number of members, 90; living out of Territory, 30; Grand □ dues $90.00.

CHIVINGTON ☐ NO. 6, CENTRAL CITY.

Time of meetings: second and fourth Wednesdays of each month.

OFFICERS.

J. T. White, W. M.
B. W. Wisebart, S. W.
E. C. Parmelee, J. W.

D. J. Martin, Treas.
G. E. Wilson, Sec'y.
J. Y. Glendinen, S. D.

W. B. Squires, J. D.
E. L. Gardner, Tyler.
Rev. B. T. Vincent, Chap.

MEMBERS.

J. N. Adams,
W. H. Allen,
T. J. Brower,
E. H. Beals,
E. H. Brown,
Thomas Barnes,
A. E. Buckmiller,
I. B. Brunel,
G. W. Buchanan,
Bela S. Buel,
H. O. Basford,
Rev. A. Barrelle,
John Boylan,
James Clark,
J. B. Cofield,
Joseph Coleman,
D. C. Collier,
W. P. Caldwell,
L. W. Chase,
Thomas Mullen,
Z. Myers,
J. S. McLane,
G. G. Norton,
T. D. Nash,
H. M. Orahood,
J. L. Pritchard,
G. A. Pugh,
F. Poznainski,
J. E. Plummer,
W. P. Pollock,
E. P. Parker,
W. Rosenfield,
H. S. Robinson,

G. B. Cornell,
N. Z. Cozens,
T. O. Clark,
R. A. Clark,
A. B. Davis,
J. J. Dunnegan,
P. H. Dunnegan,
W. T. Ellis,
H. R. Eldred,
Robert Frazer,
Matt. France,
W. G. Fairhurst,
Basil Green,
L. G. H. Greene,
D. S. Green,
Erastus Garrott,
U. B. Holloway,
Charles L. Hill,
Frank Hall,
H. J. Hammond,
A. G. Raynor,
J. M. Rank,
J. K. Rutledge,
J. H. Reed,
A. Ramos,
George Schram,
Hal. Sayr,
W. F. Sears,
L. P. Sperry,
A. M. Studer,
H. M. Teller, P. G. M.
S. F. Tappan,
D. Tooker,

R. Hutchins,
O. H. Harker,
A. Jacobs,
H. A. Johnson,
William Jones,
W. C. M. Jones,
G. W. Jacobs,
David Kline,
H. J. Kruse,
John Kip,
J. H. Kinney,
D. Loeb,
S. L. Lorah,
Benjamin Lake,
Jacob Mack,
J. C. McClellan,
L. Merchant,
P. McGraw,
J. G. Mahany,
Charles Massard,
M. Thomas,
G. J. Tracy,
J. S. Taylor,
A. Weston, P. G. M.
H. A. Woods,
Wm. Watson,
A. H. Whitehead,
L. Weil,
J. Weidman,
M. C. Wythe,
J. W. Watson,
G. B. Walker,
E. Wilder.

DIMITTED.

O. E. Colony,

C. W. Johnson,
D. W. Tilton,

Charles Massard.

FLLOWCRAFTS.

George Cassels,

J. P. Folley,
E. B. Stillings,

A. McNamee.

ENTERED APPRENTICES.

D. T. Beals,
J. C. Bruce,
James Cree,
David Ettien,

Wm. Humphrey,
L. Kennedy,
W. H. Nichols,

G. B. Reed,
N. L. Sibley,
A. Schonecker,
J. W. Wilson.

Admitted, 8; initiated, 27; passed, 27; raised, 29; dimitted, 4; rejected, 48; number of members, 107; living out of Territory, 18; Grand ☐ dues, $133.50.

UNION ⊡ NO. 7, DENVER.

Time of meetings: second and fourth Saturdays of each month.

OFFICERS.

Eli M. Ashley, W. M.	Chas. Ruter, Treas.	Rev. O. A. Willard, Chap.
O. A. Whittemore, S. W.	W. D. Anthony, Sec.	E. Millerson, S. S.
E. H. Collins, J. W.	Jonas Deitch, S. D.	C. Donnelly, J. S.
	C. J. Clark, J. D.	

MEMBERS.

J. M. Chivington, P.G.M.	L. C. Clark,	A. Cunningham,
J. C. Anderson,	John Evans,	Samuel H. Elbert, P. M.
J. R. Boyce,	Richard Leach,	Joseph Finley,
Rev. H. B. Hitchings,	John Pierce,	J. L. Bailey,
Loudon Mullin,	John Chamard,	B. F. Houx,
J. J. Johnson,	Henry Henson,	O. B. Brown, D. G. M.
F. R. Bill,	Simeon Whitely,	J. E. Stewart,
R. V. Fairbanks,	Jacob Downing,	Alfred Sayre,
N. W. Welton,	D. C. Corbin,	Rodney Curtis,
W. D. Pease,	Luther Kountze,	F. Z. Salomon,
Redwood Fisher,	M. A. Rogers,	H. C. Leach.
	G. E. Crater,	

DIMITTED.

J. D. Simpson,	M. C. White,	E. P. Parkker.

FELLOWCRAFTS.

O. H. Whittier,	J. McFadden,	C. C. Davis.

ENTERED APPRENTICES.

Daniel Witter,	D. A. Chever,	C. W. Pollard,
Luther Wilson,	J. J. Thomas,	D. P. Wilson.
	Isaac Chandler,	

Certificate granted Chancey Barbour, F. C. and Thomas Barnum, E. A. to receive degrees in other ⊡.

DIED.

John S. Fillmore, Fellowcraft.

Admitted, 3; initiated, 10; passed, 14; raised, 12; dimitted, 3; died, 1 (F. C.); rejected, 8; number of members, 44; living out of Territory, 6; Grand ⊡ dues, $57.

EMPIRE ⊡, U. D., EMPIRE CITY.

Time of meetings: first and third Saturdays of each month.

OFFICERS.

A. Mason, P. D. G. M.	John S. Jones, Treas.	W. L. Sawtell, S. D.
H. A. Haskin, S. W.	David J. Ball, Sec'y.	J. W. Martin, J. D.
John Slawson, J. W.		J. M. Smith, Tyler.

MEMBERS.

Edward James,	J. W. Drips,	G. C. Munson,
J. A. Love,	E. C. Westcoat,	Henry Nutt.
	T. J. Buchanan,	

FELLOWCRAFTS.

G. A. Smith,	G. W. Hall,	Charles King.

Initiated, 5; passed, 6; raised, 3; rejected, 1.

MONTANA ☐, U. D., VIRGINIA CITY, M. T.

Time of meetings: second and fourth Tuesdays of each month.

OFFICERS.

H. L. Hosmer, W. M.
L. W. Frary, S. W.
William Gray, J. W.

N. T. Butler, Treas.
J. R. Gilbert, Sec'y.

J. Dimsdall, S. D.
J. W. Todd, J. D.
R. E. Cook, Tyler.

MEMBERS.

R. M. Cam bell,
A. L. Kerr,p
J. S. Pendarias,

J. S. Lewis,
J. R. Bryce,
Hugh Duncan,

J. W. Hudgens,
L. C. Lee,
Charles Lange.

FELLOWCRAFT.

Thomas L. Gerham.

ENTERED APPRENTICES.

Sidney Wilson,
Philip Schenck,
Samuel Ward.

Initiated, 5; passed, 2; raised, 1.

HELENA CITY ☐ U. D., HELENA CITY, M. T.

Time of meetings: first and third Saturdays of each month.

OFFICERS.

· Cornelius Hedges, W. M.
Joel Wilson, S. W.
Louis Behm, J. W.

C. C. Farmer, Secretary,
J. C. Hutchinson, Treas.

H. McFee, S. D.
R. P. Seely, J. D.
R. Hevefend.

MEMBERS.

M. A. Moore,
G. M. Pain,

John Moffit,
Robert Lawrence,
O. B. Howe,

S. J. Perkins,
O. T. Hare.

FELLOWCRAFTS.

J. G. Sanders,
A. Fall.

ENTERED APPRENTICE.

Z. French.

Initiated, 3; passed, 2.

PROCEEDINGS

SIXTH ANNUAL COMMUNICATION

OF THE

GRAND LODGE OF COLORADO,

HELD AT CENTRAL CITY, OCT. 1, A. L. 5866.

———

The Most Worshipful Grand ▭ of Ancient, Free and Accepted Masons of Colorado met in Annual Communication at Masonic Hall, in Central City, on the first Monday, it being the first day of October, A. D. 1866, A. L. 5866, at 10 o'clock A. M.

Present—

M∴ W∴ ANDREW MASON, Grand Master.

R∴ W∴ A. J. VAN DEREN, P∴ G∴ M∴ as Deputy Grand Master.

R∴ W∴ CHASE WITHROW, Senior Grand Warden.

R∴ W∴ JAS. T. WHITE, Junior Grand Warden.

R∴ W∴ RICHARD SOPRIS, Grand Treasurer.

R∴ W∴ O. A. WHITTEMORE, Grand Secretary.

Bro. WM. A. FULLER, as Grand Chaplain.

Bro. L. N. GREENLEAF, as Senior Grand Deacon.

Bro. B. W. WISEBART, as Junior Grand Deacon.

Bros. A. M. JONES and H. A. HASKIN, as Grand Stewards.

Bro. J. K. RUTLEDGE, as Grand Tyler, and representatives from subordinate ▭.

A ▭ of Master Masons was opened.

The Grand Secretary announced that six ▭ were represented, which, being a constitutional number, the Most Wor-

20

shipful Grand ◻ of Colorado was opened in ample form, with prayer by the Grand Chaplain.

The Grand Master announced the following committee :

On Credentials.—S∴ G∴ W∴ Chase Withrow, J∴ G∴ W∴ Jas. T. White, Grand Treasurer Richard Sopris, who made the following report, which was adopted:

To the M∴ W∴ Grand ◻ of A., F. and A. M. of Colorado:

Your committee on Credentials beg leave to make the following report :

We find the following brethren present and entitled to seats and votes in this Grand ◻ :

Bro. Andrew Mason, M∴ W∴ G∴ M∴, 2 votes; Bro. Chase Withrow, R∴ W∴ S∴ G∴ W∴, 1 vote; Bro. Jas. T. White, R∴ W∴ J∴ G∴ W∴, 1 vote ; Bro. Richard Sopris, R∴ W∴ Grand Treasurer, 1 vote ; Bro. O. A. Whittemore, R∴ W∴ Grand Secretary, 1 vote; Bro. A. J. Van Deren, P∴ G∴ M∴, 1 vote.

Golden City ◻ No. 1 : Bro. E. Fellows, W∴ M∴, 1 vote.

Nevada ◻ No. 4 : Bro. A. M. Jones, W∴ M∴, 1 vote; Bro. O. T. Sparks, J∴ W∴, 1 vote.

Denver ◻ No. 5 : Bro. L. N. Greenleaf, W∴ M∴, 1 vote; Bro. A. McCune, S∴ W∴, 1 vote; Bro. F. A. Clark, J∴ W∴, 1 vote.

Chivington ◻ No. 6 : Bro. B. W. Wisebart. W∴ M∴, 1 vote ; Bro. J. Y. Glendinen, S∴ W∴, 1 vote; Bro. N. Z. Cozens, J∴ W∴, 1 vote.

Union ◻ No. 7 : Bro. O. A. Whittemore, W∴ M∴, 1 vote; Bro. W. D. Anthony, S∴ W∴, 1 vote.

Empire ◻ No. 8 : Bro. H. A. Haskin, S∴ W∴, proxy to cast entire vote of ◻, 3.   CHASE WITHROW, ⎫
                          JAS. T. WHITE,   ⎬ *Committee.*
                          R. SOPRIS.   ⎭

The reading of the minutes of the last Annual Communication was dispensed with, printed copies being in the hands of members.

The M∴ W∴ Grand Master then delivered the following address :

Brethren of the Grand ◻:

We have great reason to thank the Supreme Architect of the Universe that He has spared our lives and permitted us once more to assemble in Grand Communication and hold fraternal council as to what shall best conduce to the usefulness and prosperity of our beloved order for the coming year.

During the past Masonic year, my official acts as Grand Master have been few. On the 27th of January, I granted a dispensation to El Paso ◻, at Colorado City, with Bro. E. T. Stone as W∴ M∴, Bro. C. T. Judd, S∴ W∴, and Bro. S. K. Roberts, J∴ W∴ This dispensation was granted on the recommendation of Denver ◻ No. 5. On the 15th day of February, I granted a dispensation to Black Hawk □, at Black Hawk, with Bro. Chase Withrow W∴ M∴, Bro. Harper M. Orahood S∴ W∴, Bro. J. Wellington Nesmith J∴ W∴. This dispensation was granted on the recommendation of Chivington □ No. 6. On the petition for each of the above □, there was the constitutional number of signers.

I have not had the pleasure of visiting El Paso □, U. D., but I presume they will be present at this communication to render an account of their work. I visited Black Hawk □, U. D., and take great pleasure in saying that I found it in a prosperous condition.

A number of questions on Masonic law have been propounded to me during the past year, all of which have been answered according to the best of my ability. I received a letter from Bro. Cornelius Hedges, W∴ M∴ of Helena City □ No. 10, of Montana Territory, informing me of the organization of a Grand □ for that Territory, and asking permission to retain the charter granted to them by this Grand body at its last communication, which permission was not granted, and I requested him to return their charter to this Grand □. Montana □ No. 9 I have not heard from, but presume that they are now working under the jurisdiction of the Grand □ of Montana Territory.

The closing year finds all the □ under this jurisdiction and the order in general, in a prosperous and harmonious condition.

Before closing, I desire to return this Grand body, and the fraternity in general, my sincere thanks for the honor they have conferred upon me, and for the uniform kindness and courtesy extended to me during the past Masonic year.

I remain, yours fraternally,

ANDREW MASON, *Grand Master.*

The M∴ W∴ Grand Master then appointed the following committees :

Visiting Brethren—Bros. F. A. Clark, H. A. Haskin, O. T. Sparks.

Charters and Dispensations—P∴ G∴ M∴ A. J. Van Deren, and Bros. L. N. Greenleaf and A. M. Jones.

Finance, Mileage and Per Diem—S∴ G∴ W∴ Chase Withrow, J∴ G∴ W∴ Jas. T. White, Grand Treasurer Richard Sopris.

Grand □ was then called from labor to meet at 2 o'clock P. M.

MONDAY, 2 o'clock P. M.

Grand □ resumed labor.

Officers and members present as at morning session.

The committee on Returns and Work of ⊡ U. D., on Chartered ⊡ and on Petitions, made the following report:

To the M∴ W∴ Grand ☐ of the Most Ancient and Honorable Fraternity of Free and Accepted Masons:

Your committee on Returns and Work of ☐ U. D., on Chartered ☐ and on Petitions, respectfully report that they have examined the returns of El paso ☐ U. D., and find them incorrect, in that the minutes do not show that a constitutional number were present at any communication. We further find that the brethren of said ☐ have conferred the first, second and third degrees, and are desirous of receiving a charter from this Grand ☐; we therefore refer the same, together with the returns and minutes of said ☐, to this Grand ☐ for its consideration. Your committee have also examined the returns of Black Hawk ☐ U. D., and find the same correct. They also find that the brethren of said ☐ have conferred the first, second and third degrees, and that the Worshipful Master and Wardens of said ☐ are now present, and desire that a charter be granted and the officers installed by the M∴ W∴ Grand ☐. Your committee do therefore recommend that a charter and number be granted to said Black Hawk ☐ U. D., and that the officers be installed by the Grand ☐.

We have examined the returns of Nevada ☐ No. 4, Denver ☐ No. 5, Chivington ☐ No. 6, Union ☐ No. 7, and Empire ☐ No. 8, and find them correct. We have also examined the returns of Golden City ☐ No. 1, and find that the dates of initiation, passing and raising, are omitted, and that the names of members residing out of the Territory are not given; in all other respects correct.

Respectfully submitted,

A. J. VAN DEREN, ⎫
L. N. GREENLEAF, ⎬ *Committee.*
A. M. JONES, ⎭

Bro. Chase Withrow, of committee on Credentials, submitted the following additional report:

To the M∴ W∴ Grand ☐ of A., F. and A. M. of Colorado:

Your committee on Credentials respectfully report further, as follows: That Bro. J. F. Phillips, S∴ W∴ of Nevada ☐ No. 4, is present and entitled to a seat and vote in this Grand ☐.

CHASE WITHROW, *Chairman.*

On motion of P∴ G∴ M∴ A. J. Van Dereń, a charter was granted to Black Hawk ☐, the said ☐ to be known as Black Hawk ☐ No. 11.

On motion of P∴ G∴ M∴ A. J. Van Deren, the dispensation of El Paso ☐ was continued at the discretion of the Grand Master.

The Grand Secretary submitted the following report:

To the M∴ W∴ Grand □ of Colorado:

Your committee on Foreign Correspondence have but a very brief report to make, for the following reasons: Past Grand Masters H. M. Teller and J. M. Chivington, members of the committee, are both absent from the Territory. The proceedings of our sister Grand □, so far received, were sent some time ago to Bro. Teller, chairman, to enable him to prepare a report, and it was not until to-day that I learned of his absence. Bro. Chivington has been away for the greater part of the year.

The proceedings of our sister Grand □ have been received as follows: Arkansas, Alabama, Connecticut, Canada, California, Delaware, Florida of 1861, 1864 and 1865, Iowa, Indiana, Kansas, Kentucky, Louisiana, Maryland, Maine, Missouri, Massachusetts, New York, New Hampshire, New Jersey, Nevada, Nebraska, North Carolina, Oregon, Ohio, Texas for 1861, 1862, 1863, 1864 and 1865, Vermont, Virginia, Washington and Wisconsin.

We have been informed by W∴ M∴ of Montana □ No. 9, of the organization of a Grand □ for Montana, but nothing has been received from the officers of the new Grand □.

A circular letter has been received from Bro. Charles J. McDonald, Secretary of Grand □ of Nova Scotia, asking the recognition of their Grand □.

Since the last meeting of our Grand □, R∴ W∴ Francis L. King, Grand Secretary of the Grand □ of Indiana, R∴ W∴ W. H. Adams, Grand Secretary of the Grand □ of Pennsylvania, R∴ W∴ A. O'Sullivan, Grand Secretary of the Grand □ of Missouri, and R∴ W∴ T. D. Merrick, Grand Secretary of the Grand □ of Arkansas, have gone to their rest in the Grand □ above.

We beg to submit the following resolution, and ask its adoption:

Resolved, That the fraternal greetings of this Grand □ be extended to our sister Grand □ of Nova Scotia and Montana, and that they be welcomed into the sisterhood of Grand □.

Fraternally submitted,

O. A. WHITTEMORE.

Which report was received, and the recommendation contained therein adopted.

The Grand Secretary and Grand Treasurer submitted their accounts and reports as follows, which were received and referred to the Finance committee:

To the M∴ W∴ Grand □ of Colorado:

I have the honor to submit the following report and accompanying account. The receipts for the past year have been:

From dispensations	$ 80 00
From charter, Empire □ No. 8	20 00
From dues of □	508 50
From dues collected by Empire □ from unaffiliated brethren	1 50

Showing total receipts from all sources, of.................$610 00

I have, during the year, received several notices from the post-office at St. Joseph, Mo., informing me of packages to my address, held there for postage. I have remitted the amounts claimed and received the packages, but as proceedings of many of our sister Grand ☐ with whom we have been in correspondence have failed to reach me, I presume that they have been sent, but held at some distributing post-office for want of the necessary postage, many of our correspondents not being aware of the law requiring letter postage on all printed matter, west of Kansas.

A Grand ☐ has been established in Montana, but the charters granted at our last Annual Communication to Montana ☐ No. 9, and Helena City ☐ No. 15, have not been returned to me as required by usage and instructions from our M∴ W∴ Grand Master. All the chartered ☐ in our jurisdiction, within our own Territory, have sent in their returns and dues. Black Hawk ☐, U. D., and El Paso ☐, U. D., have returned their work and pray for charters.

Respectfully submitted,

O. A. WHITTEMORE, *Grand Secretary.*

O. A. Whittemore, Grand Secretary, in account with Grand ☐ of Colorado:

	DR.
Nov. 7, Empire ☐ No. 8, dues unaffiliated brethren.............	$ 1 50
Nov. 7, Empire ☐ No. 8, charter.............................	20 00
Dec. 1, El Paso ☐, for dispensation........................	40 00
Feb. 16, Black Hawk ☐, for dispensation....................	40 00
Oct. 1, Golden City ☐ No. 1, dues.........................	51 00
" 1, Nevada ☐ No. 4, dues...............................	64 50
" 1, Denver ☐ No. 5, dues...............................	114 00
" 1, Chivington ☐ No. 6, dues..........................	166 50
" 1, Union ☐ No. 7, dues...............................	72 00
" 1, Empire ☐ No. 8, dues..............................	40 50
	$610 00

		CR.	
Nov. 8, by paid postage..............................	$ 2 00		
May 30, by paid postage sent.........................	6 00		
June 2, " " " "	1 80		
July 5, by paid express.............................	3 10		
July 14, by paid postage received.....................	2 35		
July 17, " " " "	87		
" 17, " " " "	5 25		
" 17, " " " "	60		
" 17, " " " "	15		
Aug. 6, " " " "	94		
Sept. 27, " " " sent...................	1 42		
" 27, " " " stamps.................	1 00		
" 27, " " expense...................	75		
" 27, " " stationery.................	2 00		
" 27, " " Grand Treasurer.............	581 77	$610 00

Richard Sopris, Grand Treasurer, in account with Grand ▢ of Colorado:

DR.
To cash from Grand Secretary.................................. $619 00

CR.
By paid warrant to A. Sagendorf......................... $ 4 00
"   "   "   E. M. Ashley......................... 4 00
"   "   "   L. N. Greenleaf....................... 4 00
"   "   "   J. M. Chivington.................... 4 00
"   "   "   J. Kelley........................... 7 00
"   "   "   O. A. Whittemore.................... 104 00
"   "   "   A. Davidson......................... 10 00
"   "   "   H. M. Teller........................ 14 00
"   "   "   J. T. White......................... 14 00
"   "   "   A. J. Van Deren..................... 14 00
"   "   "   Chase Withrow....................... 14 00
"   "   "   J. F. Phillips...................... 14 00
"   "   "   Andrew Mason........................ 17 00
"   "   "   Byers & Dailey, printing, 1865....... 85 90
"   "   "   "   "   "   "   1866........ 262 90

$522 80
Balance in Treasury.................................. 96 20
————— $619 00

Respectfully submitted,

R. SOPRIS, *Grand Treasurer.*

On motion of P∴ G∴ M∴ Van Deren, the Grand Master proceeded to install Bros. Chase Withrow as Worshipful Master; Harper M. Orahood, Senior Warden; J. W. Nesmith as Junior Warden of Black Hawk ▢ No. 11, and admitted them to seats and votes in this Grand ▢, Bro. Andrew Sagendorf acting as Grand Marshal.

P∴ G∴ M∴ Van Deren moved that the first business in order when we resume labor in the morning, be the election of officers for the ensuing year.

Motion concurred in.

When the Grand ▢ was called from labor, to meet to-morrow, at 9 o'clock A. M.

———

TUESDAY, OCT. 2, A. D. 1866, A. L. 5866.

Grand ▢ resumed labor at 9 o'clock A. M., officers and members present as yesterday.

Minutes of yesterday's proceedings read and approved.

The committee on Credentials submitted an additional report, as follows:

To the M∴. W∴. Grand ☐ A., F. and A. M. of Colorado:

Your committee on Credentials beg leave to report further, that the following brethren are now present and entitled to seats and votes in this Grand ☐: Bros. Chester C. Carpenter, proxy for Bro. James Kelly, S∴. W∴. of Golden City ☐ No. 1, and G. N. Belcher, J∴. W∴. of Golden City ☐ No. 1.

Respectfully submitted,

CHASE WITHROW, *Chairman.*

Report received.

The special order of the hour being the election of officers for the ensuing year, the Grand Master appointed as tellers, Bros. F. A. Clark and J. F. Phillips.

The Grand ☐ proceeded to ballot, with the following result:

Bro. CHASE WITHROW, Black Hawk ☐ No. 11, Grand Master.
Bro. A. SAGENDORF, Denver ☐ No. 5, Deputy Grand Master.
Bro. AARON M. JONES, Nevada ☐ No. 4, Senior Grand Warden.
Bro. L. N. GREENLEAF, Denver ☐ No. 5, Junior Grand Warden.
Bro. RICHARD SOPRIS, Denver ☐ No. 5, Grand Treasurer.
Bro. ED. C. PARMELEE, Chivington ☐ No. 6, Grand Secretary.

Grand ☐ was then called from labor, to meet at half past one o'clock P. M.

TUESDAY, HALF PAST 1 O'CLOCK P. M.

Grand ☐ resumed labor, officers and members present as at morning session.

M∴. W∴. Grand Master Andrew Mason, assisted by P∴. G∴. M∴. Van Deren as Grand Marshal, then installed the Grand Master elect, M∴. W∴. Chase Withrow, who announced the following as the appointed officers:

R∴. W∴. H. B. HITCHINGS, Union ☐ No. 7, Grand Chaplain.
R∴. W∴. HENRY M. TELLER, Chivington ☐ No. 6, Grand Orator.
W∴. B. W. WISEBART, Chivington ☐ No. 6, Senior Grand Deacon.
W∴. H. A. HASKIN, Empire ☐ No. 8, Junior Grand Deacon.
W∴. E. FELLOWS, Golden City ☐ No. 1, Grand Marshal.
W∴. JAS. KELLY, Golden City ☐ No. 1, Grand Sword Bearer.
Bro. ALEX. DAVIDSON, Denver ☐ No. 5, Grand Tyler.

The Grand Master then installed the remaining officers, who assumed their stations as follows:

M∴ W∴ CHASE WITHROW, Grand Master.

R∴ W∴ A. SAGENDORF, Deputy Grand Master.

R∴ W∴ A. M. JONES, Senior Grand Warden.

R∴ W∴ L. N. GREENLEAF, Junior Grand Warden.

R∴ W∴ RICHARD SOPRIS, Grand Treasurer.

R∴ W∴ ED. C. PARMELEE, Grand Secretary.

R∴ W∴ H. B. HITCHINGS, Grand Chaplain.

R∴ W∴ HENRY M. TELLER, Grand Orator.

W∴ B. W. WISEBART, Senior Grand Deacon.

W∴ H. A. HASKIN, Junior Grand Deacon.

W∴ E. FELLOWS, Grand Marshal.

W∴ JAS. KELLY, Grand Sword Bearer.

W∴ ALEX. DAVIDSON, Grand Tyler.

On motion of P∴ G∴ M∴ Mason, it was

Resolved, That a warrant be drawn on the Treasurer for one hundred dollars, in favor of R∴ W∴ O. A. Whittemore, for services as Grand Secretary during the past Masonic year; also, a warrant for ten dollars, in favor of Bro. J. K. Rutledge, for services as Tyler during the present session of this Grand ▭.

On motion of P∴ G∴ M∴ Mason, the thanks of this Grand ▭ were tendered to Central City Chapter No. 1, Royal Arch Masons, and Chivington ▭ No. 6, for the free use of their hall during this Annual Grand Communication.

P∴ G∴ Secretary Whittemore presented the following resolution and moved its adoption:

Resolved, That the resolutions adopted November, 1863, concerning the Conservators' Association, be stricken from the standing resolutions of this Grand ▭.

Resolution lost.

D∴ G∴ M∴ Sagendorf moved that the third of the resolutions concerning the Conservators' Association, passed November, 1863, be stricken from the standing resolutions of this Grand ▭.

Motion lost.

P∴ G∴ M∴ Van Deren offered the following, which was adopted:

Resolved, That Section 41 of By-Laws pertaining to ▭, &c., be amended by adding thereto as follows: "But in cases where the report of the com-

21

mittee to whom the petition is referred be unfavorable, the report shall not be considered a rejection, and the ballot shall be spread."

P∴ G∴ M∴ Van Deren offered the following, which was adopted:

Resolved, That it is the sense of this Grand ☐ that a member of a subordinate ☐ may, by a vote of the ☐, be stricken from the roll of membership for arrearages in dues, for the space of one year.

The committee on Finance, Mileage and Per Diem, presented the following report, which was received, and the recommendation adopted:

To the M∴ W∴ Grand ☐ A., F. and A. M. of Colorado:

Your committee on Finance, Mileage and Per Diem, beg leave to make the following report:

We have examined the Grand Secretary's and Grand Treasurer's reports, and find them correct as reported to this Grand body. We also find the following Grand Officers, Past Grand Officers and representatives in attendance, and entitled to the following pay:

NAMES.	Miles traveled.	Attendance, days.	Amount.
M∴ W∴ Andrew Mason, G∴ M∴	30	2	$ 7 75
R∴ W∴ Chase Withrow, S∴ G∴ W∴	2	2	4 25
R∴ W∴ James T. White, J∴ G∴ W∴	80	2	14 00
R∴ W∴ R. Sopris, G∴ T∴	80	2	14 00
R∴ W∴ O. A. Whittemore, Grand Secretary	80	2	14 00
Br . A. J. Van Deren, P∴ G∴ M∴	......	2	4 00
Bro. E. Fellows, W∴ M∴ Golden City ☐ No. 1	50	2	10 25
Bro. A. M. Jones, W∴ M∴ Nevada ☐ No. 4	2	2	4 25
Br . L. N. Greenleaf, W∴ M∴ Denver ☐ No. 5	80	2	14 00
Bro. B. W. Wisebart, W∴ M∴ Chivington ☐ No. 6	......	2	4 00
Bro. H. A. Haskin, S∴ W∴ Empire ☐ No. 8	30	2	7 75

Respectfully submitted,

CHASE WITHROW, ⎫
JAS. T. WHITE, ⎬ *Committee.*
R. SOPRIS, ⎭

Your committee would further recommend that, as Union ☐ No. 7 has no representative who draws pay, that the S∴ W∴ of said ☐ be allowed mileage and per diem, the same as others are entitled to.

Respectfully,

CHASE WITHROW, ⎫
JAS. T. WHITE, ⎬ *Committee.*
R. SOPRIS, ⎭

P∴ G∴ M∴ Van Deren offered the following, which was adopted:

Resolved, That the thanks of this Grand ▫ be tendered to Past Grand Secretary O. A. Whittemore, for the able and faithful manner in which he has conducted the duties of his office.

P∴ G∴ M∴ Van Deren offered the following, which was adopted:

Resolved, That the thanks of this Grand ▫ be tendered to P∴ G∴ M∴ Andrew Mason, for the faithful and impartial manner in which he has performed his duties during the past year.

On motion of P∴ G∴ M∴ Mason, the resolution adopted November, 1865, reading: "*Resolved*, That it is the sense of the Grand ▫ of Colorado, that the non-payment of dues cannot work a forfeiture of Masonic standing," was stricken from the standing resolutions of this Grand ▫.

On motion of D∴ G∴ M∴ Sagendorf, it was voted that this Grand ▫ require all ▭ under dispensation to pay a fee of one dollar and fifty cents for each Mason raised.

The M∴ W∴ Grand Master announced the following committees for the ensuing Masonic year:

Foreign Correspondence.—P∴ G∴ Secretary O. A. Whittemore, P∴ G∴ M∴ H. M. Teller, P∴ G∴ M∴ A. Mason.

Jurisprudence.—P∴ G∴ M∴ A. Mason, P∴ G∴ M∴ A. J. Van Deren, D∴ G∴ M∴ A. Sagendorf.

The minutes were then read and approved, when this Annual Communication of the M∴ W∴ Grand ▫ of A., F. and A. M. of the Territory of Colorado was closed in ample form.

ED. C. PARMELEE, *Grand Secretary*.

RETURNS OF LODGES.

GOLDEN CITY ☐ NO. 1, GOLDEN CITY.

Time of meetings: first and third Saturdays of each month.

OFFICERS.

E. Fellows, W. M.
Jas. Kelly, S. W.
G. N. Belcher, J. W.

D. E. Harrison, Treas.
Owen Williams, Sec.

J. S. Scott, S. D.
J. H. Durham, J. D.
E. L. Gardner, Tyler.

MEMBERS.

Wm. Ashley,
S. M. Breath,
A. J. Butler,
J. C. Bowles,
H. M. Bussell,
Reuben Barton,
G. M. Chilcott,
Felix Crocker,
J. D. Carnes,
S. C. Clinton,
Eli Carter,
Joseph Casto,
C. C. Carpenter,
Fox Diefendorf,
D. G. Dargin,
Lewis Davis,

C. L. Eggers,
L. W. Frary,
J. M. Ferrill,
Wm. Frederick,
J. R. Gilbert,
J. B. Hendry,
Wm. R. Howell,
John F. Kirby,
John Keane,
J. B. Longdon,
J. S. Maynard,
George Morrison,
John A. Moore,
D. McCleery,
W. R. Nelson,
W. P. Pollock,

Geo. C. Peck,
J. C. Remington,
W. D. Rippy,
W. L. Rothrick,
L. L. Reno,
A. Slater,
Milo Smith,
E. B. Smith,
P. L. Smith,
John Strouse,
J. Sexton,
F. O. Sawin,
S. F. Shaffer,
Henry Stevens,
G. M. Willson,
S. B. Williams.

FELLOWCRAFT.

Wesley Teter.

ENTERED APPRENTICES

C. S. Burdsall,
J. W. Bartholomew,
M. H. Knapp,
Allen Lewis,

Lewis Mallett,
Jos. Parrott,
Barney Pratt,
A. B. Patton,

James Stevens,
Thos. Sheridan,
A. M. Wallingford,
Bruce Woodward.

DIMITTED.

William Newton.

DIED.

T. P. Boyd.

Initiated, 5; passed, 6; raised, 6; rejected, 6; number of members, 59; living out of Territory, 25; Grand ☐ dues, $51.00.

NEVADA ☐ NO. 4.

Time of meetings: second and fourth Saturdays of each month.

OFFICERS.

A. M. Jones, W. M.	B. C. Waterman, Treas.	O. H. Henry, S. D.
J. F. Phillips, S. W.	T. H. Craven, Sec.	T. Woodward, J. D.
O. T. Sparks, J. W.		J. C. Donnelly, Tyler.

MEMBERS.

P. Anderson,	Theo. Haswell,	Thos. Newlun,
Wm. F. Avery,	Robert Hughes,	Andrew Nichols,
C. S. Abbott,	F. J. Hibbard,	B. F. Pease,
A. J. Biggs,	W. H. James,	W. D. Perkins,
J. A. Burdick,	W. H. Jester,	H. K. Pearson,
J. C. Bradley,	J. Jennings,	J. C. Russell,
W. H. Belcher,	James Jones,	J. W. Ratliff,
James Baxter,	Thos. J. Johns,	J. W. Stanton,
S. G. Brown,	Perry A. Kline,	Preston Scott,
T. H. Clewell,	David Lees,	F. T. Sherman,
J. E. Craine,	Asa L. Miller,	B. F. Shaffer,
E. Crockett,	A. C. Megeath,	Isaac Sands,
B. W. Eussen,	J. H. Mitchell,	Jos. Stanley,
R. M. Foster,	Robert Milliken,	Horace Shaw,
D. L. Fairchild,	Geo. Marshall,	Wm. R. Uren,
J. E. Gregg,	Orlando North,	A. J. Van Deren, P. G. M.
E. W. Henderson,	E. B. Newnum,	C. Visscher,
D. A. Hamer,		Chase Withrow, P. M.

DIMITTED.

J. D. Ball,	C. E. Forgy,	A. Mason, P. D. G. M.
J. W. Bowles,	J. H. Gest,	J. W. Martin,
Geo. Craine,	H. A. Haskin,	J. M. Smith,
W. T. Carothers,	J. W. Lester,	W. S. Sawtell.
	Addi Vincent,	

FELLOWCRAFTS.

Chas. Alber,	J. M. Aldrich,	C. H. Merrell.
	J. F. Spaulding,	

ENTERED APPRENTICES.

Geo. W. Brock,	W. L. Ireland,	Marine Symonds,
Jos. Cooling,	Geo. W. Miller,	Abraham Stafford,
James Huff,	Wm. McFeeters,	Benair Walls.
	S. H. Wright,	

Admitted, 1; initiated, 8; passed, 6; raised, 5; rejected, 7; number of members, 61; living out of Territory, 18; Grand ☐ dues, $64.50.

DENVER ☐ NO. 5, DENVER.

Time of meetings: first and third Saturdays of each month.

OFFICERS

L. N. Greenleaf, W. M.	Geo. Tritch, Treasurer,	W. D Robinson, S. S.
A. McCune, S. W.	J. E. Gates, Secretary,	J. W. Huntington, J. S.
F. A. Clark, J. W.	G. G. Brewer, S. D.	Alex. Davidson, Tyler.
	H. H. Gillett, J. D.	

MEMBERS.

A. P. Allen,	W. R. Ford,	F. Meserve,
W. D. Arnett,	H. F. Ford,	James McNassar,
J. S. Addleman,	Henry Feurstein,	Julius Mitchell,
Moses Anker,	J. H. Gerrish,	F. A. McDonald,
A. O. Ashley,	A. Goldsmith,	Samuel Mitchell,
W. N. Byers,	W. H. Grafton,	N. H. Rice,
C. H. Blake,	C. J. Goss,	E. E. Ropes,
C. L. Bartlett,	G. H. Greenslit,	G. L. Moody,
A. Bartlett,	Jacob Goldsmith,	H. J. Rogers,
G. H. Bryant,	Geo. Gillett,	R. Sopis, P. M.
Bernard Berry,	E. S. Graves,	A. Sagendorf, P. M.
F. R. Bennett,	A. Hanaeur,	W. M. Slaughter,
N. A. Baker,	J. S. Howell,	J. J. Saville,
J. L. Bartels,	B. C. Hayman,	H. Z. Solomon,
S. H. Bowman,	Noah Hill,	Edwin Scudder,
J. M. Broadwell,	G. W. Hurtel,	M. B. Sherwood,
E. W. Cobb,	Henry Hitchings,	Wm. Stepp,
G. W. Clayton,	J. H. Hodges,	G. L. Shoup,
G. T. Clark,	Warren Hussey,	W. W. Slaughter,
C. A. Cook,	E. H. Jewett,	J. E. Tappan,
W. S. Cheesman,	Theron W. Johnson,	Nicholas Thede,
Robert Cleveland,	E. W. Kingsbury,	W. J. Thompson,
J. C. Carter,	Jerry Kershaw,	W. E. Turner,
H. S. Clark,	G. K. Kimball,	S. W. Treat,
F. M. Durkee,	Henry Kline,	J. H. Voorhies,
J. H. Dudley,	I. H. Kastor,	J. W. Webster,
W. M. Dailey,	W. M. Keith,	G. W. Webster,
J. L. Dailey,	Joseph Kline,	John Wanless,
J. H. Douglass,	J. B. Lamber,	F. R. Wagoner,
J. M. Diedenbach,		J. T. Yonker.

FELLOWCRAFTS.

Joseph Davis,	B. F. Downer,	C. F. Parkhurst.

ENTERED APPRENTICES.

C. L. Brassler,	John Good,	G. W. Lowe,
H. B. Chamberlain,	Moses Hallett,	Samuel McLelland,
W. H. Evans,	J. W. Kerr,	Wm. Nowlan.
	Joseph Lambert,	

DIMITTED.

Wm. Antes,	Wm. Gray,	Thos. Thompson,
J. R. Devor,	Isaac Louis,	Samuel Schwaub,
M. W. Edson,	A. T. Randall,	F. H. Page,
W. H. Garvin,	Geo. Richardson,	Dewitt C. Waugh.
	C. W. Smith,	

DIED.

S. L. Ireland,	T. W. Lavin,	S. H. Cook.
	L. B. McLain,	

Admitted, 7; initiated, 11; passed, 17; raised, 16; rejected, 22; number of members, 99; living out of Territory, 28; Grand ☐ dues, $114.

CHIVINGTON □ NO. 6, CENTRAL CITY.

Time of meetings : second and fourth Wednesdays of each month

OFFICERS.

B. W. Wisebart, W. M.   G. B. Walker, Treas.   Benj. Lake, S. S.
J. Y. Glendinen, S. W.   S. I. Lorah, Sec'y.   I. B. Brunell, J. S.
N. Z. Cozens, J. W.   Frank Hall, S. D.   J. K. Rutledge, Tyler.
                     W. F. Sears, J. D.

PAST MASTERS.

Allyn Weston, P. G. M.   H. M. Teller, P. G. M.   J. T. White, J. G. W.
                     L. W. Chase, P. G. Treas.

MEMBERS.

J. N. Adams,   J. P. Folley,   J. L. Pritchard,
Wm. Aitcheson,   B. Green,   Ed. C. Parmelee,
H. W. Allen,   D. S. Green,   J. E. Plummer,
T. J. Brower,   E. L. Gardner,   W. P. Pollock,
E. H. Brown,   E. Garrott,   C. W. Pollard,
T. Barnes,   U. B. Holloway,   W. Rosenfield,
John Best,   C. L. Hill,   J. M. Rank,
E. H. Beals,   H. J. Hammond,   A. Ramos,
J. Boylan,   R. Hutchins,   J. H. Reed,
G. W. Buchanan,   O. H. Harker,   A. G. Raynor,
B. S. Buell,   J. Hutchinson,   Willis Reid,
S. A. Buell,   A. Jacobs,   G. Schram,
H. O. Basford,   G. W. Jacobs,   Hal Sayr,
B. R. S. Batchell,   H. A. Johnson,   W. B. Squires,
A. E. Buckmiller,   W. Jones,   L. P. Sperry,
E. C. Beach,   W. C. M. Jones,   A. M. Studor,
G. W. Brewer,   W. J. Joblin,   H. F. Sawyer,
James Clark,   D. Kline,   E. B. Stillings,
J. B. Cofield,   H. J. Kruse,   E. W. Sinclair,
J. Coleman,   John Kip,   Clark A. Smith,
D. C. Collier,   J. H. Kinney,   S. F. Tappan,
W. P. Caldwell,   D. Loeb,   J. S. Taylor,
G. B. Cornell,   J. Mack,   M. Thomas,
R. A. Clark,   J. C. McClellan,   G. E. Thornton,
W. Z. Cozens,   L. Merchant,   G. J. Tracy,
T. O. Clark,   P. M. Martin,   D. Tooker,
G. Cassels,   D. J. Martin,   B. T. Vincent,
A. S. Cobb,   P. McGran,   H. A. Woods,
J. R. Cleaveland,   J. G. Mahany,   Wm. Watson,
H. A. Clough,   T. Mullen,   L. B. Weil,
A. B. Davis,   Z. Myers,   J. Weidman,
J. J. Dunagan,   J. S. McLain,   M. C. Wythe,
P. H. Dunagan,   V. W. McCory,   A. H. Whitehead,
F. M. Danielson,   S. Moore,   G. E. Wilson,
W. T. Ellis,   G. G. Norton,   J. W. Watson,
H. R. Eldred,   T. D. Nash,   E. Wilder,
R. Frazer,   Wm. H. Nichols,   R. Woods,
M. France,   H. M. Orahood,   I. N. Wilcoxin,
W. G. Fairhurst,   G. A. Pugh,   J. B. Zerbe.

DIMITTED.

Rev. A. Barrelle,   E. P. Parker,   F. Poznanski,
L. G. H. Greene,   H. S. Robinson.

FELLOWCRAFTS.

E. Paul Jones,   H. H. Miller,   Lee R. Seaton.
                        E. J. Vance,

ENTERED APPRENTICES.

D. T. Beals,   David Ettien,   A. Schonecker,
J. C. Bruce,   Wm. Humphrey,   N. L. Sibley,
James Cree,   L. Kennedy,   E. F. Stafford,
J. W. Cooper,   A. McNamee,   J. W. Wilson,
J. S. Ewers,   G. B. Reed,   C. J. Whitaker,

Admitted, 7; initiated, 28; passed, 23; raised, 22; rejected, 16; suspended, Geo. E. Wilson, February 28, 1866, re-instated July 11, 1866; number of members, 131; living out of Territory, 20; Grand ▢ dues, $166.50.

UNION ▢ NO. 7, DENVER.

Time of meetings: second and fourth Saturdays of each month.

OFFICERS.

O. A. Whittemore, W. M.   Luther Kountze, Treas.   H. B. Hitchings, Chap.
W. D. Anthony, S. W.   Geo. E. Crater, Sec.   M. A. Rogers, S. S.
C. J. Clarke, J. W.   H. C. Leach, S. D.   Jos. Finley, J. S.
                          J. L. Bailey, J. D.

MEMBERS.

J. C. Anderson,   Jonas Deitsch,   James A. McFadden,
Eli M. Ashley, P. M.   C. C. Davis,   John Pierce,
Francis R. Bill,   Isadore Deitsch,   W. D. Pease,
Geo. N. Billings,   John Evans,   H. L. Pitzer,
J. Sidney Brown,   S. H. Elbert, P. M.   Charles Ruter,
J. M. Chivington, P.G.M. R. V. Fairbanks,   Fred. Z. Salomon,
E. H. Collins,   Redwood Fisher,   J. E. Stewart,
D. C. Corbin,   L. B. France,   Alfred Sayre,
Langdon Clark,   J. H. Goodspeed,   J. M. Strickler,
Rodney Curtis,   Henry Henson,   Milo H. Slater,
Austin Cunningham,   B. F. Houx,   N. W. Welton,
W. S. Collins,   H. B. Haskell,   Rev. O. A. Willard,
John Chamard,   Jay J. Johnson,   Geo. Williams,
Chas. Donnelly,   C. B. Kountze,   Oscar H. Whittier,
Jacob Downing,   Loudin Mullin,   S. S. Woodbury.
                        Elisha Millerson,

DIMITTED.

O. B. Brown, D. G. M.   J. R. Boyce,   Simeon Whiteley.
                        Richard Leach,

DIED.

Joseph Finly, Steward.

ENTERED APPRENTICES.

A. W. Atkins,   C. C. Clements,   D. P. Wilson,
Isaac H. Chandler,   Geo. H. Mills,   Luther Wilson,
D. A Chever,   Daniel Witter.

Permission granted to take second and third degrees elsewhere, to Lewis Barnum and Chas. W. Pollard; admitted, 7; initiated, 10; passed, 6; raised, 7; rejected, 19; number of members, 52; living out of Territory, 4; Grand ▢ dues, $72.00.

22

EMPIRE □ NO. 8, EMPIRE.

Time of meetings : first and third Saturdays of each month.

OFFICERS.

Andrew Mason, W. M.   David J. Ball, Treas.   Geo. C. Munson, S. D.
Hiram A. Haskin, S. W.   Henry Nutt, Secretary,   E. C. Westcoat, J. D.
Wm. L. Sawtell, J. W.   J. W. Martin, Tyler.

MEMBERS.

Samuel P. Allen,   Tyler Disbrow,   Jos. A. Love,
Francis L. Andre,   J. P. Haskins,   James H. Osborn,
Chas. H. Aylesworth,   John S. Jones,   Geo. Richardson,
Thos. J. Buchanan,   Edward James,   John Slawson,
Elijah Bently,   Charles King,   J. M. Smith,
John Collom,   Benj. Kerr,   Francis M. Scott,
Jas. W. Drips,   Geo. A. Smith.

DIMITTED.

Solomon Knox.

FELLOWCRAFT.

Park Disbrow.

Admitted, 2 ; initiated, 11 ; passed, 11 ; raised, 12 ; rejected, 2 ; number
of members, 28 ; living out of Territory, 1 ; Grand □ dues, $40.50.

BLACK HAWK □ U. D., BLACK HAWK.

Time of meetings : first and third Saturdays of each month.

OFFICERS.

Chase Withrow, W. M.   G. W. Currier, Treas.   W. G. Fairhurst, S. S.
H. M. Orahood, S. W.   J. S. Taylor, Secretary,   Z. Myers, J. S.
J. W. Nesmith, J. W.   John Boylan, S. D.   A. Smith, Tyler.
                       J. E. Wertzback, J. D.

MEMBERS.

C. S. Abbott,   H. E. Hurlbut,   F. A. Rudolph,
Ira C. Barkhurst,   A. F. Hoppy,   W. H. Richardson,
E. K. Baker,   F. B. Hurlbut,   A. P. Seabury,
Geo. Cassells,   H. H. Heiser,   Geo. Schram,
R. A. Clark,   Stephen Johns,   Thos. R. Smith,
W. F. Eberlin,   J. H. Kinney,   Wm. H. Studer,
J. P. Folley,   S. P. Lathrop,   E. Wilder,
Robert Frazer,   W. M. McLaughlin,   B. Woodbury,
James Fisher,   J. H. Parsons,   J. D. Williams.
                       J. W. Richie,

ENTERED APPRENTICES.

W. N. Dickerson,   N. F. Spicer.

Initiated, 17 ; passed, 15 ; raised, 16 ; rejected, 17 ; number of members, 38.

EL PASO □ U. D., COLORADO CITY.

Time of meetings : first and third Saturdays of each month.

OFFICERS.

E. T. Stone, W. M.   N. C. Miller, Treas.   Henry White, S. D.
C. T. Judd, S. W.   E. A. Smith, Secretary,   Charles Looner, J. D.
S. K. Roberts, J. W.   T. Gertue, Tyler.

MEMBERS.

Stephen Frazier,   Henry N. Hooper,   B. C. Myers,
G. B. Frazier,   J. W. Irion,   Adam Pastors,
R. J. Frazier,   Charles Pauls.

FELLOWCRAFT.
G. H. Byan.

ENTERED APPRENTICES.

A. Botts,   E. W. Innes,   J. M. Noble,
B. S. Hall,   E. S. Randall.

Initiated, 11; passed, 6; raised, 5; number of members, 17.

TABULAR STATEMENT

OF THE WORK OF THE SEVERAL ☞ SUBORDINATE TO THE GRAND LODGE OF COLORADO, FOR THE YEAR ENDING WITH SEPTEMBER 29TH, A. D 1866, A. L. 5866, SHOWING THE ENTIRE MEMBERSHIP OF THE TERRITORY.

No. of Lodge,	LODGE.	Affiliated.	Initiated.	Passed.	Raised.	Dimitted.	Died.	Suspended.	Expelled.	Reinstated.	Rejected.	Living out of Territory.	No. of members.
1	Golden City..........	...	5	6	6	1	1	...	...	...	6	25	59
2	Summit*..........................	...	...	...	...	...	...	...	...	...	...	......	......
3	Rocky Mountain*................	...	...	...	...	...	...	...	...	...	...	......	......
4	Nevada..........................	1	8	6	5	13	...	...	...	...	7	18	61
5	Denver..........................	7	11	17	16	13	4	...	...	...	22	23	99
6	Chivington......................	7	23	23	22	5	...	1	...	1	16	20	131
7	Union...........................	7	10	6	7	4	1	...	...	...	19	4	52
8	Empire..........................	2	11	11	12	1	...	...	...	...	2	1	28
9	Montana †.......................	...	...	...	...	...	...	...	...	...	...	......	......
10	Helena City †...................	...	...	...	...	...	...	...	...	...	...	...	......
U. D.	Black Hawk....................	...	17	15	16	...	...	...	...	...	17	......	38
U. D.	El Paso........................	...	11	6	5	...	...	...	...	...	...	......	17
	Total.......................	24	96	90	89	37	6	1	...	1	89	91	485

*Extinct.
†In Montana Territory, no reports.

PROCEEDINGS

OF THE

SEVENTH ANNUAL COMMUNICATION

OF THE

GRAND LODGE OF COLORADO,

HELD AT DENVER, OCT. 7, A. L. 5867.

———

The M∴ W∴ Grand ⊏ of A., F. and A. M. of Colorado, met in Annual Communication at Masonic Hall, in Denver, on the first Monday, it being the 7th day of October, A. D. 1867, A. L. 5867, at 10 o'clock A. M.

Present—

M∴ W∴ CHASE WITHROW, Grand Master.
R∴ W∴ ANDREW SAGENDORF, Deputy Grand Master.
R∴ W∴ AARON M. JONES, Senior Grand Warden.
R∴ W∴ L. N. GREENLEAF, Junior Grand Warden.
R∴ W∴ RICHARD SOPRIS, Grand Treasurer.
R∴ W∴ ED. C. PARMELEE, Grand Secretary.
R∴ W∴ Rev. H. B. HITCHINGS, Grand Chaplain.
R∴ W∴ HENRY M. TELLER, Grand Orator.
Bro. FRANK HALL, as Senior Grand Deacon.
W∴ H. A. HASKIN, Junior Grand Deacon.
W∴ JAMES KELLY, Grand Sword Bearer.
Bro. JOHN W. WEBSTER, Grand Tyler.
P∴ G∴ M∴ A. J. VAN DEREN.
P∴ G∴ M∴ ANDREW MASON.
And representatives from six subordinate ⊏⊐.

A ⊏ of Master Masons was opened.

The Grand Secretary announced that all the ⊏⊐ in the jurisdiction but one were represented, and had paid their Grand

☐ dues, when the M∴ W∴ Grand ☐ of Colorado was opened in ample form, with prayer by the Grand Chaplain.

The M∴ W∴ Grand Master announced the following

Committee on Credentials.—P∴ G∴ M∴ Van Deren, D∴ G∴ M∴ Sagendorf, Grand Treasurer Sopris.

Grand ☐ was then called from labor to refreshment, to meet at 2 o'clock P. M.

MONDAY, 2 o'clock P. M.

Grand ☐ resumed labor, officers and members present as at morning session.

Committee on Credentials submitted the following report, which was read and adopted:

To the M∴ W∴ Grand ☐ of Colorado:

Your committee on Credentials beg leave to make the following report: We find the following brethren present, and entitled to seats and votes in this Grand ☐:

Bro. Chase Withrow, M∴ W∴ G∴ M∴, 2 votes; Bro. A. Sagendorf, R∴ W∴ D∴ G∴ M∴, 1 vote; Bro. A. M. Jones, R∴ W∴ S∴ G∴ W∴, 1 vote; Bro. L. N. Greenleaf, R∴ W∴ J∴ G∴ W∴, 1 vote; Bro. Richard Sopris, R∴ W∴ G∴ Treasurer, 1 vote; Bro. Ed. C. Parmelee, R∴ W∴ G∴ Secretary, 1 vote; Bro. H. M. Teller, P∴ G∴ M∴, 1 vote; Bro. A. J. Van Deren, P∴ G∴ M∴, 1 vote; Bro. Andrew Mason, P∴ G∴ M∴, 1 vote.

Golden City ☐ No. 1: Bro. James Kelly, W∴ M∴, 1 vote; Bro. F. O. Sawin, proxy for S∴ W∴, 1 vote; Bro. G. N. Belcher, proxy for J∴ W∴, 1 vote.

Nevada ☐ No. 4: Bro. John W. Ratliff, W∴ M∴, 1 vote; Bro. J. F. Phillips, S∴ W∴, 1 vote; Bro. B. C. Waterman, proxy for J∴ W∴, 1 vote,

Denver ☐ No. 5: Bro. F. A. Clark, W∴ M∴, 1 vote; Bro. Alvin McCune. proxy for S∴ W∴, 1 vote; Bro. S. Mitchell, proxy for J∴ W∴, 1 vote.

Chivington ☐ No. 6: Bro. Frank Hall, S∴ W∴, 1 vote; Bro. Ed. C. Parmelee, proxy for J∴ W∴, 1 vote.

Union ☐ No. 7: Bro. W. D. Anthony, W∴ M∴, 1 vote; Bro. C. J. Clarke, S∴ W∴, 1 vote; Bro. M. A. Rogers, J∴ W∴, 1 vote.

Empire ☐ No. 8: Bro. H. A. Haskin, W∴ M∴, 1 vote; Bro. George C. Munson, proxy for S∴ W∴, 1 vote; Bro. George C. Munson, proxy for J∴ W∴, 1 vote.

Black Hawk ☐ No. 11: Bro. H. M. Orahood, W∴ M∴, 1 vote; Bro. J. W. Nesmith, S∴ W∴, 1 vote; Bro. A. Smith, proxy for J∴ W∴, 1 vote.

A. J. VAN DEREN,
A. SAGENDORF, ⎬ *Committee.*
R. SOPRIS,

The M∴ W∴ Grand Master appointed the following committees :

On Visiting Brethren.—Bros. Clark, Phillips and Haskin.
On Returns and Work.—D∴ G∴ M∴ Sagendorf, S∴ G∴ W∴ Jones, Bro. Kelly.
On Appeals and Grievances.—P∴ G∴ M∴ Mason, Bros. Clark and Anthony.
On Finance, Mileage and Per Diem.—J∴ G∴ W∴ Greenleaf, Bros. Clarke and Orahood.

The M∴ W∴ Grand Master then delivered the following

ADDRESS:

Brethren of the Grand □ :

Through the mercy of the Supreme Grand Master we have been spared to meet again as a Grand □, for the purpose of reviewing our work for the past year, and making such regulations as may be necessary for the future.

During the past year my business has been of such a nature as to require my constant attention, and for this reason I have been unable to pay such attention to Masonry as I should otherwise have done, or as it deserved.

Many things denote the prosperity of the institution. I am afraid it is becoming too popular for its own prosperity. Petitions for new □ in places which have just sprung up, or that have received a fresh start from some sudden freak of fortune, are frequently presented. Those presented to me I have almost invariably refused, thinking a little delay in the matter could work no possible harm to them, and might be best for the institution.

Popularity and prosperity are not synonomous terms. When so much work is done in such haste, some of it must be badly done.

On the 17th of November, 1866, I received a letter from Bro. Whittemore, enclosing one from Bro. J. M. Ellis, W∴ M∴ of Mount Moriah □ U. D., at Great Salt Lake City, working under dispensation from the Grand □ of Nevada, enquiring whether they could get a dispensation from here if they should surrender the one they had. The reason given was that they disliked certain instructions from the Nevada Grand □ forbidding their making Masons of Mormons, or to allow them to affiliate or visit. I informed Bro. Ellis that, while I might differ in opinion with the Grand Master of Nevada, I did not think it the policy of this Grand □ to interfere with the matter ; and, inasmuch as they had a dispensation from Nevada, and were working under it, that they had better work along for another year ; then if they failed to get a charter, they could surrender their dispensation, and, if they chose, apply elsewhere.

I have received five petitions to form new □, one of which I have granted, and the other four I have refused. I received a petition for a dispensation, from Columbia City, Nov. 17th, nominating P∴ G∴ M∴ Van Deren for W∴ M∴ Bro. Van Deren informed me that he could not and did not intend to attend to the conducting of the □, and I did not think the Bro.

23

recommended for S∴ W∴ could conduct a □. The J∴ W∴ I knew nothing about. At that time also, as near as I could ascertain, they had no room suited to the practice of Masonic rites. A short time afterwards, I received another petition from the same place, and it appearing to me that the difficulties had been removed, I granted a dispensation, appointing P∴ G∴ M∴ Van Deren first W∴ W∴, Bro. Theodore Haswell first S∴ W∴, and Bro. T. J. Johns first J∴ W∴ The brethren have been at work, and as far as I can learn, have been doing good work. They will probably apply at this communication for a charter.

I received a petition for a dispensation from Canon City, July 25th, one from Georgetown Aug. 7th, 1867, and one from Dayton, Aug. 26th, 1867, all of which I refused for reasons which seemed to me sufficient; and it being so near the session of the Grand □, I recommended them to present their petitions to that body.

On the 19th of February, 1867, I granted permission to Denver □ No. 5, to spread the ballot at other than the usual time, the case appearing to be one of emergency.

On the 4th of March, 1867, I received a communication from Montezuma □ No. 209, at Santa Fe, New Mexico, asking permission to confer the degrees upon a petitioner living at Conejos, Colorado, which I granted.

Feb. 11th, 1867, Bro. J. W. Ratliff, W∴ M∴ of Nevada □ No. 4, inquired of me if he should receive the petition of a brother for affiliation, who was made in a military □ (the books and papers of which were lost or destroyed,) without his demit. I instructed him to received the petition upon the best evidence he could get.

On Dec. 28th, 1866, I granted a special dispensation to Nevada □ No. 4, to hold another election for the offices of W∴ M∴ and Tyler, and also to fill any vacancies which might occur by such election, and also to install the officers after St. John's day, for the following reason: Bro. A. M. Jones informed me that at their annual election there had been twenty votes cast, of which one brother received ten, another five, another four, and one blank. Bro. Jones decided that the brother receiving ten had a majority, and declared him elected. A question having arisen in said □, and it being referred to me, I decided it was not a valid election, and that the brother receiving ten votes out of nineteen and one blank, had not a majority of all the votes cast. The □ asked for a dispensation to elect at their next regular, which I granted as before stated.

On December 22d, I conferred the P∴ M∴ degree upon the W∴ M∴ elect, and installed the officers of Golden City □ No. 1.

This embraces the whole of my official acts during the year.

Brethren, Masonry is getting to be too much of a machine; it is treated as though it consisted merely of forms and ceremonies. This should not be. Masters of □ should strive to make their meetings interesting and attractive. Mere forms of ritual, no matter how quaint or unusual, become stale when nothing else is heard night after night. Mere making of Masons or conferring degrees is not all of Masonry. Ours is intended to be a social institution; it is intended to cultivate and mature the intellectual as well as the moral features of man's character. Masters should be selected who are competent to instruct their ☐ in something more than the ritual.

Masonry has a history; it has an object; these and many other subjects cannot be exhausted. These symbols we use and speak of so familiarly have more meaning than is expressed in the manuals. Every intelligent Mason sees more than the mere form of the block he looks upon; he is taught some moral principle by every emblem.

Something ought to be done to attract to the ☐ brethren who can instruct us. We have such men in the order, who would be glad to devote a small part of their time to imparting instruction upon Masonic subjects, which are never thought of by a large part of our Masons. The object seems to be only to have the name of a Mason—not to learn and know what Masonry is—what it teaches, and what it makes a man. The principles we profess, if correctly understood and zealously practiced, will make us better men, break off our vices and superfluities, and leave us " better fitted for that spiritual building, that house not made with hands, eternal in the heavens."

Bro. Grand Treasurer informs me that there is something over two hundred dollars on account of library fund. I would recommend that the money be invested so that we may receive some benefit, either by the purchase of books, or placing it at interest.

I thank the fraternity for the uniform courtesy which has been extended towards me during the past year, and for the honor conferred upon me at the last session of the Grand ☐.

Fraternally,
CHASE WITHROW, Grand Master.

Which on motion was received.

The petition of James A. Burdick, F. O. Johnson, Wm. W. Ware, F. F. Brune, H. K. Pearson, D. O. Darnell, J. W. Hall, David Lees, J. W. Watson, Matt France, Albert Johnson, Wm. Barton, Dubois Tooker and Andrew Mason, for a charter for a ☐ at Georgetown, to be called Washington ☐, naming Andrew Mason as W∴ M∴, Jairus W. Hall as S∴ W∴, and Dubois Tooker as J∴ W∴, and recommended by Empire ☐ No. 8, was read, and on motion of Bro. Clark, the prayer of the petition was granted, the ☐ to be known on the register as No. 12.

The following were then read:

The petition of Bro. D. H. Nichols, and fourteen others, for a dispensation for a ☐, to be called Valmont ☐, at Valmont, Boulder County. Recommended by Denver ☐ No. 5.

The petition of Bro. G. B. Frazier, and ten others, for a dispensation for a ☐, to be called Canon ☐, at Canon City, Fremont County.   Recommended by Denver ☐ No. 5.

And on motion, were referred to a special committee, consisting of P∴ G∴ M∴ Van Deren, D∴ G∴ M∴ Sagendorf, and S∴ G∴ W∴ Jones, who submitted the following report:

To the M∴ W∴ Grand ☐ of Colorado:

Your committee on Petitions for Dispensation bèg leave to submit the following report:

That in the opinion of this committee the subject matter should be referred to the M∴ W∴ G∴ M∴, whose right and prerogative it is to grant dispensations, if, in his opinion, the interests of Masonry would be thereby advanced.

A. J. VAN DEREN, ⎫
A. SAGENDORF, ⎬ *Committee.*
A. M. JONES, ⎭

Which, on motion, was received and adopted.

On motion of P∴ G∴ M∴ Teller, the fourth resolution, relating to the Conservators' Association, passed November, 1863, was stricken from the standing resolutions of this Grand ☐.

The Grand Secretary and Grand Treasurer presented the following report and accounts, which were read and referred to the committee on Finance, Mileage and Per Diem:

To the M∴ W∴ Grand ☐ of Colorado:

I have the honor to submit the following report and accounts:

The receipts for the past Masonic year have been as follows:

For dispensations..$ 40 00
"   dues from Bro. C. H. Blair.................................   2 00
"   donations to library fund.................................   8 25
"   special dispensation......................................   2 00
"   dues from ☐..   654 00
"   dues from unaffiliated brethren........................... 12 00

Making a total of......................................$718 25

I have received several notices from the postmaster at St. Louis, informing me of packages remaining in that office to my address, held there for want of pre-paid letter postage. I have sent the several amounts required, but have received a part of the packages only. The others probably have been lost on the way, as, in answer to my letters, the postmaster acknowledges the receipt of the money, and informs me he has forwarded the packages.

I have also received a bound volume containing the Ancient Constitutions, Constitution and By-Laws and Decisions of the Grand ☐ of Iowa, compiled by R∴ W∴ Bro. Parvin, Grand Secretary, which is a valuable addition to our library.

The charters of Montana ☐ No. 9, and Helena ☐ No. 10, have been returned to me in answer to letters to the Masters thereof, requesting them so to do.

All the chartered ☐ in our jurisdiction have sent in their returns and dues.

El Paso ☐ U. D., and Columbia ☐ U. D., have returned their work and paid their dues.

> Fraternally submitted,
>
> ED. C. PARMELEE, *Grand Secretary.*

ED. C. PARMELEE, *Grand Secretary, in account with Grand ☐ of Colorado:*

	GENERAL FUND.	DR.
Dec. 16, 1866. to	dispensation Columbia ☐.......................$	40 00
May 11, 1867, "	C. H. Blair, dues......	2 00
Oct. 7, " "	Golden City ☐ No. 1, dues................... .	54 00
" " "	Nevada ☐ No. 4, dues........................	73 50
" " "	Denver ☐ No. 5, dues......................	132 00
" " "	Chivington ☐ No. 6...........................	168 00
" " "	Union ☐ No. 7............... ·	82 50
" " "	Empire ☐ No. 8...............	37 50
" " "	Black Hawk ☐ No. 11.......................	51 00
" " "	El Paso ☐ U. D............................	37 50
" " "	Columbia ☐ U. D............................	18 00
" " "	Nevada ☐ No. 4, dues unaffiliated brethren.....	9 00
" " "	Union ☐ No. 7, dues unaffiliated brethren......	3 00
		$708 00

		CR.
Oct. 3, 1866, by paid	postage and stamps.................$	3 00
" " "	stationery ....·	7 50
" 31, " "	freight on books and proceedings from Denver...........................	3 00
Nov. " "	postage received.....................	72
Dec. 2, " "	postage sent..........................	10 00
Dec. 8, " "	expense proceedings 1865............	1 00
Jan. 1, 1867, "	blank record........................	5 00
Feb. 12, " "	two blank records...................	9 00
Feb. 26, " "	express on Ohio proceedings.........	75
M'ch 16, " "	postage received.....................	1 76
April 24, " "	" stamps....................	3 00
May 8, " "	" received..................	51
June 29, " "	" "	80
Aug. 11, " "	" " (4 packages)........	3 93
" 18, " "	" "	95
" 21, " "	express proceedings to chairman committee Foreign Correspondence....	75
Oct. 7, " "	Grand Treasurer......................	656 33
		$708 00

ED. C. PARMELEE, *Grand Secretary, in account with Grand □ of Colorado:*

LIBRARY FUND.   DR.

Oct. 2, 1866, to per diem donated by M∴ W∴ G∴ M∴...............$ 4 25
 " " " Bro. Wisebart..................................... 4 00
Feb. 26, 1867, to cash M∴ W∴ G∴ M∴ for special dispensation..... 2 00

                  $10 25

                CR.

Oct. 2, 1866, by Grand Treasurer's receipt....................$8 25
Oct. 7, 1867, by Grand Treasurer's receipt.................... 2 00

                  $10 25

RICHARD SOPRIS, *Grand Treasurer, in account with Grand □ of Colorodo:*

GENERAL FUND.   DR.

Oct. 3, 1866, to balance on hand..................................$ 519 12
Oct. 7, 1867, to cash of Grand Secretary......................... 656 33

                  $1175 45

                CR.

By paid warrant to Collier & Hall.....................$263 00
 " " " O. A. Whittemore.................... 114 00
 " " " J. T. White......................... 14 00
 " " " A. M. Jones......................... 4 25
 " " " A. Mason........................... 7 75
 " " " H. A. Haskin........................ 7 75
 " " " L. N. Greenleaf..................... 14 00
 " " " W. D. Anthony...................... 14 00
 " " " E. Fellows......................... 10 25
 " " " A. J. Van Deren.................... 4 25
 " " " J. K. Rutledge..................... 10 00
 " " " R. Sopris......................... 14 00
 " " " C. Withrow......................... 4 25
 " " " B. W. Wisebart..................... 4 00
 " Cash on hand..................................... 689 95

                 —$1175 45

RICHARD SOPRIS, *Grand Treasurer, in account with Grand □ of Colorado:*

LIBRARY FUND.   DR.

Oct. 5, 1866, to balance on hand.................................$197 00
 " 5, " " received of Grand Secretary...................... 8 25
 " 7, 1867, " " " " " 2 00

                  $207 25

                CR.

Oct. 7, 1867, by cash on hand............................$207 25

Bro. Whittemore, chairman of committee on Foreign Correspondence, presented the following report, which was read, and on motion, adopted and ordered printed with the proceedings of this Grand Communication:

To the M∴ W∴ Grand of Colorado:

The R∴ W∴ Grand Secretary has placed in the hands of your committee on Foreign Correspondence the proceedings of the following named Grand ⬜, received since our last Annual Grand Communication:

Alabama,	Michigan,	Tennessee,
Canada,	Minnesota,	Nebraska,
Connecticut,	Montana,	New York,
California,	Maryland,	New Jersey,
Georgia,	Nevada,	Virginia,
Iowa,	Ohio,	Washington Territory,
Illinois,	Oregon,	Wisconsin,
Kansas,	Pennsylvania,	West Virginia,
Kentucky,	Rhode Island,	Bulletin of Grand Orient
Louisiana,		of France.

The non-receipt of the proceedings of other of our sister Grand ⬜, with whom we have been in correspondence, is probably to be accounted for by their bein wihheld for want of the necessary letter postage pre-paid, required on all transient printed matter coming west of Kansas.

The Grand Secretary has been notified of such packages being held at St. Louis, and the necessary postage forwarded, but as yet the packages have not come to hand.

The review of the proceedings received has been entrusted to poor hands, absence from home most of the time since their receipt preventing that examination necessary for a report.

A cursory examination of the proceedings before us shows a general prosperity of the order, and very much that we would like to bring to the notice of this Grand ⬜, if there was time to do so.

The Grand ⬜ of Nova Scotia, recognized by us at our last Annual Grand Communication, we find to be recognized by Maine, Canada, New Hampshire, Indiana, Iowa, Maryland, Oregon and Rhode Island, while recognition is withheld by Pennsylvania and New York.

In the address of the Grand Master of Connecticut, we find the following with regard to the action of New York City ⬜ making Masons of candidates of other jurisdictions, temporarily residing in New York, which applies so nearly to similar cases of citizens of Colorado made Masons in New York, that we quote without comment:

" At the last session of this Grand ⬜, by a resolution, it became my duty to confer with the Most Worshipful Grand Master of the Grand ⬜ of the State of New York, relative to the matter of subordinate ⬜ in the City of New York receiving candidates residing in this jurisdiction. I have not, however, complied with that resolution, so far as conferring with the M∴ W∴ Grand Master is concerned, believing that nothing can be gained by any such conference, as these infractions of our rights have occurred so many times in years gone by, and so many complaints have been made by those who have preceded me, occupying the position I am now in, with no conceivable favorable result."

He states that he has been in conference with a committee, also with the D∴ G∴ M∴ for the district in which the particular case is located, but had arrived at no definite settlement of the question.

The Grand ⬜ of Iowa adopted the following resolution, by reason of the

Grand ☐ of D. C. making Masons of persons temporarily residing in that jurisdiction :

"*Resolved*, That as this Grand ☐ forbids all ☐ in this jurisdiction to make Masons of sojourners, so it also forbids them to receive or regard as regular Masons, until they shall have been healed, all persons residents of this State who may have been made Masons without the authority of the ☐ nearest their permanent residence; and that this shall be construed to apply to all persons made in military ☐."

We would recommend the adoption of a similar resolution in this jurisdiction.

The receipt of our proceedings is acknowledged by the following Grand bodies: Alabama, Connecticut, California, Georgia, Iowa, Kansas, Kentucky, Louisiana, Michigan, Maryland, Nevada, New York, New Jersey, Nebraska, Oregon, Pennsylvania, Tennessee, West Virginia, Wisconsin and Washington Territory.

Canada, Illinois, Minnesota, Rhode Island and Virginia present no report.

In the report of committee of Ohio we find no acknowledgment of receipt of our proceedings.

Brief reports of us are contained in the reports of the Grand ☐ acknowledging the receipt of our proceedings, all containing fraternal greetings, many quoting from the address of the Grand Master for 1865.

The transactions of most of the Grand ☐ have been of a local character, and all show that the fraternity is rapidly increasing.

Most of the addresses of Grand Masters caution a free use of the black ball, which by the list of rejections shows to have been done.

Harmony everywhere prevails.

Fraternally submitted,
O. A. WHITTEMORE,
For the Committee.

The following communication was then read:

DENVER, COLORADO, Oct. 5th, 1867.

Bro. Grand Secretary:

At a regular communication of Union ☐ No. 7, F. and A. M., held on Saturday, Sept. 28th, 1867, the following resolution prevailed:

"*Resolved*, By Union ☐ No. 7, F. and A. M., that the use of Masonic Hall, in Denver, be tendered to the M∴ W∴ Grand ☐ of Colorado, for their occupancy during their coming annual session, to be holden in Denver, October 7th, 1867." Yours fraternally,

REDWOOD FISHER, *Secretary.*

On motion of P∴ G∴ M∴ Teller, the Grand ☐ approved the action of the M∴ W∴ G∴ M∴ during the past year, in reference to granting dispensations.

D∴ G∴ M∴ Sagendorf moved that a committee be appointed to revise the Constitution and By-Laws of this Grand ☐.

Motion concurred in, and Grand Secretary Parmelee, J∴

G∴ W∴ Greenleaf, and P∴ G∴ M∴ Mason, were appointed said committee.

P∴ G∴ M∴ Teller moved that the election of Grand Officers be held this evening at 7½ o'clock.

Motion concurred in.

The Grand ▭ was then called from labor to refreshment, to meet at 7½ o'clock P. M.

MONDAY, 7½ o'clock P. M.

Grand ▭ resumed labor. Officers and members present as at afternoon session.

The special order of the hour being the election of officers for the ensuing Masonic year, the Grand Master appointed as Tellers, Bros. Orahood and Clarke.

The Grand ▭ proceeded to ballot, with the following result:

Bro. HENRY M. TELLER, Grand Master.
Bro. O. A. WHITTEMORE, Deputy Grand Master.
Bro. AARON M. JONES, Senior Grand Warden.
Bro. W. D. ANTHONY, Junior Grand Warden.
Bro. RICHARD SOPRIS, Grand Treasurer.
Bro. ED. C. PARMELEE, Grand Secretary.

The Grand ▭ was then called from labor to refreshment, until 9 o'clock A. M. to-morrow.

TUESDAY, 9 o'clock A. M.

Grand ▭ resumed labor. Officers and members present as at yesterday's session.

Minutes of yesterday's proceedings read and approved.

P∴ G∴ M∴ Van Deren moved that that portion of the M∴ W∴ Grand Master's address referring to library fund be referred to a special committee.

Motion concurred in, and P∴ G∴ M∴ Van Deren, Bro. Orahood and Grand Treasurer Sopris were appointed said committee.

The special committee on Constitution and By-Laws submitted the following:

24

To the M∴ W∴ Grand □ of Colorado:

The special committee on revision of the Constitution and By-Laws beg leave to submit the following report:

We recommend that the word "thirty" in the third line of article 12 of the Constitution, be stricken out, and the word "twenty" be inserted in lieu thereof; and to add to the said article the following: "and no charter shall be issued to any new □, which has not worked under dispensation a sufficient length of time, and which shall not have regularly conferred the degrees of Entered Apprentice, Fellowcraft, and Master Mason.

Also, that the word "seven" in the third line of section 12 of By-Laws be stricken out, and the word "eight" inserted in lieu thereof.

Also, that section 31 of By-Laws be amended by striking out all after the word "withdrawn" in the third line.

Fraternally submitted,

ED. C. PARMELEE,
ANDREW MASON, } Committee.
L. N. GREENLEAF,

On motion of Bro. Hall, report was received.

On motion of Bro. Orahood, the amendments therein recommended were acted upon separately.

Which several amendments were so adopted.

The committee on Finance, Mileage and Per Diem submitted the following report, which was adopted:

To the M∴ W∴ Grand □ of Colorado:

Your committee on Finance, Mileage and Per Diem beg leave to submit the following report:

We have examined the Grand Secretary's and Grand Treasurer's reports and accounts, and find them correct.

We also find the following Grand Officers, Past Grand Officers, and representatives in attendance, and entitled to the following pay:

NAMES.	Miles traveled.	Attendance, days.	Amount.
M∴ W∴ Chase Withrow, G∴ M∴	80	2	$14 00
R∴ W∴ A. Sagendorf, D∴ G∴ M∴	......	2	4 00
R∴ W∴ A. M. Jones, S∴ G∴ W∴	80	2	14 00
R∴ W∴ L. N. Greenleaf, J∴ G∴ W∴	......	2	4 00
R∴ W∴ R. Sopris, Grand Treasurer	......	2	4 00
R∴ W∴ Ed. G. Parmelee, Grand Secretary	80	2	14 00
Bro. H. M. Teller, P∴ G∴ M∴	80	2	14 00
Bro. A. J. Van Deren, P∴ G∴ M∴	80	2	14 00
Bro. A. Mason, P∴ G∴ M∴	104	2	17 00
Bro. James Kelly	24	2	7 00
Bro. J. W. Ratliff	80	2	14 00
Bro. F. A. Clark	......	2	4 00
Bro. W. D. Anthony	......	2	4 00
Bro. H. A. Haskin	104	2	17 00
Bro. H. M. Orahood	80	2	14 00

Your committee would also recommend that, as Chivington ☐ No. 6 has no representative who draws pay, that the Senior Warden of said ☐ be allowed mileage and per diem the same as others are entitled to.

Fraternally submitted,

L. N. GREENLEAF, }
HARPER M. ORAHOOD, } *Committee.*
C. J. CLARKE,

On motion of P.∴ G.∴ M.∴ Van Deren, the word "Monday," in Section 1 of By-Laws was stricken out, and the word "Tuesday" inserted in lieu thereof.

On motion of P.∴ G.∴ M.∴ Van Deren, all that portion of Section 1 of By-Laws after the words "Central City," was stricken out.

Bros. S.∴ G.∴ W.∴ and Phillips offered the following:

Resolved, That in the election for officers of this Grand ☐, and subordinate ☐ in this jurisdiction, no blank ballots shall be counted as a vote.

P.∴ G.∴ M.∴ Teller moved to amend so as to read:

Resolved, That in the election for officers of this Grand ☐ and subordinate ☐ in this jurisdiction, blank ballots shall be counted as votes.

Amendment lost.

P.∴ G.∴ M.∴ Teller offered the following substitute as an amendment to original resolution:

Resolved, That in all elections in the Grand ☐ and subordinate ☐, no person shall be declared elected unless he shall have a majority vote of all the members present.

Amendment adopted.

Resolution as amended adopted.

Bro. Orahood offered the following:

Resolved, That no representative from any subordinate ☐ in this jurisdiction shall receive more pay for mileage and per diem than is paid by the said ☐ for Grand ☐ dues.

Resolution lost.

P.∴ G.∴ M.∴ Teller offered the following:

Resolved, That no subordinate ☐ shall hereafter allow its hall, or place of holding Masonic meetings, to be used for dances or other amusements, after it shall be dedicated for Masonic purposes.

Resolution adopted.

Bros. S.∴ G.∴ W.∴ and Ratliff offered the following:

' *Resolved,* That it is at variance with the spirit of Masonry to make nominations for officers in Grand or subordinate ▱, and the practice is hereby prohibited in this Grand ▱ jurisdiction.

Resolution adopted.

Bro. Anthony offered the following:

Resolved, That the words "Territory of Colorado," in the third line of ·Section 32 of By-Laws be stricken out, and the words "jurisdiction of this Grand ▱," be inserted in lieu thereof.

Resolution adopted.

Special committee on Grand Master's Address submitted the following:

To the M∴ W∴ Grand ▱ of Colorado :

Your committee to whom was referred that portion of the Grand Master's address relating to the library fund, would most respectfully recommend that the Grand Treasurer be instructed to loan the same, at such rate of interest, and with such security, as the M∴ W∴ Grand Master shall approve.

A. J. VAN DEREN, ⎫
R. SOPRIS,   ⎬ *Committee.*
H. M. ORAHOOD,   ⎭

Which, on motion, was received and adopted.

Grand ▱ was then called from labor to refreshment, to meet at half past 2 o'clock P. M.

———

TUESDAY, 2½ o'clock P. M.

Grand ▱ resumed labor, officers and members present as at morning session.

Committee on Petitions and Work submitted the following report :

To the M∴ W∴ Grand ▱ of Colorado :

Your committee on Returns and Work beg leave to submit the following report:

We have examined and found the returns from all the ▱ in this jurisdiction in form and correct.

We have also examined the records of El Paso and Columbia ▱ U. D., and found them in due form, manifesting great care and efficiency in conducting the business of the respective ▱. And while we note with pleasure the evidence of prosperity indicated in the numbers of accessions recorded therein, we feel it our duty to warn our brethren of those ▱ against the common evil of making Masons on the grounds of quantity instead of quality.

We respectfully recommend that charters be granted to the above named ⌷.

Respectfully submitted,

A. SAGENDORF, ⎫
A. M. JONES, ⎬ *Committee.*
JAMES KELLY, ⎭

Which, on motion, was received and adopted, and charters ordered issued to said ⌷.

D∴ G∴ M∴ Sagendorf moved that El Paso ⌷ be numbered 13, and Columbia ⌷ 14; motion carried.

D∴ G∴ M∴ Sagendorf moved to amend Section 5 of By-Laws so as to read, " every ⌷ subordinate to this Grand ⌷ shall, at least ten days prior to the first day of each Annual Grand Communication, pay to the Grand Secretary," &c. &c. Motion carried.

P∴ G∴ M∴ Van Deren moved that the name of Theodore Haswell be inserted in place of A. J. Van Deren for W∴ M∴, and the name of W. T. Potter in place of Theodore Haswell for S∴ W∴, in the charter of Columbia ⌷. Motion carried.

On motion of Grand Treasurer Sopris, a warrant was ordered drawn on the treasurer for ten dollars, in favor of Bro. J. W. Webster, for services as Tyler during the present session of this Grand ⌷.

Bro. Ratliff offered the following:

Resolved, That all Past Masters in this jurisdiction are hereby declared permanent members of this Grand ⌷, and entitled to seats and votes, without mileage and per diem.

Resolution lost.

P∴ G∴ M∴ Van Deren offered the following:

Resolved, That the R∴ W∴ Grand Secretary be authorized to print 500 copies of the proceedings, 200 copies to be retained for future use, and that he be authorized to sell copies at cost of publication.

Resolution adopted.

Bro. Orahood offered the following:

Resolved, That the thanks of this Grand body be tendered to the Masonic bodies of Denver City, for the free use of their hall during this Annual Grand Communication.

Resolution adopted.

Bros. Ratliff and Phillips offered the following:

Resolved, That before application can be made to the Grand ☐ by brethren already members of a ☐, for a charter to form a new one, the applicants shall pay up all dues to their ☐, and notify them in writing that they intend applying for a charter to establish a new ☐. And in the formation of a new ☐, a Mason may hold his membership in the number to which he belongs, until the new one be chartered, when it shall immediately cease.

Resolution laid on the table.

P∴ G∴ M∴ Teller offered the following:

Resolved, That the R∴ W∴ Grand Secretary be allowed the sum of one hundred dollars for his services as Grand Secretary.

Resolution adopted.

The M∴ W∴ Grand Master-elect announced the following as the appointed officers for the ensuing year:

Bro. Rev. H. B. HITCHINGS, Grand chaplain.

Bro. Rev. B. T. VINCENT, Grand Orator.

Bro. H. M. ORAHOOD Grand Lecturer.

Bro. HAL SAYR, Grand Marshal.

Bro H. A. HASKIN, Senior Grand Deacon.

Bro. JAMES KELLY, Junior Grand Deacon.

Bro. J. W. Nesmith, Grand Sword Bearer.

Bro. J. F. PHILLIPS, Senior Grand Steward.

Bro. J. W. WEBSTER, Junior Grand Steward.

Bro. WM. F. SEARS, Grand Tyler.

M∴ W∴ Grand Master Withrow, assisted by P∴ G∴ M∴ Van Deren as Grand Marshal, then installed the Grand Master elect, and the elective and appointed officers, who assumed their respective stations.

The M∴ W∴ Grand Master announced the following committees for the ensuing Masonic year:

Jurisprudence.—P∴ G∴ M∴ Van Deren, P∴ G∴ M∴ Mason, P∴ G∴ M∴ Withrow.

Foreign Correspondence.—Bro. Frank Hall, P∴ D∴ G∴ M∴ Sagendorf, P∴ J∴ G∴ W∴ Greenleaf.

The minutes were then read and approved, when this Annual Communication of the Most Ancient and Honorable Fraternity of F. and A. M. of Colorado was closed in ample form, with prayer by the Grand Orator.

ED. C. PARMELEE, *Grand Secretary.*

RETURNS OF LODGES.

GOLDEN CITY □ NO. 1.

Time of meetings: first and third Saturdays of each month.

OFFICERS.

James Kelly, W. M.
James C. Scott, S. W.
Owen Williams, J. W.
Frank O. Sawin, Treas.
C. C. Carpenter, Sec.
D. E. Harrison, S. D.
J. C. Remington, J. D.
E. L. Gardner, Tyler.

MEMBERS.

Wm. Ashley,
Stephen Bailey,
G. N. Belcher,
Reuben Barton,
J. C. Bowles,
S. M. Breath,
H. M. Russell,
J. D. Carns,
Eli Carter,
N. F. Cheesman,
Geo. M. Chilcott,
S. C. Clinton,
Felix Crocker,
D. G. Dargin,
Lewis Davis,
Fox Diefendorf,

John H. Durham,
Chas. L. Eggers,
E. Fellows, P. M.
John M. Ferrill,
L. W. Frary, P. M.
John R. Gilbert,
John B. Hindry,
Wm. R. Howell,
John Kean,
John F. Kirby,
M. C. Kirby,
W. J. Kram,
J. B. Longan,
W. A. H. Loveland,
J. S. Maynard,
Daniel McCleery,

John A. Moore,
Geo. Morrison,
Wm. R. Nelson,
Martin Oppel,
J. H. Pinkerton,
P. P. Pollack,
Wm. D. Rippey,
M. L. Sawin,
John Saxton,
Sam. H. Shaefer,
Abram Slater,
E. B. Smith,
P. L. Smith,
Henry Stevens,
John Strouse,
S. B. Williams,

FELLOWCRAFTS.

Peter Erskins,
A. B. Patton,
Wesley Teter.

ENTERED APPRENTICES.

J. A. Bartholomew,
John Churches,
Washington Jones,
M. H. Knapp,
Allen Lewis,
Leon Mellet,
Joseph Parrott,
Barney Pratt,
Geo. W. Reeves,
Thos. Sheridan,
A. M. Wallingford,
Bruce Woodward.

DIMITTED.

A. J. Butler,
Wm. Fredericks,
L. L. Reno,
W. L. Rothrick,
Milo Smith,
Geo. M. Wilson.

NEVADA □ NO. 4.

Time of meetings: second and fourth Saturdays of each month.

OFFICERS.

John W. Ratliff, W. M.
J. F. Phillips, S. W.
Ozias T. Sparks, J. W.
B. C. Waterman, Treas.
Thos. H. Craven, Sec'y.
David A. Hamor, S. D.
Robt. Hughes, J. D.
Isaac Sands, S. S.
Joseph Codling, J. S.
C. Visscher, Tyler.

MEMBERS.

A. J. Van Deren, P. G. M.
A. M. Jones, S. G. W.
Preston Anderson,
W. F. Avery,
J. M. Aldrich,
A. J. Biggs,
J. A. Burdick,
J. C. Rradley,
W. H. Belcher,
James Baxter,
S G. Brown,
Samuel Butler,
George H. Barrett,
T. H. Clewell,
J. E. Craine,
Ed. Crockett,
J. C. Donnelly,
B. W. Eussen,
Otto Eckhart,
Wm. Emperor,

D. L. Fairchild,
J. E. Gregg,
Theo. Haswell,
O. H. Henry,
F. I. Hibbard,
I. N. Henry,
Wm. Hyndman,
Wm. H. James,
Wm. H. Jester,
Joshua Jennings,
James Jones,
T. J. Johns,
Perry A. Kline,
David Lees,
Cyrus A. Lyon,
A. L. Miller,
A. C. McGeath,
Robt. Milliken,
George Marshall,

Orlando North,
E. B. Newnam,
Thomas Newlun,
Andrew Nichols,
W. D. Perkins,
Hollis K. Pearson,
B. F. Pease,
Albert Price,
J. C. Russell,
A. C. Rupe,
James W. Stanton,
Preston Scott,
F. T. Sherman,
B. F. Shaffer,
Joseph Standley,
Horace Shaw,
Jared F. Spaulding,
Walter Scott,
Thomas Woodward,
Wm. R. Uren.

FELLOWCRAFTS.

Charles Alber,   C. H. Merrill.

ENTERED APPRENTICES.

Geo. W. Brock,
Wm. S. Downing,
James Huff,

W. L. Ireland,
Geo. W. Miller,
Wm. McFeeters,
M. Symonds,

Abraham Stafford,
B. R. Walls,
Sam. H. Wright.

DIMITTED.

Charles S. Abbott,
R. M. Foster,

E. W. Henderson,

J. H. Mitchell,
Chase Withrow.

DENVER □ NO. 5.

Time of meetings: first and third Saturdays of each month.

OFFICERS.

F. A. Clark, W. M.
G. G. Brewer, S. W.
J. E. Gates, J. W.

George Tritch, Treas.
J. W. Webster, Sec'y.
H. H. Gillett, S. D.
J. E. Le Cavalier, J. D.

W. E. Turner, S. S.
J. L. Bartels, J. S.
R. K. Frisbee, Tyler.

PAST MASTERS.

A. Sagendorf, D. G. M.   L. N. Greenleaf, J. G. W..R. Sopris, Grand Treas.

MEMBERS.

Thomas P. Ames,
A. P. Allen,
Wm. D. Arnett,
A. O. Ashley,
Moses Anker,
J. S. Addleman,
Wm. N. Byers,
Charles H. Blake,
A. H. Barker,
C. L. Bartlett,
A. Bartlett,

James H. Eames,
Wm. R. Ford,
H. F. Ford,
H. Feuerstein,
H. H. Failing,
John H. Gerrish,
A. Goldsmith,
W. H. Grafton,
George Gillett,
C. J. Goss,
Geo. H. Greenslit,

Reuben P. Lamb,
Wolf Londoner,
George L. Moody,
F. Meserve,
James McNassar, Sr.
Alvin McCune,
F. A. McDonald,
Julius Mitchell,
Samuel Mitchell,
R. O. Old,
David Parlin,

J. M. Broadwell,
Geo. H. Bryant,
Barnard Berry,
Julius Berry,
F. R. Bennett,
N. A. Baker,
S. H. Bowman,
E. W. Cobb,
Chas. A. Cook,
Geo. T. Clark,
W. S. Cheeseman,
Robert Cleveland,
J. C. Carter,
H. S. Clark,
J. G. Casey,
James Clellan,
John L. Daily,
Wm. M. Daily,
J. C. Davidson,
F. M. Durkee,
J. H. Dudley,
Alex Davidson,
J. W. Douglass,
J. M. Deidenbach,
Joseph Davis,
B. F. Downen,

A. Hanauer,
J. S. Howell,
B. C. Hayman,
George W. Hertel,
H. Hitchins,
Jas. H. Hodges,
J. M. Holland,
Charles L. Hall,
J. W. Huntington,
Warren Hussey,
R. L. Hatten,
Moses Hallet,
C. Heinebauch,
C. J. Hart,
E. H. Jewett,
Theron Johnson,
George W. Kassler,
Wm. M. Keith,
E. W. Kingsbury,
J. Kershaw,
G. K. Kimball,
Henry Kline,
I. H. Kastor,
Joseph Kline,
John B. Lamber,

N. H. Rice.
E. E. Ropes,
H. J. Rogers,
W. D. Robinson,
Wm. M. Slaughter,
J. J. Saville,
H. Z. Solomon,
Joseph Lambert,
Edwin Scudder,
M. B. Sherwood,
Wm. Stepp,
George L. Shoup,
W. W. Slaughter,
Daniel Shuts,
Adolph Schirmer,
Fred. Schirmer,
Andrew Slane,
Nicholas Thede,
W. J. Thompson,
S. W. Treat,
J. H. Voorhies,
John Wanless,
J. W. Webster,
G. W. Webster,
F. R. Waggoner,
J. T. Yonkers.

FELLOWCRAFT.

Charles F. Parkhurst.

ENTERED APPRENTICES

H. B. Chamberlain,
W. H. Evans,
John Good,
J. W. Kerr,

George N. Lowe,
Samuel McLellan,
J. Molsen,

Wm. Nowlan,
J. M. Tallman,
John Upton,
Chas. S. Wheeler.

DIMITTED.

George W. Clayton,

Jacob Goldsmith,

John E. Tappan.

DIED.

Elijah S. Graves.

CHIVINGTON ☐ NO. 6.

Time of meetings : second and fourth Wednesdays of each month.

OFFICERS.

J. Y. Glendinen, W. M.
Frank Hall, S. W.
Hal Sayr, J. W.

C. W. Pollard, Treas.
S. I. Lorah, Secretary,
E. B. Stillings, S. D.
Wm. F. Sears, J. D.

E. C. Beach, S. S.
H. F. Sawyer, J. S.
J. K. Rutledge, Tyler.

MEMBERS.

J. N. Adams,
Wm. Aitcheson,
Wm. A. Amsbury,
Wm. F. Allen,
E. H. Brown,
E. H. Beals,

O. H. Harker,
R. Hutchins,
J. Hutchinson,
Richard Harvey,
Henry Hartman,
Charles L. Hill,

J. L. Pritchard,
George A. Pugh,
Ed. C. Parmelee,
W. P. Pollock,
Wm. Rosenfield,
A. G. Raynor,

25

Thomas Barnes,
A. E. Buckmiller,
I. B. Brunell,
G. W. Buchanan,
B. S. Buell,
H. O. Basford,
B. R. S. Bachell,
S. A. Buell,
G. W. Brewer,
John A. Best,
Hugh Butler,
James Clark,
J. B. Cofield,
D. C. Collier,
Joseph Coleman,
W. P. Caldwell,
L. W. Chase, P. M.
G. B. Cornell,
N. Z. Cozens,
W. Z. Cozens,
A. S. Cobb,
J. R. Cleaveland,
H. A. Clough,
A. B. Davis,
J. J. Dunnegan,
P. H. Dunnegan,
F. M. Danielson,
Wm. T. Ellis,
H. R. Eldred,
Matt France,
E. L. Gardner,
Basil Green,
D. S. Green,
E. Garrott,
U. B. Holloway,

Charles A. Hoyt,
Vaus F. Inskeep,
A. Jacobs,
H. A. Johnson,
W. C. M. Jones,
Wm. Jones,
E. Paul Jones,
G. W. Jacobs,
Wm. J. Joblin,
C. W. Johnson,
H. J. Kruse,
David Kline,
John Kip,
John H. Kinney,
Benj. Lake,
H. N. Lynch,
Oscar Lewis,
Jacob Mack,
J. C. McClellan,
D. J. Martin,
P. M. Martin,
Philip McGran,
A. McNamee,
J. G. Mahany,
Thomas Mullen,
J. S. McLain,
Samuel Moore,
V. W. McCory,
H. H. Miller,
George Mellor,
J. P. McAvoy,
N. H. McCall,
G. G. Norton,
Wm. H. Nichols,
T. D. Nash,

J. M. Rank,
James H. Reed,
G. B. Reed,
Antonio Ramos,
A. N. Rogers,
George Schram,
W. B. Squires,
A. M. Studer,
E. W. Sinclair,
Clark A. Smith,
H. M. Teller, P. G. M.
S. F. Tappan,
D. Tooker,
M. Thomas,
George J. Tracy,
George E. Thornton,
L. C. Tolles,
B. T. Vincent,
E. J. Vance,
A. Weston, P. G. M.
H. A. Woods,
Wm. Watson,
J. T. White, P. M.
B. W. Wisebart, P. M.
L. B. Weil,
J. Weidman,
M. C. Wythe,
A. H. Whitehead,
J. W. Watson,
George E. Wilson,
George B. Walker,
Robert Woods,
I. N. Wilcoxin,
C. C. Welch,
J. B. Zerbe.

FELLOWCRAFT.

L. R. Seaton.

ENTERED APPRENTICES.

J. C. Bruce,
D. T. Beals,
J. W. Cooper,
David Ettien,

J. S. Ewers,
Wm. Humphrey,
L. Kennedy,
H. C. Palmeter,

A. Schonecker,
N. L. Sibley,
J. W. Wilson,
C. J. Whitaker.

DIMITTED.

H. W. Allen,
T. J. Brower,
John Boylan,
R. A. Clark,
Thomas O. Clark,

Robert Frazier,
J. P. Folley,
W. G. Fairhurst,
H. J. Hammond,
David Loeb,
Z. Myers,

H. M. Orahood,
Willis Reid,
L. P. Sperry,
J. S. Taylor,
E. Wilder.

DIED.

Leonard Merchant.

UNION ☐ NO. 7.

Time of meetings: second and fourth Saturdays of each month.

OFFICERS.

W. D. Anthony, W. M.   Redwood Fisher, Sec'y.   H. B. Hitchins, Chap.
C. J. Clarke, S. W.   L. B. France, S. D.   J. M. Strickler, S. S.
M. A. Rogers, J. W.   J. L. Bailey, J. D.   J. S. Brown, J. S.
Frank Palmer, Treas.   R. K. Frisbee, Tyler.

MEMBERS.

John C. Anderson,   J. H. Goodspeed,   M. H. Slater,
Eli M. Ashley, P. M.   H. B. Haskell,   George B. Stimpson,
Francis R. Bill,   Henry Henson,   N. W. Welton,
G. N. Billings,   B. F. Houx,   O. A. Willard,
J. M. Chivington, P. G. M.   Jay J. Johnson,   George Williams,
John Chamard,   Luther Kountze,   A. Cunningham,
D. A. Chever,   C. B. Kountze,   George E. Crater,
Langdon Clark,   Henry C. Leach,   C. C. Davis,
C. C. Clements,   E. G. Mathew,   Isadore Deitsch,
E. H. Collins,   Louden Mullen,   Jonas Deitsch,
W. S. Collins,   W. D. Pease,   C. J. Mahar,
D. C. Corbin,   John Pierce,   J. H. McFadden,
Rodney Curtis,   H. D. Pitzer,   Elisha Millerson,
Charles Donnelly,   Hugo Richards,   G. H. Mills,
Jacob Downing,   Charles Ruter,   H. D. Mosier,
S. H. Elbert, P. M.   F. Z. Solomon,   O. H. Whittier,
John Evans,   Alfred Sayre,   S. S. Woodbury,
R. V. Fairbanks,   J. E. Stewart,   O. A. Whittemore, P. M.

ENTERED APPRENTICES.

A. W. Atkins,   E. M. Quinby,   Daniel Witter,
J. H. Chandler,   W. W. Roberts,   Luther Wilson,
G. McKee,   D. P. Wilson.

EMPIRE ☐ NO. 8.

Time of meetings: first and third Saturdays of each month.

OFFICERS.

H. A. Haskin, W. M.   John Collom, Treas.   Geo. Richardson, S. D.
David J. Ball, S. W.   George C. Munson, Sec.   Benjamin Kerr, J. D.
Samuel P. Allen, J. W.   James W. Martin, Tyler.

MEMBERS.

Francis L. Andre,   John S. Jones,   James H. Osborn,
Chas. H. Aylsworth,   Edward James,   Wm. L. Sawtell,
T. J. Buchanan,   Charles King,   Francis M. Scott,
Elijah Bentley,   Joseph A. Love,   John Slawson,
James W. Drips,   A. Mason, P. G. M.   George A. Smith,
Tyler Disbrow,   Henry Nutt,   J. M. Smith,
J. P. Haskins,   E. C. Westcoat.

BLACK HAWK ☐ NO. 11.

Time of meetings: first and third Saturdays of each month.

OFFICERS.

H. M. Orahood, W. M.   Alonzo Smith, Treas.   Robert Frazer, S. S.
J. W. Nesmith, S. W.   F. B. Hurlbut, Sec'y.   J. D. Williams, J. D.
J. S. Taylor, J. W.   Eugene Wilder, S. D.   Wm. McLaughlin, Tyler.
   John P. Folley, J. D

MEMBERS.

Chase Withrow, G. M.
Charles S. Abbott,
John Boylan,
Ira C. Barkhurst,
E. K. Baker,
Robert A. Clark,
George Cassels,
J. N. Crawford,
Robert Cameron,
Robert Busby,
W. F. Eberlein,
Thomas Entwistle,

G. W. Fairhurst,
James Fisher,
Samuel Favere,
A. F. Hoppe,
H. H. Heiser,
S. Hutchinson,
Ed. E. Hanchet,
Stephen Johns,
James Laughran,
D. D. Leach,
Z. Myers,

J. H. Parsons,
R. L. Palmer,
J. W. Ritchie,
F. A. Rudolph,
Wm. H. Richardson,
James H. Riley,
T. R. Smith,
Wm. H. Studer,
J. E. Wurtzebach,
B. Woodbury,
J. D. Westover,
D. P. Woodruff.

FELLOWCRAFTS.

George S. Parmelee,   John H. Miller.

ENTERED APPRENTICES.

W. N. Dickerson,

N. F. Spicer,
James Mills,

R. W. Mosely.

DIED.

John Johns.

EL PASO □ U. D.

Time of meetings: second and fourth Saturdays of each month.

OFFICERS.

E. T. Stone, W. M.
C. T. Judd, S. W.
S. K. Roberts, J. W.

B. C. Myers, Treasurer,
H. N. Hooper, Sec.
E. A. Smith, S. D.
J. W. Irion, J. D.

G. B. Frazier, S. S.
N. C. Miller, J. S.
S. Gerton, Tyler.

MEMBERS.

G. H. Bryan,
Antony Bott,
E. S. Randall,
J. C. Brown,
C. M. Bryant,
C. C. Burt,
S. M. Buzzard,
M. M. Craig,
Benjamin F. Crowell,
Stephen Frazier,
R. J. Frazier,

Emile Gehrung,
E. C. Gehrung,
B. S. Hall,
E. M. Innis,
A. G. Lincoln,
John W. Lore,
Solon Mason,
W. H. McClure,
James McGee,
C. W. Myers,

J. M. Noble,
Adam Pasters,
Charles Pauls,
John Pisderez,
James Roberts,
Charles Souver,
E. F. Stafford,
W. Sweetland,
J. Weir,
Henry White,
T. T. Young.

FELLOWCRAFTS.

James Kline,   J. C. Woodbury.

COLUMBIA □ U. D.

Time of meetings: second and fourth Thursdays of each month.

OFFICERS.

A. J. Van Deren, W. M.
Theodore Haswell, S. W.
Thomas J. Johns, J. W.

Abram Mills, Treas.
George W. Carter, Sec.

O. H. Henry, S. D.
E. A. Hupper, J. D.
John Richardson, Tyler.

MEMBERS.

A. E. Berger,
W. A. Corson,
Bart. Esmond,
Henry Green,
J. W. Horner,
Troy McCleary,

W. T. Potter,
J. W. Pomeroy,
Henry Paul,
Thomas Ryalls,
J. F. Spaulding,

W. C. Slater,
Wilhelm Sommer,
M. G. Smith,
J. A. Stanton,
O. H. Tubbs,
J. W. Wigginton.

FELLOWCRAFTS.

W. R. Blore,   E. P. McClure.

ENTERED APPRENTICES.

E. H. Andrews,
Amos Bixby,

Geo. D. Cook,

L. McIntosh,
W. H. Smith.

TABULAR STATEMENT

OF THE WORK OF THE SEVERAL ☐ SUBORDINATE TO THE GRAND LODGE OF COLORADO, FOR THE YEAR ENDING OCTOBER 7TH, A. D 1867, A. L. 5867, SHOWING THE ENTIRE MEMBERSHIP OF THE TERRITORY.

No. of Lodge,	LODGES.	Affiliated.	Initiated.	Passed.	Raised.	Dimitted.	Died.	Rejected.	Living out of Territory.	No. of Members.	Gr'd Lodge dues.
1	Golden City	3	5	4	2	6	...	7	19	55	$54 00
2	Summit*	...	...	...	...	...	...	...	......	......	....
3	Rocky Mountain*	...	...	...	...	...	...	...	......	......	....
4	Nevada	2	8	8	11	5	...	5	20	69	73 50
5	Denver	9	8	7	9	3	1	18	34	122	132 00
6	Chivington	7	9	10	14	16	1	16	21	133	168 00
7	Union	2	6	6	7	...	...	10	6	61	82 50
8	Empire	...	...	...	...	...	...	...	3	28	37 50
9	Montana†	...	...	...	...	...	...	...	......	......	....
10	Helena†	...	...	...	...	...	...	...	......	......	....
11	Black Hawk	1	17	14	12	...	...	12	11	45	51 00
U. D.	El Paso	...	20	25	25	...	...	2	2	44	37 50
U. D.	Columbia	...	19	14	12	...	...	4	2	25	18 00
	Total	24	92	88	92	30	2	74	118	582	654 00
	Total last year	24	96	90	89	37	6	89	91	485	508 50
	Increase of members									97	

*Extinct.
†Under jurisdiction of Gránd ☐ of Montana.

PROCEEDINGS

OF THE

EIGHTH ANNUAL COMMUNICATION

OF THE

GRAND LODGE OF COLORADO,

HELD AT CENTRAL CITY, OCT. 6, A. L. 5868.

The M∴ W∴ Grand ☐ of Ancient, Free and Accepted Masons of Colorado met in Annual Communication at Masonic Hall, Central City, on the first Tuesday, it being the 6th day of October, A. D. 1868, A. L. 5868, at 10 o'clock A. M.

Present—

M∴ W∴ HENRY M. TELLER, Grand Master.
R∴ W∴ O. A. WHITTEMORE, Deputy Grand Master.
R∴ W∴ A. M. JONES, Senior Grand Warden.
R∴ W∴ W. D. ANTHONY, Junior Grand Warden.
R∴ W∴ RICHARD SOPRIS, Grand Treasurer.
R∴ W∴ ED. C. PARMELEE, Grand Secretary.
R∴ W∴ Rev. B. P. VINCENT, Grand Orator.
R∴ W∴ H. M. ORAHOOD, Grand Lecturer.
Bro. G. C. MUNSON, *as* Senior Grand Deacon.
Bro. B. W. WISEBART, *as* Junior Grand Deacon.
Bro. J. F. PHILLIPS, Grand Steward.
Bro. N. D. HASKELL, *as* Grand Tyler.

PAST GRAND OFFICERS.

P∴ G∴ M∴ A. J. VAN DEREN.
P∴ G∴ M∴ A. MASON.
D∴ G∴ M∴ A. SAGENDORF.
And representatives from subordinate ☐.

A ☐ of Master Masons was opened in due form.

26

The Grand Secretary announced that, the representatives from a constitutional number of ⊞ were present, when the M∴ W∴ Grand ▢ of Colorado was opened in ample form, with prayer by the R∴ W∴ Grand Orator.

On motion, the reading of the minutes of the last Annual Communication was dispensed with.

The M∴ W∴ Grand Master announced the following

Committee on Credentials.—P∴ G∴ M∴ Mason, P∴ G∴ M∴ Van Deren, and Grand Treasurer Sopris.

Who submitted the following report, which, on motion, was received and adopted:

To the M∴ W∴ Grand ▢ of Colorodo:

Your committee on Credentials beg leave to report the following brethren present, and entitled to seats and votes at this communication:

Bros. H. M. Teller, G∴ M∴, O. A. Whittemore, D∴ G∴ M∴, A. M. Jones, S∴ G∴ W∴, W. D. Anthony, J∴ G∴ W∴, R. Sopris, Grand Treasurer, Ed. C. Parmelee, Grand Secretary, A. J. Van Deren, P∴ G∴ M∴, A. Mason, P∴ G∴ M∴, A. Sagendorf, P∴ D∴ G∴ M∴.

Nevada ▢ No. 4: J. F. Phillips, W∴ M∴, T. H. Craven, S∴ W∴.

Denver ▢ No. 5: L. N. Greenleaf, W∴ M∴, and proxy for S∴ W∴, A. Sagendorf, proxy for J∴ W∴.

Chivington ▢ No. 6: B. W. Wisebart, W∴ M∴, E. C. Beach, J∴ W∴.

Union ▢ N. 7: W. D. Anthony, W∴ M∴, C. J. Clarke, S∴ W∴, H. B. Haskell, proxy for J∴ W∴.

Empire ▢ No. 8: G. C. Munson, proxy for S∴ W∴, and J∴ W∴.

Black Hawk ▢ No. 11: H. M. Orahood, W∴ M∴.

Washington ▢ No. 12: Matt. France, Proxy for W∴ M∴, Wm. W. Ware, S∴ W∴, David Lees, J∴ W∴.

Columbia ▢ No. 14: W. T. Potter, S∴ W∴, proxy for W∴ M∴, W. A. Corson, proxy for J∴ W∴.

Fraternally submitted,

ANDREW MASON, ⎫
A. J. VAN DEREN, ⎬ *Committee.*
R. SOPRIS, ⎭

The M∴ W∴ Grand Master then appointed the following committees:

On Visiting Brethren—Bros. Ware, Potter and Orahood.

On Returns and Work—P∴ G∴ M∴ Mason, P∴ G∴ M∴ Van Deren, and P∴ D∴ G∴ M∴ Sagendorf.

• *On Appeals and Grievances*—Bro. Greenleaf, Grand Treasurer Sopris, and Bro. Munson.

On Finance, Mileage and Per Diem—Bro. Phillips, J∴ G∴ W∴ Anthony, and Bro. France.

The Grand ▢ was then called from labor to refreshment until 2 o'clock P. M.

TUESDAY, 2 o'clock P. M.

Grand ▢ resumed labor. Officers and members present as at morning session.

The committee on Credentials submitted the following, which was, on motion, received and adopted:

To the M∴ W∴ Grand ▢ of Colorado:

Your committee on Credentials beg leave to further report, that the following brethren are now present, and entitled to seats and votes in this body:

Bros. James Kelly, W∴ M∴, No. 1; G. N. Belcher, S∴ W∴, No. 1; Hal. Sayr, Grand Marshal and S∴ W∴, No. 6; J. W. Nesmith, Grand Sword Bearer and S∴ W∴, No. 11.

Fraternally submitted,
ANDREW MASON,
For the Committee.

The R∴ W∴ Grand Orator, Rev. B. T. Vincent, then delivered the following

ORATION:

The oft-repeated remark that "Masonry is conservative," suggests the few sentences I give you. We have grown to dread the word *conservative*, because so many deeds in religion, society and politics have been done in that name.

In these ages of revolution, to preserve old forms and opinions is thought to be treason to civilization and is indeed liable to that charge. As every season turns its soil to gather new and luxuriant harvests, so the genius of progress scorns the fogy, and moves on to sentence old seeds to death, that new ones may grow bountifully from them. Yet, while thus civilization bears its testimony to the glory of restless and resistless progress by revolution, we dare stamp some forms of philosophy "conservative" without condemning them.

There have always been among men certain backbone forms and ideas which have kept unbroken the link with the past. Around them the flesh and blood and nerve gather, and hold and live. Depending upon the life thus spiritualizing them have they deserved favor. Otherwise, as dry skeletons, society has justly doomed them. That any form thus vitalized should be sacredly conserved is axiomatic. Among opinions and forms and powers other than the direct spiritually worshiping agencies, true Masonry holds such a place, to be conserved in form and spirit, as (1) teaching beautiful lessons by symbols, whose significant charms are, and ever will be, undiminished. For as long as men will sincerely bow before its trinity of light, and travel its rugged and hazardous, yet victorious roads, will they feel its ancient power, although in spring-like freshness; as (2) forming bonds of unity and strength which can never cease to endure while vows are binding and brotherhoods are made of true hearts; as (3) making avenues of progress, by inspiration and labor, whose doors shall never be closed while men have sympathies, and human suffering claims the full and benevolent hand.

This threefold mission of Masonry, then, having nothing narrow or contracted in its aim or nature, is backbone to human culturing enterprises, and not a feature cardinal to it needs change, or is subject to revolution. Therefore, conservatism is written over its mystic doors, and upon every ballot its truest brothers cast.

This conservatism is twofold, of construction and membership.

Masonic forms and ceremonies are essential to its existence, because the principles which sustain the order live through these symbols and lessons. Not that they do not live through others, and may not as well, but taking no place of more or less efficient systems, it exists to fill its own sphere and do its own work. Upon this account the blows which have been feebly aimed at her secrecy and independence have fallen harmless. For it is the glory of our democracy that every tub standing upon its own bottom, while it pushes none others out of their appointed way, is perpetually defended by the great enactor and executor, common sense. And further, Masonry being unostentatiously and non-interferingly cosmopolitan, has its home unmolested under every banner. Now, if men choose, in generosity and liberality, to serve truth in a certain way, they dare not be denied the privilege, though antediluvian antiquity be assumed of it while freshness of character still belongs to it. But the error fatal to some Masons and Masonry in their hands—that religion is supplanted by it—must be rebuked, for the claims of right to conserve an organization limits always the relation of that organization to the sphere of its action, viz: its adherents, which claim cannot be made of religion. *Its* spheres, demands, and privileges are *universal.* Masonry belongs to its members alone, and by them may and must be circumscribed, with its own compasses, in its own hands. Within this circle we may, we will stand, none daring to molest us or make us afraid. But this conservatism is for practical purposes, brethren, and must be so considered. The principles of our order forbid any narrow concealment of good or restrictions of influence and power. For while the *sun* shines in all its course with uninterrupted beams, and the *moon* gives freely every borrowed ray, so must the *Master*, whether subordinate, grand or supreme in Masonry, lead all who profess to follow into paths of widespread usefulness. Our conservatism must then be practical in the spheres of our work and result. And in this I think I shall fully echo all the meaning of the conservative counsel. We must *first* retain our ancient efficiency. As every symbol is dark and mysterious until the key is given to the candidate, so sacredly must we keep the keys of our immortal benefits from foul and profane hands, until, by pure renunciations, they become worthy to receive them. Hence let no old symbol in form or ceremony be lost whose power may thus be imparted; and since, as like in the criminal curiosity which checked the daily coming of the fabled golden egg, exposure shall forever break the spell and looseness steal the charms, let us not tremble before the assailants of antiquity, but keep and use, while earth shall last, what for centuries has given the shock of enlightenment, opened the scientific way to the inner chamber, and taught the beautiful significancy of the sprig of acacia to thousands. This retention of ancient efficiency in matter and manner is by incorporating it so that every Mason is a casket of Masonic purity and truth, secreting its beauty, but revealing its holy power.

The *second* method of practicing Masonic conservatism is the use of the ballot. This is a delicate but an important subject. Good men have been forbidden the blessings of Masonry by a villainous use of the ballot, and bad men have been permitted to curse her hallowed associations by its indifferent use. The Masonic standard is not theological attainment, nor educational power, nor industrial skill, but *moral* worth. The first preparation is in the *heart*. This is not to be made by Masonry, but *confirmed* by it. The Masonic temple is not a place of creeds or of schools, neither is it a moral nursery. It is where are gathered professedly moral men, who pledge themselves before God and each other to all virtue as regards the Supreme Master, the country, each other and themselves. Hence it does not assume to take men in vice and wretchedness, and initiate them for conversion, but to accept men who are *ready* to make the necessary renunciations and pledges, honoring the institution and furthering its objects by personal improvement and affectional and culturing association. It is therefore necessary for us to exercise the right of holding back any assumer who would take upon himself Masonic vows without possessing Masonic qualifications.

The method is:

(1.) To establish a perfect individual character ourselves as a basis of voting. Every man must exercise judgment for himself, and the compulsion to vote implies ability to vote justly, in holding and using the wonderful authority of a Masonic ballot. Our ballots reflect our own moral standard always, and men like ourselves we will admit, and thus, if untrue, our order disgraced by ourselves, will be ten-fold disgraced by our privileges in opening the mystic doors to the world. Now, I do not propose a standard. Masonry does not fully define it. But this I affirm to be true, the highest standard of character furnished by our age demands our adherence. It is sometimes claimed that because Mohammedan Masons are recognized as brethren, their sensual standard is true Masonry. Far from it. That may be good Masonry in the land of the Saracen, but here the standard is higher. A true Mason seeking the holiest heart and life will strive to reach its glorious summit. My brother cannot be true to Masonry without being true to Judaism. I cannot, without being true to Christianity! Each is true to Masonry, not concerning the propagation of his sect, but his highest standard of moral and religious character. This will make the ballot-box the honest receptacle of holy decisions, and will truly conserve Masonry, by accepting the good and rejecting the bad, according to the highest discovered standard. (2.) Having secured this sense of right, relentlessly we must exercise our power. Vote not by sympathies, but judgment; we want men, not bodies. Vote fearless of fault-finding brethren or outside babbling. A system is tested by faithfulness to its principles. If Masonry will not bear firm, dignified justice, its overthrow, rather than support, becomes duty. Let our faithfulness, therefore, be apparent in this, that we make our order attractive to good men, and while the bad may seek to secure its livery in which to serve their vile purposes, let us repel them by manly rejections.

Finally, let us consecrate a proper modicum of our powers to a dignified use and perpetuity of our beloved instrumentality, as modestly, silently, yet unchangeably, it goes on to accomplish its own work. Then, when the great day that shall reveal all secrets comes, it will show a pure record. The *Plumb* will prove the rectitude of its purpose. The *Level* will indicate that not by clothes, or purse, or caste, but *character*, all are one; and as the Great Hand applies a *Square* more true than ours, may the accomplishment in us all prepare for a safe submission to that perfect test in which the Master Builder shall say, "Square work and true work, just such as is needed for the Great Temple on High."

Bro Sayr moved that the R.˙. W.˙. Grand Orator be requested to furnish a copy of his oration, and that the same be published with the proceedings of this communication.

Motion concurred in.

The M.˙. W.˙. Grand Master then delivered the following

ADDRESS:

Brethren of the Grand □:

We are again, under the blessing of Divine Providence, permitted to take counsel together as to the best means of increasing our Masonic usefulness in this jurisdiction; to consider how we may best strengthen and invigorate old friendships, and create and cement new ones. But in the joy of reunion let us not forget to render thanks to the Great Master of us all for the many mercies vouchsafed to us.

On the 22d day of October, I consecrated and dedicated Washington □ No. 12, and installed the officers.

On the 7th day of November, assisted by R.˙. W.˙. Grand Lecturer, I consecrated and dedicated El Paso □ No. 13, and on the 8th day of November, the officers were installed by R.˙. W.˙. Grand Lecturer, by my direction.

At the last Annual Communication of this Grand body, the petition of Bro. G. B. Frazier and others for a □ at Canon City, was referred to the

Grand Master. Knowing that the section of country about Canon City was but sparsely settled, and that the population of the town was small, I did not feel willing to grant the dispensation. until I could make personal inquiries as to the number and character of the brethren in that section. While at El Paso □ I was informed by W∴ M∴ Bro. Stone, that the proposed W∴ M∴ and J∴ W∴, residing near Canon City, were regular attendants at the communications of El Paso □, although, in order to do so, it was necessary for them to ride a distance of not less than fifty miles through a country almost entirely uninhabited.

On the 8th day of November, I visited Canon City, and conferred with the brethren there as to their ability to support a □. I found quite a number of the brethren anxious for the establishment of a □. On my return, I met the proposed W∴ M∴ and J∴ W∴ at El Paso □. I was satisfied that while the number of brethren in the vincinity of Canon City was small, yet they had the ability and disposition to support a good □, and on the 11th day of December, being satisfied as to the ability of the proposed W∴ M∴ to take charge of the □, I granted a dispensation to the brethren of Canon City, with Bro. G. B. Frazier as W∴ M∴, Bro. B. F. Smith as S∴ W∴, and Bro. Stephen Frazier as J∴ W∴ I suppose the brethren of Canon City will apply at this term for a charter, which I presume will be cheerfully granted them.

On the 17th day of December, the officers of Denver □ No. 5 being absent, I granted a dispensation to R∴ W∴ Bro. O. A. Whittemore, D∴ G∴ M∴, to congregate the □ at the regular place before St. John's day, that an election of officeers might be had. The officers were elected, and subsequently installed by R∴ W∴ D∴ G∴ M∴

On the 13th of January, I received a petition from the brethren at Valmont, Boulder county, for a dispensation to open a new □, to be called Valmont □. Believing that the interests of the fraternity would be promoted by so doing, I granted the dispensation, with Bro. Datus E. Sutherland as W∴ M∴ On the 27th of June, I visited the □ and found it in good working order.

In January last I left the Territory, and was absent until the last of April. During that time the R∴ W∴ D∴ G∴ M∴ granted a dispensation to the brethren of Cheyenne, Dakota Territory, to open a □ with Bro. James Scott, Past Master of Golden City □ No. 1, as W∴ M∴ On my return from the East, in April, I visited the □ at Cheyenne, and found it in a prosperous condition. The inhabitants of Cheyenne are as yet quite unsettled, yet I think there is suitable material to support a good □ at that point.

The R∴ W∴ D∴ G∴ M∴ also granted a dispensation to the brethren of Pueblo and vicinity. I know nothing of the working of that □, but I am satisfied from my acquaintance with brethren of that section, that a □ can be sustained in a creditable manner at that point.

The R∴ W∴ D∴ G∴ M∴ also granted a dispensation to the brethren at Denver to open a new □, to be called Germania □. I doubt the policy of establishing another ☐ at Denver at this time. The membership of the ☐ already chartered there are not large, and I fear another ☐ will weaken those already established. I would prefer to see a few good strong ☐ in the jurisdiction than to see a large number of feeble ones.

If Nos. 5 and 7, in Denver, do not furnish the brethren of that place with sufficient facilities for the enjoyment of Masonic privileges, then it will be better to charter another ☐ there. If such facilities are not lacking, it is better to concentrate the strength in those already established. I trust no other consideration, save that of the good of the fraternity, will be considered in relation to this matter.

I am informed that the brethren of Columbia ☐ desire to change the place of holding their meetings. The most of the members residing in and about Ward have removed to other sections of the country, leaving the brethren in the vicinity of Boulder City to keep up the organization. This they cannot continue to do without considerable trouble and expense, and, therefore, they desire to move the ☐ to Boulder City, where they have made preparation by procuring suitable rooms for ☐ purposes. If this change is made it will bring Columbia ☐ within seven miles of Valmont, and I do not think both ☐ can be well supported so close together. The brethren of Valmont ☐ U. D., have shown great interest in the new ☐, and have incurred some expense in fitting up their rooms, etc., and I suppose will petition for a charter at this time. While I am anxious to serve the brethren at Valmont, I cannot recommend the granting of a charter to them if Columbia ☐ is allowed to meet at Boulder City. If no change is made in the place of meeting of Columbia ☐, I will cheerfully recommend the granting of a charter to the brethren of Valmont, for I feel they are entitled to the full confidence of this Grand ☐.

I did expect to visit Canon City and Pueblo ☐ U. D., during the month of September, and should have done so but for the Indian difficulties, which rendered it unsafe to travel in that direction.

At the last Annual Communication of this Grand body, the R∴ W∴ Grand Treasurer was authorized to loan the library fund, with such interest and security as the Grand Master might approve. The R∴ W∴ Grand Treasurer informed me that he could loan the same at two per cent. per month, and would be responsible to the Grand ☐ for the same. I approved of the interest and security. It will be well to take some action on this matter at this time. I would recommend that this fund be continued at interest until such time as the Grand ☐ may be permanently located.

The library fund is..$207 25
Interest on loan... 49 70
                                                              ————
    Total $256 95

The past year has been a prosperous one to the fraternity in most sections of this jurisdiction. The most of the ☐ have improved their financial condition since the last communication of the Grand ☐.

At the last session of the Territorial Legislature, I prepared an Act for the benefit of Masonic bodies in this Territory, which became a law on the 10th

.day of January last. The Act provides for the incorporation of Masonic
□. I would not have recommended the incorporation of any Masonic □.
I think it hardly consistent with the character of our institution. I find
quite a growing disposition among the fraternity to have the □ incorporated, and fearing that this feeling among the □ might eventually result
in some action of the Legislature which might declare all Masonic bodies
corporate bodies, I drafted the Acts referred to. No □ will derive any benefit from being incorporated, as all the real benefits to be derived by incor-
·poration can be obtained under this Act; for Section VII of the Act referred to (see Revised Statutes, page 149,) provides that "Any of the foregoing Masonic bodies duly chartered by the respective grand bodies, accord-
to the laws, constitution and usages of the Masonic fraternity, and not wishing to become a corporate body under the provisions of this Act, may take
and hold real estate for their use and benefit, by purchase, grant, devise
gift, or otherwise, in and by the name and number of said body, according
to the respective registers of the grand body under which the same may be
holden; and the presiding officer of such body, together with the Secretary
thereof, may make conveyances of any real estate belonging to such body,
when authorized by a majority of all the members of said body, under such
regulations as the said Masonic body, or its grand body, may see fit to
make; but all such conveyances shall be attested by the seal of said subordinate body. (Sec. VIII.) Should it become necessary at any time to
protect the rights of such Masonic body in and to the real estate and personal property, said body not being incorporated under this Act, the presiding officer thereof may bring suit in his own name for the benefit of the
Masonic body over which he presides, in any of the courts of record of this
Territory having original jurisdiction, and may prosecute or defend the
same in the Supreme Court of the Territory."

Thus it will be seen that all the benefits of an incorporation are obtained
without the usual embarrassments.

In this connection, I desire to call your attention to the address of the
Grand Master of New Jersey.

And now, my brethren, in returning to your hands the high power you
were pleased to intrust to my care, I do most earnestly and cordially thank
yóu for the repeated honor you have seen fit to bestow on me, and as I take
my place among the workers of this Grand □, I shall carry with me such
pleasant memories of your kindness and courtesy as shall never fade while
reason holds its sway. And, in the language I used on a former occasion,
when surrendering to you the gavel, I pledge to you, my brethren, my co-
operation with whomsoever you may elect as my successor, and may the
blessings of the Grand Master of us all be on you and yours, with all regular
Masons, and when we shall have completed our work below, may we meet
in that upper and better □, where the Supreme Architect of the Universe
presides.   H. M. TELLER,
                                        Grand Master of Masons in Colorado.

The R∴ W∴ Grand Lecturer then presented the following, which was received and ordered printed with the proceedings :

As Grand Lecturer of Colorado, I would respectfully submit the following report of my official action during the past year:

By order of the M∴ W∴ Grand Master, I accompanied him to Georgetown, in October last, and assisted in the dedication and consecration of Washington □ No. 12.

Early in November I visited El Paso □ No. 13, at Colorado City, and spent a week posting the officers and members in the work and lectures, and also assisted the M∴ M∴ Grand Master in the consecration and dedication of the □.

I found the brethren doing considerable work, and as well as could be expected, they never having been instructed in the work of this jurisdiction. I found every officer and member willing and anxious to learn the work and lectures. During the time I was with them I conferred the third degree.

I found Bro. Dr. Dickinson, a P∴ M∴ of Michigan, residing in Colorado City, very proficient in the work as adopted by this Grand □, and requested him to continue my instructions, which he promised to do.

I met Bro. Frazier, the proposed W∴ M∴ of the new □ to be organized at Canon City, but had very little time to post with him. I found him quite proficient in the lectures, and anxious to learn the work. I asked and obtained the M∴ W∴ Grand Master's permission for Bro. Frazier to post with Bro. Dickinson.

In January, Bro. Sutherland, who was recommended as W∴ M∴ of Valmont □, spent two days with me at Black Hawk, posting for that position. I then wrote a letter to Columbia □ No. 14, stating that I considered Bro. Sutherland qualified for the position, and they recommended the petition for a dispensation, which was granted by the M∴ W∴ Grand Master.

January 22d I was in Valmont, and with the S∴ W∴ of Valmont □, U. D., visited their □ room, which I found very comfortable and perfectly safe, and spent some time posting with the S∴ W∴ and members.

January 28th I visited the □ room the brethren were preparing in Cheyenne, and I found it safe and convenient for Masonic purposes.

February 5th I visited Golden City □ No. 1. The W∴ M∴ failed to receive my letter, and had no meeting called; had a very pleasant meeting with the W∴ M∴, Wardens, and a few brethren; posted on the work until a late hour.

February 20th, by invitation of the W∴ M∴ of Golden City □ No. 1, I conferred the third degree for them.

February 25th, by invitation from the S∴ W∴, who was acting Master, and the brethren, I visited Washington □ No. 12, at Georgetown; had quite a large meeting, and a very pleasant one. I staid until the 26th, and posted in most of the work with Bro. Ware, and compared with Bro. J. T. White, Past Grand Lecturer, and found our work to agree. I told Bro. Ware if he should forget any part of the work, as I had posted him, to learn it from Bro. White. The ☐ seemed to be in a prosperous condition, and doing good work.

May 11th, by invitation of Bro. Anthony, W∴ M∴ of Union ☐ No. 7, I conferred the third degree. I spent some time in comparing points of difference in Bro. Anthony's work. I found his work very near that adopted by the Grand ☐.

May 30th I was in Cheyenne, and proposed to spend a day or two posting the ☐ there, but found the W∴ M∴ and S∴ W∴ both absent, so had to leave without seeing them.

In July I spent four days with Valmont ☐; conferred the third degree for them. I left them very proficient in the work.

I made arrangements in August for visiting El Paso ☐ No. 13, Canon ☐ U. D., and Pueblo ☐ U. D., but was prevented from doing so by the Indian troubles.

In September, the M∴ W∴ Grand Master and myself intended visiting said ☐, but the Indians appearing on the road and commiting depredations again, we deemed it unsafe, and did not do so.

October 3d I attended a regular communication of Denver ☐ No. 5, but saw very little of the working of the ☐, there being no business to transact or work to do.

I have found in nearly every ☐ some things that do not conform to the work as adopted by the Grand ☐, but find the brethren always ready and willing to correct irregularities and learn the work, and am happy to state I find the ☐ working harmoniously and brotherly love prevailing, and that they are generally in a prosperous condition.

In all my official duties I have been treated by the brethren with uniform brotherly courtesy, for which I return them my sincere thanks.

Respectfully submitted,

HARPER M. ORAHOOD, *Grand Lecturer.*

The Grand Treasurer presented the following report, which was read and referred to the committee on Finance, Mileage and Per Diem:

RICHARD SOPRIS, *Grand Treasurer, in account with the M∴ W∴ Grand ☐ of Colorodo:*

LIBRARY FUND.	**DR.**
Oct. 7, 1867, to balance on hand...............................	$207 25
Oct. 6, 1868, to interest received...............................	49 72
	$256 97
	CR.
Oct. 6, 1868, by amount on hand...........................	$256 97
GENERAL FUND.	**DR.**
Oct. 7, 1867, to balance on hand...............................	$689 95

				CR.
By paid warrant to	W. D. Anthony	$	4	00
"	"	A. M. Jones	14	00
"	"	R. Sopris	4	00
"	"	A. Mason	17	00
"	"	H. A. Haskin	17	00
"	"	H. M. Orahood	14	00
"	"	Ed. C. Parmelee	14	00
"	"	L. N. Greenleaf	4	00
"	"	C. Withrow	14	00
"	"	Frank Hall	14	00
"	"	Jas. Kelly	7	00
"	"	J. W. Ratliff	14	00
"	"	Collier & Hall	13	00
"	"	F. A. Clarke	4	00
"	"	H. M. Teller	14	00
"	"	A. J. Van Deren	14	00
"	"	A Sagendorf	4	00
"	"	J. W. Webster	10	00
"	"	Ed. C. Parmelee	100	00
"	"	Collier & Hall	300	00
By amount overdrawn in 1866			9	00
By error to balance account			33	62
Oct. 6, 1868, balance on hand			34	33
			——$689	95

The Grand Secretary presented the following report and accounts, which were read and referred to a special committee, consisting of S∴ G∴ W∴ Jones, J∴ G∴ D∴ Kelly and Bro. Nesmith:

To the M∴ W∴ Grand □ of Colorado :

As soon after our last Annual Communication as possible, I had 500 copies of the proceedings of that communication printed. They have been disposed of as follows:

Six copies were sent to each of the □ in the jurisdiction. Three copies were sent to each of the Grand □ with which we are in correspondence. The customary number to each of the Grand Officers. A few have been furnished sundry Masonic periodicals, and distinguished brethren abroad. A *very* few sold, as per resolution of the Grand □, and the balance are on hand for future use.

Soon after our last communication, I addressed a circular letter to the Grand Secretaries of our sister Grand □, calling their attention to the United States Postal Law, requiring pre-paid letter postage on all transient mail matter coming west of the west line of Kansas, and am happy to say that our list of proceedings this year is more complete than before.

The Act of Congress repealing the obnoxious postal law went into effect October 1st inst., and hereafter we may reasonably expect to receive the proceedings of all of our sister Grand □, as well as the proceedings of many former years, now wanting to complete our files.

R∴ W∴ Bro. Clark, Grand Secretary of Vermont, notified me of the mailing of the proceedings of their last communication, and R∴ W∴ Bro. Hacker, Grand Secretary of Indiana, of the mailing of the reprint* of the proceedings of the Grand ☐ of Indiana, from its organization in 1817 to 1845, neither of which have as yet come to hand.

I have received from Bro. Leon Hyneman, of Philadelphia, a copy of his work entitled "World's Masonic Register," and from R∴ W∴ Bro. Sayre, Grand Secretary of Alabama, a finely bound copy of the "Code of Alabama," and from R∴ W∴ Bro. Wise, Grand Secretary of Nebraska, the reprint of the proceedings of the Grand ☐ from 1857 to 1867.

The Grand ☐ of New Brunswick and of Idaho have forwarded us the proceedings of their organization, and ask recognition by us. The proceedings received have been forwarded to the chairman of the committee on Foreign Correspondence.

Since our last communication, M∴ W∴ Bro. Charles A. Fuller, P∴ G∴ M∴ of Tennessee, a member of that Grand ☐ since 1842, and for the past sixteen years Grand Secretary, has been called to the Grand ☐ above.

All the chartered ☐ made returns and paid their dues. Canon ☐, U. D., Pueblo ☐, U. D., Valmont ☐, U. D., and Germania ☐, U. D., have returned their dispensations and work, and paid their dues,

Fraternally submitted,

ED. C. PARMELEE, *Grand Secretary.*

[Cheyenne ☐, U. D., made returns after above report was submitted.— GRAND SEC.]

Ed. C. Parmelee, Grand Secretary, in account with the M∴ W∴ Grand ☐ of Colorado:

LIBRARY FUND.					DR.
Oct. 16, 1867, to special dispensation to No. 14					$ 10 00
Dec. 4, 1867, " " " " 13					2 00
Oct. 5, 1868, " " " " 5					2 00
Oct. 5, 1868, " " " " 7					5 00
					$19 00

CR.

Oct. 5, 1868, by paid Grand Treasurer.................$19 00

GENERAL FUND.		DR.
Oct. 8, 1867, to charter, Washington ☐ No. 12		$ 60 00
Oct. 8, " " " El Paso ☐ No. 13		20 00
Oct. 9, " " " Columbia ☐ No. 14		20 00
Sept. 28, 1868, sale of proceedings		2 63
" 28, 1868, to dues. Union ☐ No. 7		96 00
" 28, 1868, " Columbia ☐ No. 14		21 00
" 29, 1868, " Washington ☐ No. 12		54 00
Oct. 2, 1868, to dues, Golden City ☐ No. 1		52 50
" 2, " " dues, Germania ☐, U. D.		9 00

*Indiana proceedings have since been received.—GRAND SEC.

Oct. 5, 1868, to dispensation, Germania ◻ U. D................... $ 40 00
  " 5,   "   "   "   Cheyenne ◻ " 40 00
  " 5,   "   "   "   Valmont ◻ " 40 00
  " 5,   "   "   "   Canon   ◻ " 40 00
  " 5,   "   "   "   Pueblo   ◻ " 40 00
  " 5,   " dues, Valmont ◻, U. D.............................   3 00
  " 5,   "   "   Empire   ◻, No. 8............................. 42 00
  " 6,   "   "   Canon   ◻, U. D............................. 15 00
  " 6,   "   "   Nenada   ◻, No. 4............................. 58 50
  " 6,   "   "   "   ◻, No. 4, from an affiliated brother.... 3 00
  " 6,   "   "   Black Hawk ◻ No. 11......................... 70 50
  " 6,   "   "   Denver   ◻ No. 5............................. 127 50
  " 6,   "   "   Chivington ◻ No. 6.......................... 144 00
  " 6,   "   "   Pueblo   ◻, U. D............................. 13 50
  " 6,   "   "   El Paso ◻, No. 13........................... 42 00
                                                              _____
                                                               $1054 13

By paid stationery, postage, etc., as per bill of items   CR.
  herewith submitted... .... $ 49 12
By paid charters, and express charges on same........   65 00
By paid Grand Treasurer...........................   940 01
                                                        _____
                                                          $1054 13
                  Fraternally submitted,
                          ED. C. PARMELEE, *Grand Secretary.*

, A petition from Columbia ◻ No. 14, for the changing of the location of that ◻ from Columbia City, Boulder county, to Boulder City, Boulder county, was read, and on motion referred to the committee on Returns and Work.

Bro. Wisebart moved that the election of Grand Officers be held this evening at 8 o'clock.

Motion concurred in.

Bro. Sayr offered the following:

Resolved, That the committee on Foreign Correspondence be **granted** further time to complete their report, and when completed, it be submitted to the M∴ W∴ Grand Master for his approval; and when approved, it be printed with the proceedings of this communication.

Resolution adopted.

P∴ D∴ G∴ M∴ Sagendorf offered the following:

Resolved, That section 1 of the By-Laws be amended by striking out **the** words, "first Tuesday of October," and inserting the words, "last **Tuesday** of September," in lieu thereof.

Resolution adopted.

Bro. Grand Secretary offered the following:

Resolved, That no ◻ in this jurisdiction shall, knowingly, hereafter recognize as a Mason any citizen of Colorado who shall be hereafter made a **Ma-**

son outside the jurisdiction of this Grand □ during his citizenship, unless by permission of the □ in whose jurisdiction he resides.

Resolution adopted.

The Grand □ was then called from labor to refreshment, to meet at 8 o'clock P. M.

TUESDAY, 8 o'clock P. M.

The Grand □ resumed labor, officers and members present as at afternoon session.

The special order of the hour being the election of officers for the ensuing Masonic year, the M∴ W∴ Grand Master appointed as tellers, Bros. Sayr and Carson.

The election was then held, resulting in the election of the following brethren:

M∴ W∴ HENRY M. TELLER, Grand Master.
R∴ W∴ ANDREW SAGENDORF, Deputy Grand Master.
R∴ W∴ BENJ. W. WISEBART, Senior Grand Warden.
R∴ W∴ WEBSTER D. ANTHONY, Junior Grand Warden.
R∴ W∴ RICHARD SOPRIS, Grand Treasurer.
R∴ W∴ ED. C. PARMELEE, Grand Secretary.

P∴ G∴ M∴ Van Deren presented the following:

To the M∴ W∴ Grand □ of Colorado :

Your committee to whom was referred the request for recognition of the M∴ W∴ Grand □ of Idaho and New Brunswick, beg leave to submit the following:

Resolved, That the fraternal greetings of this Grand □ be extended to our sister Grand □ of Idaho and New Brunswick, and that they are hereby tendered a cordial welcome into the sisterhood of Grand □.

Fraternally submitted,

A. J. VAN DEREN,)
ANDREW MASON, } *Committee.*
A. SAGENDORF,)

And on motion, the report was received and the resolution adopted.

The committee on Returns and Work submitted the following, which was read, and on motion, adopted:

To the M∴ W∴ Grand □ of Colorado :

Your committee on Returns and Work beg leave to submit the following report:

We have examined and found the returns from all the ▭ in the jurisdiction in form and correct. We have also examined the records of Canon, Cheyenne, Pueblo and Germania ▭ U. D., and found them in due form, manifesting commendable skill and efficiency, and respectfully recommend that charters be granted to the three first named. Your committee are not clear as to the propriety of granting a charter to Germania ▭, and deem it expedient to refer the matter back to this Grand body. We would also recommend that the prayer of the petitioners for the removal of Columbia ▭ No. 14, from Columbia City to Boulder City, be granted.

Fraternally submitted,

A. MASON,
A. J. VAN DEREN, } *Committee.*
A. SAGENDORF,

The Grand ▭ was then called from labor to refreshment, to meet at 8½ o'clock A. M. to-morrow.

WEDNESDAY, 8½ o'clock A. M.

Grand ▭ resumed labor, officers and members present as yesterday.

P.·. G.·. M.·. Van Deren offered the following:

Resolved, That the location of Columbia ▭ No. 14, is hereby changed from Columbia City, Boulder County, to Boulder City, Boulder County; and that charters be granted Canon ▭ U. D., at Canon City, to be known as Mount Moriah ▭ No. 15; and to Cheyenne ▭, at Cheyenne, Dacota Territory, to be No. 16; and to Pueblo ▭, at Pueblo, to be No. 17.

Resolution adopted.

Bro. Kelly offered the following:

Resolved, That the name of J. E. Gates be inserted in place of James Scott for W.·. M.·., and the name of E. B. Carling in place of J. E. Gates for S.·. W.·., in the charter of Cheyenne ▭.

Resolution adopted.

Bro J.·. G.·. W.·. Anthony offered the following:

Resolved. That a charter be granted, and the same is hereby ordered to be issued, to Germania ▭, to be called Germania ▭ No. 18.

Resolution lost.

The following communication was read:

To the M∴ W∴ *Grand* □ *of Colorado :*

At a regular communication of Chivington □ No. 6, held at Masonic Hall, September 23d, A. D. 1868, A. L. 5868, it was

Resolved, That we petition the M∴ W∴ Grand □ of Colorado to change the name of our □ from Chivington to Central No. 6.

B. W. WISEBART,

W∴ M∴ Chivington □ *No.* 6.

Attest:

    S. I. LORAH, *Secretary.*

Bro. Grand Treasurer Sopris offered the following:

WHEREAS, It is the request of the members of Chivington □ No. 6, to change the name of said □, therefore,

Resolved, That the name of Chivington be stricken out and that of Central inserted in lieu thereof, said □ to be hereafter known and recognized as Central No. 6.

Resolution adopted.

J∴ G∴ W∴ Anthony, for the committee on Finance, Mileage and Per Diem, moved that the report of the Grand Treasurer be received and adopted.   Motion concurred in.

P∴ G∴ M∴ Whittemore offered the following:

Resolved, That the R∴ W∴ Grand Secretary be authorized to have reprinted 800 copies of the past proceedings of this Grand □, *providing* the fraternity of this jurisdiction shall subscribe for 300 copies of the same, at an advance of fifty cents per copy upon actual cost. The price per copy not to exceed two dollars; 300 copies to be retained in library of the Grand □ for future use.

Resolution adopted.

P∴ G∴ M∴ Van Deren offered the following:

Resolved, That Section 32 of the By-Laws pertaining to □, be amended by striking out the word "six" in the fourth line and inserting the word "twelve" in lieu thereof.

Resolution adopted.

P∴ D∴ G∴ M∴ Sagendorf moved to amend Section 7 of the By-Laws by inserting after the word "for," at the end of the first line, the word "non-contributing."   Motion concurred in.

J∴ G∴ W∴ Anthony offered the following:

Resolved, That the W∴ M∴ and Wardens representing the several subordinate □, in this Grand □, be instructed to wear their jewels of office of their respective □, in all future attendance upon this body.

Resolution adopted.

28

Bro. Wisebart moved that the W∴ M∴ of each subordinate ▢ be appointed a committee to solicit subscriptions, to be forwarded to the Grand Secretary, for the purpose of procuring suitable Grand ▢ jewels. Motion concurred in.

The following communication was read:

MASONIC HALL, CENTRAL CITY, }
September 30, A. D. 1868, A. L. 5868. }

To the M∴ W∴ Grand ▢ of Colorado :

At the last regular meeting of Chivington ▢ No. 6, and Central City Chapter No. 1, it was

Resolved, That the use of the hall be tendered to the M∴ W∴ Grand ▢ of Colorado, for the purpose of holding its Annual Communication in October.

Fraternally,
S. I. LORAH,
Secretary of ▢ and Chapter.

Communication received, and ordered printed with the proceedings.

Bro. Wisebart offered the following :

Resolved, That all property not strictly private, belonging to Germania ▢, U. D., be given to the ▢ of Denver; and that of Valmont ▢, U. D., to Columbia ▢ No. 14.

Resolution adopted.

J∴ G∴ W∴ Anthony offered the following :

Resolved, That the thanks of this Grand ▢ be, and the same are hereby tendered to Central ▢ No. 6, and Central City Chapter No. 1, for the free use of their hall for this body.

Resolution adopted.

D∴ G∴ M∴ Whittemore moved that the resolution relative to the loaning the library fund, adopted at the last Annual Communication, be continued until otherwise ordered.

Motion concurred in.

S∴ G∴ W∴ Jones presented the following, which was read, and on motion, was received and adopted :

To the M∴ W∴ Grand ▢ of Colorado :

Your committee, to whom was referred the report and accounts of the Grand Secretary, respectfully report that they have examined the same, and find them correct.

Fraternally submitted,
A. M. JONES, } *Committee.*
JAMES KELLY, }

The committee on Finance, Mileage and Per Diem, presented the following report, which was read, and, on motion, received and adopted:

To the M∴ W∴ Grand ☐ of Colorado:
Your committee on Finance, Mileage and Per Diem, beg leave to report
the following brethren entitled to the amount set opposite their names:

NAMES.	Miles traveled.	Attendance days.	Amount
M∴ W∴ H. M. Teller, G∴ M∴	...	2	$ 4 00
M∴ W∴ A. J. Van Deren, P∴ G∴ M∴	...	2	4 00
M∴ W∴ A. Mason, P∴ G∴ M∴	30	2	7 75
R∴ W∴ O. A. Whittemore, D∴ G∴ M∴	80	2	14 00
R∴ W∴ A. Sagendorf, P∴ D∴ G∴ M∴	80	2	14 00
R∴ W∴ A. M. Jones, S∴ G∴ W∴	2	2	4 25
R∴ W∴ W. D. Anthony, J∴ G∴ W∴	80	2	14 00
R∴ W∴ R. Sopris, Grand Treasurer	80	2	14 00
R∴ W∴ Ed. C. Parmelee, Grand Secretary	40	2	9 00
Bro. J. Kelly, W∴ M∴, No. 1	50	2	10 25
Bro. J. F. Phillips, W∴ M∴, No. 4	2	2	4 25
Bro. L. N. Greenleaf, W∴ M∴, No. 5	80	2	14 00
Bro. B. W. Wisebart, W∴ M∴, No. 6	...	2	4 00
Bro. G. C. Munson, proxy, W∴ M∴, No. 8	30	2	7 75
Bro. H. M. Orahood, W∴ M∴, No. 11	2	2	4 25
Bro. Matt. France, proxy, W∴ M∴, No. 12	40	2	9 00
Bro. W. T. Potter, proxy, W∴ M∴, No. 14	56	2	11 00

Your committee would also recommend that as Union ☐ No. 7 has no
representative who draws pay, that the S∴ W∴ of said ☐ be allowed mileage and one day's attendance, amounting to $12.

Fraternally submitted,
J. F. PHILLIPS, }
W. D. ANTHONY, } *Committee.*
MATT. FRANCE, }

P∴ G∴ M∴ Van Deren offered the following:

Resolved, That a warrant be drawn on the Treasurer for ten dollars in
favor of Bro. N. D. Haskell, for services as Tyler, and a warrant for one
hundred dollars in favor of Ed. C. Parmelee, for services as Grand Secretary.

Resolution adopted.

The M∴ W∴ Grand Master announced the following as the
appointed officers for the ensuing Masonic year:

Bro. Rev. H. B. HITCHINGS, R∴ W∴ Grand Chaplain.
Bro. L. N. GREENLEAF, R∴ W∴ Grand Orator.
Bro. H. M. ORAHOOD, R∴ W∴ Grand Lecturer.
Bro. FRANK HALL, R∴ W∴ Grand Marshal.
Bro. JAMES KELLY, W∴ Senior Grand Deacon.

Bro. G. C. MUNSON, W∴ Junior Grand Deacon.

Bro. E. T. STONE, W∴ Grand Sword Bearer.

Bro. J. F. PHILLIPS, }
Bro. W. W. WARE,   } Grand Stewards.

Bro. J. L. BAILEY, Grand Tyler.

P∴ G∴ M∴ Mason, assisted by R∴ W∴ Hal Sayr, Grand Marshal, then installed the M∴ W∴ Grand Master-elect, who installed the other elective and appointed officers, who assumed their respective stations.

The Grand ▭ was then called from labor to refreshment, to meet at 2 o'clock P. M.

TUESDAY, 2 o'clock P. M.

Grand ▭ resumed labor, officers and members present as at morning session.

M∴ W∴ Grand Master announced the following committees:

On Jurisprudence.—P∴ G∴ M∴ A. J. Van Deren, P∴ G∴ M∴ A. Mason, P∴ D∴ G∴ M∴ O. A. Whittemore.

On Foreign Correspondence.—Bro. Hal Sayr, P∴ G∴ M∴ A. Mason, J∴ G∴ W∴ W. D. Anthony.

The minutes were then read and approved, when this Annual Communication of the Most Ancient and Honorable Fraternity of F. and A. M. of Colorado, was closed in ample form.

ED. C. PARMELEE, *Grand Secretary.*

RETURNS OF LODGES.

GOLDEN CITY □ NO. 1.

Time of meetings: first and third Saturdays of each month.

OFFICERS.

James Kelly, W. M.
G. N. Belcher, S. W.
C. C. Carpenter, J. W.

F. O. Sawin, Treasurer,
M. C. Kirby, Secretary,
M. L. Sawin, S. D.
J. C. Remington, J. D.

P. L. Smith, S. S.
W. J. Cram, J. S.
D. E. Harrison, Tyler.

MEMBERS.

William Ashley,
Reuben Borton,
S. M. Breath,
J. C. Bowles,
Stephen Bailey,
H. M. Bussell,
J. D. Carnes,
N. F. Cheesman,
Geo. M. Chilcott,
John Churches,
S. C. Clinton,
Felix Crocker,
Lewis Davis,
D. G. Dargin,
Fox Diefendorf,
John H. Durham,

E. L. Eggers,
Peter Eskins,
Ephram Fellows,
J. M. Ferrell,
L. W. Frary,
T. B. Gardner,
J. R. Gilbert,
Arthur C. Harris,
John B. Hendry,
Wm. Howell,
John Kean,
John F. Kirby,
J. B. Langdon,
W. A. H. Loveland,
J. S. Maynard,
John A. Moore,
Geo. Morrison,

Daniel McClary,
W. R. Nelson,
Martin Opal,
A. P. Patten,
J. H. Pinkerton,
Perry P. Pollock,
W. D. Ripley,
James S. Scott,
John Sexton,
Samuel F. Shaffer,
Abram Slater,
E. B. Smith,
Henry Stephens,
John Strouse,
Owen Williams,
S. B. Williams.

FELLOWCRAFTS.

Wesley Teter,   Geo. W. Reaves.

ENTERED APPRENTICES.

J. A. Bartholomew,
Washington Jones,
M. H. Knapp,
Allen Lewis,

Leon Mallet,
John H. Myers,
Joseph Parrott,

Barney Pratt,
Thomas Shenden,
A. M. Wallingford,
Bruce Woodward.

DIMITTED.

Eli Carter,   George C. Peck.

SUMMIT □ NO. 2.

Charter surrendered.

ROCKY MOUNTAIN □ NO. 3.
Extinct.

NEVADA □ NO. 4.

Time of meetings: second and fourth Saturdays of each month.

OFFICERS.

John F. Phillips, W. M. B. C. Waterman, Treas. Jos. Standley, S. S.
O. T. Sparks, S. W.   J. W. Ratliff, Secretary, Albert Price, J. S.
Thos. H. Craven, J. W.   D. A. Hamor, S. D.   B. W. Eussen, Tyler.
                         Wm. Emperor, J. D.

PAST MASTERS.

A. J. Van Deren, P.G.M.   A. M. Jones, S. G. W.   J. W. Ratliff.

MEMBERS.

P. Anderson,   Geo. H. Barrett,   Jas. W. Stanton,
Wm. F. Avery,   John E. Craine,   John E. Gregg,
John M. Aldrich,   Joseph Codling,   Robert Hughes,
A. J. Biggs,   Edward Crockett,   Fred. J. Hibbard,
Wm. H. Belcher,   Jas. C. Donnelly,   Wm. Hyndman,
Jas. Baxter,   Otto Eckhart,   I. N. Henry,
Silas G. Brown,   D. L. Fairchilds,   John Hatswell,
Wm. H. Jester,   E. B. Newman,   Wm. H. James,
James Jones,   Thomas Newlun,   Preston Scott,
Perry A. Kline,   Andrew Nickolls,   B. F. Schaffer,
Cyrus A. Lyon,   Dennis O'Brien,   Isaac Sands,
A. L. Miller,   Geo. W. Pepper,   Horace Shaw,
A. C. McGeath,   Wm. D. Perkins,   Walter Scott,
Robert Millikin,   B. F. Pease,   Wm. R. Uren,
Geo. Marshall,   A. C. Rupe,   Cornelius Visscher,
Orlando North,   Thomas Woodward.

FELLOWCRAFTS.

Chas. Alber,   Thos. J. Ashton,   C. H. Merrill.
                      Francis Jeffrey,

ENTERED APPRENTICES.

Geo. W. Brock,   Wm. L. Ireland,   M. Symonds,
James Huff,   G. W. Miller,   B. R. Walls.
                      Wm. McFeeters,

DIMITTED.

J. A. Burdick,   Theo. Haswell,   H. K. Pearson,
Jas. C. Bradley,   O. H. Henry,   John C. Russell,
Samuel Butler,   Joshua Jennings,   F. T. Sherman,
T. H. Clewell,   T. J. Johns,   J. F. Spaulding.
                      David Lees,

DENVER ⸗ NO. 5.

Time of meetings: first and third Saturdays of each month.

OFFICERS.

L. N. Greenleaf, W. M.   F. A. McDonald, Treas.   Joseph Kline, S. S.
J. W. Webster, S. W.   J. L. Bartels, Sec.   W. Londoner, J. S.
Samuel Mitchell, J. W.   S. H. Bowman, S. D.   A Davidson, Tyler.
                           W. E. Turner, J. D.

MEMBERS.

Thos. P. Ames,   Wm. N. Byers,   Julius Berry,
Wm. D. Arnett,   A. H. Barker,   F. R. Bennett,
A. O. Ashley,   J. M. Brodwell,   N. A. Baker,
Moses Auker,   Geo. H. Bryant,   G. G. Brewer,
J. S. Addleman,   Bernard Berry,   Chas. A. Cook.
E. W. Cobb,   J. S. Howell,   David Parlin,
F. A. Clark, P. M.   B. C. Hayman,   N. H. Rice,
Geo. T. Clark,   Geo. W. Hertel,   E. E. Ropes,
W. S. Cheesman,   H. Hitchins,   H. J. Rogers,
Robt. Cleveland,   Jas. H. Hodges,   W. D. Robinson,
J. C. Carter,   J. M. Holland,   B. W. Rogers,
H. S. Clark,   Chas. L. Hall,   Wm. M. Slaughter,
J. C. Casey,   Warren Hussey,   J. J. Saville,
Jas. Clellan,   R. L. Hatten,   H. Z. Solomon,
John L. Dailey,   Moses Hallet,   Edwin Scudder,
Wm. N. Dailey,   Clinton Himelaugh,   M. B. Sherwood,
J. C. Davidson,   C. J. Hart,   Wm. Stepp,
F. M. Durkee,   E. Hexter,   Geo. L. Shoup,
J. H. Dudley,   E. H. Jewett,   W. W. Slaughter,
J. W. Douglass,   Theron Johnson,   Daniel Sheets,
Joseph Davis,   Geo. W. Kassler,   A. Schinner,
B. F. Downen,   Wm. M. Keith,   Fred. Schirmer,
M. Deitsch,   E. W. Kingsbury,   Andrew Slane,
J. H. Eames,   J. Kershaw,   A. Sagendorf, P. M.
Wm. R. Ford,   G. K. Kimball,   R. Sopris, P. M.
H. F. Ford,   Henry Kline,   Geo. Tritch,
H. Feuerstein,   John B. Lamber,   W. J. Thompson,
H. H. Failing,   Joseph Lamber,   S. W. Treat,
Isaac Freund,   Reuben P. Lamb,   P. Trounstein,
John H. Gerrish,   J. E. Le Cavalier,   H. B. Tuttle,
A. Goldsmith,   Foster Meserve,   John Wanless,
C. J. Goss,   Jas McNassar, Sr.   G. W. Webster,
Geo. H. Greenslit,   Alvin McCune,   F. R. Wagoner,
J. E. Gates,   Julius Mitchell,   S. T. Wells,
A. Hananer,   G. L. Moody,   J. T. Yonkers.
                           R. O. Old,

FELLOWCRAFTS.

H. H. Ellis,   C. F. Parkhurst,   J. W. Richards.

ENTERED APPRENTICES.

John E. Bush,   J. W. Kerr,   Wm. Nolan,
H. B. Chamberlain,   Geo. N. Lowe,   J. M. Tallman,
W. H. Evans,   Peter A. Leyner,   John Upton,
John Good,   S. McClellan,   Chas. S. Wheeler.
                           J. Mohlsen,

DIMITTED.

A. P. Allen,	J. W. Diedenbach,	J. W. Huntington,
A. Bartlett,	H. H. Gillett,	I. H. Kaster,
C. L. Bartlett,	Geo. Gillett,	N. Thede,
Charles Blake,	W. H. Grafton,	J. H. Voorhies.

CHIVINGTON ☐ NO. 6, CENTRAL CITY.

Time of meetings: second and fourth Wednesdays of each month.

OFFICERS.

B. W. Wisebart, W. M.	J. R. Cleaveland, Treas.	W. H. Nichols, S. S.
Hal. Sayr, S. W.	S. I. Lorah, Sec'y.	Jas. Hutchinson, J. S.
E. C. Beach, J. W.	F. M. Danielson, S. D.	N. D. Haskell, Tyler.
	W. F. Sears, J. D.	

MEMBERS.

J. N. Adams,	D. S. Green,	V. W. McCory,
W. Aitcheson,	E. Garrott,	P. M. Martin,
W. A. Amsbary,	J. Y. Glendinen, P. M.	Samuel Moore,
Wm. F. Allen,	R. Hutchins,	Geo. Mellor,
Geo. H. Adams,	N. B. Holloway,	H. H. Miller,
E. H. Brown,	O. H. Harker,	N. H. McCall,
E. H. Beals,	Frank Hall,	A. McNamee,
Thos. Barnes,	Chas. L. Hill,	J. P. McAvoy,
Isaac B. Brunell,	Richard Harvey,	G. G. Norton,
B. R. S. Bachtell,	Henry Hartman,	T. D. Nash,
S. A. Buell,	C. A. Hoyt,	J. L. Pritchard,
Geo. W. Brewer,	Thos. J. Hart,	Geo. A. Pugh,
John Best,	V. F. Inskeep,	Ed. C. Parmelee,
Hugh Butler,	A. Jacobs,	Wm. P. Pollock,
James Clark,	H. A. Johnson,	C. W. Pollard,
J. B. Cofield,	W. C. M. Jones,	Thos. J. Potter,
D. C. Collier,	Wm. Jones,	A. G. Raynor,
Jos. Coleman,	E. Paul Jones,	John M. Rank,
W. P. Caldwell,	Wm. J. Joblin,	Antonio Ramos,
L. W. Chase, P. M.	C. W. Johnson,	A. N. Rogers,
G. B. Cornell,	David Kline,	G. B. Reed,
W. Z. Cozens,	H. J. Kruse,	D. M. Richards,
N. Z. Cozens,	John Kip,	Wm. B. Squires,
A. S. Cobb,	J. H. Kinney,	A. M. Studer,
H. A. Clough,	Benj. Lake,	E. B. Stillings,
A. B. Davis,	R. C. Lake,	H. F. Sawyer,
P. H. Dunnegan,	H. N. Lynch,	E. W. Sinclair,
J. J. Dunnegan,	Oscar Lewis,	Clark A. Smith,
Wm. T. Ellis,	Jacob Mack,	H. M. Teller, P. M. and
H. R. Eldred,	Philip McGren,	G. M.
E. L. Gardner,	J. G. Mahany,	S. F. Tappan,
Basil Green,	Thos. Mullen,	M. Thomas.
Geo. J. Tracy,	Jas. T. White, P. M.	Geo. E. Wilson,
L. C. Tolles,	L. B. Weil,	Geo. B. Walker,
B. T. Vincent,	H. J. Weil,	Robert Woods,
E. J. Vance,	J. Weidman,	I. N. Wilcoxin,
Allyn Weston, P. M.	M. C. Wythe,	C. C. Welch,
Wm. Watson,	A. H. Whitehead.	J. B. Zerbe.

FELLOWCRAFT.
David D. Lake.

ENTERED APPRENTICES.

J. C. Bruce,	J. S. Ewers,	A. Schonecker,
D. T. Beals,	Wm. Humphrey,	N. L. Sibley,
J. W. Cooper,	H. J. Hawley,	J. W. Wilson,
David Ettien,	H. C. Palmeter,	C. J. Whitaker.

DIMITTED.

A. E. Buckmiller,	Geo. W. Jacobs,	Geo. Schram,
G. W. Buchanan,	J. C. McClellan,	D. Tooker,
Bela S. Buell,	D. J. Martin,	Geo. E. Thornton,
H. O. Basford,	J. S. McLane,	H. A. Woods,
Matt. France,	Wm. Rosenfield,	J. W. Watson.
	James H. Reed,	

DIED.
J. K. Rutledge.

Name changed to Central □.

UNION □ NO. 7, DENVER.

Time of meetings: second and fourth Saturdays of each month.

OFFICERS.

W. D. Anthony, W. M.	E. G. Matthews, Sec.	H. B. Hitchings, Chap.
C. J. Clarke, S. W.	Rodney Curtis, S. D.	Geo. N. Billings, S. S.
L. B. France, J. W.	J. L. Bailey, J. D.	C. C. Davis, J. S.
Frank Palmer, Treas.		R. Sopris, Tyler.

MEMBERS.

J. C. Anderson,	John Evans,	C. C. McLenore,
Eli M. Ashley, P. M.	R. W. Fairbanks,	W. D. Pease,
Francis R. Bill,	Redwood Fisher,	John Pierce,
J. Sidney Brown,	J. H. Goodspeed,	H. L. Pitzer,
H. L. Bailey,	Henry Henson,	Wm. S. Peabody,
D. A. Chever,	H. B. Haskell,	E. M. Quinby,
J. M. Chivington, P.G.M.	B. F. Houx,	Hugo Richards,
C. C. Clements,	M. L. Horr,	Chas. Ruter,
Langdon Clark,	H. M. Harrington,	M. A. Rogers,
John Chamard,	Jay J. Johnson,	F. Z. Solomon,
E. H Collins,	Luther Kountze,	Alfred Sayre,
W. S. Collins,	Chas. B. Kountze,	Milo H. Slater,
D. C. Corbin,	Henry C. Leach,	Geo. B. Stimpson,
A. Cunningham,	Julius Londoner,	J. M. Strickler,
Geo. E. Crater,	C. J. Mahar,	N. W. Welton,
David J. Cook,	J. A. McFadden,	Geo. Williams,
Chas. Donnelly,	Elisha Millison,	O. H. Whittier,
Jacob Downing,	G. H. Mills,	S. S. Woodbury,
Jonas Deitsch,	H. D. Mosher,	O. A. Whittemore, P. M.
Isadore Deitsch,	Louden Mullin,	Daniel Witter,
S. H. Elbert, P. M.	John H. Martin,	Peter Winne.

29

FELLOWCRAFT.

W. W. Roberts.

ENTERED APPRENTICES.

Alex. W. Atkins,   Harry G. Elder,   Luther Wilson,
I. H. Chandler,   Jonas C. Higley,   D. P. Wilson,
I. L. Craft,   F. D. Hetrich,   Geo. F. Wanless.
          G. McKee,

DIMITTED.

John E. Stewart,   O. A. Willard.

EMPIRE ☐ NO. 8, EMPIRE.

Time of meetings: first and third Saturdays of each month.

OFFICERS.

H. A. Haskin, W. M.   John Collom, Treas.   E. C. Westcoat, S. D.
Geo. C. Munson, S. W.   Tyler Disbrow, Sec.   Elijah Bently, J. D.
Henry Nutt, J. W.   .   C. H. Aylesworth, Tyler.

MEMBERS.

F. L. Andre,   Albert O. Griggs,   Jas. W. Martin,
S. P. Allen,   J. P. Haskins,   Jas. H. Osborn,
David J. Ball,   Edward James,   Geo. Richardson,
A. S. Carpenter,   Charles King,   Wm. L. Sawtell,
Jas. P. Davis,   Benj. Kerr,   John Slawson,
J. W. Drips,   Joseph A. Love,   Geo. A. Smith,
Don C. Dailey,   A. Mason, P. M.   Robert H. Taylor,
Edgar Freeman,   Cornelius Wilkins.

DIMITTED.

John S. Jones,   Francis M. Scott,   Jothan M. Smith.

MONTANA ☐ NO 9, VIRGINIA CITY.

Now Montana ☐ No. 2, under jurisdiction of M∴ W∴ Grand ☐ of Montana.

HELENA CITY ☐ NO. 10, HELENA CITY.

Now Helena ☐ NO. 3, under the jurisdiction of M∴ W∴ Grand ☐ of Montana.

BLACK HAWK ☐ NO. 11, BLACK HAWK.

Time of meetings: first and third Saturdays of each month.

OFFICERS.

H. M. Orahood, W. M.   Alonzo Smith, Treas.   Robert Frazer, S. S.
J. W. Nesmith, S. W.   D. D. Leach, Sec'y.   W. H. Richardson, J. D.
J. N. Crawford, J. W.   John Boylan. S. D.   W. G. Fairhurst, Tyler.
          E. E. Hanchet, J. D.

MEMBERS.

Chas. S. Abbott,
Ira C. Barkhurst,
E. K. Baker,
Robert Busby,
James Fisher,
Samuel Farver,
John P. Folley,
H. H. Farnum, Jr.
A. F. Hoppe,
H. H. Heiser,
S. Hutchinson,
F. B. Hurlbut,
Ed. C. Hughes,
Stephen Johns,
James Loughran,

S. H. Bradley,
R. A. Clark,
Geo. Cassels,
Robert Cameron,
Z. Myers,
Wm. McLaughlin,
John H. Miller,
James Mills,
R. W. Mosely,
J. H. Parsons,
Geo. S. Parmelee,
John W. Ritchie,
F. A. Rudolph,
Jas. H. Riley,
Wm. H. Studer,
John D. Smails,

H. P. Cowenhoven,
Geo. E. Congdon,
Wm. F. Eberlin,
Thomas Entwistle,
John Simmons,
Jacob Tallman,
J. S. Taylor,
Wm. H. Vernon,
Chase Withrow, P. M.
 and P. G. M.
J. E. Wertzebach,
Benj. Woodbury,
Eugene Wilder,
J. D. Westover,
D. P. Woodruff.

ENTERED APPRENTICES.

Wm. N. Dickerson,   N. F. Spicer.

DIMITTED.

R. L. Palmer,   T. R. Smith.

WASHINGTON □ NO. 12, GEORGETOWN.

Time of meetings: second and fourth Saturdays of each month.

OFFICERS.

Jairus W. Hall, W. M.
W. Wm. Ware, S. W.
David Lees, J. W.

H. K. Pearson, Treas.
Matt. France, Sec'y.

Jas. A. Burdick, S. D.
H. C. Chapin, J. D.
Jas. D. Allen, Tyler.

MEMBERS.

Wm. Barton,
C. W. Bramel,
E. E. Burlingame,
G. W. Buchanan,
A. W. Brownell,
F. F. Brune,
A. F. Curtis,
Alexander Cree,
Adam D. Cooper,
B. F. Darrah,

W. S. Downing,
D. O. Darnell,
E. R. Evans,
A. C. Fellows,
Dennis Faivre,
D. W. Glaze,
W. H. Henderson,
J. R. Hambel,
W. N. Hutchinson,
Demetrius Hill,
Albert Johnson,

F. C. Johnson,
John Murley,
M. P. Parker,
Daniel Roberts,
David T. Rigsby,
J. M. Smith,
D. Tooker,
Geo. E. Thornton,
Samuel Todd,
J. W. Watson.

FELLOWCRAFTS.

Wm. Burris,   C. W. Dennison,   Austin B. Rae.

ENTERED APPRENTICES.

John Fillins,
Conrad Hansen,
Geo. L. Sites,

L. F. Zates.

DIMITTED.

Andrew Mason, P. M.

EL PASO □ NO. 13, COLORADO CITY.

Time of meetings: second and fourth Saturdays of each month.

OFFICERS.

E. T. Stone, W. M.
B. C. Crowell, S. W.
S. M. Buzzard, J. W.

C. W. Myers, Treas.
E. S. Randall, Sec.
C. T. Judd, S. D.
A. Bott, J. D.

John Love, S. S.
T. T. Young, J. S.
James Roberts, Tyler.

MEMBERS.

O. M. Bryant,
G. A. Bryant,
J. C. Brown,
C. C. Burt,
M. M. Craig,
T. Gerton,
E. C. Gherung,
Emile Gherung,

Z. Gill,
B. S. Hall,
J. W. Iron,
A. G. Lincoln,
Solon Mason,
Aaron Mason,
B. C. Myers,
James McGee,

John Pisdirez,
James Rime,
S. R. Roberts,
Wm. Sweetland,
E. A. Smith,
Henry White,
J. C. Woodbury,
J. Weir.

FELLOWCRAFT.

Levi Van Schyock.

ENTERED APPRENTICE.

D. C. Guire.

DIMITTED.

G. B. Frazier,
R. J. Frazier,

W. H. McClure,
J. M. Noble,

Chas. Pauls,
E. A. Stafford.

COLUMBIA □ NO. 14, COLUMBIA CITY.

Time of meetings: second and fourth Thursdays of each month.

OFFICERS.

T. Haswell, W. M.
W. T. Potter, S. W.
O. H. Henry, J. W.

Abram Mills, Treas.
Henry Paul, Sec.
Wm. C. Slater, S. D.
J. A. Stanton, J. D.

Henry Green, S. S.
W. Sommer, J. S.
A. E. Berger, Tyler.

MEMBERS.

E. H. Andrews,
W. R. Blore,
Geo. W. Carter,

Geo. D. Cook,
W. A. Carson,
T. J. Johns,
E. P. McClure,

L. McIntosh,
M. G. Smith,
J. W. Wigginton.

FELLOWCRAFTS.

John Davis,

A. W. Peters,

W. H. Smith.

ENTERED APPRENTICE.

Amos Bixby.

DIMITTED.

T. McCleary,   B. F. Slaughter.

DIED.

E. F. Mason.

Location of □ changed to Boulder City, Boulder County.

CANON ☐ U. D. CANON CITY.

Time of meetings : first and third Fridays of each month.

OFFICERS.

G. B. Frazier, W. M.   W. H. McClure, Treas.   H. H. Marsh, S. S.
B. F. Smith, S. W.   W. R. Fowler, Sec.   B. F. Rockyfellow, J. S.
Stephen Frazier, J. W.   R. J. Frazier, S. D.   G. W. Depp, Tyler.
                           Charles Pauls, J. D.

MEMBERS.

N. M. Burroug s,   H. J. Frazier,   Aug. Sartor,
S. M. Cox,   h   Lewis Jones,   W. H. Thompson,
M. Mills Craig,   B. F. Moore,   H. C. Vaughn,
J. H. Depp,.   J. H. Nelson,   S. D. Webster,
Henry Dunn,   Geo. T. Phillips,   S. R. West.
                        John Ritchie,

ENTERED APPRENTICES.

A. T. Seabring,   Jas. A. McCanlas.

Chartered as Mount Moriah ☐ No. 15.

PUEBLO ☐ U. D., PUEBLO.

Time of meetings : second and fourth Wednesdays of each month.

OFFICERS.

C. J. Hart, W. M.   F. R. Donnelly, Treas.   P. R. Thombs, S. D.
A. Bartlett, S. W.   J. D. Miller, Sec.   L. R. Graves, J. D.
P. Craig,, J. W.   R. N. Daniels, Tyler.

MEMBERS.

M. Anker,   C. C. Burt,   J. W. O. Snyder,
D. B. Berry,   D. G. Gallatin,   J. J. Thomas,
M. Beshoar,   E. F. Stafford,   R. T. Warrant.

FELLOWCRAFT.

W. Keeling.

ENTERED APPRENTICES.

H. Matzdorff,   James J. Nolan,   F. Spilleke.
                     H. O. Rettberg,

Chartered as No. 17.

CHEYENNE ☐ U. D., CHEYENNE.

Time of meetings : first and third Saturdays of each month.

OFFICERS.

J. S. Scott, W. M.   L. B. Weil, Treas.   Orlando North, S. D.
J. E. Gates, S. W.   S. J. Scriber, Sec.   W. D. Robinson, J. D.
Jay J. Johnson, J. W.   J. H. Hayford, Tyler.

MEMBERS.

N. A. Baker,	John Harper,	David Shackman,
A. C. Beckwith,	T. J. Johns,	R. W. Twiet,
N. K. Boswell,	H. P. Jussen,	J. H. Voorheis,
E. B. Carling,	W. D. Pease,	A. Walters,
C. H. Collins,	W. W. Slaughter,	Geo. Williams.

Chartered as No. 16.

VALMONT □, VALMONT.

Time of meetings: first and third Saturdays of each month.

OFFICERS.

D. E. Sutherland, W. M.	H. H. Jacobs, Sec.	A. P. Allen, Chap.
John W. Ritchie, S. W.	H. W. Allen, S. D.	Henry Grace, S. S.
H. R. Eldred, J. W.	David Parlen, J. D.	Wm. Howell, J. S
Wm. M. Barney, Treas.		T. J. Jones, Tyler.

MEMBERS.

W. W. Baldwin,	C. H. Gardner,	S. Peck,
Freeman Belcher,	P. D. Goss,	Wm. Shepherd,
E. J. Coffman,	H. E. Hurlbut,	E. G. Slifer,
Robert Florman,	Abram Lemmex,	G. W. Webster,
	David Nickels,	

ENTERED APPRENTICES.

A. S. Lewis,   Oscar Pears.

Dispensation surrendered.;

GERMANIA □ U. D., DENVER.

Time of meetings: first and third Mondays of each month.

OFFICERS.

Sam. H. Elbert, W. M.	H. Feuerstine, Treas.	P. Zehner, S. S.
J. E. Wurtzebach, S. W.	F. Schirmer, Sec.	Wm. Barth, J. S.
Julius L. Bartels, J. W.	Jos. Klein, S. D.	R. Sopris, Tyler.
	Julius Mitchell, J. D.	

MEMBERS.

F. A. Brocker,	Peter Fischer,	C. F. Leimer,
J. Q. Charles,	Peter Gottesleben,	Conrad Walbrach.
	H. H. T. Grill,	

ENTERED APPRENTICES

John C. Kaufmann,   Wm. Vanenderb.

Dispensation surrendered.

TABULAR STATEMENT

OF THE WORK OF THE SEVERAL ⟨⟩ SUBORDINATE TO THE GRAND LODGE OF COLORADO, FOR THE YEAR ENDING SEPTEMBER 26TH, A. D 1868, A. L. 5868, SHOWING THE ENTIRE MEMBERSHIP OF THE TERRITORY.

No. of Lodge,	LODGE.	Affiliated.	Initiated	Passed	Raised	Dimitted.	Died.	Suspended.	Expelled.	Reinstated.	Rejected.	Living out of Territory.	No. of Members.	No. of F. C.	No. of E. A.
1	Golden City	1	2	3	3	2	...	...	...	...	...	24	60	2	11
4	Nevada	...	4	4	3	13	...	...	...	...	2	20	59	4	7
5	Denver	3	8	6	4	12	..	...	...	...	5	31	116	3	13
6	Chivington	1	7	6	5	16	1	...	...	...	9	26	123	1	12
7	Union.	3	11	9	8	2	...	...	...	...	8	9	73	1	10
8	Empire	...	7	7	7	3	...	...	...	...	...	3	31	...	...
11	Black Hawk	3	6	8	10	2	...	...	...	...	10	8	55	...	2
12	Washington	7	26	23	20	1	...	...	...	...	11	8	39	3	4
13	El Paso	1	3	2	3	6	...	...	...	...	3	......	34	1	1
14	Columbia	...	3	7	6	2	1	...	...	...	1	6	20	3	1
U. D.	Canon	...	12	10	10	...	...	...	...	...	1	......	26	...	2
U. D.	Cheyenne	...	3	3	3	...	...	...	...	...	...	......	23	...	...
U. D.	Pueblo	...	8	4	4	...	...	...	...	...	4	2	17	...	4
U. D.	Valmont	...	4	2	2	...	...	...	...	...	1	2	24	...	2
U. D.	Germania	...	8	6	6	...	...	...	...	...	2	......	17	...	2
	Total	19	112	100	94	50	2	...	...	...	57	134	717	18	71
	Total last year	24	92	88	92	30	2	...	...	...	74	118	582	...	...
	Increase	...	......	......	...	...	...	...	..	...	...	......	135	...	...

REPORT

ON

MASONIC CORRESPONDENCE.

—◦◦◦◦—

To the M∴ W∴ Grand ▢ of Colorado, A., F. and A. M.:

Your committee, appointed at the last annual communication of this Grand ▢, respectfully present the subjoined report of their pleasant rambles through the ever blooming and richly fruitful fields of Masonic periodical literature.

The review herewith presented embraces only such matters as were esteemed most worthy of being reproduced for the instruction of our craftsmen whose Masonic experience has been acquired in a limited jurisdiction, and a few cases of brief analysis. The committee has met with no little embarrassment in perfecting the delicate culling process they have been called to perform. The field is so broad, so replete with eloquent and noble thoughts, so freighted with Masonic learning and essential instruction, as to render the work of concentration extremely difficult. The custom which is universally accepted, of submitting in alphabetical order with more or less elaborateness of review, the annual transactions of the various Grand ▢ whose chronicles have been received, is fixed upon for obvious reasons, the chief of which is the vast amount of statistical intelligence derived from it. Want of funds has hitherto obliged us to circumscribe the volume of our annual publications to the smallest possible compass. Recognizing this unfortunate condition of our financial affairs, your committee have been governed by considerations of economy in their treatment of those subjects which comprise this report, and have endeavored to comprehend as much information as possible within the space allotted them.

Proceedings have been received from the following named jurisdictions, which, for the sake of convenience, are arranged in tabular form, covering name, date of annual communication, membership, etc., etc., so far as the same can be ascertained:

30

TABLE OF STATISTICS.

GRAND LODGES.	Date of Communication	Members.	Initiations.	Rejections.	Deaths.	Suspensions.	Expulsions.	No. of Lodges.	Receipts.
Arkansas	Nov. 4, 1867	6784	817	......	135	71	2	216	$4264 20
Alabama	Dec, 2, 1867	9707	755	258	179	653	35	140	5358 00
California	Oct. 8, 1867	7500	850	259	125	5	4	152	16245 90
Canada	July 10, 1867	7000	1165	......	86	183	...	193	6923 86
Connecticut	May 8, 1867	10629	860	......	95	3	12	83	1783 5o
Delaware	June 27, 1867	868	97	24	5	5	...	17	228 00
District of Columbia	May 7, 1867	2288	523	176	26	1	1	16	4098 50
Georgia	Oct. 30, 1867	14164	961	299	153	584	...	262	13742 24
Illinois	Oct. 1, 1867	28184	4051	......	231	173	82	560	22622 75
Iowa	June 4, 1867	8468	1381	......	63	87	22	193	8411 80
*Idaho	Dec. 16, 1867	....	......	......	....	....	...	......	
Kansas	Oct. 15, 1867	2042	423	128	18	73	4	62	1310 75
Louisiana	Feb. 10, 1868	6711	767	......	193	2	6	117	7291 29
Maine	May 5, 1868	13001	1672	733	148	8	3	147	6431 28
Massachusetts	Dec. 11, 1867	17136	2285	......	....	....	...	......	
Maryland	Nov. 18, 1867	4387	207	......	24	......	6	57	5340 17
Michigan	Jan. 9, 1868	16861	2656	606	130	126	48	242	1206 65
†Minnesota	Oct. 22, 1867	....	......	......	....	....	...	......	
Missouri	Oct. 14, 1867	12500	2211	1178	175	113	53	250	11426 82
Mississippi	Jan. 20, 1868	8378	882	......	191	1804	18	213	12272 85
Montana	Oct. 7, 1867	355	96	40	1	......	5	12	854 00
Nebraska	June 19, 1867	595	140	54	6	8	1	15	316 60
Nevada	Sept. 17, 1867	705	155	77	7	20	2	10	2045 77
†New Brunswick	Jan. 22, 1868	....	......	......	....	....	...	......	
New Hampshire	Dec. 27, 1866	5005	805	......	....	......	...	66	4465 13
New Jersey	Jan. 16, 1867	5986	350	......	80	76	6	80	3844 00
New York	June 4, 1867	51331	7111	2478	558	53	56	542	62164 59
North Carolina	Dec. 2, 1867	9254	866	424	118	21	19	203	2701 25
Nova Scotia	June 21, 1867	....	......	......	....	....	...	17	408 12
Ohio	Oct. 15, 1867	20225	3260	......	....	....	...	355	124 20
Oregon	June 24, 1867	1099	144	88	7	26	6	38	2828 60
Rhode Island	June 25, 1867	2684	330	144	25	2	2	22	1212 62
South Carolina	Nov. 19, 1867	....	......	48	....	1	5	116	1418 00
Tennessee	Oct. 7, 1867	15790	2553	......	154	105	44	289	10991 10
Texas	June 8, 1868	....	......	......	....	....	...	73	
Virginia	Dec. 9, 1867	....	......	......	....	....	...	......	5667 01
Washington	Sept. 18, 1867	353	29	8	......	2	..	11	903 81
Wisconsin	June 11, 1867	7074	1232	597	53	63	12	154	4800 00

*Organized December 16, 1867.
†No statistics.

It is to be regretted that some of the Grand Secretaries have permitted their reports to be published unaccompanied with a statistical summary of their contents. In compiling the foregoing table great difficulty has been experienced in tracing out the information sought. It would seem to require but a slight effort for each Secretary to prepare a recapitulation of the facts referred to, and it would be of inestimable service to the various committees in making up their exhibits on correspondence. This department is becoming, we rejoice to say, one of the most important and interesting of our Masonic chronicles. Its good works are manifest, and appear to meet with thorough appreciation from the craft everywhere. As Masons, no less than as individuals, we have acquired an almost inordinate fondness for remarkable comparisons. Through the well-directed labors of these committees, we are enabled each year to review the progress of Masonry in the several States and Territories, ofttimes obtaining an enlarged conception of the glorious work as it flourishes among the enlightened nations of Europe, where many thousands of skillful operatives are employed upon our boundless Masonic temple. We compare them one with the other, and each with our own, and, inspired with the spirit of emulation, direct our energies to the elevation of our own order to the exalted station of the most deserving.

Our report covers the published transactions of thirty-eight Grand ☐. Several bulletins issued by the Grand Orient, of France, are also on the Secretary's table, but the committee being ignorant of the language in which they are printed, and having failed to obtain translations, have omitted them.

Asking your indulgence for the prolixity of our preliminary observations, we take up in the regular order of business the last annual register of the Grand ☐ of

ARKANSAS.

The twenty-ninth communication transpired on Monday, November 4, 1867, in the Masonic Temple at Little Rock, the capital of the State, Grand Master E. H. English presiding. Upon calling the roll of subordinate ☐, eighty responded through representatives. The address is a masterly production, full of lofty eloquence, profound Masonic precepts, and interesting historical truths. We regret that the want of space precludes the possibility of giving more than a hasty synopsis of this very able paper. Considerable attention is devoted to the favorite child of the brotherhood, "St. John's College," an institution founded by their charities and maintained by voluntary contributions. Its successful operation was seriously disturbed by the late war, but with the return of peace, efforts are being made to place it once more upon a firm footing, and by the inauguration of judicious educational systems, enable it to become one of the best schools of learning in the State. A new library, to replace the large and valuable one destroyed during the war, is in process of collection, as also a full complement of chemical, philosophical and astronomical apparata. For more than five years the college has been closed, but the light of education is again kindled within its walls, to burn, let us hope, through many peaceful, prosperous and happy generations.

Bro. English takes great pleasure in making the declaration that "the Masons of the North, rising above the passions and prejudices engendered by the late unhappy war, have sent bread into the South to feed her impoverished and starving families.

To this fund the Grand ☐ of New York alone contributed five thousand dollars. From this auspicious commencement, may we not confidently look for the early and complete restoration of our beloved union, through the benign influence of the ever-living tenets of our Masonic profession, "Brotherly love, relief and truth?" Their power is mightier than bayonets or conventional laws, their strength to reconstruct and save, more potent than the shock of battling armies. Between the Masons of the North and South there is no division. They stand now as they have ever stood, upon the same eternal principles, are governed by the same immutable laws. Through the soothing influence of fraternal exchanges, the storms of bat-' tle, and the wild frenzy of passion, excited by strife and confusion, are forgotten, and we meet now, as we have always met, upon the broad level of an indivisible union.

Among the laws of the Grand □ is one which prohibits subordinate □ from making By-Laws. A uniform code has been established, and by its wise provisions all minor bodies are controlled. Under this code a Master Mason may be a member of two or more □, provided he pays dues in each. The Grand Master has decided that " when a member of a □ joins in a petition for a new □, and a dispensation is granted, he becomes a member of the same, on payment of all dues to the □ of which he was a member at the time of signing. But if he be a *Warden* of the old □ when the dispensation is granted, he must remain a Warden until his term of office expires."

Referring to Masonic trials, Bro. English says : " I am aware of no power in the Worshipful Master of a □, a Deputy Grand Master, or the Grand Master himself, to set aside its judgment of expulsion, and proceed to try the accused *de novo*, on account of an error in the trial. The □ itself, may grant the expelled a new trial when the application is made in the proper time, if there are good grounds for it. But when no application is made for a new trial, or if made, refused, the only remedy left the expelled is an appeal to the Grand □."

During the current year no less than seventy-three members were tried on various charges, of whom seventy-one were suspended and two expelled.

Fourteen dispensations were granted for the formation of new □. It was decided in committee, whose report was adopted, that "after a non-affiliated Mason has applied for membership and been rejected, he had all the rights of Masonry in the □ except that of voting."

The report of the committee on Foreign Correspondence, prepared by Bro. Samuel W. Williams, is among the best received. Bro. Mason's address of that year is characterized as " short, and devoted to matters of a local character." The review covers one hundred and twenty-four closely printed pages, and is edited with rare ability.

The ballot for Grand Officers resulted in the re-election of E. H. English, Grand Master, and W. D. Blocher, Grand Secretary.

ALABAMA.

The forty-seventh annual communication of the Grand □ of Alabama began in the city of Montgomery, December 2, 1867, and continued in session four days. With one exception, a full complement of Grand Officers was present, and one hundred and forty □ represented. The address delivered by Grand Master Wilson Williams is sound, terse, and altogether sensible, conveying much valuable advice, and giving a number of important decisions. He acknowledges with expressions of gratitude, the receipt of contributions from the fraternity in all parts of the north, east and west, toward the relief of their destitute, whose substance had been destroyed by the war. The report of the Finance committee, to whom this part of the address was referred, shows the amount so received to be $3,511.55, giving the names of the persons and ☐ by whom remitted, and testifying their appreciation in the following noble words: " Just emerging from a long and disastrous civil strife, in which clouds and darkness were round about us, with the war echoes and their wail of woe still ringing in our ears, and longing for peace and tranquility, we gathered our clans of scattered craftsmen to comfort those that mourned, and give aid to the destitute; we could not give aid to the afflicted, for *they* mourned those that were not, and exhausted our means ere the work of relief was well begun. Thus, powerless to succor, the voice of cheer comes to us from our northern brethren—enemies in war, in peace, friends—and the hand of charity is extended to a fallen foe. They bid us welcome to their hearts, and give of their substance to relieve our necessities. We accept, with grateful hearts, the aid thus tendered, and in these acts of fraternal sympathy we recognize the influence of that noble tenet of our time-honored order—'Brotherly love, relief and truth.' By it the gulf of strife is bridged over, and we enter a land of peace and harmony, where our feet tread the sacred pavement of the ☐. Would that Masonry were universal; then would all enemies be subdued, and the nations learn war no more."

The Grand Master informs his ☐ that he has received numerous applications for dispensations to confer the degrees upon maimed persons, but in every case had refused to grant them. In opening his chapter of decisions he says: " It is a well established law of Masonry that everything that contravenes the moral law is a violation of Masonic law, and everything that effects the relation of man to God, his neighbor or himself, is the proper subject of ☐ jurisdiction and Masonic investigation." Also, " that when a Mason commits an offense against the moral and divine laws, the ☐ should not wait for the adjudication of such offense by any other tribunal, either church or state, but to investigate for itself, and dispose of it as justice may demand, regardless of what others may do or say."

Now, one and all acknowledge this to be true Masonic reasoning, yet there are men in every ☐—scores of them in every jurisdiction throughout the world—who live in open and notorious violation of its every principle. They are covered with Masonic crimes, and each day adds to the number; yet our lips are sealed, not a word of remonstrance is uttered, nor a step taken to prevent the hideous accumulation of sins. We throw open the doors of our ☐, take them to our bosoms, extend to them the right hand of fellowship upon the sacred floor of Masonry, and present them to our guests as worthy and upright men, upon whose hearts all the holy mysteries of our brotherhood are stamped in ineffaceable characters. Among the profane their conduct heaps obloquy upon the order, and among the good, the just and pure, spreads distrust and excites hostile criticism. Our precious creed is forgotten or ignored, all the solemn obligations which bind us together are trampled under foot, all the ennobling precepts taught in the

▢ thrown to the winds. Is it not time that we enforced our laws or abolished them?

Bro. Williams decides that when the W∴M∴ shall prefer charges against a brother he should not be allowed to preside at the trial, or appoint any person to supercede the Senior Warden, whose place is in the East. It has been held by prominent Masons in Colorodo that a member cannot legally be suspended from the rights of membership for the non-payment of ▢ dues. This, of course, depends entirely upon the local laws, but we find hundreds of suspensions for this cause upon the records of Grand ▢ throughout the United States.

Among the resolutions passed is one which authorizes the appointment of a special committee to inquire into, and report upon, the expediency of forming a Masonic Life Insurance Company, under the patronage and control of the Grand ▢. The committee were unable to submit a report during the session, and so recommended that the business be referred to a special commission, with instructions to present the result of their deliberations at the next Grand Communication. And why should not the proposition meet with universal favor? These insurance corporations are flourishing everywhere, amassing immense fortunes, and accomplishing a world of good. Why not adopt them among ourselves, and thus insure to the profit of the order at large as well as to individuals. Under proper laws its influence would promote, to a very great extent, the most vital interests of the order. Create libraries, erect temples, furnish and maintain them, relieve the distressed, and in every way enlarge our field of usefulness. It might not be expedient in Colorado, at this time, but in most of the larger States the scheme would be successful.

Another authorizes the Grand Secretary to procure photographs, at the expense of the Grand treasury, of all the present and Past Grand Masters that are living, which strikes us as being a very laudable transaction.

The Masonic Code of Alabama, which was prepared by a committee appointed at the previous communication, was submitted, adopted, and a thousand copies ordered printed, one of which is now in the hands of your committee. It is a handsome volume of one hundred and sixty-eight pages containing a historical synopsis of the Grand ▢ from its organization to date; the act of incorporation; Constitution, Laws and Regulations; old charges of the Free and Accepted Masons; a digest of the resolutions, edicts and authoritative reports adopted from time to time; form of keeping the minutes of subordinate ▢, etc., etc. The work has been splendidly executed, and is one which reflects the highest credit upon the committee who performed it, and upon the Grand body that gave it to the craft.

Many indigent orphans of deceased Masons are being educated at the expense of subordinate ▢.

The report of the Treasurer shows a cash surplus on hand of $7,520.58, six thousand of which was ordered to be invested in gold, and measures were adopted to prevent the further accumulation of funds. To this end Grand ▢ dues were reduced from fifty cents to ten cents per capita.

The report of the committee on Foreign Correspondence covers seventy-six pages, and goes into an exhaustive analysis of the transactions of thirty-eight Grand ▭. The work exhibits considerable ability on the part of its editor, Bro. W. C. Penick.

The ballot for officers resulted in the election of M∴ W∴ Geo. D. Norris, Grand Master, and Bro. Daniel Sayre, Grand Secretary.

CALIFORNIA.

The M∴ W∴ Grand ▭ of the State of California commenced its eighteenth annual communication, in the city of San Francisco, on the 8th of October, 1867. Grand Master Gilbert B. Claiborne presided in the East. His address, congratulating the ▭ on the continued happy and prosperous condition of its affairs at home and abroad, says: "The relations existing between our jurisdiction and other Masonic bodies are of the most fraternal character." Acknowledges the organization of Grand bodies in Montana Territory, Nova Scotia and West Virginia; alludes to the dissensions between the Grand ▭ of East and West Virginia, and gives the opinion 'that the consent of a majority of the chartered ▭ in new domain should first be obtained before a new Grand ▭ can be formed, and that the ▭ proposing to assume and exercise sovereign powers, should have first honestly discharged themselves of former allegiance." It refers to the fact that conflicts have arisen between the Grand and subordinate ▭ of California, the latter "having refused to respond to the demand of the executive requiring them to report to him in what manner certain regulations of the Grand ▭, promulgated for their guidance, had been obeyed;" but that all questions of difference had been amicably adjusted, and perfect harmony restored. During the year five dispensations for the creation of new ▭ have been granted. There is no express regulation in this jurisdiction forbidding subordinate ▭ from holding meetings and engaging in work on the Sabbath day, but Bro. Claiborne emphatically declares that the practice "is entirely inconsistent with the teachings of Masonry." He also decides that a petition, signed with a cross-mark, is *prima facie* evidence that the party petitioning cannot write his name, and under their regulations such person is unfit to be made a Mason. He animadverts with some severity on the proceedings of various Grand bodies which have granted dispensations to army ▭ to meet and work the degrees. The operations of this class of ▭ have been characterized by a looseness and irregularity which amounts to lawlessness, and by their agency persons are now wandering over the country claiming the right to be received and acknowledged as Masons, while they are destitute of the ability to convince Masons of the claim they set up. He advises that when one of these army Masons makes application to be received into any of the ▭ of California, as a condition precedent to an examination, proof shall be required under the seal of the Grand ▭ from which the dispensation emanated, that the ▭ by which he was made was legally established, and that his name is upon the rolls thereof. The members are exhorted to observe great care in the examination of strangers. If a person cannot produce the most convincing proof of his Masonic ability he should be rejected. They are especially cautioned against assuming the right to conduct examinations without authority from the Master. "The Master himself," he says, and truly, "is responsible for the admission of all visitors within the □ which he governs."

The Grand Secretary, Bro. A. G. Abell, who has held the position for the last twelve or fifteen years, presents the transactions of his office for the current year. Among other things is exhibited a fine catalogue of Masonic publications that have been added to the library, in all, ninety-two volumes, making the aggregate now on hand four hundred and sixty-seven. The Grand □ is congratulated upon having what is believed to be the largest and most complete collection of pure Masonic works to be found upon this continent.

The report of the committee on Foreign Correspondence comprehends the proceedings of thirty-seven Grand bodies. We would gladly follow their wanderings through the rich fields explored, would time or space permit. But as our bounds are inflexibly prescribed, it must be our object to confine our labors to matters of general instructiveness alone. One of these days, when we shall have attained the strength and dignity of our more prosperous neighbors, we will enter the lists and compete with them for the higher prizes in the fields of literature. At present we can only observe, with admiring eyes, united with earnest heart wishes, the rapid strides of those who go before, pray for their prosperity, and lend our feeble encouragement in pushing forward the great progressive car of Freemasonry.

A memorial from the Masonic board of relief of the city of San Francisco was presented, praying that the Grand □ levy a tax upon each member of the order throughout the State, to be paid in as Grand □ dues, for the purpose of creating a general charity fund. The reasons assigned were that the city of San Francisco, being the principal commercial seaport of the coast, naturally receives a large majority of all the Masons from other jurisdictions, who arrive in the State requiring Masonic assistance. The petitioners believe that the onerous burdens thus annually thrown upon the city alone should be shared by the fraternity at large. The memorial was referred to a committee, whose report was favorable to the proposition. The gross receipts for the year, as exhibited by the Finance committee, were $11,722.45. All the principal officers are salaried. The appropriations for the year provide the sum of $6,600 for the salary of the Secretary, and incidental expenses of his office. An assistant Secretary receives $1,200, and the Grand Treasurer and Tyler are each paid $100.

A committee was appointed to devise and procure a suitable testimonial for presentation to P∴ G∴ M∴ Gilbert B. Claiborne, as an expression of the high appreciation in which his eminent services are held. It was likewise resolved that the retiring Grand Master be requested to sit for his portrait, and that the Secretary be instructed to have it suitably framed and hung in the office of the Grand □.

M∴ W∴ William Abraham Davies was elected Grand Master, and R∴ W∴ Alexander G. Abell re-elected Grand Secretary.

CONNECTICUT.

The seventy-ninth annual communication of the Grand □ of Connecticut transpired in the city of Hartford on the 8th of May, 1867. The several stations were filled by the regular Grand Officers. Grand Master E. S. Quintard's address is brief, reviewing, in sharp, terse sentences, his official acts performed during the past year; quoting decisions, and recording the general progress of the order within the State. He refers ˙to a slight collision which had occurred between himself and the Grand Master of New York, relative to the matter of subordinate ⊡ in the city of New York receiving candidates residing in the neighboring jurisdiction. In this connection it may be proper to say, this complaint is by no means a new one, nor is it confined exclusively to the Grand □ of Connecticut. Several others, including our own, have entered protests against the unjust exercise of power assumed by the ⊡ of New York. A number of persons who had been repeatedly rejected by a subordinate □ in Colorado, were received and made Masons in New York without reference to the action taken here. This is all wrong. If a citizen of this Territory is pronounced unfit to be invested ˙with the sacred rights and privileges of our order by the only legitimate tribunal acknowledged among Masons in such cases, and he subsequently transfers his application to a □ within the city of New York without having quitted his residence in the jurisdiction to which he first applied, and is there received and made a Mason, there can be no question as to the right of such □ to complain of injustice. In other States the remedy applied is to require proof of fixed residence within the jurisdiction of one, two, or more years, and is the most efficacious we can think of. Colorado is several thousand miles from the Atlantic city, and if the committees to whom such petitions were referred were anxious to perform their duties, a line to the Secretary of the jurisdiction from which the applicant hailed, would enable them to present him in his true character, by defining his standing in the community where he last resided. Even this would in some measure neutralize the bitterness created by the opposite course.

The Grand Master commends to the officers and brethren a careful examination of, and familiar acquaintance with, the Constitution and By-Laws of the Grand □, in order to save themselves and him much useless annoyance, growing out of disputed cases that are constantly arising among craftsmen.

The Grand Master is daily called on to decide questions of law which might readily be discovered by consulting the standing regulations to which all have free access. He decides that a petition when once presented cannot be withdrawn. It must stand the inflexible test of the ballot. The petitioner cannot be regarded in any other light, symbolically, than as a stone brought up for the building, and must either be accepted or rejected.

The committee appointed at the preceding session to examine an appeal for recognition from the newly organized Grand □ of Nova Scotia, submitted their views at considerable length. It appears from correspondence obtained that the Grand □ of Scotland, from which the ⊡ of Nova Scotia

derived their powers, had refused its consent to their proposed separation
from the parent government, and therefore the committee were of the impression that the Grand □ of Connecticut could not properly acknowledge
the existence of a Grand body whose allegiance to another jurisdiction had
not been dissolved. This report was accepted.

A resolution was passed accepting the abridgment of "Masonic Laws and
Practice," prepared by Bro. Luke A. Lockwood, repealing the old code and
adopting the new. Also, one recommending the *National Freemason* to the
patronage of the brethren throughout the State.

Bro. John W. Paul, Grand Secretary, presented a very full and well
written report on Foreign Correspondence. He expresses deep regret for
the serious injury done to Masonry through the pernicious operations of
Army □, and says, "the evil was so immeasurably great as to convince the
true craftsman that they were a curse rather than a blessing." He is likewise apprehensive that the order is growing too rapidly for its honor or
safety, owing principally to the prevailing desire of □ to fill the purse of
the Treasurer, rather than to build up and strengthen the moral character
of the institution.

Referring to the unfortunate postal restrictions imposed upon us by Congress, whereby we have failed to receive copies of Grand □ transactions,
he observes, with a degree of sadness, "*We* think that to be compelled to
live in Colorado is hardship enough ; but if we were there, and cut off from
all communication with the world, we should be compelled to exclaim, 'My
punishment is greater than I can bear.'" There's compassion for you. But
we are under no obligations to our very estimable brother of Connecticut
for his commiseration. We have lived in his State ; in fact, grew up among
its mountains and barren stony fields. We feel inclined, after ten years liberty in the great West, to thank the Almighty Disposer of human events
that our lot was not forever cast in the little State of Connecticut. Here
we have plenty of room to move about in. Our Territory is nearly as large
as all New England put together. The spirit of progress circulates freely
amongst us, and nerves to the execution of heroic deeds. (No allusions intended to *monstrous deeds* for mining property.) We stand beside the colossal enterprise of the world, breathe the purest atmosphere under heaven,
have planted temples of liberty and civilization upon the so-called American desert, and upon the loftiest peaks of the Rocky Mountains, ten thousand feet above tide-water, and are opening beneath them the treasure-house
of nations. Is it, then, so great a misfortune to live in Colorado, even
though we may occasionally be deprived of a few of life's luxuries, as Bro.
Paul represents it to be ? We think not.

The embargo upon printed matter is now removed, and free intercourse
with the distant shores of our country restored. Congratulate us and keep
sending your Masonic literature, for we love it more ardently than any
other, because of its scarcity.

The election of Grand Officers resulted in the election of M∴ W∴ William
Storer, of West Hartford, Grand Master, and Joseph K. Wheeler, of the
same place, Grand Secretary.

CANADA.

The pamphlet before us from this jurisdiction embraces the transactions of two special and one regular grand communication; the first two having been convened for the purpose of laying the foundation stones of churches. The twelfth annual was held in the city of Kingston, on the 10th, 11th and 12th days of July, 1867. Grand Master Wm. M. Wilson gives a thorough review of the condition of the order, including the progress of present and projected enterprises. He refers in eloquent terms to the completion of the great bond of union between the kingdom of Great Britain and her American colonies, exemplified by the Atlantic telegraph; also to the fact of the new political union of those colonies, whereby two Grand ☐ were thrown into one jurisdiction. To obviate the difficulty, and to reconcile all dissensions that have arisen, and which are likely to arise, under the new colonial establishment, he suggests the propriety of organizing one general Grand ☐, having provincial Grand ☐ in each province. The erection of a building for Grand ☐ purposes was likewise proposed. Fourteen dispensations for the formation of new ☐ have been granted during the year, but no decisions of importance rendered. Finances seem to be flourishing in a very gratifying manner, since the fund on hand amounts to $22,759,67, all invested in paying securities. Each of the district deputies submitted reports on Masonic affairs within their respective limits.

The committee on Foreign Correspondence review our proceedings for 1866 *in extenso*, giving all the important resolutions passed at the session of that year, in full, though without comment.

DELAWARE.

The sixty-first annual communication of the Grand ☐ of this State was held on the 27th of June, 1867, in the city of Wilmington. If the gross libel upon the fraternity enunciated by the committee on Foreign Correspondence, could justly be contemplated as representing the sentiment of the Grand ☐ of Delaware, we should feel warranted in making short work of the little pamphlet before us with its own words: "We have examined her proceedings *with great care*, and find nothing in them of interest to this Grand ☐," merely adding—or any other. The committee, by its contemptuous treatment of sister Grand bodies, has insulted the entire Masonic brotherhood. How any man could have perused the thirty or forty volumes of Grand ☐ transactions, issued during the year in which their senseless report was made, without finding anything of interest, is beyond our comprehension. On the contrary, however, it is a matter of astonishment that the committees of our class should be able to execute even a tolerable abridgment of their contents in the narrow space of one or two hundred compactly printed pages. Each is an encyclopedia of useful knowledge, glowing with warmth and beauty. The man who could coldly declare that there is nothing in them of interest to the craft, betrays a soul incapable of appreciating, in the slightest degree, either the colossal proportions or the historic grandeur of Freemasonry. Its records cannot be written in three

soulless, metallic lines.   But we must remember that Masonry in Delaware
has slept for nearly half a century, and it is only through the continual
hammering of its progressive Grand Master, Daniel McClintock, that a feeble rattle is at length heard among its dry bones. He proposes to wake
them up, straighten things out and force them to stand living and erect before the world and their brethren.   He tells us that their records have been
wantonly destroyed, the edicts of the Grand □ set at defiance, proceedings
from year to year used for kindling fires, their ☞ all at sixes and sevens,
finances deranged, etc., etc. ; the whole practically illustrating " confusion
worse confounded."   It may be said, we are too harsh and uncharitable
toward our brethren of Delaware, but we answer, the record is from their
own lips.   We are but endeavoring to assist Bro. McClintock to reduce
chaos to order. If he is denied help at home, he should have it from abroad.
His re-election gives the assurance that the next register from that quarter
will exhibit an improved condition of things.   Meanwhile he has our best
wishes for the complete triumph of his undertaking, in which is involved
the redemption from ruin of a rapidly decaying temple.

DISTRICT OF COLUMBIA.

Every facility is afforded the Grand □ of this district for convening its
assemblies at pleasure. The order, though numerically large, is not so
widely scattered as in other jurisdictions, but is confined within a small
circle of territory, and the space from centre to circumference is easily and
quickly spanned.   Hence the frequency of their special communications.
Whenever an important building, church edifice or public work is to be
founded, the Grand □ is invited to contribute the beautiful ceremonies of
the order at its inauguration, and generally accepts. Nine of these specials
were held in 1867, together with the semi-annual and regular annual sessions.   The latter occurred on the 5th of November, in the city of Washington, M∴ W∴ R. B. Donaldson acting as Grand Master. His address is
short, and mostly confined to local business. In alluding to the death of
the Grand Master, which occurred on the 4th of September, he says : "No
words of mine, brethren, can give additional lustre to the memory of one
so beloved by his brethren, and so worthy the exalted position to which he
had been so often called in this Grand □ ; nor can words assuage the grief
we feel; yet, if I possessed the ability, I would gladly pronounce before
you, and before the world, an eulogy that would in some measure do justice to his character and worth as a man and a Mason. That duty devolves
upon a distinguished brother—far better qualified for its fulfillment than
myself; and I am, therefore, content to place upon record my own feelings,
faintly and imperfectly expressed, in view of the loss we have all sustained
in the removal from earth of our beloved brother, and late Most Worshipful
Grand Master, George C. Whiting."

The eulogy, followed by appropriate resolutions, was subsequently pronounced by P∴ G∴ M∴ B. B. French.

Communications were read from the Grand Orients of France, Peru and

Italy, referring to various matters which, at this late day, would be of no material interest if reproduced.

The committee on Foreign Correspondence publish a very full and able report, in which our Grand body is remembered.

Bro. B. B. French presented to the Grand □ an interesting relic of the early days of our republic, in the form of a fragment of sperm candle, which was carried by P∴ G∴ M∴ Alexander McCormick, on the occasion of the funeral of our illustrious brother, General George Washington. The thanks of the □ were returned for the valuable gift.

GEORGIA, 1867.

The journal, though handsomely printed, is badly soiled by numerous typographical and orthographical errors that have escaped the eye of the proof-reader. The *style* of the work, however, is faultless, and the superior intellectual tone which pervades the various reports that cover a majority of the three hundred and thirty-six pages, overcomes every minor objection, and elicits our heartiest admiration. This is especially true of the report on Foreign Correspondence, compiled by Bro. Geo. L. Barry. It sparkles with "thoughts that breathe and words that burn," glows with touching pathos, and flashes with ire as occasion demands. He makes no attempt to disguise his antipathy toward Bro. Guilbert, of Iowa, and in replying to the hyberbolical thunders of the northwestern dictator, employs language in the highest degree emphatic. While we earnestly deprecate both the words used and the peculiar aggravations that called them forth, we are compelled to acknowledge that the "soft answer which turneth away wrath" was hardly to be expected from our brother of Georgia. Both sides of the controversy evince the intensest political feelings and sectional hatred. Both are highly reprehensible, because both are Masons, and it is with Masonry alone that they are privileged to deal while clothed in the vestments of their respective Grand □.

The opening exercises differ slightly from our method. The Grand □ assembles without the Grand Master, one of his Deputies occupying the Grand East, by whom the □ is opened in ample form. The Most Worshipful Grand Master is then announced, from the Tyler's door, enters, and is received with private grand honors, after which he is conducted to the throne. This striking and beautiful ceremony is worthy universal adoption.

The address is a worthy expression of true Masonic principles, and one that awakens our liveliest sensibilities. It is mild, calm, dignified and conciliatory, dispensing light and instruction, avoiding every thought of injustice, covering the faults of the erring with the broad mantle of Masonic charity, and giving us a multitude of new ideas upon the subject which is so near and dear to all our hearts. Speaking of the objects of these annual conventions, he says: " These communications are considered by some as simply intended for the delegates to make their annual returns, pay dues, elect officers, receive their mileage and per diem, and return home no more enlightened than if they had not been here. If this is all we have assembled for, our time will be most unprofitably spent. Permit me to admonish you, as faithful representatives, that we are assembled for a more noble purpose —for the purpose of counseling together in the noble work of elevating humanity, alleviating distress, disseminating the pure principles of virtue, and especially to render ourselves more capable of dispensing true Masonic light and knowledge to the craft." He alludes to the restoration, by the Grand Master of Ohio, of a □ Bible, taken from Atlanta by a Federal soldier at the time of Sherman's entry. Also, the charter of Newborn □, taken when the army passed through Georgia, returned by the Grand Secretary of Indiana. It is proper to say, however, that neither of these articles were abstracted by Masons. The testimony is abundant which exonerates the craftsmen of our armies from any share in the sacriligious desecration of □ in the South.

Grand Master Harris further admonishes his brethren to "recollect that it is not the business of Masonry to engage in political strife. Masonry cannot have anything to do with a brother's political or religious opinions. Divest yourselves of all those feelings and prejudices which, if indulged, might in the least disturb the harmony of our deliberations." Again, "remember that we are engaged in a work of benevolence and love, and are admonished to emulate each other in striving to see 'who can best work and best agree.'"

ILLINOIS.

We might easily gather sufficient information from the twenty-seventh journal of the Grand □ of Illinois, to fill fifty pages, if we had them to give. There is so much that we wish to copy, yet cannot find room for, as to make the effort to condense exceedingly unsatisfactory. But since we are unable to do this mammoth jurisdiction—the second largest in the Uuited States—full justice, our brethren will please accept the will for the deed, kindly remembering our youthfulness and temporal feebleness.

Their committee on Foreign Correspondence jumped nimbly over our heads, scarcely noticing that we were there at all. The review is from the facile pen of our distinguished brother, James H. Matheny, whom it has never been our good fortune to meet. Still our respect for him reached the boiling point after perusing the splendid work of his intellect. We shall ask his illustrious successor, Bro. H. G. Reynolds, to handle us less gingerly in his coming report.

Grand Master Gorin's address is an estimable compendium of the transactions of his office during the twelve months last past. He speaks of the destitution then prevailing in the South, caused by the devastations of civil strife, and of his appeals to the □ and brethren of Illinois for contributions to alleviate the distress of the poor of these States. "A few individuals," he says, "and thank God, very few, objected and refused to give anything toward this noble object, because, perhaps, they might keep some poor fellow-being from starvation, who had participated in the late rebellion. No true Mason—no man possessed of any of the milk of human kindness, would ever stop to inquire what were the antecedents of the father of the child who would call on him for bread, and who was starving for the want of it." In which opinion we heartily concur. It was our martyr President who said : " With malice toward none, with charity for all, with firmness in the right as God gives us to see the right, let us strive to finish the work we are in, to bind up the nation's wounds, to care for him who shall have borne the battle, and for his widow and his orphan, do all which may achieve and cherish a just and lasting peace among ourselves and with all nations." As Masons, these noble, thrilling words should teach us our duty ; to forget all wrongs, forgive all men, and bury deep in the soil of oblivion all remembrances of the conflict which has cost so much blood and suffering, retaining only the remembrance of our fraternal ties.

Three memorial pages are inscribed to the memory of deceased Worshipful brethren Michael I. Noyes, Jonathan Young and Charles R. Starkweather.

The Grand Master pronounces, as should every one, against the use of Masonic emblems for the purpose of advertising or attracting business, and recommends the expulsion of members who so use them. He thinks "the matter of avouchments in ⌑ is greatly abused," and recommends that "the Grand Master be authorized to enforce the secrecy of the ballot, and punish by suspension from office, or by closing a ⌑ until a meeting of the Grand ⌑, for every infraction of the well known rule respecting the ballot." Condemns, in unmeasured terms, the manufacture and sale of cypher works, asking for such legislation as will effectually eradicate the evil; takes a strong position against the so-called Masonic gift enterprises, and all other kindred swindles, however elaborately disguised. " The jurisdiction," he says, " is becoming too large and unwieldy for the control of one man," and suggests that the State be divided into sub-districts, and Deputy Grand Masters elected to each of them. He asks, also, that some provision be made for the erection of a Grand ⌑ building. A committee was subsequently appointed, who submitted an elaborate argument in favor of the proposition, together with plans for raising the requisite funds. It was deemed advisable, however, to postpone definite action thereon until the next annual, and in the meantime submit the matter to the consideration of subordinate ⌑.

A committee was appointed to examine a recent Masonic work entitled, " A General History of Freemasonry," by Emanuel Rebold, a distinguished brother of the Grand Orient of France. Their report is emphatically adverse to its reliability, and denunciatory of the " Atheistical virus of the writer." Rebold is evidently not a " success" as a Masonic historian.

From the list of reformatory resolutions offered, we select the following :

" *Resolved*, That each applicant for the degrees shall have been a resident of the State of Illinois at least two years before he can be initiated."

Many other Grand ⌑ would do well to lay down this wholesome regulation, which would in some measure prevent the frequent collisions on jurisdictional questions.

" *Resolved*, That hereafter no petition for initiation shall be balloted on until the same has been three months before the ⌑, and no Entered Apprentice shall be passed in a less time than three months from the time of his initiation ; and no Fellowcraft shall be raised to the sublime degree of Master Mason in less time than six months from his passing, unless by dispensation."

Laid over for one year.

M∴ W∴ Bro. Jerome B. Gorin, of Decatur, was re-chosen Grand Master, and Bro. H. G. Reynolds, of Springfield, Grand Secretary.

IOWA, 1867.

The Grand Master being absent, the twenty-fourth annual communication was opened on the 4th day of June, by R∴ W∴ Reuben Mickel, D∴ G∴ M∴, acting as Grand Master.

The committee on Credentials reported one hundred and nineteen ⌑ represented.

The address was read by the Grand Secretary. Among its recommendations we find one which deserves more than passing notice, since it is likely, sooner or later, to agitate the entire fabric of Freemasonry on this continent. We have deemed proper, therefore, to insert the major portion of the Grand Master's observations, as also the subsequent action taken thereon by the Grand ⌑.

Bro. Peck (Grand Master) remarks that he has repeatedly been applied to to know " if he was empowered to grant dispensations for ⌑ to those of the negro race, and had of course been under the necessity of informing them that we are not allowed to recognize them as Masons, but consider them clandestine."

But he evidently believes this restriction to be unjust, unwise, and totally inconsistent with the spirit of the new political epoch upon which the nation has entered, for he asks : " In consideration of the new position in which they (the negroes) have been placed, and the recognition of the constitutional declaration now being forced upon us, that all men are created free and equal, does it not become us as Masons to weigh well our relations and duty toward them as members of the same order ?"

He then proceeds to set up in support of his position, the rather imperfect argument, that should the white Masons of Iowa fall into distress, and call upon the negro ⌑ already established in the State, for assistance, it would be cheerfully answered. Other jurisdictions permitted the introduction of Indians into their ⌑, and he asks : " Do recent developments indicate that they are so much more elevated in moral habits and Christianity than the negro race as to entitle them to this preference, and that they will make more worthy and creditable members of our order ?"

Instead of this weakly reasoning, he should have put it upon the broad moral grounds of right and justice. It cannot be denied that the prejudice against the negro that for a thousand years has been universal, has been softened, and in a great measure removed, by the irresistible logic of recent events. We acknowledge now, without equivocation, that we have acted most cruelly toward a people who have the same rights to the pursuit of happiness and civilization under God's laws that we have. But the same reasons why we should now give them free exercise of their political rights under the new governmental establishment do not, in our opinion, apply with equal force to Masonry. But let us follow the train of Bro. Peck's reflections further. He argues that the negroes are rising rapidly in moral and intellectual worth, in consequence of the new order of things, and fails to see why preparation for true Masonic life may not as well be made under a dark skin as under one of fairer shade, and then asks: "Do you not recognize in this question a new duty devolving upon us?" He does not recommend hasty action, "only early consideration of it," and suggests the propriety of appointing "a special committee to report upon it at the next annual communication." We now pursue the subject through its reception by the Grand ⊏, for the advantage of future reference. This portion of the address was referred to a special committee, who submitted the following: "The official acts of our M∴ W∴ Grand Master, as set forth in his address, we most cordially approve and indorse. We, however, deem it our privilege and our duty to dissent from the suggestions and recommendations of the M∴ W∴ Grand master respecting 'our relations Masonically to negro Masons, and respecting granting dispensations for the formation of negro ⊏,' and present the subjoined objections, neither of which, in our opinion, will bear analysis, except, perhaps, the first:

1. "This question, if introduced into the Masonic body, would be the entering wedge to rend asunder, beyond the power of recovery, the Masonic love and harmony that now does, and always should, exist among us." Here they should have stopped, for the reasons which follow are unworthy of educated and liberal minds.

2. "The ancient constitutions declare that a candidate for Masonic honors must be free-born, of good report, etc. This alone is of sufficient importance to cause us to reflect and be cautious.

3. "We should, as a Grand body, by such a movement subject ourselves (and that justly) to the most severe and indefensible criticisms from our sister Grand ⊏ that can be readily conceived, and instead of our Masonic thermometer standing at a temperate and healthy degree as it now does, we should, in a short time, fall below zero.

"In view of the foregoing we would recommend the adoption of the following resolution:

"*Resolved*, By this Grand ⊏, that in consideration of the dignity that she is in duty bound to maintain toward herself, and the respect she has for her subordinates and individual Masons within her jurisdiction, we deem it unwise and imprudent to entertain any action in relation to the recognition *as regular*, either negro ⊏ or negro Masons."

On the third day of the session—this report having been made on the morning of the second—Bro. Playter, hoping to bring the business to some definite conclusion, offered this:

"*Resolved*, That that part of the Grand Mrster's (Peck) address relating to the recognition of colored Masons and colored ⊏, be recommitted to a special committee of three, whose duty it shall be to give the subject a candid and impartial investigation, and report to the next session of the Grand ☐ the result of their deliberations."

Which was, on motion, "*laid on the table*," and there the matter ended. We have searched in vain through subsequent transactions in pursuit of further light from this dark subject. But notwithstanding our failure, we feel well assured that this is not the last of it, and shall watch the future action of this Grand ☐ narrowly, with the expectation of meeting it again.

We find a growing sentiment among the more prominent jurisdictions of the country in favor of building temples exclusively for Grand ☐ purposes. The Grand ☐ of Iowa, with many others, has such a proposition under consideration.

The Grand Master decides that Entered Apprentices and Fellowcrafts can have no place in Masonic processions under the practice in that jurisdiction. A resolution was adopted appropriating one hundred dollars from the Grand ☐ funds in aid of the " Soldiers' Orphans' Home."

P∴ G∴ M∴ Guilbert prepared the report on Foreign Correspondence, in characteristic style, in which we see vastly more to admire than to condemn. Every page bristles with quotations, Masonic and otherwise, interwoven with a vast amount of originality and sound reasoning. Long familiarity with all the written and unwritten chronicles of Freemasonry, together with his great interest in all the proceedings of the fraternity in his own State, have rendered him peculiarly well fitted for the arduous duties of this department.

M∴ W∴ Reuben Mickel was chosen Grand Master, and T. S. Parvin, Grand Secretary.

IDAHO.

A convention to organize a Grand ☐ in the Territory of Idaho was held in Idaho City, on the sixteenth day of December, 1867. P∴ M∴ George H. Coe was chosen chairman, and W∴ M∴ P. E. Edmonson appointed Secretary. Representatives from four chartered ☐ were present.

As standing resolutions the following were adopted:

"*Resolved*, That one ballot on a petition to be made a Mason—if clear— entitles the applicant to three degrees of symbolic Masonry. *Provided*, he may be arrested in his degrees upon proof of unmasonic conduct.

"*Resolved*, That any non-affiliated Mason living within the jurisdiction of this Grand ☐, who shall fail or neglect to contribute a sum equal to his monthly dues, for a longer period than six months, when able to do so, shall not be entitled to any of the rights and privileges of ☐.

"*Resolved*, That this Grand ☐ prohibits the practice of holding membership in more than one ☐ at the same time.

"*Resolved*, That when any expelled or indefinitely suspended Mason shall desire to be restored to the rights and privileges of Masonry, he shall petition the ☐ of which he was a member at the time of his expulsion or suspension, for their approval of his petition, and if said ☐ shall approve the petition by a vote of all its members present at any regular meeting, the

Secretary shall furnish the Grand Secretary with a certificate of the fact. *Provided*, however, that in case any □ shall refuse its approbation, the petitioner may appeal from its action, and the Grand □ shall consider it as in other cases of appeal. But no subordinate □ has authority to restore or reinstate an expelled or indefinitely suspended member.

"*Resolved*, That the annual communication of this Grand □ commence its sessions on the first Monday in November of each year."

W∴ Bro. Geo. H. Coe was elected Grand Master, and P. E. Edmonson, Grand Secretary.

Thus another bright sister is added to the brilliant galaxy of American Grand □. We give her cordial welcome, united with our best wishes, for unlimited prosperity throughout all succeeding generations. Being now successfully launched upon the universal ocean of Freemasonry, may she glide peacefully onward, gathering to herself a multitude of honors through the consummation of good works.

KANSAS.

The twelfth annual communication of the Grand □ of Kansas was held in the city of Leavenworth, on Tuesday, October 15, 1867, the stations being filled by the regular Grand Officers. To provide for the filling of certain vacancies, reported by the committee on Credentials, one of their number offered the following, which was adopted:

"*Resolved*, That when a subordinate □ is not otherwise represented, the oldest Past Master present, provided he is a member of such subordinate □, shall represent it."

The Grand Master, in his excellent address, urges upon the brethren the necessity for the adoption of more stringent measures to secure perfect uniformity of work in the jurisdiction, and to this end recommends the appointment of a "Board of Custodians," in number to correspond with the sub-districts of the State, and the location of a member in each. The Grand □, after deciding upon what work shall be used (the Preston-Webb was subsequently adopted), shall enjoin the members of the board to learn it thoroughly, and afterward enforce its practice in their respective districts, permitting no innovations whatever.

He submitted to the committee on Grievances sundry papers covering a case of trespass preferred against a Kansas □, by a □ in New York City. It is the old story—"You have been using material which belonged to me." He suggests, as a remedy for difficulties of this kind, that every Grand □ in the United States adopt a regulation making it incompetent for any subordinate □ in its jurisdiction, knowingly, to receive and act upon the petition or confer the degrees of Masonry upon any candidate who had been previously rejected by any □ in the United States, without first receiving the consent of the □ so rejecting the candidate. Further on, we shall have occason to digest this very laudable suggestion at some length, in connection with another of similar import.

He is unalterably opposed to conferring the degrees upon maimed persons; had been asked for a dispensation to confer them upon a person who had an anchylosed knee joint, but refused to grant it.

We give the more important of his decisions in brief:

A petition cannot be withdrawn after it is presented and received by the □. A □ may tax its members for legitimate □ purposes.

Negro Masons and □ are clandestine. Brethren have no right to visit such pretended □.

A □ cannot reconsider the vote by which a brother has been expelled, but may, by unanimous vote, restore the expelled to the privileges of Masonry.

An expelled Mason cannot sit in the □ from which he has been expelled during the pendency of an appeal to the Grand □.

A Master Mason, of good standing, may dimit from the □ of which he is a member without withdrawing from the jurisdiction.

The practice of conferring either of the three degrees upon several candidates at one and the same time, is deemed an innovation upon the ancient usages of the order.

A candidate who has received the Entered Apprentice and Fellowcraft degrees in one State, and the Master Mason in another, under proper regulations, becomes a member of the □ in which the last degree was conferred by signing its By-Laws.

Sixteen dispensations for new □ had been granted during the year. In the Foreign Correspondence report we find extracted from the proceedings of the Grand □ of South Carolina the following strictures upon the action of our Grand □ in relation to rejected candidates:

"The regulation, of which this (the rule which permits the rejected applicant, after one year's interval, to apply to any other □ for initiation) is a violation—is one of those borrowed by our speculative system from the operative institution upon which it has been founded. Nearly a thousand years ago, the Gothic Constitutions, adopted when the order was both operative and speculative, declared that a 'brother shall not supplant his fellow in the work;' and the axiom has repeatedly been renewed, in subseqent regulations, so that it is now an acknowledged landmark of Masonry, that one □ shall not interfere with another. The candidate who has applied to a □ becomes forever the property of that □. He is the material presented to it for its living temple, if fitting for the tools of the craftsmen, to be used; if not, to be reserved until time and opportunity shall render it worthy of acceptance. But to permit a candidate to range from □ to □; to be rejected annually by every □ that is shrewd enough to discover his want of qualifications, until, at last, one less competent to judge, or less stringent in its demands, shall haply make the 'rejected stone the head of the corner,' is to transform our □ into rival shops for custom, and to give to unworthy candidates advantages for intrusion into the order which, in any jurisdiction which adopts such a course, must lead to conflicts between □, and to consequent injury to the institution. It is to be hoped that subsequent reflection will lead the Grand □ of Colorado to remove this mischievous facility which it has given for the admission of unworthy aspirants, by thus permitting them, on their rejection by one ☐, to continue, year after year, their application to other ☐."

We do not claim, by our adoption of the regulation referred to, that its operation should be either permanent or universal. Under the circumstances that existed here at the time of its incorporation among our rules of government, our Grand ☐ believed itself fully warranted in granting this privilege to rejected applicants. We are free to confess that we do not indorse the proposition, but, with our brother of South Carolina, believe the Grand ☐ of Colorado should take early occasion to reverse its action in this particular. We hold, with him, that a stone, when once brought up for the building, whether it be accepted or rejected, becomes the exclusive property of the jurisdiction to which application was first made, and that no other should ever be permitted to make use of its rejected material, without first having obtained the consent of the original possessor. The very fact of rejection implies unfitness, and if unfit for one temple, we must assume that it is unfit for any. It may be said, the rule is too severe, and that its rigid enforcement would prevent many worthy men from becoming Masons, as it is fully understood that rejections are sometimes made on personal grounds alone, in defiance of Masonic principles. To this we answer, any ☐ whose consent may be asked by a sister jurisdiction to the initiating, passing and raising of a rejected candidate may, by the unanimous vote of the members present, virtually traverse its original decision, and thus do justice to one she has treated unjustly by granting the application. But, if she refuses, it is safe to conclude that the applicant should, under no circumstances, be permitted to become a member of the order. We permit one who has been rejected the right to apply again and again, after the expiration of certain probationary terms, and not unfrequently accept, on the second or third trial, that which was refused on the first. The rule suggested is the same, differing only in the mode of application. As a further safeguard, it would be wise to require of each accepted candidate for the degrees that, prior to being prepared for initiation, he shall make oath that he has never been rejected by any ☐ in the United States, nor in any of the Territories thereof. This, together with the remedy suggested by the Grand Master of Kansas, respecting the action of the grand jurisdictions, would, we are convinced, effectually close the door against all attempts at intrusion, and afford the most ample satisfaction to the fraternity everywhere.

A communication was read by the Grand Secretary, from the M∴ W∴ Grand ☐ of Pennsylvania, announcing the death of its Most Worshipful Grand Master, Bro. John L. Goddard, when a resolution expressing condolence was passed.

A memorial page is dedicated to the memory of M∴ W∴ Jacob Sagui, Past Grand Master of Kansas, who died in Atchison, June 14, 1867.

M∴ W∴ M. S. Adams was chosen Grand Master, and R∴ W∴ E. T. Carr, Grand Secretary. The next annual was voted to be held in Lawrence.

LOUISIANA.

The journal shows that the brethren of this jurisdiction are but just emerging from the demoralization incidental to the blighting prevalence of war and confusion. We rejoice to learn that the ▱ all over the State are being impregnated with new vitality, and are entering upon a more progressive epoch than they have heretofore known. The fifty-sixth annual communication of the Grand ▱ was begun in the city of New Orleans, on the 10th day of February, 1868, being opened in ample form by the M∴ W∴ Grand Master, Abel J. Norwood. Fifty chartered ▱ were represented. The address is devoted entirely to local affairs. The Grand Master had been absent most of the year, and the duties of his office had therefore devolved upon his Deputy. Relative to the practice of granting dispensations, he says: "It is true that no dispensation ought to be granted for the formation of a new ▱ to brethren not qualified for the work, or in any locality where the good of Masonry will not be subserved, but the Grand Officers can know little or nothing of these matters, and if an error should be committed in the first place, it should and ought to be remedied by withholding a charter," which seems to us very much like cautioning a man against carelessness, after he has fallen and broken his neck. In this we beg to differ with our distinguished brother of Louisiana. We believe it is the duty of every Grand Master to inform himself thoroughly in regard to the qualifications of those brethren who aspire to the chief offices in a new ▱ which he is asked to create, in order that errors may be avoided. If circumstances will not permit him to make personal examination of the applicants, it would appear to be his duty to delegate his powers to a commission of well-informed brethren, selected from the chartered ▱ nearest the locality in which the new ▱ is desired, and on receipt of their report proceed as shall seem wise and just. We cannot regard his proposition to act blindly in the premises, and, if it turns out badly, to shift the whole business upon the Grand ▱, as anything less than a desire to escape a responsibility which properly belongs to his office.

The Deputy Grand Master reports that "the condition of the ▱ in this Masonic district, if not altogether what it should be, is probably better than at any previous time. As a general thing, more care is taken in the preliminary investigations, a greater desire and effort to do correct work, and not so much zeal to increase their numbers, although there can be no doubt there is yet much room for improvement." Also that W∴ Bro. J. C. Gordy, who was authorized to visit all the ▱ in the jurisdiction, lecture and teach them the work, had performed that duty to the entire satisfaction of all concerned. He recommends that Bro. Gordy be retained in the position. Many flattering testimonials to his worth and efficiency as a lecturer and teacher are paid by the ▱ he had visited.

A parcel of ground has been purchased as a site of a new Masonic Temple, as the old one had become inadequate for the present demands of the order. We give place to the more important resolutions adopted:

"*Resolved*, That the regulation of this Grand ▱, adopted February 15th,

1859, providing 'that no one made in a clandestine □ can be affiliated with, or healed by, our ▭, but must come in as a profane, or by a special dispensation from the Grand □ in each particular case as it may arise,' remains in full force and vigor.

"*Resolved*, That every Mason in this jurisdiction is strictly forbidden to display Masonic emblems on sign boards, business cards, or advertisements, and the ▭ are hereby directed to discipline any brother who continues to do so after being duly warned to discontinue the same.

"*Resolved*, That all ▭ are strictly forbidden to confer the first section of the first and second degrees on more than one candidate at the same time."

Henry R. Swasey is Grand Master, and J. C. Batchelor, M. D., Grand Secretary.

MAINE.

Our brethren of Maine assembled in grand communication in the city of Portland, May 5th, 1868. Let us see what they are doing for the advancement of our glorious cause away up in the north-east corner of New England, the cradle of Masonry in America. The great fire in Portland swept away several □, with all their properties, but they have risen, Phœnix-like, from the ashes, and are again speeding hopefully onward. Their journal for the last year is full of interesting passages, which we have scored extensively, probably more than we shall be permitted to transplant. It is our purpose, however, to stretch our limits to the utmost, in order to give our young craftsmen the full benefit of the teachings of the venerable masters whose doings we take so much pleasure in reading.

The Foreign Correspondence is intensely good. Smooth, musical and vigorous, it is in the highest degree entertaining. Now that we, for the first time, are brought into the field with these experienced and gifted veterans, we feel how weak we are, and how little of Masonry we really know. From associations with them, we hope to acquire that knowledge and strength which will enable us to guide and instruct our less informed brethren, and year by year, as we become more and more familiar with our eminent preceptors, be better qualified for teaching the sublime principles of our noble order to those who have not possessed the same advantages.

We give the Grand Master's address in brief. In most of the ▭ harmony and brotherly love continued to prevail. Much more attention is being paid to the study of the laws and regulations of the Grand □ than formerly, as also to the investigation of the real character of the applicants for the degrees. He urges the necessity of providing cheerful and attractive □ rooms, as the effect upon the initiates and the brethren generally is in every way beneficial. The call for new ▭ had not been so great as during the previous year. He had been invited to consecrate the newly organized Grand □ of New Brunswick, but could not attend. This question had been asked: "Is it necessary for a re-elected Master to be re-installed?" He had answered: "While it is not absolutely necessary, because he would hold over by virtue of his previous installation, I have invariably held that he ought to be installed. This is the uniform practice in the Grand ▢, and should be initiated in every subordinate ▢. It is a well settled principle that no officer can act as such until he is installed, and unless a re-elected Master is re-installed, he does not act by virtue of his last election, but of the former." He is opposed to making nominations of officers to be voted for at the annual ▢ elections. Laying corner stones of public edifices, and dedication of halls, like the constituting of new ▢, can only be done by the Grand Master or his proxy. Candidates rejected in another State cannot legally be made Masons in Maine without the consent of the proper authority in the jurisdiction where rejected. This decision is made on the principle of the old law that no ▢ can interfere with the business of another ▢. Here is a case in point: "A candidate is rejected by a ▢ having jurisdiction, although he lived in a town where there is no ▢. Subsequently a ▢ is erected in the town where he lives, and he desires to be initiated. The new ▢ must have the consent of the old ▢ on account of the law of rejections, and the old ▢ must have the consent of the other, on account of the law of jurisdiction. In other words, neither ▢ can act upon his case without the consent of the other, and either can take him with the consent of the other." He says, some action is desirable in regard to non-affiliated Masons who are enjoying all the privileges of the institution, and contribute nothing to its welfare, or much to its honor, and proposes that they be made to pay something. He refers at considerable length to the renewal by our enemies of their warfare against the fraternity, and says: "Already, in the west, a portentous cloud appears to be gathering—destined, in the hopes of our enemies, to overwhelm the institution, and sweep the last vestige of Masonry from our land. In connection with this event it has been painful for me to notice in many of the newly started Masonic periodicals of our day, what I cannot but regard as an unwise course, in engaging in controversy with the men who assail us, and endeavoring to write down them and their acts, in articles not to be commended in their spirit or language by any true friend of the order. Much as I regret that we have no Masonic press in our State, I have the satisfaction thereby of knowing that we do not publish to the world anything which may afford strength and capital to our enemies by furnishing them with an excuse or a pretense for continuing their unprovoked attacks upon our fraternity."

Again: "It cannot be denied that during the past few years our doors have been too easily opened to those who would gain admission—and especially during the time of war, when it was thought that every man who was a patriot was worthy of all the honor we could confer upon him—and thus we have received many into our ranks that have not brought honor or benefit to us. The tendency of this has been to cause a laxity in discipline, and in too many cases have palpable violations of Masonic duty been permitted to pass by without rebuke or other action thereon to the detriment of the order. Herein lies the principal—indeed the only—danger to the institution, and if Masonry is ever put down and swept away, it must be by the indiscretions and irregularities of its friends; for if we are true to the principles of the order as delivered to us by the fathers of the craft, no human power can prevail against us.   Violations of the laws of Masonry, neglect of its duties in the affairs of life, and disregard of its teachings must be made more thoroughly matters of discipline." He believes in compelling every brother to conform to the principles of the order, and if the exercise of charity and kindness toward the erring fails to produce the desired effect, they should be cut off without ceremony.

The Grand □ of New Brunswick is recognized by resolution.   Another was passed requesting Masters of ▭ to urge upon non-affiliated Masons the propriety of being connected with the ▭, and if they refuse, to charge them a fee for each entrance.   The Constitution was amended by inserting this clause: "No candidate whose application may be rejected by a □ shall be initiated in any □ under this jurisdiction, other than the one which rejected him, unless the □ recommend him to another □ by a unanimous vote—the vote to be taken by secret ballot."   Almost a copy of the Kansas regulation, and one which we hope to see adopted by every Grand □ in the nation.

The committee on Foreign Correspondence review the transactions of forty-four Grand bodies, including our own for 1865, 1866 and 1867, wherein we find the following criticism upon our action in regard to the severance of the ▭ of Montana, who held charters from this jurisdiction, at the time of the erection of the Grand □ of Montana: "Two ▭, chartered by this (Colorado) Grand □, in Montana, united in forming the Grand □ of that Territory.   Thereupon this (our) Grand □ required a surrender of their charters, and enters the ▭ on its register as extinct.   This action is founded upon the idea that when a new Grand □ is formed, it constituents must surrender their old charters and take new ones.   This is not according to the ancient practice, and is erroneous in principle. The proper course is to have the charters indorsed by the new Grand □.   The ▭ should continue their existence. If they surrender their charters they at once cease to exist. They cannot have two charters at the same time, and it inevitably follows that if they surrender their charters they put an end to their existence as ▭, and the *new* charters are for *new* ▭.   When the Grand □ of Maine was formed, the subordinates retained their charters, and are still working under them." Our predecessors, in making this disposition of the question, acted upon the best information then at hand.   At the time we were wholly inexperienced in such matters, and being without books or authorities, in a great measure cut off from cummunication with the civilized world, by Congress and by Indians, it is not surprising that our action should have been ill-advised. We learn wisdom through experience, and while we can hardly expect to escape both Scylla and Charybdis in all our voyaging, we shall be guided in the future, as in the past, by the best light which may be afforded.

Bro. Drummond, who writes the report, has taken considerable pains to discover the origin and progress of negro Masonry in this county, From his remarks upon the subject, we glean the following: "We had supposed

that the craft were quite familiar with the fact that there is a national organization of colored men, in the nature of a National Grand □, with Grand
□ and subordinates in many of the States. But we find that there is a lack
of information upon this subject. For this reason, and because these □
are rapidly increasing, and because their relations, actual and possible, to
Masonry, have been warmly discussed, we propose to give the results of our
investigations. The military □ in the British army, in the war of the Revolution, between 1775 and 1782, initiated many men of color into the mysteries of Masonry. There were quite a number in Boston, but the □ there
declined to recognize them, or admit others. In 1782, Prince Hall, and
others, went to England, and were there made Masons, and in 1784 a warrant was granted to them for a □ in Boston, with the further authority to
establish new □; this □ was enrolled as No. 459, in the grand registry of
England. But the granting of this charter was an invasion of the jurisdiction of the Grand □ of Massachusetts. It was, therefore, recalled, but a
copy of it was kept by the □, and, though it was no longer any authority
for them, they continued to work as a □, many of those made in the military □ having joined them. After a time this □ in Boston resolved itself
into a Grand □, and issued dispensations and charters. Three □ having
been thus chartered in Pennsylvania, a Grand □ was organized for that
State, and afterwards a General Grand □. But they were not exempt from
internal dissensions, and another Grand □ was established in Philadelphia
in 1832. Other □ adhered to the Prince Hall (Boston) Grand □. In 1847,
delegates from these three bodies met in convention, and formed a National
Grand □, which has since met regularly tri-ennially (the last time in 1865).
Their proceedings for 1856, 1862 and 1865 have been published. In 1865,
they had Grand □ in Massachusetts, Rhode Island, New York, New Jersey, Pennsylvania, Delaware, Maryland, District of Columbia, Ohio, Indiana, Michigan and California. Since then, Grand □ have also been organized in Virginia, Missouri, Illinois, Kentucky, and perhaps other States. In
each of these States there are not less than three □, and in some about
twenty. The whole number of members returned in 1865 was 2,356. The
membership of Ohio Grand □ increased from about 250 in 1865, to 556 in
1867. But they also have their troubles. A Grand □ was formed in Louisiana called Eureka Grand □. The latter is not recognized by the others;
what the questions at issue are we do not know. We also learn that the
clandestine Supreme Council in Louisiana issues charters to □ which receive colored men as initiates. Quite a lively contest is going on between
the Grand □ and the National Grand □, or the National Grand Master.
The latter claim authority, etc., which the former claim. This conflict of
authority has caused a sharp discussion, in which acts of the National Grand
Master are strongly denounced. There is no doubt that they are forming □
in nearly all of the States, and that the membership is rapidly increasing."
Having given this interesting compilation of facts, Bro. Drummond proceeds to argue the question of our right to recognize them as regular organizations, going back through all the laws and usages of the order, and rak-

ing up evidence to prove that we can in no manner be justified in effecting the amalgamation. We should be glad to follow him through to the end; but want of space forbids. The elephant will soon be thrown upon our hands, however, and we shall all be obliged to take a part in his disposal. Our object, therefore, in transcribing Bro. Drummond's historian facts was for the purpose of laying a solid foundation upon which to build future discussion.

M∴ W∴ Timothy J. Murray was elected Grand Master, and Ira Berry, Grand Secretary.

MASSACHUSETTS.

The journal for 1867 is devoted principally to matters connected with the construction of the new Masonic temple in the city of Boston, and the collection of means to pay for the same. The universal world has heard more or less respecting this wonderful edifice, the splendor of its exterior, and the matchless beauty of its interior, embellishments, and doubtless has wondered whether the marvelous grandeur of the original temple, built by our first Grand Master for King Solomon, was equal or inferior to the one which has just been dedicated at the "hub." We are told that it is actually the finest structure of the kind in the world. It was commenced in June, 1864, and completed in June, 1867. We extract a few particulars in regard to its cost, etc., from the Grand Master's address. He says: "The singular architectural properties of the building, its elaborate finish, and the beauty of its embellishments, elicited the universal admiration and praise of the vast multitudes which the occasion had called together to witness the ceremony of its dedication; and, I may add, that the unanimous testimony of gentlemen of taste and culture now is, that it is one of the most beautiful and classical specimens of architectural skill in the country. At least thirty thousand persons have visited it since it was first thrown open to public inspection, and it is not known to me that any other individual judgment has been passed upon it either in its details or as a whole, than that of unqualified approbation."

The Auditing committee, at the annual meeting of the Grand □, made a full and detailed statement, by which it appears that the whole cost of the temple, including interest and insurance, is $418,532.03; and the cost of the furniture, including the organ, is $35,000. Making a total cost of $453,-532.03. The amount in the sinking fund for the payment of the debt is $24,997, which, together with $42,000 in bonds on hand unsold, and $6,-530.73 in cash on hand, makes $73,527.73, to be applied to its liquidation. This leaves the net liabilities $399,713.29. Which vast sum is to be reduced by the proceeds of a capitation tax of $1.00 levied upon each member of the fraternity of the State, each year for thirteen years. There are in the State 16,000 affiliated Masons. This tax, together with other revenues ordered to be applied to the sinking fund, would give, in the period named, a gross product of $320,240. One or two subordinate ⊏⊐ have protested against the tax, but the Grand □ seems inflexible in its determination to enforce its payment. The dedication ceremonies were highly impressive, and the procession that followed constituted the most imposing pageant ever witnessed in this country. The number in line is placed at ten thousand. Forty-seven brass bands furnished the music for the occasion. The column was escorted by grand and subordinate encampments of Knights Templar from Massachusetts, Rhode Island, New York, New Hampshire, Maine, Connecticut and District of Columbia. Then followed guests from abroad; the subordinate □ of Massachusetts, and finally the Most Worshipful Grand □. In an open barouche, drawn by six horses, were seated his excellency, the President of the United States, and Most Worshipful Grand Master Charles C. Dame. They were surrounded by a special guard of honor, composed of the the eighth company of Boston Encampment Knights Templar, bearing red cross lances. In the evening a grand banquet was held in the Egyptian Hall of the temple, where every luxury that could tempt the appetite or charm the eye was spread out in endless profusion. Each guest, as he entered the splendid banqueting hall, was provided with a boquet of beautiful flowers, and flowers of every variety adorned the tables. Speeches were made by Bros. Andrew Johnson, Gen. Rousseau, N. P. Banks, and other distinguished brethren.

The third quarterly communication was held September 11, at which time it was decided not to acknowledge the Grand □ of Nova Scotia, for reasons similar to those which we have already given as governing the Grand □ of Connecticut in her refusal to accept the same organization. Two important amendments to the Constitution were proposed and referred to the appropriate committee. They read as follows: "Any candidate whose application has been rejected, who shall be initiated in any □ whatever, without the recommendation aforesaid, shall be deemed a clandestine Mason, and shall not visit any □ within this jurisdiction; and the members of □ are hereby forbid holding Masonic intercourse with such initiates." The "recommendation aforesaid" refers to the consent of the □ rejecting. "Any person having his place of residence within this State who shall be initiated in any □ in any other State or Territory, without having first obtained the consent of the □ having jurisdiction, shall be deemed a clandestine Mason, and shall not visit any □ within this jurisdiction without first being formally healed."

The Grand Master states that there are now attached to the Grand □ 164 chartered □, and seven working under dispensation. During the past year there had been 2,506 initiates—105 more than the previous year. On the 1st of September, 1867, the total number of members in the State was 17,160, being an increase of 1,040 over the returns of the one preceding.

R∴ W∴ Bro. Marshall P. Wilder presented an interesting account of his visit to the World's Convention of Masons, held under the auspices of the Grand Orient of France, during the Universal Exposition.

R∴ W∴ Bro. Winslow Lewis presented to the M∴ W∴ Grand □ a portrait of his Royal Highness, Prince Frederick, Grand Master of the Grand □ of the Netherlands, who completed the fiftieth anniversary of his Grand Mastership in 1866. The portrait was ordered to be hung in the temple.

MARYLAND.

The Grand Master informs his ☐ that harmony and good will have prevailed throughout the Masonic State since the last annual, and that everything is prosperous. The new temple being erected in the city of Baltimore was progressing rapidly, and soon would be completed. He wastes very little time in eloquent rhapsodies, or feverish rhetorical display. After reciting the customary congratulatory paragraphs, he marches straight into the practical business of the session; tells what he has done in the past twelve months, winding up with a few sensible suggestions in the way of needed legislation. The proceedings relate wholly to local affairs, which would have no interest for us if transcribed.

Bro. John Coates was chosen Grand Master, and Jacob H. Medairy, Grand Secretary.

MICHIGAN

Has a vigorous and cultivated Grand Master, who penetrates deeply into the ethical philosophy of Freemasonry, and brings to the surface many wise deductions, which are forced upon the attention of all his hearers and readers. He impresses the initiate with a multitude of new reflections, and fixes in his mind the fact that the beautiful ceremonies through which he has passed in the different stages of his advancement, comprise but a small portion of the stupendous architecture of our Masonic edifice. His address is one that should be read by every Mason in the land. It covers twenty-eight printed pages, and is one of the ablest documents of the kind it has ever been our pleasure to peruse. We observe that the Grand ☐ before which it was delivered were so struck with its beauty and instructiveness that they at once voted the publication of four thousand extra copies for general distribution. In it are embraced all matters pertaining to the welfare of the craft, valuable historical researches, suggestions for the better government of the jurisdiction, and a forcible defense of the institution in response to the vituperative charges hurled against it by sectarian fanatics, whose knowledge of our profession extends no further than to the simple fact of its existence, and that it wields more power than any other human organization. It would appear that their principal aim in provoking hostile criticism is for the purpose of raising themselves from the obscurity in which, without some powerful lever of this kind, their whole lives would inevitably have been passed. They cannot be so stupid as to believe that their efforts to destroy us will be successful. An institution which has endured for three thousand years or more, through the civil and political convulsions of all ages, escaping " the ruthless hand of ignorance and the devastations of war," and upon which " the utmost exertions of human genius have been employed," from the beginning to the present time, is not to be undermined or thrown down by the feeble cackling of a few ecclesiastical and political geese.

We feel with our brother of Michigan, " that if we are only true to ourselves, we can stand the shock of the universal world, and emerge from every storm with unshattered ranks and a sublimer faith in the principles we profess."

He had granted eighteen dispensations for new □; had, in three cases, admitted to membership brethren whose dimits were lost or destroyed, they having produced conclusive evidence of such loss. We give some of his decisions in brief:

That a petitioner who had been declared unworthy must stand the test of the ballot notwithstanding the adverse report of the Investigating committee.

That a Mason under sentence of suspension may be tried by his □ for offenses committed subsequent to such sentence.

That a brother who has been raised or admitted to membership upon dimit, subsequent to a sentence of suspension, is competent to sit on any committee of the □. A suspended brother cannot be admitted into the □. He must appear by agent or attorney.

An unaffiliated Mason has no rights in connection with our □; cannot prefer charges against a member, nor act as counsel for him.

It is proper to state, however, that the committee on Jurisprudence, to whom this part of the address was referred, dissented from this opinion. A resolution was subsequently adopted which will be inserted in the proper place. "A Mason becoming dissatisfied with the action of his □ declared that he would prevent any more initiations, and since then every applicant had been black-balled." It is decided that such conduct is unmasonic, and that charges should be preferred against him, and, if found guilty, he should be suspended or expelled.

When a petitioner has been rejected the brother casting the black ball cannot, by waiving his objection, revive the petition. It dies with the adverse ballot, and the petitioner must await the expiration of the lawful probationary term, as in other cases of rejection.

The Grand Master notices that in several grand jurisdictions a system of life insurance has been adopted among the brethren, and commends the subject to the favorable consideration of his □. The plan is something like this: Any Master Mason in good standing may become a member by signing the By-Laws, and paying six dollars. He must keep the Secretary of the corporation advised of his post office address, and every birth or death in his family, and shall pay the sum of one dollar and ten cents into the treasury within thirty days after receiving from the Secretary notice of the death of a member of the corporation. His membership and interest become forfeited by a breach of these requirements. The benefits are that when a member dies, his widow, or other persons who may previously have been designated, shall receive, within thirty days after the Secretary has received notice of such death, as many dollars as there are members of the corporation.

This resolution relative to the rights of non-affiliated Masons was adopted:

"*Resolved*, That accusations or charges against members of □ cannot be received from non-affiliated Masons, except in case of charges against a member of a □ by leave granted by a vote of such □, and in case of charges against a subordinate □ by leave of the Grand □."

The Grand □ of Michigan recognizes and welcomes the Grand □ of Nova Scotia by complimentary resolution.

This case has arisen : A brother had been tried before a □ on a charge of murder, was convicted and expelled. He was also tried in the civil courts, but acquitted. He appeals from the sentence of expulsion. The testimony taken by the □ is brought before the committee on Grievances of the Grand □, who report that "the evidence raises a very strong presumption of guilt, so much so that we recommend that the action of the □ be sustained." This is stern Masonic justice.

The report on Foreign Correspondence, written by Bro. Fenton, Grand Secretary, is a faithful abstract of the proceedings of all the prominent Grand □ in the United States, and the Grand Orient of France.

MINNESOTA.

We are in receipt of an elegantly printed and judiciously compiled volume of ninety pages from the Minnesota jurisdiction, which brings from the great Northwest cheering intelligence of the progress of our institution in that distant region. The brethren, we are told, are working harmoniously together, their numbers increasing, the work uniformly good, and all are striving for the advancement of the cause on the purest Masonic principles. The annual communication for 1867 began in St. Paul on the 22d of October, and continued three days. The Grand Master gives a lengthy address. By it we learn that the degrees have been conferred by the various subordinates with greater care than formerly, and that an increased determination is manifested to inquire more particularly into the moral, physical, intellectual and social qualifications of those seeking admission. By the constant practice of this essential precaution, none but worthy men will ever be enrolled among the builders. No report on Foreign Correspondence has been rendered since 1862. In this respect the Grand □ of Minnesota has been almost as negligent as ours of Colorado, the only difference being that we never have had any. The writer has undertaken to present a partial review of current Masonic events, in the hope that through *his* endeavors those who may succeed him in this department will be stimulated to perform greater and more acceptable works. But, at the session of 1866, Bro. S. Y. McMasters, Grand Chaplain, was induced to accept the charge of this duty, and has given us a brief, but exceedingly well-written report, which we shall notice further on.

The Grand Master refers with pathetic tenderness to the appeals made to him for assistance from destitute brethren at the South. He says to his brethren: "In this, their great hour of need, we should fulfill that great mission that Masonry teaches, which is to feed the hungry and destitute; to clothe the naked; to soothe and cherish the disconsolate; to bind up the wounds of the broken-hearted; and, in the spirit of Masonry, forgive the errors of the past, remembering that to forget is noble, to forgive, divine; that indiscretion in them should not destroy humanity in us." He had issuéd a circular to the ◻ and brethren, calling upon them to give heed to this touching appeal from the South. They responded by sending him the generous sum of $2,292.65.

It appears that one Albert Carpenter, an unworthy member of the order, had been.traveling through the State soliciting charity, and the Grand Master, believing him to be an impostor, warned the faithful to put no faith in his representations. The Grand ◻ of Nova Scotia was denied recognition on grounds similar to those given by Massachusetts and Connecticut. Memorial pages are inscribed to deceased Worshipful brethren John L. Goddard, Grand Master of Pennsylvania, and George Carlyle Whiting, late Grand Master of the District of Columbia.

Bro. McMasters speaks kindly of us, while confessing that he has heard nothing from us since 1861, though why later transactions have not been received he is not informed. We must tell him that Congress, in one of its sessions for 1864, enacted a bit of pleasantry which for four years deprived us of the privileges enjoyed by the States of the Union, of sending or receiving any printed matter through overland mails, unless letter postage was prepaid thereon, and through the operation of this unjust regulation we were cut off from communicating with the brethren east of the Missouri. Happily this restriction is now removed. Of our first journal he says: "Of course, little material could be contained in the proceedings of a Grand ◻ at its first communication, beyond the routine of elections and the necessary laying out of work for the future. No important reports of committees appear; and we are glad to observe that there was no 'hot haste' in the way of legislating in advance of experience. We all rejoice to extend the hand of fellowship to this young member of the Masonic commonwealth, and wish her a happy and glorious career in the noble cause in which she has enlisted. By the Foreign Correspondence of other Grand ◻, we hear cheering accounts of Colorado as late as November 6, 1865. So far as appears, all was then satisfactory." To which we reply, *Util Gracias, Senor.*

MISSOURI

Mourns the death of her Grand Secretary and Past Grand Master, Anthony O'Sullivan, one of the most distinguished Masons and Masonic jurists in the United States. He had for many years been recognized as the great leader of the fraternity in Missouri, and his reputation for Masonic erudition was widely acknowledged and respected among the eminent preceptors of other States. He had filled all the principal offices in the Grand ◻, besides acquiring much distinction in the higher orders for his indefatigable devotion to the best interests of Freemasonry in all its departments. The cholera swept him away, as it did thousands of others, during its terrible visitation in 1866. The Grand Master gives a large part of his very elaborate address to his virtues and his distinguished services, in which the full measure of praise is heaped upon his memory. But the most remarkable feature of this somewhat singular paper is found in a decision which takes the ground that a ▢ of Masons is necessarily a ▢ of *Master Masons;* that is to say, a ▢ can neither be opened nor closed in legal form except it be done on the Master Mason degree. It assumes that in order to reach the Fellowcraft and Entered Apprentice degrees in a proper manner, the ▢ must first be opened on the last degree, and then, if there be work to do in the inferior ▭, the ▢ must descend to them, and when the work is finished recede to its original position, and then close the labors of the session. In accordance with this opinion an edict was issued to all the ▭, commanding them to enforce it. The official promulgation of this document, directed as it was against many of their long established regulations, called out sharp criticisms, and provoked the most acrimonious opposition, as might have been expected. In process of time it came before the Grand ▢, and was then referred to a select committee, who, out of respect to the Grand Master, compromised the matter by changing the phraseology, but without altering the spirit of the edict. This the Grand ▢ was not disposed to accept, and the following resolution expressing the will of the majority was, after long discussion, adopted:

" *Resolved*, That it is the order of this Grand ▢ that a ▢ of Entered Apprentices and Fellowcrafts are Master Masons at labor in those degrees; and as the Grand ▢ has decided that a ▢ cannot meet and open with a smaller number than *seven Master Masons and members* of the ▢, this definition of a ▢ empowers any ▢, *when* seven Master Masons are present, to open and work on the Entered Apprentice or Fellowcraft degrees, and to be closed upon those degrees, without opening on the third degree."

We conclude from this that the teachings of the "Masonic Solon"—as Bro. Anthony O'Sullivan is styled—have not been sown upon barren soil. The Grand ▢ recognized the danger of the precedent sought to be established, and quickly applied the remedy.

Bro. George Frank Gouley, upon whose shoulders the mantle of O'Sullivan has fallen, upon the latter's decease was appointed Grand Secretary, and it would seem that no better selection could have been made. At the succeeding communication the appointment was confirmed, and Bro. Gouley elected to the position in which he has since become distinguished. In his report on Correspondence we find an extract from the report of Bro. Penick, of Alabama, for 1866, which was given in reply to some assertions respecting the antiquity of Freemasonry, made by the Grand Orator of Iowa, who avers that "there is both history and tradition which lead me to believe that as far back as ten hundred and forty-four years before Christ, there existed secret societies called 'The Dionysiac Band of Workmen.' These societies originated in Egypt, and migrated to Tyre some time before the building of the Temple." He then argues from these premises that the institution of Freemasonry, as established by Hiram and King Solomon, and by them transmitted to succeeding ages, sprang directly from the intro-

34

duction of these workmen. But Bro. Penick has searched the records, and finds that Masonry (not the Dionysiac mysteries) "existed more than one hundred and thirty years before King Solomon laid the foundations of the Temple, and that it existed during the time of the Trojan war." "King Solomon," he says, "commenced the Temple 1012 B. C. This carries the existence of Masonry to 1143 B. C." Bro. Penick considers these teachings esoteric, however. To which Bro. Gouley adds: "The best compromise we have been able to make upon this question of 'antiquity' is simply this : That almost all ancient nations possessed the elements of secret societies in some shape or other—but the principal and most influential of all, both in their moral and operative character, were those of Egypt; and as the chief builders came from that country, and the Tyrian artists being a secret society, and Hiram, their chief, being the great workman at the Temple, that it was there that the moral beauties of the system and order were perfectly developed, and that at the Temple was given the momentum of an operative craft possessing symbols of morality, from which our order was born." The question now is, which of the three has the best of it ? We don't propose to decide between them, but if any other brother has further light to shed upon the subject, we shall read it with pleasure.

MISSISSIPPI.

We fiftieth annual communication was held in the city of Natchez, commencing January 20, 1867. The address is short, and confined exclusively to matters of internal economy. The Grand Master says fifty years ago only three ▱ were working in the State, and these held charters from different and distant jurisdictions. Having decided to form a Grand ▱, they met in convention and perfected an organization, from which had sprung, in the half century just closed, more than three hundred subordinate ▱, and the original trio were still represented in the councils of the Grand ▱. With but few exceptions, nothing had occurred to disturb the peace, or interrupt the harmony of their labors. He calls attention to the vast amount of destitution and suffering among the brethren in the State, and urges those around him to take active measures for their relief.

There was no report on Foreign Correspondence.

Thomas S. Gathright was elected Grand Master, and D. P. Porter, Grand Secretary.

MONTANA.

Our brethren of Montana, a portion of whom were but recently attached to the Grand ▱ of Colorado, appear to be working vigorously and harmoniously, each officer putting forth his best endeavors for the elevation of their jurisdiction to a standard which shall command the respect of sister Grand bodies throughout the world. Their journal shows this to be true. It is prepared with great skill, handsomely printed, and the reports therein demonstrate the fact that in respect of talents, the writers are not inferior to the best in the land. We pass by without comment the unkind reflections upon our Grand □ made by Bro. W. F. Sanders, their Grand Secretary, and chairman on Foreign Correspondence. If he is satisfied that he has treated us with the fraternal courtesy which should be shown when there is no cause for the indulgence of petty spite, let him live by that assurance. We shall not stoop to return evil for evil.

Grand Master Hull writes briefly. We extract the annexed paragraph, as showing the state of the order in his jurisdiction:

"I have the pleasure to state that in our Territory Masonry is in the most flourishing condition. The utmost degree of concord and harmony characterizes the craft, and the brethren are united in their efforts to strengthen, perpetuate and extend our cherished institution, and diffuse the blessings and privileges to be derived from a firm adherence to its precepts."

Bro. N. P. Langford, Grand Historian, presented an admirable epitome of the rise and progress of Masonic institutions in the Territory. The first □ was opened by himself and two other Master Masons, on the crest of a lofty mountain, one beautiful day (date not given) while they were *en route* from the State to the mining districts. The order, from small beginnings, had flourished and grown strong, even in the midst of the anarchy and confusion which marked the early settlement of the Territory. The result of their heroic efforts is seen in the present prosperous condition of their affairs. Leander W. Frary was chosen Grand Master, and W. F. Sanders, Grand Secretary.

NEBRASKA.

This Grand □ entered upon the tenth year of its existence June 19, 1867. In the volume handed us for dissection, are compiled printed transactions for ten years past, so arranged, we presume, for greater convenience of reference. We shall deal only with the last, however. Early in the session, while arranging preliminaries, it was found necessary to adopt a restriction something like this: It is held to be improper and unmasonic for any brother to whom the proxy of a Worshipful Master or Warden has been given, to transfer the same to a third brother, and the resolution declares that no such brother shall be entitled either to a vote or a seat in the Grand □.

The Grand Master's decisions are unimportant. He intimates, in the course of his observations, that there appears to be a desire on the part of some brethren to *modernize* the ancient craft work, to ignore ancient landmarks, laws, usages and customs, and to introduce numberless innovations, all of which is strongly reprehended. He considers the Preston-Webb work, under which the fraternity of Nebraska have always operated, the most authentic form extant, and recommends the most rigid adherence to it in all its details. This is also the opinion of the committee appointed on "Uniformity of Work," who submitted a long report on the subject. This resolution was adopted:

"*Resolved*, That it is not lawful for a □, in restoring to membership a brother who has been suspended, to charge him dues for the time intervening between his suspension and restoration."

Measures were taken for the creation of a sinking fund, to be applied, at some future time, to the erection of a Masonic Orphan Asylum. To this end a Grand ☐ tax of one dollar was levied upon each member in the State. The sum of one hundred and fifty dollars was donated for the relief of destitute brethren residing in Georgia.

Bro. Wise, chairman on Foreign Correspondence, in reviewing our proceedings for 1866, detects a ridiculous error in our By-Laws for the regulation of subordinate ☐, and proceeds in the gentlest manner to direct our attention to it. We thank him heartily for letting us off so easily. He says: "Our attention is attracted by the peculiar wording of the 35th section: ' No ☐ working under the jurisdiction of this Grand ☐ shall be allowed to do any work *irregularly, unless it be by dispensation from the Grand Master,*' " etc., etc. We acknowledge the corn, Bro. Wise, and in explanation have to say that the By-Law was, by its framers, designed to read, "out of the regular order," in place of "*irregularly,*" but through some inadvertence, was inserted as you found it. It may have been a mistake of the printer, but probably not. At least we are not quite prepared for a vigorous fight with the typos who "set it up," which would be the inevitable consequence of laying it to them.

NEVADA.

Ten warranted ☐ were represented at the third annual communication, which began September 17, 1867. The Grand Master refers to a petition from Mount Moriah ☐, U. D., at Great Salt Lake City, which, we understand, has sought admission into every jurisdiction in the West, without effect, beginning with that of Nevada. Her appeal to the Grand ☐ of Montana being disrespectfully worded, was sent back with a stinging reprimand. Grand Master Currie says: "Immediately after the close of our last communication, I endorsed the dispensation to Mount Moriah ☐, at Salt Lake City, in accordance with the vote of the Grand ☐, continuing said dispensation for one year. I have reason to believe that the ☐ and its officers have yielded a ready obedience to the instructions of my predecessor, and the behests of the Grand ☐," and recommends that a charter be granted if applied for. The matter being referred to the committee on charters, they report the papers from the ☐ regular and neatly kept, and that they " would have taken pleasure in recommending that a charter be granted had it not been for the spirit of insubordination manifested in the lengthy communication from the officers of the ☐, which accompanies the petition; in which, after a great amount of special pleading, they attempt to dictate terms to this Grand ☐ by declining a charter unless the edict of the last Grand Communication concerning Mormon Masons be repealed, and the ☐ is allowed to judge as to who shall or shall not be admitted." They (the committee) then set forth the fact that the officers of this ☐, on receiving their dispensation, were instructed " that the laws of the land have declared polygamy a crime, and that the Mormons of Utah Territory have openly and defiantly declared their intention to resist the enforcement of the law, whenever the government shall make the attempt; and that polygamy is a moral and social sore which it is the duty of Masonry to discountenance," and therefore the admission of Mormons to the □ is forbidden. This the petitioners objected to. While they disapproved of the doctrine on which the Mormon Church was founded, they insisted that there were very many members of it who believed in the one-wife principle, practiced it, and in their daily walks were just and upright men, who, if admitted to the mysteries of Masonry, would adorn the order. But our brethren of Nevada failed to see it in that light, and so passed the following resolution:

"*Resolved*, That this Grand □, in view of the unsatisfactory state of society in Great Salt Lake City, and the improper spirit manifested in the communication from the officers of Mount Moriah □, U. D., does not deem it expedient, or for the good of Masonry, to grant a charter to the brethren of Mount Moriah □, U. D., as prayed for."

Grand Master Currie had granted three dispensations to re-ballot upon the petitions of candidates within a less time than that prescribed by the Constitution. In one case "the brother casting the black-ball had, in open □, acknowledged that he cast the ballot under a misapprehension, and moved that the dispensation be prayed for, which was concurred in by the □." Another was in a case of mistaken identity. On a second ballot the candidates were accepted and became very worthy members. Peace and harmony prevailed. No dispensations for new □ had been granted. The growth of the order was gradual, but of the most healthy character. The Grand □ of Nova Scotia is recognized and welcomed to the Masonic sisterhood with great cordiality.

John C. Currie was re-elected Grand Master, and Wm. A. M. Van Bokkelen, Grand Secretary.

NEW BRUNSWICK.

On the 16th day of August, 1867, the various □ in the British Province of New Brunswick met in the city of St. John, for the purpose of taking into consideration the propriety of forming an independent Grand □, which should be entirely disconnected from the jurisdiction under which they had hitherto acted. Seven subordinates assembled with full representations. The chairman, on calling the convention to order, explained its object, and, in the course of his remarks, said: "In view of the fact that the *exclusive* right of erecting □ in this province could no longer be maintained by the Grand □ of England, Scotland and Ireland, this meeting was called to consider whether or not it was desirable that a convention be held to discuss the courses open to the □ in New Brunswick, viz: To form an independent Grand □, or to unite with the Grand □ of Canada, preparatory to the formation of a Grand □ for the Dominion." After some discussion, a circular was authorized to be addressed to all the □ of the province, notifying them of the will of the convention. On the 9th of October following, the ☐ again assembled in convention, and organized a Grand ☐, elected officers and installed them. On the 22d of January, 1868 the Grand ☐ thus created held its first regular communication. The Grand Master, in addressing his ☐, recapitulates the events through which the brethren had passed to reach their present status, and congratulates them upon the unanimity of their action and the good results thus far obtained. The work adopted was the same as received from the Past Grand Lecturer of Massachusetts, several years ago, and which the Grand Master declares will be rigidly adhered to in all the ☐ under the jurisdiction, and that he should issue no warrants for the erection of new ☐, unless the proposed officers were prepared to conduct the ritual according to the form adopted. It was deemed desirable that a site for a Grand ☐ temple be selected as soon as possible, and a building constructed thereon. Just prior to the close of the session it was

"*Resolved*, That the Most Worshipful Master be requested to take immediate steps to establish fraternal relations between the Grand ☐ and the Grand ☐ in this Dominion, in the United States, in Great Britain and Ireland, on the continent of Europe and in South America, either by an interchange of representative with such Grand ☐, or in such other way as he may deem advisable."

We believe most of the Grand bodies in the United States have extended a cordial welcome to New Brunswick, and that she is now firmly established among the family of American Grand ☐.

NEW HAMPSHIRE.

This Grand ☐ met in annual convention at the city of Concord (fitting place), June 12, 1867. The Grand Master reports having granted dispensations for three new ☐, and that, so far as his observations had extended, the affairs of the jurisdiction were never so prosperous. The address relates almost exclusively to home matters, which it would be idle to recapitulate, since many of the subjects treated have already been thoroughly digested in our review of other journals. Ten deputies rendered reports, and, so far as we were enabled to discover by a hasty glance over their transactions, no material derangement of the usual happy order of things had taken place in any of the sub-departments. The institution is growing gradually—which means healthily.

It was resolved, "that a rejected candidate should not be permitted to petition a second time within the space of twelve months, and that all applicants must have resided in the jurisdiction to which application is made, twelve months prior to the date of petition."

A committee, appointed at the last annual session of the Grand ☐ to consider and report their findings respecting the status of Masons made in army ☐, declare that, "as they understand it, these men are Masons, and no earthly power can fix any other judgment upon them, except as a punishment for some Masonic crime of which they have been duly convicted;"

that, while the granting of dispensations for army ⌑ was of doubtful expediency, it had been done through the regularly constituted channels, and could not, therefore, be revoked, or the proceedings had thereunder, annulled. And in this view of the case we must all readily concur. It is impossible, as we regard it, to destroy or to ignore the rights that have been acquired under this class of dispensations. The ⌑ so constituted had the same authority, and, per consequence, the same right, to make Masons as any other ⌑ working under the like power, unless specially restricted from so doing by the provisions of the instrument granted. And the obligations to recognize them as regular Masons are just as binding upon us as any others known among us. The error we all admit, but it is one for which there is no remedy.

The sum of one hundred dollars was appropriated for the benefit of necessitous ⌑ in the Southern States.

Bro. John J. Bell, for the committee on Foreign Correspondence, thus reviews our journals for 1865–6, the principal criticism being upon our action in installing the officers of the Empire ⌑ before the Grand ⌑. He says: "Although this practice would seem to have been adopted in some jurisdictions, it could never have been deemed 'regular here, nor can we understand the reasoning upon which it is justified. Until the charter is granted, there is no ⌑ which can elect officers; until the ⌑ is formally instituted, consecrated, and its officers duly installed, it is but an *inchoate* body which can do no Masonic act. At least, these are the views of our Grand ⌑, and which are found in Masonic text-books. Necessity, which knows no law, may have overriden the usages of the craft, but we deem it a serious innovation, and wish that the craft everywhere would return to the old safe track of abiding by the ancient landmarks."

Although the writer was not a member of the Grand ⌑ of Colorado when the proceeding of which Bro. Bell complains was had, he presumes, from the well known Masonic ability of those who composed the Grand ⌑ on that occasion, that they acted upon a well established precedent. Had this authority been wanting, the officers of Empire ⌑ would not have been so installed. Personally, our judgment is in harmony with the position assumed by our brother of New Hampshire—that no ⌑ under dispensation has the right to anticipate a charter and to elect officers to serve under it.

He thinks our resolution declaring that non-payment of dues cannot work a forfeiture of Masonic standing, which was repealed, and its place supplied by another to the effect that "a member of a subordinate ⌑ may, by a vote of a ⌑, be stricken from the roll of membership for arrearages in dues for the space of one year, somewhat faulty, that is, we were wrong in both cases." As he conceives it, we should have steered between the two, for he says: "Non-payment of dues is a Masonic crime, for it is, or may be, defrauding the ⌑ of what properly belongs to it, but no penalty should be inflicted without notice and trial. The infliction of so severe a penalty as deprivation of membership by a mere vote of the ⌑ is inconsistent with the first principles of justice." And why so, we ask? Our By-Laws are open to the inspection of every member, and duty to his □ requires that he shall familiarize himself with all the provisions. The amount of dues for the support of the □ is fixed in plain terms. It is a law that he shall, in common with all other members, contribute toward the payment of these expenses. The penalty for refusing or neglecting so to do is also set forth. Everything is as plain as it could be made if weeks were absorbed in defining and trying the matter. By refusing or neglecting to pay, he becomes amenable to the law and its penalty. There is no need of a trial to establish the fact. If poor, and unable to pay, ten words of explanation to his □ will insure charitable consideration of his case, and, if the appeal is well founded, prompt remission of the amount. This opinion may not be founded upon any fixed law, but it seems to us the common-sense view in which we shall find many supporters outside of our own jurisdiction.

[NOTE.—A recent examination of our proceedings for 1867 shows that the resolution referred to was at that session modified so as to require notice and trial.]

NEW JERSEY.

Eighth annual communication held at Trenton, January 16 and 17, 1867, sixty-eight ☐ represented, Grand Master Silas Whitehead occupying the throne. His address is a model of excellence. He refers in feeling terms to the death of Past Grand Master Edward Stewart, upon whose life and character he pronounces an eloquent eulogium, enumerating his distinguished services, his long devotion to Masonic principles, and his influence for good among the craft. "Much of the prosperity of the Masonic institution in this jurisdiction," he says, "is attributable to his labors. He took charge of the craft at the time of great despondency and gloom, and, by his energy and enthusiasm, infused new life and ambition in the brethren." His remains were interred with full Masonic honors, and a memorial page in the Grand □ journal is inscribed to his memory.

With one or two exceptions, the Grand Master had met no obstruction to the faithful discharge of the arduous responsibilities of his office. In order to reach a proper understanding of the exception, we quote: "The Grand □ at its last annual communication, by unanimous vote, adopted the report of its committee on Masonic Jurisprudence, in which occurs the following language: ˙

"From the tenor of decisions Nos. 7 and 8, your committee are led to believe one or more ☐ in this jurisdiction are using the work known as 'Conservators' Work,' and also using a ritual written or printed in cipher. The former is directly opposed to resolution of this Grand □, and the latter, in violation of their obligations. The committee believe that, if such practices are permitted, much damage will accrue to the Grand □ and to Masonry, and therefore recommend that the M∴ W∴ Grand Master *be directed to require the warrants, and to suspend any □ that is guilty of such practices.*"

He had found one □ using this prohibited work, and, refusing to use any other, he had issued an edict stopping its further operation. ⋅ Subsequently, it was visited by the Grand Lecturer, who instructed the officers in the standard work of the jurisdiction, and they showing proper contrition for past errors, the edict was revoked.

We were considerably amused by Bro. Whitehead's ludicrous description of his □ as it appeared in the immeasurable variety of costumes displayed upon the persons of the officers. Hear him: "Aprons with square and round corners, white aprons, and aprons whose whiteness is marred by printer's ink, aprons bound with blue, and aprons not bound, aprons of cotton, of linen, of silk, of satin, of velvet, and, alas! too rarely, aprons of pure white lambskin; jewels pendant from the collar, and jewels pendant from the lappel of the coat, broad blue ribbons, and narrow blue ribbons, white collars, and blue collars, collars with gorgeous fringe, and collars without gorgeous fringe, collars of silk, of satin, of velvet, and no collars at all; collars glittering with tinsel embroidery, with tinsel rosettes, and with tinsel stars—all combine to present a view as variegated and brilliant as the changing combinations of a kaleidoscope. By nothing in nature or art is the unmeaning glitter of the Masonic clothing of the officers of our subordinate □ equaled, unless perhaps it be by the 'purple and fine linen,' the 'sounding brass and tinkling cymbals' which adorn the persons of the Grand Officers."

No dispensations for new □ had been granted, but several petitions for them were on the Secretary's table, awaiting action by the Grand □.

Here we approach a subject which we feel called upon to give all the space required, for it is one of the most important that has yet come to our notice. If the opinions respecting incorporated □ given by Grand Master Whitehead, and quoted by us, are correct, and applicable to all jurisdictions, we cannot employ our space to better advantage than by giving them. It seems that several □ in New Jersey had made application to the Legislature of that State for acts of incorporation. Of these proceedings the Grand Master says: "When a □ is incorporated by an act of the legislature, it becomes a subject of the laws of the State, just as an individual citizen, with certain exceptions. It not only acquires the right to hold and convey real estate, and invest personal property in the □ name, but it also renders itself liable to be sued in its corporate capacity, and submits itself and its concerns to the supervision and control of the courts of law. By the rules of government of our institution, a brother who feels himself aggrieved by the action of his □ has the right of appeal to the Grand □. If, however, he should be fractious, and indisposed to submit himself to the adjudication of the Grand □, he has the power, if the □ be incorporated, to appeal directly to the judicial tribunals. If he has been expelled from his □ for a Masonic offence justifying such punishment, the courts of law have the power—denied by some of the ablest and wisest of Masonic writers, even to the Grand □ itself—to restore the offending brother into full and complete membership in the □ from which he has been expelled."

"Again, in cases of incorporated societies, courts of law have the power to inquire and adjudicate upon the right of a member to an office, the functions of which he may be exercising. Thus a defeated candidate for the office of Worshipful Master in a subordinate ▭, instead of appealing to the Grand ▭, may appeal to the courts of law. If the court should be satisfied that he has been irregularly elected, it has the power to eject him from his office, and place his opponent in his place. It is to be borne in mind that a judge, when considering questions which may arise in connection with an incorporated ▭, regards the case from a different stand-point than that from which a Mason views it. The judge knows nothing about the binding force of secret obligations. He does not allow his judgment to be influenced by the fact that the society of Freemasons was instituted for the purpose of fostering virtue, morality and brotherly love. He neither knows nor cares anything about the immutable character of ancient landmarks. He sees before him a citizen who has acquired certain rights in an incorporated company, which rights the law is bound to protect. And, for the purpose of ascertaining and protecting these rights, he brings to bear upon the case the same rules of law which he would apply in the case of a stockholder in a bank or an insurance company. It is plain that the application of such rules is subversive of the structure of Masonic government. It sweeps away the appellate jurisdiction of the Grand ▭ and the Grand Master, and subordinates the Masonic to the civil authorities upon questions strictly Masonic."

The committee on Foreign Correspondence make a short review of the principal transactions—among them, ours for 1865 and 1866. Bro. Wm. Silas Whitehead was re-elected Grand Master, and Joseph H. Hough, Grand Secretary.

NEW YORK.

Annual communication, June 4, 1867; five hundred and thirty-eight ▭ represented. Grand Master Robert D. Holmes, in the Grand East. The address, as might be expected, is the perfection of rhetoric and good sense. It shows the writer to be a man thoroughly fitted to preside over the first Masonic jurisdiction in the nation. We regret to find that even a slight dissension has arisen in the ranks of the faithful. It appears from the remarks of the Grand Master, that a convention of Masons had been held in the city of Brooklyn, with a view to taking into consideration the modi-fication of the extra fees demanded from initiates by Grand ▭ regulation, and for the purpose of nominating, in advance of the Grand Communica-tion, a brother for the office of Deputy Grand Master. The convention issued a circular letter, addressed to every ▭ in the State, asking its co-operation for the abolition of the odious tax, etc. This proceeding the Grand Master deemed out of order and unlawful, and says he would have issued an edict forbidding its promulgation, had he been apprised of it in time to do so. The Grand ▭ committee, to whom the subject was given for investiga-tion, review the matter carefully, reporting as follows: "It is not meant that the brethren of the ▭ should be muzzled in respect to any regulation or other measures affecting the interests of the whole fraternity. On the contrary, the old regulations expressly provide for the instruction of the representative by his constituents, and ▱ may instruct their Master and Wardens how to vote on any particular question, and perhaps it may extend to the selection of Grand ▱ officers." But the committee are nevertheless of the opinion that these things have a direct tendency to disturb unity and concord, produce unwise combinations, heart-burnings and petty jealousies, and therefore wisely pronounce against them.

By resolution, subordinate ▱ were forbidden to confer the degrees on any person for less fees than those prescribed by the By-Laws.

A brother representing subordinate ▱ No. 601, submitted for the consideration of the Grand ▱ the following:

. "*Question of Law.*—A member of a ▱ is placed upon trial, charges of gross unmasonic conduct having been preferred against him. The trial is had, and the brother is indefinitely suspended. He appeals to the Grand ▱, his case is referred to the committee on Appeals, and said committee report recommending a resolution restoring him to the rights and privileges of Masonry, but not to membership in his ▱. The Grand ▱ adopt the report and resolution. Under such decision the brother is admitted to another ▱ by application. ·

"*Question.*—Is it in conformity with the constitution of Masonry for the Grand ▱ to restore a suspended member of a ▱ to the rights and privileges of Masonry, but not to membership in his ▱?"

And here the answer—the italics are ours:

"The committee suppose it to be a well-settled law, that *an expulsion alone* terminates the connection of a brother with his ▱, and that if subsequently restored, it can only be to the rights and privileges of Masonry, and not to membership in his particular ▱. But the effect of suspension is far different. The connection is not severed, but is only held in abeyance for a time. It may be for a definite or indefinite period; whatever it may be, when that period expires, or is terminated, the brother is restored and returns to all his former relations with his ▱ and to the fraternity. *We therefore answer the interrogatory in the negative.*"   •

One Fitzgerald Tisdall, publisher of a Masonic weekly newspaper, had been tried upon charges of a grave and serious nature by a commission of brethren appointed by the Grand Master, found guilty, and expelled from all the rights and privileges of Masonry. He appeals to the Grand ▱, and the decision *is sustained.* It had been his habit to publish libelous articles upon the Grand Master and many other officers and members of the Grand ▱.

The committee on "Unfinished Business" of the preceding session, reported the result of their findings respecting the expediency of establishing a regulation proposed by the Grand Master, and running as follows: "That a series of questions should be written or printed by each subordinate ▱, and be presented to every candidate for initiation, requiring his answer to each in writing with his signature attached, to be returned to the ▱ where his application had been made."

Here follow the interrogatories:

"Q. Where were you born?

"Q. What is your age?

"Q. What is your occupation?

"Q. How long have you lived in the State of New York?

"Q. How long in the town, city, county or village in which you now reside?

"Q. Have you ever, to your knowledge, been proposed as a candidate and rejected in a Masonic □; and if so, when and in what □?

"Q. Do you believe in the existence of one ever-living and true God?

"Q. Do you know of any physical, legal or moral reason which should prevent you from becoming a Freemason?

"Your committee, fully realizing the importance of the suggestions here made, feel that the course indicated by the Grand Master ought to be made imperative on all subordinate ▭ in this jurisdiction, and recommend the adoption of the following resolution:

"*Resolved*, That it shall be made the imperative duty on the part of every subordinate □ in this jurisdiction, to present in print or writing the above and foregoing questions to every candidate for initiation in it, upon his application, requiring him to answer each and every of them in writing, and to state that he does so on his honor as a man; and that the said questions and answers so signed shall be returned to and become the property and part of the records of the □, before any ballot shall be taken upon the application."

We are glad to see that this very important and long needed regulation was adopted, and is now one of the standing laws of the Grand □, one which we hope to see inscribed upon the records of every Grand □ in the world.

The jurisdiction of New York is assuming enormous proportions, so much so as to be regarded as too unwieldy for management by one man, or one Grand □. Bro. Holmes suggests that provincial Grand ▭ be established in various sub-districts, possessing limited powers, and paying allegiance to the one supreme Grand □. The committee in charge of the plan reject it as impracticable, and substitute "a board of revision," so constituted as to be efficient and impartial, and to bring redress and relief speedier and nearer, hence cheaper, to any brother; "a system which, without conflict with existing provisions, may, if adopted, go into effect immediately."

The Grand □, by resolution, disavows and denounces as "gross and wicked impositions, all gift concerts or other gift enterprises purporting to be in aid of the 'Hall and Asylum Fund,' or of any other Masonic charity; that all such schemes, being in the nature of lotteries, are subversive of the laws of the State, and deserving of the severest condemnation of all good Masons."

We get a kindly notice from the committee on Foreign Correspondence, who review us for 1865-6, concluding the latter with this flattering compliment: "The indications are that this young Grand □ will take a prominent position among the Grand ⌑ of the country." Thus it is seen that the lion *will* sometimes condescend to pat the weasel, and tell him how big he will grow to be one of these days—" almost as big as *me*—ahem !" This is not "sarcastical"—mind you.

NORTH CAROLINA.

This Grand ⌑ convened December 2, 1867, in the city of Raleigh, and remained in session four days.

Grand Master Reade being absent there was no address, but among the appendixes we find the concluding portion of an instrument bearing that character, which was written for the occasion, and why not read at the proper time, is beyond our power to explain.

Bro. R. W. Lassiter pronounces an eloquent eulogy upon the memory of the late Grand Secretary, William F. Bain, giving a short sketch of his life, and bestowing a high tribute of praise upon his Masonic virtues, and his usefulness to the fraternity.

The Grand ⌑ having previously adopted what is known as the "Stephenson Work," which had been examined and approved by a large number of the most learned and zealous Masons in the State, it was resolved that the Grand Master be authorized to appoint a committee of three intelligent and prudent Masons, who should be required, upon accepting the office, to learn the work directly from Bro. Stephenson, and when thoroughly learned, he (Bro. S.) should give certificates to that effect, when they were to be commissioned as "Custodians of the Work," by the Grand Master. They are to hold office for the term of three years, and have power to instruct and commission lecturers, who, in the discharge of their duties, are required to enforce its adoption and practice in all the sub-⌑. Each lecturer must hold a certificate of qualification from the board of custodians, showing his fitness to teach the newly established work. This plan of operation should, and undoubtedly will, insure perfect uniformity of labor throughout the State.

Maimed people appear to be causing our brethren of the south a deal of trouble by their persistent efforts to squeeze themselves, or be squeezed, into the fraternity in defiance of regulations. Here is an unfortunate case of this nature: A worthy man had been initiated as an Entered Apprentice. He shortly afterward received a wound which deprived him of his right arm. The ⌑ asks whether it is proper to confer the remaining degrees upon him, and receives the answer that it is not.

The Worshipful Master of a certain ⌑ causes to be rejected a petition for initiation signed with a cross-mark. The subject is taken to the Grand ⌑, and the Worshipful Master's ruling is there approved.

The Grand ⌑ of Nova Scotia is recognized and welcomed to the American sisterhood.

There was no report on Foreign Correspondence.

NOVA SCOTIA

Seems to have had a prodigious and somewhat desperate struggle for independence with the "old mother" of Scotland. On the 30th of November, 1866, after the secession of the majority of subordinate □ in the province, the Provincial Grand Master for Nova Scotia, acting under orders from the Grand □ of Scotland, constituted and appointed certain new officers to carry on the so-called Provincial Grand □, and evidently with the design of taking the starch out of the seceders. The latter, however, resisted this encroachment upon their sovereign rights. They claimed that it was not only illegal, but insulting, and by resolution demanded of the mother □, in the most emphatic language, the immediate revocation of the order, and that the officers appointed be declared illegal and clandestine.

Now, if the old lady has the least particle of Scotch spunk she *wont do it*. All this occurred at a quarterly communication held December 14, 1866.

The annual communication for 1867 began at Halifax on the 21st of June. The Grand Master takes the opportunity to reiterate the oft-repeated declaration that "the great and crying evil we are called upon to remedy at the present day is that of unffiliation, an evil that is felt in all parts of the world." What *shall* we do with our stray sheep, seems to remain an unsolved question, and the chances are in favor of an increase, rather than a decrease, of the gnawing cancer.

Here is the next blot found by him upon our Masonic escutcheon: "The last evil to which I shall at present call your attention is the irregularity which is daily seen in the attendance of both officers and members on the stated meetings of □. How often do we visit □ and find perhaps half the stations filled by brethren not belonging to the particular □ open, or, if members of the □, not at all capable of filling the positions with credit to themselves and honor to the fraternity. How often does even a good Master, one who understands his own portion of the work, have to blush for very shame at the bungling manner in which some of his officers perform their duties, when, perhaps, visitors may be present who have come to criticise the work, or to acquire knowledge. How few □ are there in which every officer knows his duty, and takes a just pride in being always in his place at the appointed hour." The reproach will aptly fit many of our Colorado □, and for that reason we have given it entire.

There was a short but good report on Foreign Correspondence.

OHIO.

At the grand communication held October 15, 1867, two hundred and eighty-five □ were represented. The Grand Master enumerates his official acts for the year. It had been made his duty to set several new □ in motion, but in several cases it had been done by proxy. Before proceeding to constitute the Point Pleasant □, it had come to his knowledge "that the brethren of the □, after the surrender of the dispensation issued to them, had met and conferred the degree of Entered Apprentice on one candidate, and that of Master Mason on another. Immediately revoked the charter granted them by you at your last annual communication," but subsequently ascertained that the irregularities proceeded from ignorance of the law, and a mistaken notion of their powers, and permitted them to resume work, but required the □ to heal the candidates who had been illegally entered and raised.

Relative to the powers of □ "Under Dispensation," he says: "It has been asserted that they are invested with the privileges and prerogatives of chartered □, except the election of officers and representation in the Grand □. But the assertion is not supported either by authority or reason. All writers on Masonic jurisprudence agree that □ under dispensation are the creatures of the Grand Master, derive all their powers from him, are subject to his will for their continuance, and during their existence act simply as his proxies. The landmarks confer on him the right or prerogative to summon any legal number of his brethren, and with them to make Masons. His power to grant dispensations to open and hold □ rests on this prerogative." In support of this reasoning he cites the fact that □ under dispensation cannot adopt By-Laws unless required by the Grand □ to do so. Cannot elect officers nor install them, nor can they admit members, because there is no such thing as membership in a □ of this character, etc., etc.

During the past year the number of petitions for new □ had been unusually large. A majority of them had been granted, though in some cases he had doubted the propriety of so doing; refers to and approves the conclusions formed by the Grand Master of New Jersey respecting the incorporation of subordinate □; denounces gift enterprises; had found one □ in Ohio engaged in promoting one, and threatened to revoke its charter if the practice was continued; says Masters of □ should be high-toned, moral men, examples of the virtues which they are called to impress upon others. "The eminent stations which they occupy give notoriety to any departure from the line of rectitude;" thinks no man who is not well-read in Masonic law, history, jurisprudence, usages and customs, has a right to be an aspirant for the position of Worshipful Master of a □."

Their journal is a neat production, nicely arranged by a very competent Secretary in the most compact and comprehensive manner.

Bro. Enoch T. Carson, chairman of Foreign Correspondence, gives us a very readable review of the transactions of twenty-seven American Grand □.

OREGON.

The seventeenth annual communication occurred June 24, 1867, in the city of Portland, twenty-six □ being present. Three dispensations to confer the degrees in less time than the laws prescribe, had been issued by the Grand Master. He had visited many □, and regrets that circumstances would not permit him to exchange fraternal greetings with all. Harmony and good feeling prevailed, and peace and prosperity crowned the labors of the craft on all sides. All reports are short and to the point.

The journal is made up of local affairs, with one exception, which we regret to find occupying a prominent place upon its otherwise creditable pages. The neighboring jurisdictions of Oregon and Washington seem to have fallen into the vile habit of abusing each other like pot-house politicians, over a matter which ought to have been settled with a dozen courteous words.

It is to be hoped that an amicable adjustment will be effected before the publication of their next annual registers; for it gives the outside world, which has no interest in, or understanding of, the controversy, a bad impression of their Masonry.

RHODE ISLAND.

The journal for this jurisdiction is exceedingly brief, stiff and formal, containing but little material beyond the ordinary routine of Grand □ exercises, to interest the reader. We shall therefore glance hastily over its pages, hoping that next year will bring us one more voluminous and entertaining.

The Grand Master administers much wholesome advice to the brethren under his charge; admonishing them to shun the evils which arise from too great a desire to increase their numbers; commends them for the care they have exercised in this direction during the past year, and says, "a larger amount of work has been done than in any previous year, and if the number of rejections is any indication of the care used in selecting the material, we may presume that greater attention than heretofore has been given to this subject."

In the chapter of decisions rendered, we find this: "That members of a □ uniting in a petition for a new □, do not lose their rights and privileges as members of the former until regularly dimitted therefrom." The contrary opinion obtains in many States, but this view of the subject seems to us the only correct one.

There was no report on Foreign Correspondence.

Thomas A. Doyle, of Providence, is Grand Master, and Charles D. Greene, of the same place, Grand Secretary.

SOUTH CAROLINA.

Annual communication held in the city of Charleston, November 19, 1867. Ex-Governor James L. Orr is Grand Master, and R. S. Bruns Grand Secretary. We find many other illustrious names in the list of Grand Officers, men who have a place in the political annals of our country.

Bro. Orr had issued dispensations for opening nine new □. He alludes to the death of Bro. Joseph Rasky, who in his last will and testament devises his entire estate, real and personal, to the Grand □ of South Carolina, in trust for the use and benefit of the families of deceased Master Masons within that jurisdiction. No decisions appear in the address. The Grand Lecturer reports having visited eighty-five □ in his official "grand rounds," affording them such instruction as was found to be necessary. He had made no change in the work, having taught that in which he had been instructed by Bro. A. G. Mackey, and which has always been the authorized work of the State.

Bro. R. S. Bruns gives us a brilliant report on Foreign Correspondence.

It is evident from the absence of any mention of our Grand □, that our journals have not been received.

TENNESSEE.

Fifty-fourth annual held in the city of Nashville, October 7, 1867; a large number of subordinate □ present.

We find the following beautiful paragraph in the address:

" Impressed with a sense of the moral duty which every Mason owes to the fraternity, to accept without hesitation and perform with diligence any and all labor which the confidence of his brethren may intrust to him, I entered upon, and, as far as willing hands could do, have discharged my trust. I have been but a single workman in the quarry, and returning now from my labor, I offer but a single block, an unimportant stone in the great temple of our King. The field where I have labored is one of hallowed associations, and is all aglow with the memory of grand old masters who have preceded me. Their bodies have returned—many of them—to the earth from whence they came; their names are recorded in our hearts, and the memory of their virtues and noble examples survive to us still. Upright and just to all men, and true in their instincts to the moral excellence taught in our order, their lives are the beautiful designs left upon the trestle-board for the workmen that survive."

How beautiful and impressive, and what a noble tribute to the teachers who have gone to the assistance of the Supreme Grand Master, in adorning the Heavenly Temple.

Speaking of the presence in our order of bad men, whose disgraceful examples bring shame upon us before the world, he says: "If we cannot devise some strict precautionary measures of preventing such characters from getting into our □, then must we not, for the preservation of our ancient purity, devise some means of putting them out?"

He had given an opinion in response to an inquiry of which the annexed is the substance:

The Master of a certain □ reported that a member of his □, who was under charges for some unmasonic act, *publicly* black balled a candidate for initiation, having previously declared his intention to do so. The person so rejected was an excellent citizen, worthy all respect and confidence. The questions asked by the Worshipful Master of the □ in which this scene occurred, in submitting the case, are three-fold:

1. Is a member under charges for unmasonic conduct entitled to vote on a ballot for initiation or advancement?

2. If he is not entitled to vote, but wrongfully do so, and casts a black ball, does this illegal vote reject the candidate?

3. If this illegal vote does not reject the candidate, can he be initiated without another ballot?

And are thus answered:

1. A member under charges is not entitled to any privileges, except that

of an impartial trial, and therefore cannot vote on a ballot for initiation or advancement.

2. If but one black ball appears, and that be cast by the member under charges, the candidate is elected, the illegal vote being a nullity.

8. The petitioner is entitled to receive the degrees, having been constitutionally ‌elected.

Bro. Chas. A. Fuller gives us a good report on Foreign Correspondence. Joseph M. Anderson is Grand Master, and Chas. A. Fuller, Grand Secretary.

TEXAS.

The Grand □ of Texas has scarcely recovered from the terrible consequences of civil strife in which, like all other institutions of the State, political, commercial, religious, it bore an active part, not as an institution perhaps, but in the individual force of its members. It could not be expected that Masonry would escape the excitements and attendant disruptions of the universal storm. □ were swept away, their members scattered, peaceful avocations abandoned for the more violent pursuits of war, and to this day the □ thus broken up have not been rebuilt. The Grand Master does not refer to the disasters of war, only to those of the awful pestilence which came after. Listen: "The past season," he says, "was one of unusual sickness, and within the bounds of our jurisdiction the bills of mortality are summed up by the hundreds and thousands, and, especially along our southern border and sea coast, the angel of death appeared to overshadow the whole land. Men deserted their usual avocations, and occupied themselves in nursing the sick and burying the dead. * * * We are called upon to mourn the loss of two of our Past Grand Officers since last we met in grand communication." He had not issued a single dispensation for a new □, nor for conferring the degrees during the year, although many applications had been made for them. He disbelieves in the precedent which permits these things to be done in an indiscriminate manner, and says it needs no long argument to prove the injudiciousness of the practice. His time had been for months occupied in nursing the sick in the late epidemic, and he had finally fallen ill himself, recovering just in time to reach the Grand □ before the opening of the session. He warns his brethren not to become aspirants for the office of Grand Master, under the impression that they would possess a sinecure.

It is decided in this jurisdiction that, in the absence of the Worshipful Master of a □, he is held responsible by the Grand □ for any irregularities which may be committed by his representative. For instance: The Worshipful Master of a certain □ being absent, a stated meeting was presided over by the Junior Warden. The minutes of the preceding meeting were read and adopted by the □, and, on the order of the presiding officer to bring forward the minutes for his approval, the Secretary obeyed, but did so under protest, for the reason that the presiding officer was not the officer who presided at the meeting at which the minutes just read were made out and transcribed. This protest was overruled by the Worshipful Master *pro tem.*, and from this overruling an appeal was taken. The committee on Appeals and Grievances, after stating the case briefly, decide as follows:

"The appeal is not well taken. When the Warden presides in the absence of his superiors, he is invested with all the powers and authority of the Master *pro tem.* The presiding officer of a □ is responsible to the Grand □, as well for a correct record as for any other work pertaining to, or done in, the □."

The same committee unhesitatingly declare that it is improper, as a general rule, for a □ to accord Masonic burial to a deceased non-affiliated Mason. "When," they say, "a Mason voluntarily ostracises himself from the order, and seeks to relieve himself from the active duties and responsibilities of Masonry by withdrawing his membership from the □, he is not entitled upon his demise to demand Masonic sepulture." In all of which we heartily concur.

Peter Gray, of Houston, was chosen Grand Master, and George H. Bringhurst, of the same place, Grand Secretary.

VIRGINIA.

The Grand □ of this State met on the 9th of December, 1867. The address is confined to local affairs. The subjoined resolution, submitted by the committee on Jurisprudence, passed:

"*Resolved,* That it is inexpedient to require or authorize the Master of a subordinate □ to refer petitions for initiation or membership to a select committee, to make inquiry into the character of the applicant, but that it is the imperative duty of the Master, Wardens and members of each □ to make such inquiries."

All good Masters and Wardens who are mindful of the responsibilities imposed by the offices they hold will do this any way, whether required by regulation or not. We cannot exercise too great a degree of caution in the selection of members, and where all manifest equal interest in discovering the exact status of the applicant, some one will be sure to find out the truth. It seems to us, if every Master would take the trouble to impress this duty upon the minds of members, in open □, whenever an applicant is presented, to make the investigation one of general interest, we should be less often deceived in the character of the material that is brought up for the building.

WASHINGTON.

The Grand □ of this Territory commenced its tenth annual communication at Olympia, September 18, 1867. Grand Officers and representatives from six chartered □ were present. The Grand Master found some difficulty in bringing the brethren of Walla Walla □ to a proper comprehension of the fact that they were a Masonic, and not a political organization. One would naturally imbibe the impression, from reading his allusions to the transactions of that □, that it was made the forum for all sorts of political discussions; that the admission of members, and all other matters relating to its government, were conducted with a view to the gratification of political spite, and for the promotion of party supremacy. But, after a good deal of trouble, the Grand Master succeeded in reducing the chaotic elements to order. New officers were placed in the several stations, and peace resumed its wonted reign.

He reports having granted four dispensations to confer degrees out of the usual order. Also, that a party who claimed to have been initiated, passed and raised in a Pennsylvania ☐, had applied for admission into one of the sub-☐ of Washington jurisdiction, but, on examination, was found to possess scarcely any remembrance of the ceremonies or lectures pertaining to the degree, and was therefore rejected. He then applied to the Secretary of the ☐ in which he was made, and received a certificate to the effect that a person bearing his name was enrolled upon his membership register. But, of course, the Worshipful Master of the Washington ☐ is no better off than before, for the question of identity steps in to block proceedings. There is but one way for a Mason to make himself known among the workmen. Failing in this, he must necessarily "go over among the rubbish."

In balloting for officers, the proceedings show that Bro. H. A. Atkins was elected Grand Master, and, on the vote being announced, arose and peremptorily declined the honor.

It is claimed, in nearly all jurisdictions, that no member has a right to ask for, nor decline, an office, but we incline to the belief that with every established rule there are exceptions which are entitled to as much respect as the rule itself. Bro. Atkins plead business engagements which would prevent his acceptance of the position. Surely, no man should assume an office knowing that he cannot discharge its duties.

The balloting was resumed, and Bro. James Biles was chosen Grand Master.

WISCONSIN.

We have before us the twenty-fourth journal of this Grand ☐, for the annual communication held in the city of Milwaukee, June 11, 1867.

Grand Master Youngs being absent through sickness, his address was read by Bro. H. L. Palmer. The organization and progress of the Grand ☐, and of the order generally, from its inception to the present time, is traced with manifest pride and enthusiasm. He says: "Let us for a moment contrast our present condition and prospects with that little band who, though weak in numbers, were strong in faith and earnest of purpose, who met at Madison, in the year 1843, and there solemnly 'resolved that it is expedient to form a Grand ☐ in the Territory of Wisconsin.' That little band was composed of but seven members, the representatives of the only three ☐ in the Territory, whose combined membership was less than seventy-five. Yet to-day, after the lapse of less than a quarter of a century, we meet in grand communication a goodly number of over three hundred representatives of the one hundred and seventy different ☐ scattered over the entire length and breadth of our noble State, from each of whom we hear the welcome tidings of peace and happiness among their members, and of a degree of harmony and prosperity unparalleled in our history.   In view of this and many other blessings which have been so kindly bestowed upon us, it well becomes us to render thanksgiving to Him who has ever had our beloved order in His kind keeping—the Supreme Grand Master of us all."

The Grand Lecturer says he has visited seventy-one ☐ and instructed them in the standard work.   He had found peace and harmony on every side.   "It is well known," says his report, " that but a few years have passed since it was required that our initiates should be well versed in the ritual prior to advancement ; hence, many of the ☐ which were organized prior to that time have but few members who are capable of correctly rehearsing the ritual and conferring the degrees, whereas, those which have been more recently organized, and have complied with the edict of the Grand ☐ with reference to proficiency prior to advancement, are much better qualified to impart Masonic instruction and practice our rites than are most of the older ☐."

Harlow Pease is Grand Master, and W. T. Palmer, Grand Secretary.

CONCLUSION.

And thus we close our labors in the ripe, rich harvests of Masonic literature. On looking back through the sheaves we have gathered and bound together, we realize that many valuable grains of instruction have been added to our store, and are likewise conscious that much of equal value is left upon the field which could not be brought to the garners of the husbandman without crowding them to overflowing.

It has been our pleasure to peruse more than four thousand pages of Masonic proceedings, and to take from them the sweets of wisdom for the use and benefit of those in whose service we have been employed.   A large portion of the work has been accomplished in " pain and tribulation "—all of it under circumstances hostile to elaborate composition.   As we lay aside the pen and submit our handiwork to the wise judgment of our peers in the Masonic congress here assembled, there is but one regret in our hearts— that we cannot present a more acceptable offering.   We ask your indulgence, however, for the manifold imperfections, the errors of " omission and commission " visible in these hastily written folios.   Our object was to collect and arrange in comprehensive form such features of general information as should come before us, and in this manner lead the " less informed brethren " to a more perfect understanding of the Masonic order, its history, jurisprudence, and the incomparable grandeur of its progressive movements throughout our beloved land.

Like the great body of our members, we have paid too little attention to the *study* of our profession. This neglect is in a great measure attributable to the scarcity of Masonic publications in our midst, there being no libraries which contain books of this character, and but few volumes in the hands of individual members. It is greatly to be desired—is, in fact, a necessity—that measures should be taken to secure the early establishment of a Masonic library at some central point in the Territory for the use of Grand □ committees. Without assistance of this kind, it is a difficult task for such committees to bring forth creditable works.

Invoking the blessing of the Supreme Grand Master to rest upon and crown all our efforts for the promotion of friendship, morality and brotherly love, and the material advancement of our ancient and honorable fraternity, we abdicate the high position in which your confidence placed us, and resume our accustomed stations among the ranks of the faithful.

Respectfully, FRANK HALL,
For the Committee.

PROCEEDINGS

OF THE

GRAND LODGE OF COLORADO,

HELD AT DENVER, SEPT. 28, A. L. 5869.

NINTH ANNUAL COMMUNICATION.

The Most Ancient and Honorable Fraternity of Free and Accepted Masons of Colorado, met in Annual Communication at Masonic Hall, in Denver, on the last Tuesday, it being the 28th day, of September, A. D. 1869, A. L. 5869, at 10 o'clock A. M.

Officers present—

M∴ W∴ HENRY M. TELLER, Grand Master.
R∴ W∴ B. W. WISEBART, Senior Grand Warden.
Bro. J. A. BURDICK, *as* Junior Grand Warden.
R∴ W∴ RICHARD SOPRIS, Grand Treasurer.
R∴ W∴ ED. C. PARMELEE, Grand Secretary.
R∴ W∴ L. N. GREENLEAF, Grand Orator.
W∴ JAMES KELLY, Senior Grand Deacon.
W∴ J. W. NESMITH, *as* Junior Grand Deacon.
W∴ E. T. STONE, Grand Sword Bearer.
Bro. J. F. PHILLIPS, } Grand Stewards.
Bro. WM. W. WARE, }
Bro. A. T. RANDALL, *as* Grand Tyler.

PAST GRAND OFFICERS.

P∴ G∴ M∴ ANDREW MASON.
P∴ D∴ G∴ M∴ O. A. WHITTEMORE.
And representatives from subordinate ⌑.

A ⌑ of Master Masons was opened in due form.

37

In reply to the M∴ W∴ Grand Master, the Grand Secretary announced that the representatives from a constitutional number of ▭ were present, and had made returns and paid the dues of their respective ▭.

When the M∴ W∴ Grand ▭ of Colorado was opened in ample form, with prayer by P∴ D∴ G∴ M∴ Whittemore.

The M∴ W∴ Grand Master appointed as committee on Credentials, P∴ G∴ M∴ Mason, P∴ D∴ G∴ M∴ Whittemore, and S∴ G∴ W∴ Wisebart, who, after consultation, submitted the following report, which was received and adopted:

To the M∴ W∴ Grand ▭ of Colorado:

Your committee on Credentials beg leave to submit the following report:

We find the following brethren present, and entitled to seats and votes:

Bros. H. M. Teller, G∴ M∴; B. W. Wisebart, S∴ G∴ W∴; R. Sopris, Grand Treasurer; Ed. C. Parmelee, Grand Secretary; A. Mason, P∴ G∴ M∴; O. A. Whittemore, P∴ D∴ G∴ M∴ '

No. 1: Bros. James Kelley, W∴ M∴; James Scott, proxy for S∴ W∴.

No. 4: Bros. J. F. Phillips, proxy for W∴ M∴; D. A. Hamor, S∴ W∴ and proxy for J∴ W∴.

No. 5: Bros. L. N. Greenleaf, W∴ M∴; J. W. Webster, S∴ W∴; Samuel Bowman, J∴ W∴.

No. 6: Bros. Hal. Sayr, W∴ M∴; Jas. Hutchinson, proxy for S∴ W∴; Wm. J. Joblin, proxy for J∴ W∴.

No. 7: Sam. H. Elbert, W∴ M∴; L. B. France, S∴ W∴; Milo H. Slater, J∴ W∴.

No. 8: Bros. Andrew Mason, W∴ M∴, and proxy for S∴ W∴; Henry Nutt, proxy for J∴ W∴.

No. 12: Bros. William W. Ware, W∴ M∴; James A. Burdick, S∴ W∴; A. W. Brownell, proxy for J∴ W∴.

No. 13: Bro. E. T. Stone, W∴ M∴.

No. 14: Bros. W. T. Potter, W∴ M∴; Orin H. Henry, S∴ W∴; A. W. Harris, proxy for J∴ W∴.

No. 15: Bros. Gideon B. Frazier, W∴ M∴, and proxy for S∴ W∴; S. D. Webster, proxy for J∴ W∴.

No. 16: Bro. E. B. Carling, S∴ W∴.

No. 17: Bros. C. J. Hart, W∴ M∴, and proxy for J∴ W∴; A. Bartlett, S∴ W∴. Fraternally submitted,

ANDREW MASON, }
BENJ. W. WISEBART, } *Committee.*
O. A. WHITTEMORE, }

The M∴ W∴ Grand Master appointed the following committees:

On Visiting Brethren—Bros. Greenleaf, Hart and Stone.

On Returns and Work—Bros. P∴ G∴ M∴ Mason, P∴ D∴ G∴ M∴ Whittemore, and Kelly.

On Finance, Mileage and Per Diem—Bros. Sayr, Frazier and Potter.

On Appeals and Grievances—Bros. Elbert, Phillips and Ware.

The Grand ▭ was then called from labor to refreshment until two o'clock P. M.

TUESDAY, 2 o'clock P. M.

Grand ▭ resumed labor; M∴ W∴ Grand Master Teller in the East.

The committee on Credentials submitted the following additional report :

To the M∴ W∴ Grand ▭ of Colorado :

Your committee on Credentials beg leave to report the following brethren as present and entitled to seats and votes in this Grand ▭ :

Bros. W. D. Anthony, Junior Grand Warden; A. J. Van Deren, Past Grand Master; Chase Withrow, Past Grand Master.

　　　　　　　　　ANDREW MASON, *Chairman.*

Report received and adopted, and the brethren appeared in their respective stations.

The Grand Treasurer presented the following report and accounts, which were read and referred to committee on Finance :

　　　　　　　　　DENVER, September 28, 1869.

To the M∴ W∴ Grand ▭ of A., F. and A. M. of Colorado :

I have the honor herewith to submit my annual report as Treasurer of the Grand ▭ of Colorado for the year ending September 28, 1869, which shows the balance in my hands to date, as follows :

In general fund.... ....$602 83
In library fund. 350 22

　　　Total balance on hand...........................$953 05

All of which is fraternally submitted,

　　　　　　　　　R. SOPRIS, *Grand Treasurer.*

R. SOPRIS, *Grand Treasurer, in account with Grand* ▭ *A., F. and A. M.:*

　　　　　　GENERAL FUND.　　　　　　　　DR.

Oct. 6, 1868. To balance on hand...............................$ 34 83
 "   "   "   " amount received of Grand Secretary........... 940 00

　　　　　　　　　　　　　　　　　　　　　$974 83

CR.

Oct. 6, 1868, by paid warrants Nos. 88 to 107 inclusive....$271 50
"   "   "   J. K. Moore, printing............... 100 00
"   "   balance on hand......................... 602 83
                                                        ————
                                                       $974 33

R. SOPRIS, *Grand Treasurer, in account with Grand □ A., F. and A. M.:*

LIBRARY FUND.   DR.
Oct. 6, 1868, to balance on hand...............................$256 97
"   "   " received of Grand Secretary...................... 27 00
Sept. 28, 1869, to interest on $283.97 from October 6, 1868, to date,
2 per cent. per month... 66 25
                                                            ————
                                                           $350 22
                                                        CR.
Sept. 28, 1869, by balance on hand.....................$350 22

The Grand Secretary presented the following report and accounts, which were read and referred to the committee on Finance:

To the M∴ W∴ Grand □ of Colorado:

Immediately after our last communication I wrote several publishing houses for estimates for republishing proceeding of this Grand □, as contemplated in resolution offered by Bro. D∴ G∴ M∴ Whittemore. Bro. C. Moore, of the Fraternal Publishing Company, of Cincinnati, Ohio, was the only one from whom I received reply. I also wrote all the □ in the jurisdiction to ascertain the number of copies each would subscribe for. Nevada No. 4, Empire No. 8, Washington No. 12, and Pueblo No. 17, only, returned answers, and subscribed for eighty-four copies.

After long delay awaiting subscriptions, and for the report of committee on Foreign Correspondence, I sent manuscript in March last, to Bro. Moore for publication. Bro. J. K. Moore, secretary of said company, acknowledged receipt of manuscript, and the accompanying draft promising to have proceedings printed as soon as possible. Not hearing from there I wrote several letters to ascertain the cause. In June last I received a letter from said J. K. Moore, promising to have proceedings out in two or three weeks, since which time I have not heard from him or said company, as they do not *condescend* to answer my letters, which I suppose is the said company's style of doing business.

On the 20th inst. I received a letter, with bill enclosed, from the Elm Street Printing Company, of Cincinnati, dated Sept. 10th inst., stating that the proceedings had been shipped to me by express, directed to Central City. The box arrived there, was taken from the express office, opened, and six copies only forwarded to me at Georgetown, Saturday last.

None of the □ have made returns of the amount, if any, collected for the purpose of procuring suitable Grand □ jewels.

I have received during the past year a reprint of proceedings of Grand □ of Indiana, from its organization in 1817, to 1845 inclusive; also, Vol. 4 of proceedings of Grand □ of Iowa, making a complete file of proceedings

of that Grand ☐ from its organization in 1844, to 1868; also, Vol. 2 of reprint of proceedings of Grand ☐ of New Hampshire, from 1842 to 1856 ;*
also, of Bro. Jesse B. Anthony, of Troy, N. Y., a pamphlet containing a review of the proceedings of the Grand ☐ of New York from its organization
in 1781, to 1852 inclusive, and the following monthly publications: The
Freemason, of St. Louis, the *Masonic Monthly*, of Boston, the *American Freemason*, of Cincinnati, the *Masons' Home Book*, of Philadelphia, the *Bulletin
of the Grand Orient of France;* also, the weekly New York *Courier*, together
with sample copies of various other Masonic publications.

The proceedings of our sister Grand ☐ have been forwarded to the
chairman of the committee on Foreign Correspondence as received.

Since our last communication, Bro. Simri Rose, Grand Secretary of the
Grand ☐ of Georgia since 1845, has been summoned from labor to rest.
Bro. Rose had, I think, three seniors in term of service in the office of
Grand Secretary, viz: Bro. John Dove, of Virginia; Bro. Joseph H.
Hough, of New Jersey; and Bro. Theo. S. Parvin, of Iowa.

I have been called upon to issue several certificates to members of extinct ☐, and to certify to numerous diplomas. Considering the small
balance in our treasury, I would suggest the propriety of this body pre-
scribing suitable fees for such services.

Several of the ☐ failed to furnish this office with a list of their officers,
as required by section twenty-five of our By-Laws. But *two* ☐ complied
with section five of the By-Laws in regard to the time of making their
reports, and but *one* as regards time of paying their Grand ☐ dues.

A majority of the returns of subordinate ☐ are incorrect in some particular—showing great carelessness in their preparation, especially in the
spelling of names of members, and in the recapitulation. None give the
full names of all the brethren, and a part only arranging them in alphabetical order. I was compelled to send back some of the returns for cor-
rection, and others ought to have been, but were not received in season to
do so.

I endeavored to prepare statistical tables from the annual returns, showing the work of the various ☐ since the formation of the Grand ☐, but
found it impossible so to do on account of the vast number of errors in
them.   Fraternally submitted,

                        ED. C. PARMELEE, *Grand Secretary.*

ED. C. PARMELEE, *Grand Secretary, in account with the Grand ☐ of Colorado:*

GENERAL FUND.   DR.

To cash received for charters..	$ 60	00
" " "	of ☐ for dues..	871	50
" " "	of members of Summit ☐, No. 2, and for certifi-		
	cates issued..	15	00
" " "	for sale of proceedings............................	1	00
Total..	$947	50

*Vol. 1 has never been received.—GRAND SECRETARY.

By paid freight and express charges....................$ 9 50
"   "   postage and stationery.........................   16 80
"   "   Grand Treasurer..............................   914 20
"   "   refunded overpaid dues........................   7 50

    Total...$947 50

As per detailed statement herewith submitted.

[Black Hawk ☐ No. 11 made returns and paid dues after above report was submitted. —GRAND SEC.]

Ed. C. Parmelee, Grand Secretary, in account with Grand ☐ of Colorado:

LIBRARY FUND.   DR.
Oct. 6, 1868, to donation of Bro. Teller...........................$ 4 00
Oct. 6, 1868, to donation of Bro. Wisebart......................... 4 00
Sept. 28, 1869, to received of Grand Master for special dispensations. 6 00

    $14 00

CR.
Oct. 6, 1868, by paid Grand Treasurer.......................$ 8 00
Sept. 28, 1869, by cash on hand............................ 6 00

    $14 00

Bro. Sayr offered the following, which was adopted :

Resolved, That the Grand representative system be approved by this Grand ☐, and our Grand Officers are hereby authorized to reciprocate such appointments in each particular, the Grand Secretary keeping a record of all such appointments.

Bro. Ed. C. Parmelee submitted his credentials as the representative of the M∴ W∴ Grand ☐ of Missouri, near this Grand ☐, and on motion, was fraternally received and acknowledged as such.

The M∴ W∴ Grand Master then delivered the following

ADDRESS:

Brethren of the Grand ☐:

It is with peculiar pleasure that I extend you a fraternal greeting on this our ninth Annual Grand Communication, Let us return thanks to the Supreme Architect of the Universe for the manifold blessings we have enjoyed during the past Masonic year.

During the past year my official acts have been few and unimportant. I granted a dispensation to Columbia ☐ No. 14, to ballot on the application of a number of brethren for affiliation on the same day the petitions were presented. I did this at the request of the brethren of Columbia ☐, who were anxious that the applicants might become members in time to take part in the annual election for officers. I at the same time granted a dispensation to said Columbia ☐ to elect the Worshipful Master from among the brethren who had not served as Warden. This I did at the earnest request of Bro. Potter, who had served as Warden of the □. There was no resident member eligible except Bro. Potter, and that brother resided a distance of thirty miles from the □. I therefore thought it best to give the brethren an opportunity to elect some one else if they desired. Bro. Potter was elected to the entire satisfaction of the □.

In January last I received a petition from the brethren at Granite, Lake county, for a dispensation to open a □. The petition was presented to me on the eve of my departure for the east, and I therefore deferred action on it until my return in April. After consultation with the R∴ W∴ Deputy Grand Master, and R∴ W∴ Senior Grand Warden, I determined not to grant the request. I was induced to reject this application for various reasons. The brethren of Granite furnished me no evidence of the ability of the proposed Worshipful Master to confer the degrees and take charge of a □. Neither was I satisfied that there was suitable Masonic material in the neighborhood to justify the formation of a □. While I was yet undetermined whether to grant the dispensation or refuse it, I was urged by one of the brethren to grant it because they had already incurred considerable expense, and were then in debt. If there had been no other objection to granting the dispensation except this, I should have refused it. A □ cannot make a worse start than to be in debt, and if there is not sufficient interest taken among the brethren to see that the □ starts out of debt, I think it well to let them wait.

In May last I also received a petition from a number of brethren at Idaho, Clear Creek county, for a dispensation to open a □. In this case I was fully satisfied as to the ability of the proposed Worshipful Master to confer the degrees and to take charge of a □. The proposed Worshipful Master had served several years as Master of a □, and was well instructed in the work and lectures. The brethren had made arrangements for a suitable place to meet and would have commenced out of debt, yet owing to the sparseness of the population in that vicinity, and the uncertainty of many of the brethren remaining in that place, I thought it best to refuse the dispensation. I did so with great reluctance. I am anxious that the brethren of every section shall enjoy the blessings of Masonic intercourse with one another, and in a new jurisdiction, like ours, it is not strange that the brethren should desire to see the number of □ increased, yet I do not think it best to fill the jurisdiction with weak □. The great expense attendant on supporting a □ in this new country often renders it a burden instead of a benefit, and perhaps a few brethren are compelled to keep up the □ at quite a sacrifice. The demands of the □ for money to meet the current expenses, such as rent, lights and fuel, become so pressing that when a petition is presented the brethren think more of the advantage to be derived by the candidate's election in a pecuniary view, than of the qualifications which should recommend him to be made a Mason. It is impossible for a small □, embarrassed with debts, to do justice to the fraternity at large. I trust that no one will think that I am losing sight of the fact that the strength of a □ does not consist in numbers, or the amount in its treasury, but in the virtue, zeal and intelligence of its members.

I also received a petition from the brethren at South Pass City for a dispensation to open a □, but as it did not come to my hands until within a month I refused it. I will call the attention of the brethren of this Grand □ to Section 11 of our By-Laws, which provides what the petition for a dispensation shall contain, and that such petition shall be accompanied by the recommendation of the nearest □ certifying the truth of the statements contained in the petition. It is the duty of the □ whose recommendation accompanies the petition to carefully investigate the case, determine everything that the petition alleges in the affirmative, and must know in a Masonic way that all the petitioners are Master Masons, and that there is one Past Master on the petition, and certify that the statements in the petition are true, and recommend the granting of the dispensation. This is necessary to enable the Grand Master to form a correct opinion of the propriety of granting a dispensation.

In April last I received a communication from Bro. Moses Anker, of Denver No. 5. He complained that he had not been allowed to visit Pueblo □ No. 17. The facts, as I understand them from Bro. Anker's letter, and from the officers of No. 17, are, one of the members of No. 17 objected to sitting in □ with Bro. Anker, and the Worshipful Master informed Bro. Anker that he could not visit the □ until the objection was withdrawn. I sustained the ruling of the Worshipful Master. I have also learned that a case of like character occurred in Mount Moriah □ No. 14, with like ruling by the Worshipful Master. I think that the rule is well settled that a visiting brother cannot unseat a member.

The brethren of Pueblo □ No. 17, expelled one Wm. H. Chapman for conduct unbecoming a Mason, and I approved the action of the □ in so doing.

＊   ＊   ＊   ＊   ＊   ＊   ＊   ＊   ＊

In accordance with the resolution of the Grand □ in its last Annual Communication, Columbia □ No. 14 has been removed to Boulder City, and I am gratified to state that the □ is in a flourishing condition.

The Grand □ library fund, amounting to $350.22, is in the hands of the R∴ W∴ Grand Treasurer. I would recommend, as I did on a former occasion, that this fund be kept at interest until such times as the Grand □ shall be permanently located, and I would suggest to the brethren the propriety of increasing that fund by such donations as they may feel able from time to time to make.

At the last Annual Communication the R∴ W∴ Grand Secretary was authorized to reprint 800 copies of the proceedings of the Grand □ since its organization, provided the fraternity would subscribe for 300 copies. I am informed by the R∴ W∴ Grand Secretary that the requisite number of subscriptions not being obtained, he did not reprint. It is to be regretted that the brethren did not take sufficient interest in this matter to subscribe for the requisite number of the reprint. The expense, when divided among the brethren of the fraternity, is trifling, yet entirely too much for the Grand ▢ at this time. The proceedings of our first and second Annual Grand Communications were published in limited quantities, and the demand has long since exceeded the supply. I presume it is safe to say that not one member in ten, could, if he desired so to do, provide himself with copies of the first and second Annual Communications of this Grand ▢, and I trust this matter will not be dropped until the brethren have taken sufficient interest in it to justify the reprinting of the proceedings.

I desire to call the attention of the brethren to one of the standing resolutions of this Grand ▢, adopted in November, 1865, which makes it the "imperative duty of the subordinate ▢ in the jurisdiction to restrain as far as possible the Masonic crime of intemperance by trial and suspension or expulsion, as the case may require." The vice of intemperance prevails to an alarming extent among the fraternity in this jurisdiction. It is to be regretted that so many of the brethren have forgotten that the virtue of temperance should be the constant practice of every Mason, and daily bring disgrace and reproach, not only on themselves, but on the institution of Freemasonry. I trust the Worshipful Masters of the subordinate ▢ will endeavor by all means in their power, to comply with the requirements of this resolution, ever remembering that due allowance must be made for the weakness of humanity, and that they are not to "aggravate the offenses of their brethren but judge with candor, admonish with friendship, and reprehend with justice, tempered with mercy."

*   *   *   *   *   *   *   *   *

It is with sorrow I announce to this Grand ▢ the death of Past Grand Master Allyn Weston. Bro. Weston died after a short illness, at Brooklyn, in the State of New York, on the 12th of May last. Bro. Weston was, at the time of his death, a permanent member of this Grand ▢, having been its first Grand Lecturer and its second Grand Master. In 1863 Bro. Weston removed to the State of New York and resided there until his death. The Grand Master of New York appointed a committee to convey the remains of our distinguished brother to the home of his father in Massachusetts. The brethren of this jurisdiction will long remember Bro. Weston as an accomplished gentleman, and earnest and intelligent Mason; and very much of the Masonic zeal which has been exhibited among the fraternity in this jurisdiction was, in a great measure, due to the example set them by our deceased brother. I trust this Grand body will take suitable steps to do honor to the memory of our beloved brother.

The press of professional business has been such that during the past year I have not been able to supervise the work, and give that close personal examination to the condition of the various ▢ I had hoped to do, yet I have no hesitation in saying that the ▢ in all parts of this jurisdiction are doing well; that with few exceptions harmony exists in all the subordinate ▢ among the brethren. Our numbers have increased by the admission of good and worthy men, and the financial condition of the various ▢ im-

38

proves year by year, and I trust the day is not far distant when every ☐ in this jurisdiction will be out of debt.

I desire again to thank the members and officers of this Grand ☐ for the kindness and courtesy which they have extended to me. During the three years I have served you as Grand Master, I can recall no instance when I have failed to receive that hearty, cordial support, and cheerful co-operation which it has ever pleased you to yield to the Grand Master of Masons in this jurisdiction.

*   *   *   *   *   *   *   *   *

May the blessings of Heaven rest on you and all regular Masons, and when we shall have done with things below, may we find ready admission into that Celestial ☐ above, where the Supreme Architect of the Universe presides.   H. M. TELLER,
Grand Master of Masons in Colorado.

On motion of P∴ G∴ M∴ Withrow, that portion of the M∴ W∴ Grand Master's address referring to the death of P∴ G∴ M∴ Weston, was referred to a special committee, consisting of P∴ G∴ M∴ Withrow, P∴ G∴ M∴ Van Deren, and P∴ G∴ M∴ Mason.

On motion of P∴ G∴ M∴ Mason, that portion of the M∴ W∴ Grand Master's address referring to the library fund, was referred to the Finance committee.

Bro. J. C. Hart, W∴ M∴ of Pueblo ☐ No. 17, presented a copy of the charges against Bro. Wm. H. Chapman, and the proceedings of the trial held by the ☐, which were read ; and, on motion, the action of Pueblo ☐ No. 17, expelling Wm. H. Chapman, an Entered Apprentice of said ☐, from all the rights and privileges of Masonry, was sustained.

The following was read and ordered published with the proceedings :

At a regular communication of Denver ☐ No. 5, A., F. & A. M., held Saturday evening, Sept. 18th, A. L, 5869, it was, upon motion,

Resolved, That the use of the Masonic Hall be tendered to the Grand ☐ of Colorado during its ensuing session.

                                   B. W. ROGERS, *Secretary.*

Bro. Greenleaf offered the following, which was adopted unanimously :

Resolved, That it is the sense of this Grand ☐, that whenever the admission of a visiting brother is objected to by a member of a subordinate ☐ within this jurisdiction, the Master shall refuse to admit such visiting brother; and that the rulings of the Masters of Mount Moriah ☐ No. 15, and Pueblo ☐ No. 17 be, and the same are hereby sustained.   •

P∴ D∴ G∴ M∴ Whittemore offered a resolution, which, after amendment, was adopted, as follows:

Resolved, That all subordinate ☐ within the jurisdiction of this Grand ☐, be instructed not to receive a petition for affiliation from any brother holding membership outside of this jurisdiction, unless accompanied by a dimit or a certificate of good standing from the ☐ of which the petitioner was last a member.

S∴ G∴ W∴ Wisebart moved that the election of officers for the ensuing Masonic year, be held at 8 o'clock this evening,

Motion concurred in.

Bro. Sayr, chairman of committee on Foreign Correspondence, reported that he had prepared a report, but by an oversight had left it at Central, and was unable to present it to the Grand ☐.

Bro. J∴ G∴ W∴ Anthony moved that the report on Correspondence be printed with the proceedings of this communication.

Motion concurred in.

P∴ G∴ M∴ Mason, for the committee on Credentials, verbally reported Bros. J. W. Nesmith, Worshipful Master; John Boylan, Senior Warden; and Robert Frazer, proxy for Junior Warden, of Black Hawk ☐, No. 11, as present and entitled to seats and votes in this Grand ☐.

Report received and adopted.

The Grand ☐ was then called from labor to refreshment until 8 o'clock P. M.

TUESDAY, 8 o'clock P. M.

Grand ☐ resumed labor; Grand Master Teller in the East.

This being the appointed time for the election of officers for the ensuing, Masonic year, the M∴ W∴ Grand Master appointed as tellers Bros. Sayr and Hart.

The election was then held, resulting in the election of

Bro. HENRY M. TELLER, M∴ W∴ Grand Master;
Bro. RICHARD SOPRIS, R∴ W∴ Deputy Grand Master;
Bro. WEBSTER D. ANTHONY, R∴ W∴ Senior Grand Warden;
Bro. HAL. SAYR, R∴ W∴ Junior Grand Warden;
Bro. WM. W. WARE, R∴ W∴ Grand Treasurer;
Bro. ED. C. PARMELEE, R∴ W∴ Grand Secretary.

Past Deputy Grand Master Whittemore moved that the following be stricken from the standing resolutions of this Grand □:

Resolved, That it is at variance with the spirit of Masonry to make nominations for officers in Grand or subordinate ⌼, and the practice is hereby prohibited in this Grand □ jurisdiction.

Motion lost.

Past Deputy Grand Master Whittemore moved that the following be stricken from the standing resolutions of this Grand □:.

WHEREAS, Attempts are being made to force upon sister Grand ⌼ the institution known as the "Conservator's Association," contrary to and in violation of the ancient cardinal principles and regulations of our beloved order, therefore be it

Resolved, 1st. That the M∴ W∴ Grand □ of Colorado solemnly declare the said Association a corrupt organization, treasonable to the institution of Masonry, and subversive of its sacred interests, honor and perpetuation.

2d. That the M∴ W∴ Grand □ of Colorado peremptorily interdict and forbid the introduction of the above-mentioned work or organization in any Masonic body in this Grand jurisdiction.

3d. That no Mason, subject or adhering to said Association, shall be allowed to sit in or visit this Grand □, or any subordinate □ thereunder, or hold affiliation with, or be recognized by, any Mason in this jurisdiction.

Motion concurred in.

The Grand □ was then called from labor to refreshment to meet at 9 o'clock A. M. to-morrow.

WEDNESDAY, 9 o'CLOCK A. M.

Grand □ resumed labor, G∴ M∴ Teller in the East, officers and members present as yesterday.

Yesterday's proceedings read and approved.

The M∴ W∴ Grand Master-elect annnounced the following as the appointed officers for the ensuing Masonic year:

Bro. Rev. WM. A. AMSBARY, Grand Chaplain.
Bro. Rev. JOHN L. PECK, Grand Orator.
Bro. CHASE WITHROW, Grand Lecturer.
Bro. JOHN L. DAILEY, Grand Marshal.
Bro. C. J. HART, Senior Grand Deacon.
Bro. E. T. STONE, Junior Grand Deacon.
Bro. G. B. FRAZIER, Grand Sword Bearer.
Bro. D. A. HAMOR, Senior Grand Steward.
Bro. J. A. BURDICK, Junior Grand Steward.
Bro. NOAH D. HASKELL, Grand Tyler.

P∴ G∴ M∴ Mason, assisted by P∴ D∴ G∴ M∴ Whittemore as Grand Marshal, then installed M∴ W∴ Henry M. Teller Grand Master-elect, who installed the other elective and appointed officers, who assumed their respective stations.

The special committee on the death of P∴ G∴ M∴ Weston presented the following report, which was read, and on motion, received and adopted:

To the M∴ W∴ Grand ☐ of Colorado :

Your committee appointed to draft resolutions expressive of the feelings of this Grand ☐ upon the death of P∴ G∴ M∴ Allyn Weston, respectfully report the following:

WHEREAS, It has pleased Almighty God to remove by death our brother Allyn Weston, Past Grand Master of Masons of Colorado, and, whereas, we feel deeply the loss Masonry has sustained, therefore,

Resolved, That by the death of P∴ G∴ M∴ Weston, Masonry has lost one of its brightest lights, and, that Colorado Masonry has lost a brother, who, identified as he was, with the early history of Masonry in the Territory, will ever be remembered with the warmest fraternal respect.

Resolved, That a committee of one be appointed by the Grand Master to collect the principal facts connected with Bro. Weston's Masonic history in Colorado, and that after approval by the Grand Master, they be published with the proceedings of this Grand ☐, and that when so published, the Grand Secretary be directed to forward copies to the relatives of Bro. Weston.

Resolved, That as a suitable token of our respect, a page of our printed proceedings be set apart to his memory.

Respectfully submitted,

CHASE WITHROW, ⎫
ANDREW MASON, ⎬ *Committee.*
A. J. VAN DEREN, ⎭

The committee on Returns and Work submitted the following report, which was, on motion, received and adopted:

To the M∴ W∴ Grand □ of Colorado:

Your committee appointed on Returns and Work of ▣, beg leave to report that they find in the returns of Denver □, No. 5, R. O. Old, W. M. Slaughter and John Wanlass reported as out of the Territory. Believing the language, "out of the Territory," to mean out of the jurisdiction of the Grand □, we think the members above named should not be exempt from Grand □ dues, as some or all of them are known to be within the jurisdiction of ▣ subordinate to this Grand □; W. M. Slaughter being at Georgetown; R. O. Old now in Denver; and John Wanlass a resident at Laramie, and within this jurisdiction. W. W. Slaughter, returned as a member of No. 5, is also reported as an member and officer of No. 16, and was, we think, dimitted from No. 5 when No. 16 was chartered.

In the returns of Central □, No. 6, we find E. L. Gardner, now in Denver, reported as out of the Territory; and L. B. Weil is reported as a member of No. 6, and out of the Territory; also on returns of Cheyenne □, No. 16, as a member. If a charter member of Cheyenne □, we think he should be returned as dimitted from No. 6.

The returns of the other ▣ we find correct.

Respectfully submitted,

ANDREW MASON, ⎫
JAMES KELLY, ⎬ *Committee.*
O. A. WHITTEMORE, ⎭

The committee on Finance, Mileage and Per Diem submitted the following report, which was, on motion, received and adopted:

To the M∴ W∴ Grand □ of Colorado:

Your committee on Finance, Mileage and Per Diem beg leave to submit the following report:

We have examined the Grand Secretary's and Grand Treasurer's reports and accounts, and find them correct. We also find the following Grand Officers, Past Grand Officers and representatives in attendance and entitled to the following pay:

M∴ W∴ H. M. Teller, Grand Master............................$14 00
∴ W∴ B. W. Wisebart, Senior Grand Warden................... 14 00
R∴ W∴ W. D. Anthony, Junior Grand Warden................. 4 00
∴ W∴ R. Sopris, Grand Treasurer............................. 5 50
∴ W∴ Ed. C. Parmelee, Grand Secretary....................... 16 50
∴ W∴ Andrew Mason, Past Grand Master....................... 16 50
∴ W∴ A. J. Van Deren, Past Grand Master.................... 14 00
∴ W∴ Chase Withrow, Past Grand Master...................... 7 75
R∴ W∴ O. A. Whittemore, Past Deputy Grand Master........... 4 00
Bro. James Kelly, No. 1..................................... 7 75
Bro. J. F. Phillips, No. 4.................................. 14 25
Bro. L. N. Greenleaf, No. 5................................. 4 00

Bro. Hal. Sayr, No. 6... 14 60
Bro. S. H. Elbert, No. 7.......................... .... 4 00
Bro. J. W. Nesmith, No. 11...................................... 13 75
Bro. W. W. Ware, No. 12... 16 50
Bro. E. T. Stone, No. 13............................ .... 22 75
Bro. W. T. Potter, No. 14.. 11 00
Bro. G. B. Frazier, No. 15.. 35 25
Bro. E. B. Carling, No. 16.. 31 50
Bro. C. J. Hart, No. 17.........:................................. 31 50

Fraternally submitted,

HAL. SAYR,   ⎫
G. B. FRAZIER, ⎬ *Committee.*
W. F. POTTER, ⎭

Deputy Grand Master Sopris moved that the Grand Secretary be allowed one hundred and fifty dollars for his services for the past Masonic year.

Motion concurred in.

Past Deputy Grand Master Whittemore offered the following:

Resolved, That the R∴ W∴ Grand Secretary be authorized to have reprinted eight hundred copies of the past proceedings of this Grand ☐, *providing* the fraternity of this jurisdiction shall subscribe for three hundred copies of the same, at an advance of fifty cents per copy upon the actual cost; the price per copy not to exceed two dollars; three hundred copies to be retained in the library of the Grand ☐ for future use.

Resolution adopted.

S∴ G∴ W∴ Anthony offered the following:

Resolved, That the Secretary call the roll of ☐, and that the representatives present announce what number of copies of the reprint of our proceedings will be taken by their respective ☐.

Resolution adopted.

Upon the roll of ☐ being called, the representatives present subscribed for 354 copies of said reprint.

P∴ G∴ M∴ Van Deren moved that the following be stricken from the standing resolutions of this Grand ☐:

Resolved, That no proxies issued in blank by the Worshipful Master or Wardens of any subordinate ☐ in this jurisdiction, shall be received, or entitle the holders thereof to a vote in this Grand body.

Motion concurred in.

P∴ G∴ M∴ Withrow offered the following:

Resolved, That the Grand Secretary be authorized to collect a fee of one dollar for each certificate of standing issued to members of defunct ⌑, and a like sum for each other certificate, not otherwise provided for, given by him under the seal of the Grand ⌑, and that the amount so received be paid into the library fund.

Resolution adopted.

P∴ G∴ M∴ Mason offered the following:

Resolved, That the thanks of this Grand ⌑ are hereby tendered to the Masonic bodies of Denver for the free use of their hall during this Grand Annual Communication.

Resolution adopted.

P∴ G∴ M∴ Van Deren moved that a committee be appointed to select a design, and procure a set of jewels for this Grand ⌑, and that a warrant be drawn on the Treasurer for that purpose, in a sum of not to exceed three hundred dollars.

Motion concurred in, and P∴ G∴ M∴ Van Deren, S∴ G∴ W∴ Anthony, and P∴ G∴ M∴ Mason were appointed said committee.

On motion, a warrant was ordered drawn on the Treasurer for ten dollars, in favor of Bro. A. T. Randall, for services as Grand Tyler.

The M∴ W∴ Grand Master announced the following standing committees:

On Jurisprudence.—P∴ G∴ M∴ Andrew Mason, P∴ G∴ M∴ Chase Withrow, P∴ G∴ M∴ A. J. Van Deren.

On Foreign Correspondence.—P∴ J∴ G∴ W∴ L. N. Greenleaf, P∴ D∴ G∴ M∴ O. A. Whittemore, Bro. James Kelly.

The minutes were then read and approved, when the ninth Annual Communication of the Most Ancient and Honorable Fraternity of Free and Accepted Masons of Colorado was closed in ample form, with prayer by the R∴ W∴ Grand Orator.

ED. C. PARMELEE, *Grand Secretary.*

RETURNS OF LODGES.

GOLDEN CITY □ NO. 1, GOLDEN CITY.

Regular meetings: first and third Saturdays of each month.

OFFICERS.

James Kelly, W. M.
C. C. Carpenter, S. W.
F. O. Sawin, J. W.

Arthur C. Harris, Treas.
M. C. Kirby, Sec.

D. E. Harrison, S. D.
J. C. Remington, J. D.
John Churches, Tyler.

MEMBERS.

G. N. Belcher,
M. L. Sawin,
Perry L. Smith,
W. J. Cram,
Fox Diefendorf,
Reuben Borton,
S. M. Breath,
J. M. Ferrell,
E. B. Smith,
Daniel McClary,
Samuel F. Shafer,
John B. Hendry,
L. M. Frary,
S. B. Williams,
John Sexton,
D. G. Dargen,

J. S. Maynard,
W. A. H. Loveland,
John Kean,
Lewis Davis,
J. C. Bowles,
Henry Stephens,
J. R. Gilbert,
Geo. Morrison,
James Scott,
Ephram Fellows,
Perry P. Pollock,
J. B. Langdon,
W. D. Ripley,
W. R. Nelson,
S. C. Clinton,
Felix Crocker,
Abram Slater,

Martin Opal,
J. D. Carns,
Stephen Bailey,
John Strouse,
John H. Durham,
H. M. Bussell,
Wm. Ashley,
Owen Williams,
William Howell,
E. L. Eggers,
N. F. Cheesman,
T. B. Gardner,
Peter Eskins,
G. W. Reeves,
A. P. Patton,
A. R. Roney.

FELLOWCRAFT.

Wesley Teter.

ENTERED APPRENTICES.

J. A. Bartholomew,
G. W. Jones,
M. H. Knapp,
Allen Lewis,

Leon Mallett,
Joseph Parrott,
Barney Pratt,
Thomas Shenden,
A. M. Wallingford,

Bruce Woodward,
John H. Myers,
H. Biggs,
W. H. Curry.

DIMITTED.

John A. Moore,
John F. Kirby,

G. M. Chilcott,

J. H. Pinkerton,
G. C. Peck.

SUMMIT □ NO. 2, PARKVILLE,

Charter Surrendered.

ROCKY MOUNTAIN ☐ NO. 3, GOLD HILL.

Extinct.

NEVADA ☐ NO. 4, NEVADA.

Regular meetings: second and fourth Saturdays of each month.

OFFICERS.

T. H. Craven, W. M.
D. A. Hamor, S. W.
B. F. Shaffer, J. W.

B. C. Waterman, Treas.
C. Visscher, Sec.
Wm. Emperor, S. D.
I. N. Henry, J. D.

Thos. Woodward, S. S.
Robert Hughes, J. S.
J. W. Ratliff, Tyler.

MEMBERS.

A. J. Van Deren, P.G.M.
A. M. Jones, P. S. G. W.
J. F. Phillips, P. M.
Preston Anderson,
W. F. Avery,
J. M. Aldrich,
Thos. J. Ashton,
A. J. Biggs,
W. H. Belcher,
James Baxter,
S. G. Brown,
Geo. H. Barrett,
J. E. Craine,
Edward Crockett,
Joseph Codling,
J. C. Donnelly,
B. W. Eussen,
Otto Eckhardt,

D. L. Fairchild,
Wm. Finley,
J. E. Gregg,
F. I. Hibbard,
Wm. Hyndman,
John Hatswell,
W. S. Haswell,
Michael Hattenbach,
W. H. James,
James Jones,
W. H. Jester,
Francis Jeffrey,
Perry A. Kline,
C. A. Lyon,
A. L. Miller,
Robert Millikin,
George Marshall,
Orlando North,
Thomas Newlun,

Andrew Nichols,
Dennis O'Brien,
G. W. Pepper,
W. D. Purkins,
B. F. Pease,
Albert Price,
I. M. Parsons,
A. C. Rupe,
John Rutherford,
J. W. Stanton,
Joseph Standley,
Isaac Sands,
Horace Shaw,
Walter Scott,
J. A. Shanstron,
P. G. Shanstron,
O. T. Sparks,
A. W. Tucker.

FELLOWCRAFT.

James Trezise.

DIMITTED.

W. R. Uren, E. B. Newman.

DIED.

A. C. McGeath, Preston Scott.

DENVER ☐, NO. 5, DENVER.

Regular meetings: first and third Saturdays in each month.

OFFICERS.

L. N. Greenleaf, W. M.
J. W. Webster, S. W.
S. H. Bowman, J. W.

Geo. Tritch, Treas.
B. W. Rogers, Sec.
W. Londener, S. D.
J. E. Le Cavelier, J. D.

N. H. Rice, S. S.
P. Tunnstein, J. S.
A. T. Randall, Tyler.

MEMBERS.

T. P. Ames,
W. D. Arnedt,
A. O. Ashley,
J. S. Addleman,
W. N. Byers,
A. H. Barker,
G. H. Bryant,
J. M. Broadwell,
Bernard Berry,
J. L. Bartells,
Julius Berry,
F. R. Bennett,
G. G. Brewer,
L. E. Bussell,
O. Brooks,
C. A. Cook,
E. W. Cobb,
F. A. Clark, P. M.
G. T. Clark,
W. S. Cheesman,
R. Cleveland,
H. T. Clarke,
J. G. Casey,
James Clellan,
H. A. Clough,
J. L. Daily,
Wm. M. Daily,
J. C. Davidson,
F. M. Durkee,
A. Davidson,
J. H. Dudley,
J. W. Douglass,
M. Deitsch,
J. H. Eames,

W. R. Ford,
H. T. Ford,
H. Feurstein,
H. H. Farling,
I. Friend,
J. H. Garrish,
A. Goldsmith,
C. J. Goss,
G. H. Greenslip,
A. Hanauer,
J. S. Howell,
B. C. Hayman,
G. W. Hertell,
H. Hitchins,
J. H. Hodges,
J. M. Holland,
C. L. Hall,
Warren Hussey,
R. L. Hattan,
M. Hallett,
C. Hinebaugh,
E. H. Jewett,
T. W. Johnson,
G. W. Kassler,
W. N. Keith,
E. W. Kingsbury,
J. Kershaw,
G. K. Kimball,
H. Kline,
Joseph Kline,
J. B. Lamber,
J. Lambert,
F. Meserve,

James McNasser,
A. McCune,
Julius Mitchell,
G. L. Moody,
Samuel Mitchell,
F. A. McDonald,
L. McCarty,
R. O. Old,
David Parlin,
E. E. Ropes,
H. J. Rogers,
J. W. Richards,
W. M. Slaughter,
J. J. Seville,
H. Z. Solamon,
E. Scudder,
M. B. Sherwood,
Wm. Stepp,
G. L. Shoup,
W. W. Slaughter,
A. Shinner,
A. Slane,
F. Shirmer,
A. Sagendorf, P. M.
R. Sopris,
W. E. Turner,
W. J. Thompson,
S. W. Treat,
H. B. Tuttle,
John Wanlass,
G. W. Webster,
F. R. Waggoner,
S. T. Wells,
J. T. Yonkers.

FELLOWCRAFTS.

J. E. Bush,

Henry Levison,

C. F. Parkhurst.

ENTERED APPRENTICES.

H. B. Chamberlin,
W. H. Evans,
T. B. Farmer,
John Good,
J. W. Kerr,

G. N. Lowe,
S. McClellan,
J. Molson,
M. C. McGuire,
Wm. Nolan,

G. W. Perkins,
H. N. Shannon,
J. N. Talman,
John Upton,
C. S. Wheeler.

Permission granted P. A. Leiner, E. A., and H. H. Ellis, F. C., to receive degrees in other ⬜.

DIMITTED.

M. Anker,
N. A. Baker,
J. C. Carter,

B. F. Downen,
J. E. Gates,
C. J. Hart,
E. Hexter,

R. P. Laub,
W. D. Robinson,
Daniel Shuts.

CENTRAL □ NO. 6, CENTRAL CITY.

Regular meetings: second and fourth Wednesdays of each month.

OFFICERS.

Hal Sayr, W. M.
Elam C. Beach, S. W.
Hugh Butler, J. W.

J. R. Cleaveland, Treas.
Samuel I. Lorah, Sec.
William F. Sears, S. D.
James Hutchinson, J. D.

Richard C. Lake, S. S.
John Best, J. S.
*Noah D. Haskell, Tyler.

MEMBERS.

J. N. Adams,
G. H. Adams,
Wm. Aitcheson,
Wm. A. Amsbury,
Wm. F. Allen,
E. H. Beals,
E. H. Brown,
Thos. Barnes,
I. B. Brunell,
B. R. S. Bachtel,
Sam. A. Buell,
Geo. W. Brewer,
James Clark,
J. B. Cofield,
Joseph Coleman,
D. C. Collier,
W. P. Caldwell,
L. W. Chase, P. M.
G. B. Cornell,
N. Z. Cozens,
W. Z. Cozens,
A. S. Cobb,
H. A. Clough,
Marcus Crohn,
Thos. J. Campbell,
A. B. Davis,
J. J. Dunnegan,
P. H. Dunnegan,
F. M. Danielson,
J. V. Dexter,
Wm. T. Ellis,
H. R. Eldred,
E. L. Gardner,
Basil Green,
David S. Green,
J. Y. Glendinen, P. M.
E. Garrott,
U. B. Holloway,
Charles L. Hill,
Frank Hall,

R. Hutchins,
R. Harvey,
C. A. Hoyt,
H. Hartman,
H. J. Hawley,
V. T. Inskeep,
A. Jacobs,
H. A. Johnson,
Chas. W. Johnson,
Chas. Johnson,
William Jones,
W. C. M. Jones,
E. Paul Jones,
W. J. Joblin,
David Kline,
John Kip,
H. J. Kruse,
John H. Kinney,
Benj. Lake,
David D. Lake,
H. N. Lynch,
Oscar Lewis,
Jacob Mack,
Philip McGren,
J. G. Mahany,
Thos. Mullen,
V. W. McCory,
Phil. M. Martin,
Samuel Moore,
George Mellor,
H. H. Miller,
N. H. McCall,
A. McNamee,
J. P. McAvoy,
G. J. W. Mabee, jr.
John S. D. Manville,
G. G. Norton,
T. D. Nash,
W. H. Nichols,

J. L. Pritchard,
G. A. Pugh,
Ed. C. Parmelee,
W. P. Pollock,
C. W. Pollard,
Thos. H. Potter,
A. G. Raynor,
J. M. Rank,
A. Ramos,
A. N. Rogers,
D. M. Richards,
G. B. Reed,
W. B. Squires,
A. M. Studer,
E. B. Stillings,
H. T. Sawyer,
E. W. Sinclair,
Clark A. Smith,
John H. Schweder,
Romeo D. Strang,
H. M. Teller, G. M.
S. F. Tappan,
Morris Thomas,
Geo. J. Tracy,
L. C. Tolles,
Richard Temby,
B. T. Vincent,
Em. J. Vance,
Wm. Watson,
J. T. White, P. M.
B. W. Wisebart, P. M.
L. B. Weil,
H. L. Weil,
M. C. Wythe.
A. H. Whitehead,
Geo. E. Wilson,
Geo. B. Walker,
Robert Woods,
I. N. Wilcoxin,
C. C. Welch.

FELLOWCRAFTS.

Henry Jewell,   William Tennis.

*Not a member.

ENTERED APPRENTICES.

John C. Bruce,
D. T. Beals,
J. W. Cooper,
David Ettien,

J. S. Ewers,
Wm. Humphrey,
Moses Hall,
N. D. Owen,
H. C. Palmeter,

A. Schonecker,
N. L. Sibley,
J. W. Wilson,
C. J. Whitaker.

DIMITTED.

O. H. Harker,   J. B. Zerbe.

DIED.

Thos. J. Hart,   Jacob Weidman,   Allyn Weston, P. G. M.

UNION □ NO. 7, DENVER.

Regular meetings: second and fourth Saturdays of each month.

OFFICERS.

Sam. H. Elbert, W. M.
L. B. France, S. W.
Milo H. Slater, J. W.

Frank Palmer, Treas.
O. A. Whittemore, Sec.
E. A. Willoughby, S. D.
D. J. Cook, J. D.

W. W. Denniston, S. S.
H. L. Bailey, J. S.
*A. T. Randall, Tyler.

MEMBERS.

John C. Anderson,
Eli M. Ashley, P. M.
W. D. Anthony, P. M.
Joseph L. Bailey,
Geo. N. Billings,
J. S. Brown,
F. A. Brocker,
Alex. H. Boyd,
L. F. Bartels,
E. H. Collins,
J. M. Chivington, P.G.M.
D. C. Corbin,
John Chamard,
Clarance J. Clarke,
Geo. E. Crater,
Rodney Curtis,
Austin Cunningham,
Wm. S. Collins,
C. C. Clements,
D. A. Chever,
J. Q. Charles,
Charles Donnelly,
Jacob Downing,
Jonas Deitsch,
C. C. Davis,
Isadore Deitsch,

John Evans,
R. V. Fairbank,
Redwood Fisher,
J. H. Goodspeed,
Justin A. Goodhue,
P. A. Gottesleben,
Christ. C. Gird,
Henry Henson,
B. F. Houx,
H. B. Haskell,
M. L. Horr,
H. M. Herrington,
George Hurney,
Jonas C. Higley,
Samuel N. Hoyt,
Chas. B. Kountze,
Wm. F. Knowlton,
Henry C. Leach,
Julias Londoner,
Chas. F. Leimer,
Loudon Mullin,
Elisha Millison,
James A. McFadden,
E. C. Mathews,
Con. J. Mahar,

Geo. H. Mills,
H. D. Moshier,
John H. Martin,
C. C. McLemore,
Ferdinand Meyer,
D. C. Oaks,
John Pierce,
W. D. Pease,
H. L. Pitzer,
Wm. S. Peabody,
J. M. Quimby,
Chas. Ruter,
M. A. Rogers,
Hugo Richards,
F. Z. Solomon,
Alfred Sayer,
J. M. Strickler,
Geo. B. Stimpson,
N. W. Welton,
George Williams,
Oscar H. Whittier,
S. S. Woodbury,
Daniel Witler,
Peter Winne,
John Walker,
R. W. Woodbury.

---

*Not a member.

FELLOWCRAFTS.

Harry G. Elder, Frank Hetrick, W. W. Roberts.

ENTERED APPRENTICES.

Alex. W. Atkins, John G. Melvin, D. P. Wilson,
J. L. Craft, George McKee, Geo. F. Wanlass.
      Luther Wilson,

DIMITTED.

H. B. Hitchings, Luther Kountze, Jay J. Johnson.

Stricken from rolls for non-payment of dues, Francis R. Bell and Langdon Clark.

Permission granted T. B. Davis, E. A., to receive degrees in Canada.

EMPIRE ☐ NO. 8, EMPIRE.

Regular meetings: first and third Saturdays of each month.

OFFICERS.

Andrew Mason, W. M. John Collom, Treas. R. W. Taylor, S. S.
Hiram A. Haskin, S. W. David J. Ball, Sec. Edgar Freeman, J. S.
Saml. P. Allen, J. W. E. C. Westcoat, S. D. Jas. H. Osborn, Tyler.
      Don C. Daily, J. D.

MEMBERS.

Francis L. Andre, Albert O. Griggs, James W. Martin,
Chas. H. Aylesworth, J. P. Haskins, Henry Nutt,
Elijah Bently, Charles King, George Richardson,
A. S. Carpenter, Benjamin Kerr, Wm. L. Sawtell,
James W. Drips, James Kirkland, George A. Smith,
James P. Davis, Joseph A. Love, Cornelius Wilkins.
      George C. Munson,

ENTERED APPRENTICE.

F. Newton Bogue.

DIMITTED.

Edward James, John Slawson.

DIED.

Tyler Disbrow.

MONTANA ☐ NO 9, VIRGINIA CITY.

Now Montana ☐ No. 2, under jurisdiction of M∴ W∴ Grand ☐ of Montana.

HELENA CITY ☐ NO. 10, HELENA CITY.

Now Helena ☐ NO. 3, under the jurisdiction of M∴ W∴ Grand ☐ of Montana.

BLACK HAWK □ NO. 11, BLACK HAWK.

Regular meetings: second and fourth Thursdays in each month.

OFFICERS.

J. W. Nesmith, W. M.   R. W. Mosley, Treas.   J. D. Westover, S. D.
John Boylan, S. W.   Geo. E. Congdon, Sec'y.   W. H. Richardson, J. D.
————, J. W.   Jno. H. Riley, Steward.

MEMBERS.

Chase Withrow, P. G. M.   Robt. Frazer,   James Mills,
H. M. Orahood, P. M.   James Fisher,   J. H. Parsons,
Chas. S. Abbott,   H. H. Farnum, Jr.   Geo. S. Parmelee,
Ed. K. Baker,   —— Fitz Simmons,   John W. Ritchie,
Ira C. Barkhurst,   Patrick Flanigan,   F. A. Rudolph,
John B. Ballard,   Samuel Farrer,   Alonzo Smith,
W. J. Barker,   Frank B. Hurlbut,   Wm. H. Studer,
R. Busby,   A. F. Hoppe,   John D. Smails,
S. H. Bradley,   H. H. Helser,   George Scott,
Geo. Cassels,   Ed. C. Hughes,   J. M. Sutter,
Robert Cameron,   Spence Hutchinson,   J. S. Taylor,
H. P. Cowenhoven,   David A. Irvine,   Jacob Tallman,
Ambrose B. Clark,   Stephen Johns,   W. H. Vernon,
Adelbert Crum,   D. D. Leach,   Palemon Wiley,
W. F. Eberlin,   James Laughran,   Eugene Wilder,
Thos. Entwistle,   Chas. Leitzman,   Benj. Woodbury,
W. G. Fairhurst,   Zeph Myres,   J. D. Williams.
   Wm. McLaughlin,

DIMITTED.

John Simmons,   John P. Folley,   J. E. Wurtzebach,
J. N. Crawford,   Ed. E. Hanchett,   D. P. Woodruff.

DIED.

Robert A. Clark, J. W.

WASHINGTON □ NO. 12, GEORGETOWN.

Regular meetings: second and fourth Saturdays in each month.

OFFICERS.

W. W. Ware, W. M.   M. P. Parker, Treas.   D. W. Glaze, S. S.
Jas. A. Burdick, S. W.   C. W. Bramel, Sec'y.   Daniel Roberts, J. S.
H. C. Chapin, J. W.   D. T. Rigsby, S. D.   Jotham Smith, Tyler.
   Wm. S. Downing, J. D.

MEMBERS.

James D. Allen,   Benj. F. Darrah,   Joseph Hough,
Schuyler D. Austin,   Chas. W. Denison,   Martin Hensi,
Wm. Barton,   Elias R. Evans,   Albert Johnson,
E. E. Burlingame,   Matt. France,   David Lees,
A. W. Brownell,   Almond C. Fellows,   John Murley,
G. W. Buchanan,   Dennis Faivre,   H. K. Pearson,
Wm. Burris,   John Fillins,   Austin B. Rea,
Chas. T. Bellamy,   Jairus W. Hall,   Geo. L. Sites,
Henry Boyer,   W. N. Hutchinson,   Theo. F. Simmons,
A. F. Curtis,   John R. Hamble,   Dubois Tooker,
Alexander Cree,   Denetrius Hill,   Geo. E. Thornton,
Adam D. Cooper,   Conrad Hanson,   Samuel Todd.

FELLOWCRAFT.

John A. Higgins.

ENTERED APPRENTICE.

L. F. Yates.

SUSPENDED.

Wm. H. Henderson.

EL PASO ☐ NO. 13, COLORADO CITY.

Regular meetings: second and fourth Saturdays of each month.

OFFICERS.

E. T. Stone, W. M.   C. W. Myers, Treas.   John W. Love, S. S.
B. F. Crowell, S. W.   J. C. Brown, Sec'y.   T. T. Young, J. S.
S. M. Buzzard, J. W.   David Spielman, S. D.   James Roberts, Tyler.
                         Solon Mason, J. D.

MEMBERS.

G. S. Barlow,   Jacob Gill,   David McShane,
C. M. Bryant,   D. C. Guier,   S. K. Roberts,
Geo. H. Bryant,   B. S. Hall,   E. S. Randall,
A. Bott,   J. W. Irion,   E. A. Smith,
Seth Beason,   C. T. Judd,   Wm. Sweetland,
Robert Finley,   James Kime,   John Pesdirs,
Emile Gehrung,   A. G. Lincoln,   J. C. Woodbury,
E. C. Gehrung,   Aaron Mason,   J. B. Weir.

FELLOWCRAFT.

L. Van Schyock.

DIMITTED.

B. C. Myers,   J. M. Noble,   James McGee.

COLUMBIA ☐ NO. 14, BOULDER CITY.

Regular meetings: second and fourth Saturdays of each month.

OFFICERS.

Willie T. Potter, W. M. M. G. Smith. Treas.   Elijah H. Andrews, S. S.
Oren H. Henry, S. W.   Henry Paul, Sec.   Wilhelm Sommer, J. S.
D. E. Sutherland, J. W. William C. Slater, S. D. Thos. J. Jones, Tyler.
                         Henry Green, J. D.

MEMBERS.

Wm. M. Barney,   Theodore Haswell,   Oscar Pierce,
Freeman Belcher,   Thos. J. Hill,   John W. Ritchie,
Andrew Berger,   Thos. J. Johns,   Daniel A. Robinson,
Wm. R. Blore,   George La Point,   Thomas Ryalls,
David Bock,   Peter A. Leyner,   Benj. H. Slaughter,

Geo. W. Carter,
Geo. F. Chase,
Wm. A. Corson,
John Davis,
Oliver T. Hamlin,
A. W. Harris,

David J. Lykins,
Edmond P. McClure,
Lemuel McIntosh,
Abram Mills,
David Parlan,
Anson W. Peters,

Esrom G. Slifer,
Watler H. Smith,
George C. Squires,
John A. Stanton,
George W. Webster,
John W. Wigginton.

FELLOWCRAFTS.

Joshua E. Chapman,

A. S. Lewis,
M. L. McCaslin,

Jas. P. Maxwell.

ENTERED APPRENTICES.

Budd Sylramus,

George D. Harmon,

Chas. N. Hockaday.

DIMITTED.

George D. Cook.

MOUNT MORIAH □ NO. 15, CANON CITY.

Regular meetings: Friday preceding each ☉.

OFFICERS.

G. B. Frazier, W. M.
B. F. Smith, S. W.
S. Frazier, J. W.

W. H. McClure, Treas.
S. M. Cox, Sec.
R. J. Frazier, S. D.
C. Pauls, J. D.

S. D. Webster, S. S.
W. H. Thompson, J. S.
G. W. Depp, Tyler.

MEMBERS.

H. M. Burroughs,
John A. Binckley,
M. Mills Craig,
Henry Dunn,
J. H. Depp,
W. R. Fowler,

H. J. Frazier,
S. C. Hall,
Lewis Jones,
O. W. Jowens,
B. F. Moore,
B. F. Rockafellow,

John Richey,
A. Sartor,
H. C. Vaughn,
J. H. Nelson,
G. T. Phillips,
John Witcher.

FELLOWCRAFTS.

J. A. McCanlas,   A. I. Seabring.

DIMITTED.

S. R. West.

DIED.

H. H. Marsh.

CHEYENNE □ NO. 16, CHEYENNE.

Regular meetings: first and third Saturdays of each month.

OFFICERS.

J. E. Gates, W. M.
E. B. Carling, S. W.
J. H. Hayford, J. W.

W. W. Slaughter, Treas.
J. P. Johnson, Sec

H. P. Jenson, S. D.
W. D. Robinson, J. D.
*James Kime, Tyler.

*Not a member.

MEMBERS.

F. E. Addome,
A. M. Appel,
N. A. Baker,
W. W. Barnett,
F. H. Barroll,
A. C. Beckwith,
N. K. Boswell,
A. J. Botsford,
W. E. Campbell,
C. H. Collins,
Thomas Conroy,
W. F. Corbett,

Ben Hamberger,
R. G. Harlow,
W. H. Harlow,
John Harper,
E. P. Johnson,
J. J. Johnson,
J. G. McAdams,
Walter Mackay,
J. H. McMinn,
James A. Mundell,
H. Newman,
Orlando North,

A. D. Palmer,
E. F. Passage,
W. D. Pease,
S. J. Scriber,
David Shackman,
A. D. Shakespear,
C. D. Sherman,
R. W. Trout,
Abraham Walters,
L. B. Weil,
Chas. H. Whittelsey,
George Williams.

FELLOWCRAFTS.

Milton Askew,
O. C. Barnard,

Wm. P. Davis,
Chas. L. Howell,
W. G. Jamison,

James N. Slaughter,
E. P. Snow.

ENTERED APPRENTICES.

Frederick Beckelman,
Thomas L. Brent,
Joseph W. Cooke,

Hugh Hughes,
Josiah Heyser,

H. S. Rembaugh,
Andrew Schoonmaker,
D. J. Shaw.

DIMITTED.

T. J. Johns,
L. S. Moe,

S. Grant Moore,

James S. Scott,
J. H. Voorheis.

PUEBLO ☐ NO. 17, PUEBLO.

Regular meetings : second and fourth Wednesdays of each month.

OFFICERS.

C. J. Hart, W. M.
A. Bartlett, S. W.
P. Craig, J. W.

James Rice, Treas.
J. D. Miller, Sec'y.
P. R. Thombs, S. D.
D. B. Berry, J. D.

R. N. Daniels, S. S.
Geo. Ebbets, J. S.
————, Tyler.

MEMBERS.

Z. G. Allen,
Chauncey C. Burt,
Lewis Barnum,
John N. Brown,
Michael Beshoar,
Augustus Beach,
Charles H. Blake,
Ferd. W. Barndollar,
D. Coleman,
John W. Felch,

Charles Goodnight,
G. F. Hall,
James S. Hunt,
Charles Holmes,
Amasa A. Johnson,
Weldon Keeling,
H. Matzdorff,
Samuel H. McBride,
George W. Morgan,
John B. Rice,

Alexander Reed,
J. W. O. Snyder,
George W. Stout,
John J. Thomas,
M. D. Thatcher,
Elias Veatch,
R. T. Warrant,
Franklin Walker,
R. W. Winbourn,
Otto Winneka.

FELLOWCRAFTS.

Charles B. Adams,

Franklin Murray,

James H. Warrant.

ENTERED APPRENTICES.

Robert F. Bagby,
William K. Carlile,
Peter K. Dotson,
Samuel Eckstein,
George Gilbert,
James J. Nolan,
Mark B. Price,
H. O. Rettberg,
F. Spilleke,
M. F. Steele,
James E. Smith,
John B. Williams.

DIMITTED.

Martin Maher, Lewis Pegg.

EXPELLED.

Wm. H. Chapman, E. A.

TABULAR STATEMENT

OF THE WORK OF THE SEVERAL ⌑ SUBORDINATE TO THE GRAND ⌑ OF COLORADO, FOR THE YEAR ENDING SEPTEMBER 18, A. D. 1869, A. L. 5869, SHOWING THE ENTIRE MEMBERSHIP OF THE TERRITORY.

No.	LODGE.	Affiliated.	Initiated.	Passed.	Raised.	Dimitted.	Died.	Stricken from roll.	Suspended.	Expelled.	Rejected.	Living out of jurisdiction.	No. of Members.	No. of Fellowcrafts.	No. of E. A.
1	Golden City	1	2	......	1	5	...	...	...	...	4	20	57	1	13
4	Nevada	...	2	9	1	10	2	...	...	...	4	17	65	1	...
5	Denver	1		4			...	...	...	...	3	37	111	3	15
6	Central	1	1	10	2	3	...	...	...	...	11	40	128	2	13
7	Union	1		9	3	6	...	2	...	...	2	9	86	3	7
8	Empire	...		1		1	...	...	...	...	......		29		1
11	Black Hawk	2		9		1	...	...	...	...	15	5	59	...	...
12	Washington	5		8	1	...	...	...	1	...	12		46	1	1
13	El Paso			4		3	...	...	...	...	1	2	34	1	...
14	Columbia	1	1	15	1	5	...	...	...	...	10	7	43	4	3
15	Mount Moriah	...		4			1	...	...	...	4	......	28	2	...
16	Cheyenne	8	2	24	1		...	...	...	...	34	10	43	7	8
17	Pueblo	7		19			...	...	...	*1	8	......	39	3	12
	Total	46	132	116	107	42	8	2	1	1	108	147	768	28	73
	Total last year	19	112	100	94	59	2				57	134	717	18	71
	Increase	27	20	16	13		6				51	13	51	10	2

*Entered Apprentice.

GRAND OFFICERS

ELECTED SINCE THE ORGANIZATION OF THE GRAND ▢ OF
COLORADO, AUGUST 2, A∴ L∴ 5861.

August, 1861.

J. M. Chivington, G. M. Jas. Ewing, S. G. W.* Eli Carter, G. Treas.*
S. M. Robbins, D. G. M.* J. M. Holt, J. G. W.* O. A. Whittemore, G. Sec.

December, 1861.

J. M. Chivington, G. M. P. S. Pfouts, S. G. W.* O. B. Brown, G. Treas.*
Andrew Mason, D.G.M. M. C. White, J. G. W.* O. A. Whittemore, G. Sec.

1862.

Allyn Weston, G. M.† J. M. Van Deren, S.G.W.* O. B. Brown, G. Treas.*
M. C. White, D. G. M.* Richard Sopris, J.G.W. O. A. Whittemore, G. Sec.

1863.

Henry M. Teller, G. M. O. B. Brown, S. G. W.* L. W. Frary, G. Treas.*
A. J. Van Deren, D.G.M. J. H. Gest, J. G. W.* O. A. Whittemore, G. Sec.

1864.

A. J. Van Deren, G. M. A. Sagendorf, S. G. W. L. W. Chase, G. Treas.
O. B. Brown, D. G. M.* Chase Withrow, J. G. W. O. A. Whittemore, G. Sec.

1865.

Andrew Mason, G. M. Chase Withrow, S. G. W. Richard Sopris, G.Treas.
O. B. Brown, D. G. M.* Jas. T. White, J. G. W. O. A. Whittemore, G. Sec.

1866.

Chase Withrow, G. M. Aaron M. Jones, S. G.W. Richard Sopris, G. Treas.
A. Sagendorf, D. G. M. L. N. Greenleaf, J. G.W. Ed. C. Parmelee, G. Sec.

1867.

Henry M. Teller, G. M. Aaron M. Jones, S.G.W. Richard Sopris, G. Treas.
O.A.Whittemore, D.G.M W. D. Anthony, J.G.W. Ed. C. Parmelee, G. Sec.

1868.

Henry M. Teller, G. M. B. W. Wisebart. S. G. W. Richard Sopris, G. Treas.
A. Sagendorf, D. G. M. W. D. Anthony, J. G. W. Ed. C. Parmelee, G. Sec.

1869.

Henry M. Teller, G. M. W. D. Anthony, S.G.W. Wm. W. Ware, G. Treas.
Richard Sopris, D. G. M. Hal. Sayr, J. G. W. Ed. C. Parmelee, G. Sec.

---

*Dimitted.   †Dead.

GRAND LODGES

IN COMMUNICATION WITH THE GRAND ☐ OF COLORADO, WITH THEIR GRAND SECRETARIES AND THEIR PLACE OF RESIDENCE, COMPILED FROM THE LATEST INTELLIGENCE RECEIVED.

IN NORTH AMERICA.

GRAND LODGES.	GRAND SECRETARIES.	RESIDENCES.	ORGANIZED.
Alabama	Daniel Sayre	Montgomery	June 14, 1821
Arkansas	William D. Blocher	Little Rock	February 22, 1832
California	Alex. G. Abell	San Francisco	April 18, 1850
Canada	Thomas B. Harris	Hamilton	October 10, 1855
Connecticut	Joseph K. Wheeler	Hartford	July 8, 1789
Delaware	John P. Allmond	Wilmington	June 6, 1806
Dist. Columbia	Noble D. Larner	Washington	December 11, 1810
Florida	Dewitt C. Dawkins	Jacksonville	July 5, 1830
Georgia	J. E. Blackshear	Macon	December 16, 1786
Illinois	Orlin H. Minor	Springfield	April 6, 1840
Indiana	John M. Bramwell	Indianapolis	January 12, 1818
Iowa	Theo. S. Parvin	Iowa City	January 8, 1844
Idaho Territory	P. E. Edmondson	Idaho City	December 16, 1867
Kansas	E. T. Carr	Fort Leavenworth	March 17, 1856
Kentucky	John M. S. McCorkle	Greensburg	October 13, 1800
Louisiana	James C. Batchelor	New Orleans	July 11, 1812
Maine	Ira Berry	Portland	June 1, 1820
Maryland	Jacob H. Medairy	Baltimore	April 17, 1787
Massachusetts	Solon Thornton	Boston	April 30, 1733
Michigan	James Fenton	Detroit	June 28, 1826
Minnesota	William S. Combs	St. Paul	February 23, 1853
Mississippi	J. L. Power	Jackson	July 27, 1818
Missouri	Geo. Frank Gouley	St. Louis	April 23, 1821
Montana	Sol. Star	Helena	January 24, 1866
Nebraska	J. N. Wise	Plattsmouth	September 23, 1857
Nevada	W.A.M.VanBokkelen	Virginia City	January 16, 1865
New Brunswick	Wm. F. Bunting	St. Johns	October 9, 1867
New Hampshire	Horace Chase	Hopkinton	July 8, 1789
New Jersey	Joseph H. Hough	Trenton	December 18, 1786
New York	James M. Austin	New York	September 5, 1781
North Carolina	D. W. Bain	Raleigh	January 14, 1771
Nova Scotia	Charles J. Macdonald	Halifax	June 21, 1866
Oregon	J. E. Hurford	Portland	August 16, 1851
Ohio	John D. Caldwell	Cincinnati	January 7, 1808
Pennsylvania	John Thompson	Philadelphia	June 20, 1764
Rhode Island	Charles D. Greene	Providence	June 25, 1791
South Carolina	Robert S. Bruns	Charleston	March 24, 1787
Tennessee	John Frizzell	Nashville	October 14, 1794
Texas	Geo. H. Bringhurst	Houston	December 20, 1837
Vermont	Henry Clark	Poultney	October 14, 1794
Virginia	John Dove	Richmond	May 6, 1777
Washington	Thomas M. Reed	Olympia	December 9, 1858
West Virginia	Thomas H. Logan	Wheeling	April 12, 1865
Wisconsin	Wm. T. Palmer	Milwaukee	December 18, 1843

ABROAD.

Grand Orient of France...———Thevenot......16 Rue Cadet, Paris.

OBITUARY.

ALLYN WESTON, Past Grand Master of Colorado, was born at Duxbury, Mass., Nov. 3d, 1825. He graduated at Harvard College, and studied law with Judge Barton, of Worcester. He afterwards married Miss Mary P. Paine, of Worcester, and practiced law at Milford, Mass., until the death of his wife, when he moved to Detroit, Mich., where he received his Masonic degrees, while editing the *Daily Advertiser*, of that place.

He then started and edited the "*Ashler*, a Masonic Magazine," for about six years, during which time he moved it to Chicago, Ill. In 1860, he sold his interest in the *Ashler*, and came to Colorado and resumed the practice of law at Central City. He was one of the founders, and the first Master, of Central (then Chivington) ☐ No. 6, at Central City, and was elected Grand Master in 1862. In the fall of 1863, he went to New York City, where he resided until his death, which occurred May 12th, 1869.

Bro. Weston was an efficient, zealous and intelligent Mason, and to his firmness and ability, while Grand Master, Masonry in Colorado owes much of its present prosperity.

Having a fine education, good ability, and dignified manners, he was fitted to adorn any circle. He left an only daughter, and a large circle of friends, who regret his early death.

THIS PAGE IS DEDICATED

TO THE MEMORY OF

Right Worshipful Allyn Weston,

PAST GRAND MASTER OF COLORADO,

And Member of Central Lodge No. 6.

Born

AT DUXBURY, MASS., NOV. 3, 1825.

Died

AT BROOKLYN, N. Y., MAY, 12, 1869.

---

*AGED FORTY-THREE YEARS, SIX MONTHS
AND NINE DAYS.*

REPORT

ON

MASONIC CORRESPONDENCE.

————◆◆◆————

To the Most Worshipful Grand ☐ of A., F. and A. M. of the Territory of Colorado :

Owing to the incessant demands of private business I have not, during the year, been able to devote any time to an examination of the proceedings of other Grand ☞ for the purpose of making a report thereon; and now, ten days previous to our Annual Grand Communication, with a lack of time even for necessary attention to my own business, I commence the perusal of reports, the examination of which, to do them full and ample justice, should occupy days where it is impossible for me to devote hours.

I, as chairman of the committee, have, since our last Grand Communication, received the proceedings of the following Grand ☞ :

Alabama,	Kentucky,	North Carolina,
Arkansas,	Louisiana,	Nevada,
California,	Massachusetts,	Ohio,
Canada,	Maryland,	Oregon,
Connecticut,	Michigan,	Pennsylvania,
Delaware,	Missouri,	Rhode Island,
District of Columbia,	Mississippi,	South Carolina,
Florida,	Minnesota,	Texas,
Georgia,	Maine,	Tennessee,
Idaho,	New York,	Vermont,
Illinois,	New Hampshire,	Virginia,
Indiana,	New Jersey,	West Virginia,
Iowa,	New Brunswick,	Wisconsin,
Kansas,		Washington Territory.

Making a total of forty-one Grand bodies with which we are in communication.

ALABAMA.

This Grand ☐ met in annual communication at Montgomery, December 7, 1868, M∴ W∴ Grand Master George D. Norris presiding.

Two hundred subordinate ☞ were represented, with an aggregate membership of 10,428.

The work of the year was as follows: Initiated, 696; passed, 646; raised 649.

The following beautiful encomium of Masonry appears in the address of the Grand Master:

"Loaded with the charms of antiquity, interesting by a thousand associations of history, heroism and romance, the order yet possesses all the health and life of novelty, all the liberality and benevolence of reform. It exists in the body and bosom of the people; it catches their sentiments, is modified by their thoughts, and changes with their manners. It partakes of their improvement, and adapts itself to all the various changes of man. Within its shadow the rich and the poor meet on terms of equality; the one forgets his wealth and his pride, and the other forgets his poverty and his sorrow. Their sympathies, ever otherwise asunder, are here mingled together, and they go forth into the world again, conscious that opposition in rank cannot with them create hostility of feeling. They loose the artificial distinctions of society, and assume the pure, original and kindly intercourse of fellow-men. The great man finds familiar friendship in walks of society where his name would otherwise never have been uttered, but with awe; and the obscure poor man finds himself exciting interest and acquiring importance among those whose looks hitherto have been bent upon him with coldness and condescension. There they learn how frail is solitary, unassociated man; how much he requires attention and support; how often the favor and caprices of fortune may change his circumstances and his hopes; how long the blessings of life may linger around the footsteps of the aged, and how soon the cup of pleasure may be dashed from the lips of the young. Oh, in this life of change, who would not seek a brotherhood not subject to mutation or decay; a brotherhood replenished and vivified in each succeeding generation; filling the places of the dead with the souls of the living, and supplying the failing wisdom of the old by the fresh ardor and fire of the young; a brotherhood which has gleaned its maxims from ancient sciences, from the lessons of history, and from the impulses of humanity.

"Our order, founded upon truth, has for its maker and builder, God. Then how proper and important is it for us to give unto our Great and Glorious Master Builder our whole hearts in adoration, praise, and thanksgiving, for his wondrous work, and grace, and goodness, to the children of men. Not unto us—not unto us, but unto Him be all the praise, adoration, grace, and glory."

M∴ W∴ Bro. George D. Norris was elected Grand Master, and R∴ W∴ Bro. Daniel Sayre, Grand Secretary, for the ensuing year. A very readable report of committee on Foreign Correspondence accompanies these proceedings.

ARKANSAS.

This Grand ☐ met in annual communication at Little Rock, Nov. 16, 1868, M∴ W∴ Grand Master E. H. English, presiding.

Ninety-eight subordinate ☐ were represented, with an aggregate membership of 7,676.

The work of the year was : Initiated, 677 ; passed, 541 ; raised, 461.

From the Grand Master's address we clip the following story, with his preface :

" Not long since a venerable Hebrew brother told me a story, which I had never heard before ; and which he said he learned, when a boy, in the fatherland, from his aged uncle, who was a Mason, and who assured him that he had it in a very ancient parchment manuscript, which had never been printed. Pleased with the story, I said to him that I would tell it to the Grand ▭ some day, and let it be printed, as it was no secret. So I give it to you now for what it is worth. It is the story of ' Solomon, the Raven and the Worm.'

Solomon, the most wise, was sitting in a grove, near his rural palace, observing a raven feeding her young. Whilst she was off in search of food, telling a servant to bring him a glass bowl, he placed it over her nest so as to cover the young birds. When she returned to the nest, the young ravens opened their mouths to receive the supplies which the mother was accustomed to bring them ; and she, meeting with the transparent obstruction, fluttered about it for some time in vain attempts to reach her imprisoned children. Vexed, she made repeated but ineffectual efforts to break the vessel with her beak. Despairing of success in this mode of attack, she lighted upon a limb near by, and sat for some time, seeming to meditate. Then leaping into the air, and spreading her black wings, she moved off with rapid flight in the direction of an island in the Mediterranean sea. Our Grand Master, who had watched with interest all her movements, sat waiting for her return. Finally see came, bearing in her beak a large white worm ; and placing it on the rim of the nest, near the edge of the bowl, it crawled over the vessel, and along its track the glass instantly cracked, as if cut by a diamond, parted, and fell to the ground !

The masons were in the quarries preparing stones for the temple. They used the drill and the wedge, but the process of parting the stones by these simple implements was tedious. The idea flashed upon the mind of Solomon that, by the instinct of the raven, Providence had placed in his hands a wonderful, but more effective instrument. Taking the worm to the quarries, he placed it upon a great stone which the laborers had heaved out from the mountain ; it crawled across it, and, to the amazement of the wise men, the stone opened along its path, and tumbled apart. Thousands of stones were thus separated into suitable rough ashlers, to be finished by the chisels and the mallets of the craftsmen.

Such is the substance of the story. It may be a mere fable. It may be that the insect excreted from its body some mysterious chemical substance, that parted the glass and the stone. Or it may be that Providence, who confounds the wisdom of men by using simple means to effect great purposes, supplied to Solomon this wonderful little craftsman, to aid in the great work of erecting a temple for His worship.

Be this as it may, I have repeated this " strange story " to illustrate the fact that Solomon, like Job, was a student of the book of nature, from every great page of which—whether he looked upon the sea, into the air, upon the earth, all teeming with life, or up into the heavens, sparkling with the lamps of night—he learned, as all Masons may, lessons of wisdom."

M∴ W∴ Bro. Elbert H. English was elected Grand Master, and R∴ W∴ Bro. William D. Blocher was elected Grand Secretary for the ensuing year.

The committee on Foreign Correspondence made quite a lengthy report, which contains a good deal of valuable Masonic information.

From their review of the proceedings of Mississippi, we clip the following : ·

"It is a rule recognized in many, if not all Masonic jurisdictions, that a Mason cannot hold membership in two □ at the same time (except it be honorary.) The Grand □ of Massachusetts, New Hampshire, Maryland, Kentucky, Missouri, Wisconsin, New Jersey, and the Grand □ of England, have adopted regulations to that effect. The impropriety would seem to be apparent, as one instance may demonstrate : A Mason, being a member of two □, might be the Master of one ; the other □ might arraign, and try and suspend him, and thereby deprive the other □ of its Master."

CALIFORNIA.

This Grand □ met in annual communication at San Francisco, Oct. 18, 1869, M∴ W∴ Grand Master William A. Davis, presiding.

One hundred and thirty-five chartered and four U. D. □ were represented, with an aggregate membership of 8,106. The work of the year was: Initiated, 817 ; passed, 822 ; raised, 821.

The following from the Grand Master's address, relative to jurisdictional rights, we heartily commend :

"At the last annual communication of the Grand □ of New York, it was resolved that it shall be made an imperative duty on the part of subordinate □ to present, in print or writing, the following questions to every candidate for initiation, requiring him to answer in writing each question, and to state that he does so upon his honor as a man ; the said questions and answers to be returned to and become the property of the □ before any ballot shall be taken upon his petition :

"'Where were you born? What is your age ? What is your occupation? How long have you lived in the State of New York? How long in the town, city, county, or village in which you now reside? Have you ever, to your knowledge, been proposed as a candidate and rejected in a Masonic □, and if so, when, and in what □ ? Do you believe in the existence of one ever-living and true God? Do you know of any physical, legal, or moral reason which should prevent you from becoming a Freemason?'

"This, it seems to me, is a sure preventive of the evils it is designed to cure ; and, at the same time, furnishes an indisputable cause for discipline in cases of misrepresentation or false statement."

M∴ W∴ Bro. Charles Marsh was elected Grand Master, and R∴ W∴ Bro. Alexander G. Abell was elected Grand Secretary.

A voluminous and well-written report, by the committee on Foreign Correspondence, forms a part of these proceedings.

CANADA.

This Grand □ met in annual communication at London, July 8th, 1868, M∴ W∴ Grand Master William Mercer Wilson, presiding.

One hundred and seventy subordinate ☐ were represented, with an aggregate membership of 8,022. The work of the past year was : Initiated, 1,243; passed, 1,138; raised, 1,042.

The address of the Grand Master relates almost wholly to local matters.

The committee on Foreign Correspondence review briefly the proceedings of thirty-six Grand bodies.

M∴ W∴ Bro. A. A. Stevenson was elected Grand Master, and R∴ W∴ Thomas B. Harris, Grand Secretary.

CONNECTICUT.

This Grand □ met in annual communication at New Haven, May 12, 1869, M∴ W∴ Grand Master William Storer, presiding.

One hundred and six subordinate ☐ were represented, with an aggregate membership of 12,784. Work of the year: Initiated, 943; passed, 900; raised, 881.

The address of the Grand Master is quite lengthy, giving a full account of his official duties performed during the year.

The report of the committee on Foreign Correspondence is voluminous and interesting. From the conclusion we quote :

" A black cloud, no bigger than a man's hand, has arisen, and threatens death and destruction to all secret societies. A cloud full of thunder and brimstone, which was conceived in the brains of a few old ladies, wearing breeches, who were recently assembled in grand convention at Pittsburg, where they resolved that it was advisable to put an end to all this humbuggery of assisting brethren in distress, and 'doing unto others as you would that they should do unto you.' In fact, they are fully persuaded in their own minds, that if the earth should continue to revolve on its axis, and not in precise accordance with their views, then the whole machinery must be stopped. All we have to say to them is, when they succeed in overthrowing the Masonic institution, we hope they will write us; but are fully persuaded it will not be while there are 'hungry ones to be fed,' 'naked ones to be clothed,' the 'sick and afflicted to be attended,' the 'widow to be consoled,' and the 'fatherless to be comforted.' "

M∴ W∴ Bro. Amos E. Cobb was elected Grand Master, and R∴ W∴ Bro. Joseph K. Wheeler, Grand Secretary.

DISTRICT OF COLUMBIA.

This Grand □ met in annual communication at Washington, Nov. 3d, 1868, M∴ W∴ Grand Master B. B. French, presiding.

Sixteen subordinate ☐ were represented, with an aggregate membership of 2,990. The work of the year was: Initiated, 235; passed, 244; raised, 289.

The following is from the address of the Grand Master:

"Let us remember that although we are brethren, we are men, and subject to all the frailties of humanity. That we may all err, for it is the characteristic of mortality; and while we know that 'to err is human,' let us never forget the remainder of the poet's sentiment, 'to forgive, divine.'

"The time will never come on this earth, until the arrival of the millenium, when men will not be found going wrong. We are all the subjects of passion, of prejudice, of indiscretion. If we mean to live harmoniously, we must exercise charity, we must subdue passion, and we must look upon the failings of our fellow men, and especially of our brothers, as to be forgiven instead of to be reproached and trumpeted to the world.

"'Then gently scan your brother man,
    And gentler sister woman,
Though ye may gang a kenning wrang,
    To step aside is human.'

"This was said by a poet and a brother Mason; and now, when we cannot disguise the fact that feelings do exist among the brethren of this jurisdiction that are not creditable to the craft, let us all strive to overcome them ourselves, and to earnestly inculcate the sentiments expressed in these quotations, and cast the mantle of charity and forgiveness over the errors of our misguided brethren."

The proceedings of this Grand ☐ contain a concise review of the proceedings of thirty-six Grand bodies, including Colorado.

M∴ W∴ Bro. R. B. Donaldson was elected Grand Master, and R∴ W∴ Bro. Noble D. Larner, Grand Secretary.

DELAWARE.

This Grand ☐ met in annual communication at Wilmington, June 27, 1868, M∴ W∴ Grand Master Daniel McClintock, presiding.

Seventeen subordinate ☐ were represented, with an aggregate membership of 922.

The work of the year was; Initiated, 92; passed, 64; raised, 59.

We clip the following decision from the address of the Grand Master, in case of persons applying for degrees who have been rejected in other jurisdictions:

"I received a communication from the Master of one of the ☐, stating that a petition had been received by his ☐, and after it had been referred to a committee, it was ascertained that the applicant had been rejected by a ☐ in a sister jurisdiction. Now, he wishes to know, whether, under the circumstances, they have jurisdiction in the matter.

"This question is one, in which we all, individually, may sometime be deeply interested, and one which I hope the Grand ☐ will determine.

"I hold the opinion, in this instance, that they could not act upon the petition without the consent of the ☐ by which he was rejected. What right have we, although perhaps personally interested, to force a profane upon a brother Mason, when there may be hidden in the past something that will forever debar Masonic intercourse between the two? Are the benefits of Masonry for Masons, or for profanes? Is there not now, too much estrangement occurring between individual Masons, and would not an act of this kind only increase it? If you will concede that this cannot be done between ☐ of the same jurisdiction, which I believe is an undisputed point, what right, I ask, have we to inflict such an injury upon a sister-jurisdiction? Are we not all members of a common family, of the same faith and order, having the same object and end in view? This is a subject, my brethren, to which too little attention is paid; and while in this instance, we might be unable to find spot or blemish, evidently some one has had, or thought he had, good and sufficient reasons for his opposition. The right of secret ballot, we concede to all. The right to pry into, or demand the motives of a brother's vote, we do not possess. I further claim, that any member has the right to object, and the Worshipful Master to exclude, any one presenting himself for admission who had been formerly rejected by that ☐, and received the degrees elsewhere, lest the harmony of the ☐ be disturbed thereby.

"I think it would be well, when a petition is received, for the committee having it in charge, if the applicant formerly resided in another jurisdiction, to make some inquiries as whether he had ever been rejected, as well as to his character."

The committee on Foreign Correspondence review briefly the proceedings of thirty-five Grand bodies.

M∴ W∴ Bro. E. J. Horner was elected Grand Master, and R∴ W∴ Bro. J. P. Allmond, Grand Secretary.

FLORIDA.

This Grand ☐ met in annual communication at Tallahassee, January 13, 1868, M∴ W∴ Grand Master Henry J. Stewart, presiding.

Forty-four subordinate ☐ were represented, with an aggregate membership of 1,783. The work of the year was: Raised, 225.

From the address of the Grand Master we take the following:

" We are taught in our Masonic infancy to live soberly, to be temperate, in short, to avoid intemperance.

" Are we living up to this teaching when we make so frequent use of the intoxicating bowl? Brethren, it is a dangerous, unmasonic vice. Let us beware, then, and 'touch not, taste not, handle not, the unclean thing.' Profane swearing is a vice. By reference to the Book, one of our great lights, we find that we are not to 'take the name of the Lord in vain.. Violating the holy Sabbath is also a vice. In that same Book are we strictly enjoined to 'remember the Sabbath day to keep it holy.'

" Gaming is an offense, not only against Masonry, but it is made a high crime by our legislature. Statute after statute has been enacted to punish and put down this detestable vice. These vices are in direct violation of the holy commands of the Almighty, forbidden by the laws of our State, and condemned by the laws and edicts of Masonry. Then, brethren, may

42

we not, can we not, once again make the effort to devise some plan by which these vices may be abolished among the members of our noble fraternity ?"

There was no report by the committee on Foreign Correspondence. M∴ W∴ Bro. Dewitt C. Dawkins was elected Grand Master, and R∴ W∴ Bro. Hugh A. Corley, Grand Secretary.

GEORGIA.

This Grand □ met in annual communication at Macon, October 27, 1868; M∴ W∴ Grand Master John Harris, presiding.

There were represented two hundred and fifty-two subordinate □, the aggregate membership of which was 13,167. Work of the year, 922 initiated, and 628 raised.

The address of the Grand Master is devoted exclusively to local matters.

The committee on Foreign Correspondence make an interesting report, covering seventy-five pages of the Grand □ proceedings, giving a review of the proceedings of upwards of thirty Grand bodies.

M∴ W∴ Bro. Samuel Lawrence was elected Grand Master, and R∴ W∴ Bro. S. Rose, Grand Secretary.

ILLINOIS.

This Grand □ met in annual communication at Springfield, October 6, 1868; M∴ W∴ Grand Master Jerome R. Gorin, presiding.

Five hundred and seventy-two subordinate □ were represented, the aggregate membership of which was 28,262. The work of the past year was: Initiated, 3,971; passed, 3,678; raised, 3,572. Increase of the year, 2,152.

The Grand Master's address relates wholly to local matters,

An interesting report by the committee on Foreign Correspondence appears with the other proceedings of this Grand □. Want of time forbids us making copious extracts therefrom.

M∴ W∴ Bro. Harmon G. Reynolds was elected Grand Master, and R∴ W∴ Bro. Orlin H. Miner, Grand Secretary.

INDIANA.

This Grand □ met in annual communication at Indianapolis, May 25, 1869; M∴ W∴ Grand Master Martin H. Rice, presiding.

Three hundred and eighty-one chartered and thirty-one U. D. □ were represented. Aggregate membership, 21,205. Work of past year: Initiated, 2,801; passed, 2,183; raised, 2,183.

From the address of the Grand Master we take as follows :

" The institution of Masonry is not a mere experiment, but a permanent growth of the ages. Its mission in the world may be assumed as a permanent mission; and its objects as beyond the necessity of mere defense. The institution is now presented to the world with a growing confidence in the vitality and fruitfulness of its organic history. It is better understood by

Masons themselves, and is consequently presented with greater distinctness, and with less seeming antagonism, and exclusiveness, and zeal, without knowledge. Many who have looked with suspicion upon the order, as claiming more than can possibly pertain to any human institution ; even the supplanting of the necessity of anything outside of the order, either for morality, religion or civilization, have found that Masonry as presented by her best and ablest advocate, is the handmaid of all that is good, beautiful and true, and not the exclusive owner of the sunlight, the love, or the redeeming merits of that God, who binds to Himself in golden chains, the whole human family.

" The object of Masonry is not the same as the church or the state. It has a peculiar mission of its own, and by the distinct presentation of that mission, so that all may see it, the less will be the suspicion in the world against the institution, and the more plainly will its peculiar merits be manifested, and unfolded in fruits of beauty, richness and delight. Masonry is not a religious or a political body. It is not exclusively or primarily a a teacher of morality, or politics, in the sense of practically applying the moral principles of any religion, or the practical principles of any civil government, but in common with all religions, and all state authority, it starts with the fact of the brotherhood of the human race ; and believing that to think over problems that relate to action between man and man, without proceeding to act, is to become speedily paralyzed ; it acts, and its action is a society ; The mysteries of mutual, fraternal action, do not yield up their secrets of light, while we

" ' Sit apart, holding no form of society,
But contemplating all.'

"The formative principle of Masonry finds its illustration in that principle of science, by which the most minute, and apparently isolated facts, resolve themselves into systems ; these systems again are bound together in still wider systems ; complex laws, as we ascend higher in the scale of being, unfold their complex operations, and assume simpler forms. And so we go from infinite diversity, to a higher and higher unity, until we find all reduced to a unity of one universe, beneath the throne of one God.

"From this fundamental principle of science, springs the development of mind, in the activity of thought, and the various applications of the conclusions gained.

"In the brotherhood of man, and the fatherhood of God, is the unity of one human family ; and this principle is the formative principle of Masonry. The realization of this sublime fact developes obligations, moral, religious and political. But Masonry aims not at the presentment or enforcement of obligations abstractly considered, only at the inculcation of the family relationship, from which spring morality, religion, civil obedience and progress. Other organizations and instrumentalities, divine and human, have their legitimate place in the world's history, to which Masonry claims only to be the handmaid, and from which Masonry welcomes light and truth, and all elements that tend to the realization and perfection of the brotherhood that it is her peculiar mission to insist upon, and illustrate.

"'For so the whole round earth, is every way
Bound by golden chains, about the feet of God.'"

No report from committee on Foreign Correspondence.

M∴ W∴ Bro. Martin H. Rice was elected Grand Master, and R∴ W∴ Bro. John M. Bramwell was elected Grand Secretary.

IOWA.

This Grand ☐ met in annual communication at Des Moines, June 2d, 1868, M∴ W∴ Grand Master Reuben Mickel, presiding.

Two hundred and thirty-two chartered and seven U. D. ☞ were represented, with an aggregate membership of 9,774. The work of the past year was: Initiated, 1,467; passed, 1,327; raised, 1,265.

The Grand Master's address is confined to local matters.

There is no report from the committee on Foreign Correspondence.

From the address of the Grand Orator we would gladly make extracts, could we do so without in a measure destroying its beauty, and want of room forbids its entire insertion.

M∴ W∴ Bro. Reuben Mickel was re-elected Grand Master, and R∴ W∴ Bro. T. S. Parvin, Grand Secretary.

IDAHO TERRITORY.

This Grand ☐ held its first annual communication at Idaho City, June 22, 1868. Four chartered and one U. D. ☐ represented.

M∴ W∴ Geo. H. Coe was elected Grand Master, and R∴ W∴ P. E. Edmondson, Grand Secretary.

KANSAS.

This Grand ☐ met in annual communication at Lawrence, October 20, 1868; M∴ W∴ Grand Master M. S. Adams, presiding.

Forty-eight subordinate ☞ were represented, with a total membership of 2,645. The work of the past year was: Initiated, 435; passed, 385; raised, 361.

The Grand Master's address relates to local matters only. The following is one of the many decisions of the Grand Master during the year:

"I hold the correct rule to be, that candidates rejected in another State cannot legally be made Masons in this State, without the consent of the proper authorities where the rejection occurred. According to some of the old Constitutions, no ☐ could 'initiate into the mysteries of the craft any person whomsoever, without being satisfied, by test or otherwise, that the candidate has not made application to any other ☐ and been rejected.' In my judgment, before the candidate for the mysteries of Masonry is admitted into the ☐, he should satisfy the brethren, by a declaration made on his honor as a man, that he has never made application to any other ☐ for the degrees of Masonry and been rejected; or, if rejected, the consent of the □ so rejecting should always be obtained before the degrees are conferred."

The report of the committee on Foreign Correspondence is a review in brief of the proceedings of thirty-five Grand bodies, including those of Colorado.

M∴ W∴ Bro. J. H. Brown was elected Grand Master, and R∴ W∴ Bro. E. T. Carr was elected Grand Secretary.

KENTUCKY.

This Grand □ held its annual communication at Louisville, October 19, 1868; M∴ W∴ Grand Master Elisha S. Fitch, presiding.

Three hundred and five chartered and fifteen U. D. ▭ represented. Aggregate membership, 18,972. Work of the year: Initiated, 2,070.

The address of the Grand Master is quite lengthy, and is devoted principally to matters concerning that jurisdiction.

The report of the committee on Foreign Correspondence is short, reviewing concisely the proceedings of thirty-one Grand bodies.

M∴ W∴ Bro. Elisha S. Fitch was elected Grand Master, and R∴ W∴ Bro. J. M. S. McCorkle, Grand Secretary.

LOUISIANA.

This Grand □ met in annual communication at New Orleans, February 8, 1869; M∴ W∴ Grand Master Henry R. Swasey, presiding.

Ninety-four chartered and four U. D. ▭ represented. Aggregate membership, 6,099. Work of the year: Initiated, 602; passed, 518; raised, 490.

The Grand Master's address treats almost exclusively of local matters.

The report of the committee on Foreign Correspondence is lengthy, ably reviewing the proceedings of thirty-nine Grand bodies. Want of space forbids us making copious extracts.

M∴ W∴ Bro. Samuel M. Todd was elected Grand Master, and R∴ W∴ Bro. James C. Batchelor, Grand Secretary.

MASSACHUSETTS.

This Grand □ met in annual communication at Boston, December 9, 1868; M∴ W∴ Grand Master Charles C. Dana, presiding.

One hundred and seventy-one ▭ were represented, with a total membership of 18,364. Work of the year: 2,094 persons made Masons.

The address of the Grand Master is devoted exclusively to local matters. There is no report on Foreign Correspondence.

M∴ W∴ Bro. William Sewall Gardner was elected Grand Master, and R∴ W∴ Bro. Solon Thornton, Grand Secretary.

MAINE.

This Grand □ met in annual communication at Portland, May 4, 1869; M∴ W∴ Grand Master Timothy J. Murray, presiding.

One hundred and forty-eight ▭ were represented, with an aggregate membership of 14,121. Work of the year was: 1,348 persons made Masons.

The Grand Master's address deals in home matters to the exclusion of all else.

The committee on Foreign Correspondence acknowledge the receipt of the proceedings of forty-four Grand ▭.

M∴ W∴ Bro. John H. Lynde was elected Grand Master, and R∴ W∴ Bro. Ira Berry, Grand Secretary.

MARYLAND.

This Grand ▭ met in annual communication at Baltimore, November 16th, 1868, M∴ W∴ Grand Master John Coates presiding.

Fifty-three subordinate ▭ were represented, with an aggregate membership of 4,609.

The work of the year was: 458 persons made Masons.

The address of the M∴ W∴ Grand Master treats only of home matters.

The committee on Foreign Correspondence made an extended report, reviewing the proceedings of forty-one Grand ▭, including Colorado.

M∴ W∴ Bro. A. T. Metcalf was elected Grand Master, and R∴ W∴ Bro. James Fenton Grand Secretary.

MICHIGAN.

This Grand ▭ met in annual communication at Detroit, January 13th, 1869, M∴ W∴ Grand Master S. C. Coffinbury, presiding.

Two hundred and thirty-four subordinate ▭ were represented, with an aggregate membership of 18,016. The work of the year was: 2,337 persons made Masons.

The following we clip from the Grand Master's address:

"*Brethren of the Grand* ▭ :

"This Grand body has again met under the most auspicious and congratulatory circumstances. The working-tools of our order have been actively employed in our jurisdiction since we last met in annual communication, and our labors have been crowned with signal success and flattering rewards. Peace has prevailed within our mystic precincts, and harmony rests on our sacred altars. Many new members have been added to our brotherhood by initiation within the year, which shows an increasing respect for our order among the intelligent of our fellow-men, and that the more Masonry, its objects, its aims, its pretensions, and its effects, are discussed and agitated by its enemies, the more favorably it impresses itself upon the moral sentiment of the age. It has been observed that the accessions to our order during the last year, and, perhaps, a part of the preceding year, have been, as a general thing, a high order of men, embracing not only some who are deservedly distinguished for their prominence as citizens and members of society, but who are justly eminent for their moral stability and pure integrity. The active business men, the worthy mechanics and laborers, the professional classes, the youth and the middle aged, have long been seeking the peaceful asylum of our order; but recently the more aged philosopher, the gray-haired moralist, and the profound thinker, have sought our school of ethics. Men who have struggled through professional, political, and pecuniary conflicts, with honor, seek our temple, sit down at our altar, and breathe freely in its atmosphere of pure morals, as they rest from their protracted struggle of life, giving dignity to Masonry, while they become useful laborers among us."

Also, the following:

"Intemperate habits in the use of strong drinks among our brothers ought to be severely punished by our ▭. There is no excuse or palliation that can now be offered for it; and I trust that, in a short time, drunkenness will be unknown among Masons. Our order owes it to mankind, as well as to herself as a moral institution, to wash her hands before the world of these plague spots, so incompatible with her professions of moral purity. Drunkenness in a Mason is such a compromise with dignity, manhood, and individual sovereignty, as to render its victim entirely unworthy of the title of Freemason. No man can be free who is a slave to his passions, his lusts, or his appetites. True manhood, the spirit of freedom, and the force of independence, are manifested in openly meeting our seducing lusts, appetites and passions, and without aid from others, but by force of our own moral will, wrestling with, and conquering them. In the victory over his own passions, by force of his own will, is embodied the true greatness of virtue. He who has met himself in such a conflict, who has battled with himself, and has arisen, freed from moral bondage, may well be called a Freemason, and may well claim our highest approval and commendation. But, when all mankind are growing wiser and better, and when our institution is tendering her aid, as a moral instrument in the great work of humanity, the brother who will embarrass her efforts, reproach her good name and bring her into shame and scandal by his drunkenness and immorality, is unworthy the honored title of Freemason."

The committee on Foreign Correspondence review in brief the proceedings of thirty-eight Grand ▭.

M∴ W∴ Bro. A. T. Metcalf was elected Grand Master, and R∴ W∴ Bro. James Fenton Grand Secretary.

MISSISSIPPI.

This Grand ▭ met in annual communication at Jackson, January 18, 1869; M∴ W∴ Grand Master Thos. S. Gathright, presiding.

One hundred and eighty-two subordinate ▭ were represented, with a total membership of 9,606. The work of the year was: Initiated, 714; passed, 586; raised, 578.

From the opening of the Grand Master's address we take the following:

" *Brethren of the Grand* ▭ :—

"It is a distinguished mark of the Divine favor that permits us to come together at this time. Into the twelve months that have passed away since we last met in Grand annual communication, there has crowded as much of bitter disappointment and sorrow, suspense and anxiety, as has filled the measure of any other period of equal extent in the annals of this Grand ▢. Our people have been chastened; and but for the promise made specially to them, the lengthened shadows of coming events, now falling around them, would inspire anything but hope. Our brethren constitute the great body of the intelligent citizenship in the common-wealth, and when we say our people are chastised, we may listen for the cry of Masons in distress. The war draped all our door-posts with mourn-ing, and planted weeds upon our hearth-stones. The losses in property, resulting from the war, impoverished our land. With an energy isolated and peculiar to our race, our brethren, oppressed by past results, but hope-ful for the future, began to struggle for a competency. During the last year, many of them reached the crisis of their pecuniary obligations, to find the proceeds of a year's labor inadequate to give relief.

"Many of our most beloved and distinguished brethren have staggered under their burdens. are stooping to receive more, while others have shaken off the debris of former prosperity, and girded themselves for a new career. *Brethren, it is a time to trust in God.*

"In seasons of prosperity, and in times of political harmony and good fellowship, it was delightful to assemble once a year in Grand ▢ and counsel together, and enjoy for a few brief days that charming fraternal communion known only among Masons. It was sweet then. How much more so now! How much does even the anticipation of a reunion soften the rigor of our cares during the passing year! How much more than heretofore does it suggest itself to us, as a special blessing, to assemble and commune with each other?"

As a matter of general Masonic interest, we clip the following from the report of the committee on Foreign Correspondence:

"We clip the following account of negro ▢, their origin and true status, from the proceedings of New York, and which are credited, by the com-mittee, to Bro. Bokkolen. We make no apology for its insertion, as it sup-plies a page in Masonic history on a subject eliciting a very general interest at present, and cannot fail to command a careful perusal:

"'HISTORY OF NEGRO LODGES.

"'In 1784, certain colored persons residing in Boston petitioned the Grand Master of England for a charter. The charter, dated September 29, 1784, was granted to Prince Hall, Boston Smith, Thomas Sanderson and several others, all colored men, under the name of African ▢, No. 459. The charter, however, was not received in Boston till the year 1787. It was an ordinary charter, in the usual form, and conferred no other privi-leges than those usually granted by such instruments. Of its proceedings from this time until 1827, we have no definite information, at which time we find it actively at work under the Mastership of Mr. John T. Hilton, claiming the powers and prerogatives of a Grand ▢, under the name of Prince Hall Grand ▢ of Ancient York Masonry, which powers it must have assumed as early as 1812, in which year it is said to have granted a charter for Boyer □, No. 1 (coloréd), in the city of New York. It was stricken from the registry of the Grand □ of England in 1818, and its lawful existence was then, of course, terminated, had it ever been anything other than an irregular organization. On surrendering the charter, *which was never returned to it*, a copy was kept, and after the □ had been dormant for several years, it was revived, *with this copy*, by the persons who were in possession of it. Its original establishment in Boston was a violation of the jurisdictional rights of the Grand □ of Massachusetts, which was organized in 1733, fifty-one years before the charter of this colored □ was granted by the Grand □ of England; and, therefore, waiving the question of color, it could never have been recognized by that or any other Masonic body, as a lawful □. Whether this or any of its numerous progeny—for from it have sprung all the negro □ in the United States claiming to be Masonic associations—are truly Masonic associations, we have no means of judging; if they be so, they are clandestine and irregular, and with them no Mason can hold Masonic intercourse or communication.

"'Our information as to the organization, at the present time, of the *so-called* negro Masonic □, is as follows: First, there is a National Grand □ at Philadelphia, having under its jurisdiction Grand □ (with subordinates) in the States of Massachusetts, Rhode Island, New York, New Jersey, Pennsylvania, Delaware, Maryland, District of Columbia, Ohio, Michigan, Indiana, Louisiana, Virginia and California. Second, there are subordinates in nearly all the Western and Eastern States not named above, except Maine, New Hampshire and Vermont; and in the following Southern States, to-wit; North Carolina, South Carolina, Georgia and Kentucky. Third, there is a Grand Chapter, Grand Encampment, Grand Consistory 32d and Supreme Council. From an incident which happened in San Francisco, in connection with the celebration of the last 4th of July, we learn that there is a schism in the African fraternity, the members mutually declaring the others as clandestine and irregular, the merits of which we understand to be as follows: In 1847 the National Grand □ referred to above, was organized. At one of the annual elections, John T. Hilton, the same as mentioned above as the Master of the Boston □ in 1827, and one Jacob Jenkins, were candidates for National Grand Master. Hilton was declared elected. Jenkins and his supporters seceded, and formed an independent organization known as the State Rights Grand □. This organization has Grand □ in New York, Pennsylvania and Maryland, and subordinates in several other States, California among the number.'"

M∴ W∴ Bro. Thos. S. Gathright was re-elected Grand Master, and R∴ W∴ Bro. J. L. Power, Grand Secretary.

MISSOURI.

This Grand □ met in annual communication at St. Louis, Oct. 12, 1868, M∴ W∴ Grand Master Wm. E. Dunscomb, presiding.

Three hundred subordinate □ were represented, with an aggregate membership of 14,497. The work of the year was: Initiated, 1,825; passed, 1,649; raised, 1,574.

The following is the opening of the Grand Master's address:

"*Brethren of the M∴ W∴ Grand □ of Missouri:*

"Another Masonic year is about to close, and yet another about to open. We meet to congratulate each other over the successes, to weave the cypress wreath for the sorrows, and to throw the mantle of forgiveness over the errors of the one, and to bind hearts and hands together anew for the labors of the other. We meet for the first time in this noble Temple, about to be consecrated to the glorious traditions, and yet more glorious offices of Masonry. Let us thus early in our annual convocation seek to catch the spirit which speaks forth from these lofty walls and splendid decorations, telling of effort wisely put forth, of means wisely expended in behalf of the great principles which bind us together, and apply ourselves in the spirit of true and earnest brotherhood to the duties now before us."

The report of the committee on Foreign Correspondence reviews the proceedings of thirty-seven Grand □, including Colorado.

M∴ W∴ Bro. John D. Vincil was elected Grand Master, and R∴ W∴ Bro. Geo. Frank Gouley, Grand Secretary.

MINNESOTA.

This Grand □ met in annual communication at St. Paul, January 12th, 1869, M∴ W∴ Grand Master C. W. Nash, presiding.

Sixty-one subordinate □ were represented. No statistics of the State given.

We clip from the address of the Grand Master as follows:

"Civilization, like most choice plants of the garden of nature, had its birth in the sunny south, under a genial sky. But as tropical plants attract the attention of the enterprising Northman, and are borne to more northern gardens, and by dint of enterprise, and the appliances of more labored art, are often developed into greater beauty than in their native soil, so the civilizations of the south are often found in greater perfection in the higher latitudes than in the countries that gave them birth.

"If oriental tradition is to be credited, long, long centuries 'before Hesiod wrote or Homer sang,' there was, comparatively, a high order of civilization in India. Temples and palaces were reared, and Sanscrit literature, like the early light of the morning, shot its rays far west and north gave shape to the language and arts of old Egypt; caught the keen eye of the Phœnician Cadmus, and by his practical genius was afterwards borne into Greece; and thence, taking the wings of the morning, flew to the remotest bounds of the earth. This may not be all true, but there are many known facts in the progress of civilization which go far to vindicate it against the charge of absurdity, or serious improbability. It is not to be questioned that India, and Persia, and Babylon, were long the seats and centres of enterprise, and some sorts of commerce, and of power; nor is it questioned that many of the arts and sciences had their birth in those sunny regions. But tropical civilization at home soon runs into luxury, effeminacy and despotism; and to escape annihilation, must seek a purer atmosphere in the less genial climes of more northern regions; or, lowering their tone of lordly pretension, must consent to live under the more practical control of northern minds. So it has ever been; and so, I presume, it will ever be.

"On a promontory of the eastern shore of the Mediterranean, in 33¼° north latitude, ever since the time ' when the memory of man runneth not to the contrary,' has stood the old city of Tyre. Some twenty miles farther up the coast lay Sidon, and between them lay the old city of Sarepta; many other cities were near. All these people are commonly known by the generic name of Phœnicians; sometimes, in the Old Testament, they are called Sidonians, from Sidon; sometimes Tyrians, from Tyrus or Tyre. They claim to be of Shemitish origin, or to have descended from Shem, the second son of Noah. If this be so, they must have come into possession of the country by conquest; for as we understand, the sons of *Ham* were the first occupants of that region. The inspired narrative runs: ' The sons of Ham were Cush, and Mizraim, and Phut, and Canaan,' * * * 'and Canaan begat Sidon, his first-born,' and as the name, Sidon, was attached to one of the Phœnician cities, there arises a strong presumption that the sons of Ham had first possession of that region of country, and that they were subsequently driven out by a colony of the sons of Shem, who became the Tyrians and Sidonians of history; and this (that they were an importation from abroad) becomes the more probable from the fact, that in the times of David and Solomon, they were, in all the arts of civilized life, far in advance of all the other nations of Canaan and the Mediterranean, excepting, perhaps, the Egyptians. It is hardly probable that two or three comparatively small cities, standing in the very heart and centre of western barbarism, should have loomed up in such majesty and grandeur as did Tyre and Sidon, without having derived their civilization from some other and more highly civilized part of the world. Nay, there arises a strong presumption, in the absence of all history, that they, *themselves*, the people, were derived from some more civilized people than any known in that quarter of the globe. Let us hear their own story. They say they were a colony of foreigners, and had, at an early period, expelled the original Tyrians and Sidonians. They had not been derived from Egypt, as some have surmised. They distinctly claim to have come from the shores of the Persian Gulf, or from some part of that remote region of the south, where it is certain that many of the Shemites did settle; and it is not a little remarkable that the historian, Strabo, tells us distinctly, that in the isles of Tyrus and Aradus, in the Persian Gulf, were found temples similar to those of the Phœnicians, and that the inhabitants of these isles claimed the cities of Tyrus and Aradus, on the coast of Phœnicia, as colonies of theirs. This is a most suggestive fact in history: that Tyrus and Aradus, now called Tyre and Ruad, or Ravad, should be claimed as colonies of two cities, or islands, of the same name in the Persian Gulf, and that their own people should acknowledge the relation, and even boast of it. At what time, and by what route they came, we have no means of knowing. It is possible that they may have come by way of Egypt, and lent their architectural skill in rearing the temples and mausoleums of her many cities, and thence have come to Phœnicia, either by land or water, as the Philistines, who settled a little lower down the Mediterranean coast, are known to have done; though I believe it is not known whether the Philistines are to be traced back any further than Egypt.

"Of the early enlightenment of the Phœnicians, including Tyre and Sidon, there can be no question. In commercial enterprise, they far outstripped all the known nations of the earth. They were long the only maritime people known, and sent their commodities to all the countries of the Mediterranean. Not only did they distribute their own commodities, which were chiefly cedar lumber, glass, and their peculiar shell-fish, from which the finest purple dye was obtained, but they received, overland, by caravans, and sent abroad, by sea, all the lighter and more valuable productions of Babylon, Persia, India, and Southern Arabia. They planted colonies in Africa, Spain, Sicily and Malta. Carthage, in Africa, was a Phœnician city founded by Dido, the sister of Pygmalion. They also worked, from their own hills, iron and copper; but the cedar of Mount Libanus was their great staple commodity. It is also known that they imported tin from Britain; and Herodotus asserts that in their trading excursions on the western coast of Africa, they certainly doubled the Cape of Good Hope, and cruised on the eastern coast, in the ·Indian ocean. In the prophecies of the Old Testament, Tyre and Sidon are both spoken of as being great in wealth and commercial importance. The prophet Isaiah calls Tyre 'The merchant city, * * whose merchants were princes; whose traffickers were the honorable of the earth.'

"Thus far I have digressed for the purpose of showing the probable derivation of the Tyrians and Sidonians, and the progress which they had made in the arts of civilization when they first appear in history, which is about the time of Joshua, 1450 B. C. Of course they must have been there long before; for their temples and public edifices were then such as to command the admiration of the world.

"Close beside them, and in immediate proximity, the providence of God had planted the Israelitish nation. The difference between these two peoples was very great. Israel were a plain, pastoral, and in some measure agricultural people, without knowledge of arts or sciences, and without commercial relations with any nation under Heaven, while the Phœnicians were, as I have already described them. The Phœnicians were also idolaters, while Israel was favored with the revelations of God, and a true religion. Side by side they lived—without conflict—for these Phœnicians were not warlike—without intimacy, so far as we are informed, for 400 years. At length, when David is firmly seated on the throne of Israel and Judah, and has commanded the respect of all the nations around him, the great Hiram, King of Tyre, sends him a message of congratulation, and his hearty recognition of the Israelitish monarchy. David has just burst on the eye of the astonished world as a star of the first magnitude in the constellation of oriental monarchs; and King Hiram is proud to do him honor. In proof of his sincerity, and according to royal usage, he sends, at the same time, costly presents, chiefly of cedar lumber from the mountains of Libanus, with carpenters and masons, to build him a royal palace, fit residence for a great king. The kindness is accepted, and in due time the palace is erected in the 'city of David,' on Mount Zion. Thus began the intimacy between Jerusalem and Tyre.

"Twenty-nine years passed away. David slept with his fathers, and Solomon, his son, reigned in his stead. It was in the heart of Solomon, as it had been in the heart of David, to build a temple to the honor of his God. Now Israel had rest from war, and the time had come for the prosecution of this noble enterprise. King Hiram, the friend of David, was dead, and his son, after a short reign, had passed away, but his grandson, Hiram, son of Ababaal, sat then on the thrones of Tyre and Sidon, united in one. He had inherited the hereditary affection for David, and now that David was dead, and Solomon on his throne, he sent an embassy of condolence to the new king on the death of his father, and of congratulation on his own accession to the throne of Israel. Solomon had reason to know the value of such a friendship, and especially of the architectural skill of the Phœnicians, and of their wise master-builders. So at once he made known his purpose to build a house for the services of religion—a temple to his God —and made this request to Hiram: 'Now therefore command thou that they hew me cedar trees out of Lebanon; and my servants shall be with thy servants, and unto thee will I give hire for thy servants, according to all that thou shalt appoint; for thou knowest that there is not among us any that can skill to hew timber like unto the Sidonians.' The proposal met with the cordial approval of the Phœnician king; and he rejoiced greatly, and said: 'Blessed be the Lord this day, which hath given unto David a wise son over this great people.' The details were soon arranged. The timber was to be procured in Mount Lebanon, brought down to the coast and sent forward by rafts or floats to the place that should be named (which was Joppa, or Jaffa); and the Phœnician workmen were to accompany it, or in due time to be ready to superintend the erection of the building. For this service Solomon was to remunerate him in corn, wine and oil; thus exchanging the commodities of one country for the commodities and skill of another; and this, so far as we know, was the first commercial treaty into which the Israelitish nation ever entered. Cedar trees and fir trees, and Phœnician skill, were exchanged for the agricultural commodities of Israel.

"Immediately the compact, or treaty, went into operation; Solomon should give to Hiram, or to his men—laborers—20,000 measures of beaten wheat, and 20,000 measures of barley, and 20,000 baths of wine, and 20,000 baths of oil, (each one of these *measures* is supposed to have been about thirty bushels) and besides this, to Hiram himself, for the use of his own household, every year, 20,000 measures of wheat, and 20 measures of pure oil.

"At once, 30,000 men of Israel were in the mountains of Lebanon, employed in the work; 10,000 were to work a month, and then go home for two months, and then 10,000 more take their place for another month; and thus, the work went on. These men of Israel were employed in merely cutting down the trees, which Hiram's men hewed into form. Then Solomon sent 70,000 men that 'bore burdens,' or in other words, carted the timber down to the coast, and 80,000 that were hewers (of stone), or quarrymen in the mountains.

"Here were thrown together people of different nationalities, diverse languages, and opposing interests. But it became necessary that they should speak, at least on some subjects, a common language, like the language of modern science, and that their interests, as far as possible, should be harmonized. Accordingly, a society was organized, the object of which was to unite strangers as friends,—to enable them to understand each other in technical language,—though speaking different vernacular tongues, and to unite people of different nationalities into a band of brothers. In this society, it is tolerably clear that the God of Israel was to be recognized, and the law of Moses received as the rule of faith and morals. When Solomon first proposed the alliance, Hiram rapturously exclaimed, 'Blessed be the *Lord*, this day!' &c. This was equivalent to an acknowledgment of Israel's God; and many think that Hiram had embraced the Jewish faith, since Israel's God, alone, was called *the Lord*. Israel, I presume, was to furnish the moral and religious elements of the society, while the Phœnicians were to teach the arts and sciences; and all were pledged to be good men, and to continue as apprentices and craftsmen in the art, until they should be accomplished workmen.

"The work went bravely forward; and at the end of seven years, the temple was completed, and dedicated to Israel's God; and Israel was scarcely more joyful at its dedication than were the men of Tyre. Of the incidents and accidents which befel them in the progress of the work, we need not speak. *One* noble Giblenite, we know, never saw the completion of the temple. The two kings, Solomon and Hiram, had taken the society under their royal patronage, and one of them generally presided in its deliberation,—perhaps always on great occasions;—or perhaps there was *another*, greatly honored by them both, who, during his life, often acted in their absence. It was a polytechnic institute, in which morals, religion, and all the arts, especially those connected with architecture, were thoroughly taught; their principles taught by night, in secret lectures, and exemplified by day, as the work went forward. What proportion of the laborers ever became wise master-builders, we have no means of knowing; but when the temple, and palaces, and other Hebrew works, were completed, there was one of the noblest bands of accomplished workmen the world had ever seen; and the Greek masters owned, in after ages, that to them they were indebted for the proudest achievements of Grecian skill in architecture.

Whether this be true or not, it is, at least, certain that these men became *travelers*, and went abroad in search of employment and wages; and the secret words, grips and signs which they had learned at Jerusalem, as the modern diploma, enabled them to make themselves known to all brethren, as apprentices, craftsmen, or masters, of that school. Thus, even in the time of Solomon, they built, not only the temple, but two or more palaces, and cities all over the land of Israel; and, also, the walls that enclosed Jerusalem; constructed the tent of the Bedouin Arab, and made home a place to be desired among all the nations around.

"As years sped, so went these men of enterprise to all lands. They fell in with the westward bound train from Scythia and Gothland; and Greece, and Italy, and all the States of southern Europe, shared in the benefits which they had to confer on humanity. Carthage was also built by them, in Africa. In short, they carried abroad the arts of civilization; and thus the religion of God, and the enterprise of the Phœnicians, united—going hand in hand in one grand race of enterprise and of mercy—have fallen in with the Gospel of Christ, and spread the light of truth and of the arts in all the earth. The sailors of Tyre also assisted Solomon in navigating his ships from his navy yard at the head of the bay of Akaba to Ophir.

"Such was the origin, and such the operative period, of Masonry.

"How long these societies continued to be made up of operatives, we have no means of knowing; but gradually, builders became capitalists, and men of leisure, and of letters; and for this, they were not excluded from the society which they loved; and their sons were admitted, without having learned the trades of Masons and builders. Gradually the temples of science, and of the arts, and of religion, were thrown open to all classes of men. The wall of partition between Jews and Gentiles was effectually broken down by the Gospel of the Redeemer, and at length, all men who sought the moral and social influence of these societies, if found worthy, were permitted to enter."

The committee on Foreign Correspondence review the proceedings of thirty-six Grand ⊠, ours included.

M∴ W∴ Bro. C. W. Nash was elected Grand Master, and R∴ W∴ Bro W. S. Cowles Grand Secretary.

NEW YORK.

This Grand ☐ met in annual communication at New York city, June 2, 1868; M∴ W∴ Grand Master Stephen H. Johnson, presiding.

Six hundred and thirty-five subordinate ⊠ were represented, with an aggregate membership of 70,333. The work of the year was: 8,855 persons made Masons.

The Grand Master's address is devoted wholly to local matters.

The committee on Foreign Correspondence review the proceedings of forty-three Grand ⊠, Colorado included.

M∴ W∴ Bro. James Gibson was elected Grand Master, and R∴ W∴ Bro. James M. Austin, Grand Secretary.

NEW HAMPSHIRE.

This Grand ☐ met in annual communication at Manchester, June 10, 1868; M∴, W∴ Grand Master John H. Rowell, presiding.

Sixty-seven subordinate ☐ were represented, with a total membership of 6,032. The work of the year was: 706 persons made Masons.

The Grand Master's address is exclusively of local importance.

The committee on Foreign Correspondence review the proceedings of thirty-eight Grand ☐.

M∴ W∴ Bro. Alexander M. Winn was elected Grand Master, and R∴ W∴ Bro. Horace Chase, Grand Secretary.

NEVADA.

This Grand ☐ met in annual communication at Virginia City, September 15, 1868; M∴ W∴ Grand Master John C. Currie, presiding.

There were represented ten chartered and two U. D. ☐, with a membership of 921. The work of the year was: Initiated, 145; passed, 135; raised, 137.

The address of the Grand Master speaks of local matters only.

The report of the committee on Foreign Correspondence is well written, covering seventy-seven pages of the proceedings, and containing a large amount of valuable information.

M∴ W∴ Bro. Geo. W. Hopkins was elected Grand Master, and R∴ W∴ Bro. Wm. A. M. Van Bokkelen, Grand Secretary.

NEW BRUNSWICK.

This Grand ☐ held its first annual communication at St. John, September 23, 1868; M∴, W∴ Grand Master B. Lester Peters, presiding.

Twenty-four ☐ were represented, with an aggregate membership of 1312.

The address of the Grand Master is devoted to his official duties performed. No report on Foreign Correspondence.

M∴ W∴ Bro. B. Lester Peters was re-elected Grand Master, and R∴ W∴ Bro. Wm. F. Bunting, Grand Secretary.

NEW JERSEY.

This Grand ☐ met in annual communication at Trenton, January 20, 1869; M∴ W∴ Henry R. Cannon, presiding.

Ninety-eight subordinate ☐ were represented, with a total membership of 7,729. No statistics given.

The Grand Master's address is wholly devoted to local interests.

The proceedings of thirty-nine Grand ☐ are ably reviewed by the committee on Correspondence.

M∴ W∴ Bro. Henry R. Cannon was re-elected Grand Master, and R∴ W∴ Bro. Joseph H. Hough, Grand Secretary.

NORTH CAROLINA.

This Grand ☐ met in annual communication at Raleigh, December 7, 1868; M∴ W∴ Grand Master R. W. Best, presiding.

One hundred and seventy-four subordinate ☐ were represented. Aggregate membership of the State, 8,944. The work of the year was: Initiated, 559; passed, 461; raised, 551.

We clip from the address of the Grand Master as follows:

"During the late war, too many of us let our zeal and sympathy get the upper hand of our judgment, and in looking over the returns of the subordinate ☐ for those years, one would almost conclude that the 'black balls' in the ☐ had been thrown away, or, at least, they were too seldom brought into requisition, the result of which we are now reaping; for it gives me sorrow to say it, yet it is nevertheless true, that a very large per cent. of those came into the order for mercenary or selfish motives, and since those motives have been accomplished they are but drones in the great hive of Masonry, for they neither work themselves, take no interest in the order, pay no dues, and never attend the ☐, except on festive occasions, and, instead of contributing to the great work, they hinder those who try to do their duty. The first duty of a ☐ is to amputate or cut off all such. There is too much shallow indulgence and mock charity in some of our ☐; there are innumerable parasites climbing in and through the temple, bent on plunder, and eager for destruction, if foiled in their designs. We may say of all such, 'strike them off,' and let those who love the work of the Great Architect go forward in the lofty and ennobling design. Yes, we repeat, 'cut them off,' for they are as much out of place in a Masonic ☐ as a viper in a nursery. Masonry is not elevated by numbers. Ten good and true Masons in a ☐ are worth more to the institution than a hundred such as I have mentioned, and if the black balls were brought more into use it would result in good. If the subordinate ☐ were to receive no new members during the next year, but devote the whole of that time in purging their ☐ of unworthy and offending members, and of the straightening of their finances, I venture the assertion that Masonry would be in greater repute than ever before."

The report of the committee on Correspondence is a review of the proceedings of forty-three Grand ☐.

M∴ W∴ Bro. Robert B. Vance was elected Grand Master, and R∴ W∴ Bro. Donald W. Bain Grand Secretary.

OHIO.

This Grand ☐ met in annual communication at Dayton, October 20, 1868, M∴ W∴ Grand Master Howard Matthews, presiding. Two hundred and sixty-five subordinate ☐ were represented. No statistics.

The Grand Master's address is devoted exclusively to home matters.

The committee on Correspondence review the proceedings of thirty-two Grand ☐, including Colorado.

44

M∴ W∴ Bro. Howard Matthews was elected Grand Master, and R∴ W∴ Bro. John D. Caldwell, Grand Secretary.

OREGON.

This Grand ☐ met in annual communication at Portland, on the 22d of June, 1868, M∴ W∴ Grand Master Avery A. Smith, presiding.

Twenty-six chartered and four U. D. ☐ represented, with an aggregate membership of 1,203. Work of the year was: Initiated, 164; passed, 161; raised, 157.

The following we quote from the address of the Grand Master:

"I am also, sorry to say, brethren, that profanity has been, and is now, indulged in by many members of the Masonic institution to such an extent that my attention has been called to it during the past year by persons in and out of the order. And I regret to say there are a few who even reject the teachings of that 'Great Light' which should be the guide of every Mason's faith and practice. This evil, so prevalent at the present time, should receive the consideration of this and all other Grand ☐ of Masons, if they would exert that moral power and influence which the intelligent, the good, the true in society should wield over others, and which Masons should seek after above all things else. A Mason who believes it right for him to curse and swear and utter the name of God in any other manner than with that awe and reverence due from the creature to his Creator, ignores the moral law and is false to his professions and his duty, and is of greater injury to Masonry than all the anti-Masons in the world, with all their slanderous vituperations.

"The moral teachings of that 'Book of the Law,' which we teach, is given to us by God himself, is obligatory upon every individual Mason who kneels at our altars, and we say its claims should be enforced. That law is the supreme law of Masonry, and no Mason can reject or neglect its teachings without rendering himself amenable to discipline. It should never be forgotten that moral worth and moral influence constitute the strength of a ☐ of Masons, and if the claims of those precepts were enforced there would be little cause of complaint. Nay, in that event Masonry would only be second in influence to religion itself. Then, brethren, we would present such an array of moral worth, and wield such a moral influence that the divine mission of Masonry would soon be felt in the world and tell gloriously on the condition of man. Then we would realize what is contemplated in our teachings. Then might the world point to Masonry as an institution to which the burthened heart could pour out its sorrows, and to whom the distressed might prefer their suit—whose hand is guided by justice, and whose heart is expanded by benevolence. Let this achievement be the great object of each and every brother; let each strive for this till the great object is attained, that Masonry may be a light and an influence in the world, that mankind and society may be made better for our having lived Masons.

"Then, my brethren, in view of the evils that exist at this time, let us with greater vigilance guard the entrance, and not suffer the principles of the fraternity to be abused with impunity by the profligate, or trampled upon by the profane. There is no vice more odious, none more degrading, none in whose train follows more numerous evils. This indulgence is without apology, without justification, while it is a direct and palpable violation of one of the cardinal virtues of our beloved order. Then let me admonish you to wipe away from the institution this reproach from this time onward, by saying to the profane when they approach the threshold of our mystic temple, thus far mayest thou go and no farther."

The committee on Foreign Correspondence review the proceedings of thirty-eight Grand ⌑, including Colorado.

M∴ W∴ Bro. A. A. Smith was elected Grand Master, and R∴ W∴ Bro. Hurford, Grand Secretary.

PENNSYLVANIA.

This Grand ⌑ met in annual communication at Philadelphia, December 2, 1868, M∴ W∴ Grand Master Richard Vaux, presiding.

Two hundred and twenty-nine subordinate ⌑ were represented. Aggregate membership of the State, 26,140. Work of the year: 3,681 persons made Masons.

We clip from the address of the Grand Master the following:

"Thus it is Freemasonry grows; thus are her borders enlarged and her stakes strengthened. Without wishing to assume 'to be holier than thou,' we would, in the most fraternal solicitude for the real welfare of the craft everywhere, beg leave to remark, that the greatest danger to which Freemasonry is now exposed, *is from enemies within, not those without.* Making members of the craft, is not necessarily making Masons. There is too great a desire to increase the number of members, for peradventure the number of Masons is not thereby increased. Strict trial, severe tests, careful examination, thorough investigation into fitness; caution, prudence, due consideration, and above all, moral courage to do the duty which these virtues demand, are now essential in all ⌑ as precedent conditions to a favorable report on those who apply for the rights and privileges of Masonry. These are the guards which are stationed at every portal of the Temple. Woe unto that man, who by deceit or lack of examination, passes them unchallenged —but woe to those who are thus made their associates. Once destroy the harmony of fraternal unity in the craft, and the enemy is thus in our very midst."

And from the conclusion of the report of the committee on Foreign Correspondence, this:

" Ages have rolled away since they who founded Masonry have rested from their labors. They have left upon the pages of history no record of their names. But their work still endures. Their children and their children's children have perpetuated it. Philosophical, political, and religious systems have arisen, and grown to greatness, side by side with *Freemasonry*, and then have vanished away. They taught false doctrines, or propagated unsubstantial dogmas or theories inconsistent with the enlightenment and progress of social existence. But, standing under the shadow of uncounted years, *Masonry* still exists, endowed with all the strength and vigor of its youth, and all the maturity of its manhood, only because its teachings and examples are inherently good, and calculated to ameliorate the condition of man in every position of life, and in every form of society. We believe Masonry is destined to endure until there shall no longer exist on earth either sin, suffering, or sorrow, and until unbounded love shall dwell in every heart, and peace shall hold her sway over every land."

M∴ W∴ Bro. Richard Vaux was elected Grand Master, and R∴ W∴ Bro. John Thompson, Grand Secretary.

RHODE ISLAND.

This Grand ☐ met in annual communication at Pawtucket, August 6th, 1868, M∴ W∴ Grand Master Thomas A. Doyle, presiding.

Fifteen subordinate ☐ were represented, with an aggregate membership of 3,013. The work of the year was: Initiated, 281; passed, 282; raised, 276.

The Grand Master's address is short, and devoted to home matters.

There was no report by the committee on Foreign Correspondence.

M∴ W∴ Bro. Thomas A. Doyle was elected Grand Master, and R∴ W∴ Bro. Charles D. Greene, Grand Secretary.

SOUTH CAROLINA.

This Grand ☐ met in annual communication at Charleston, Nov. 17th, 1868, R∴ W∴ Deputy Grand Master James Connor, presiding.

One hundred and thirteen subordinate ☐ were represented. The aggregate membership of the State is not given, nor are there any statistics of the work of the year.

No address by the Grand or Deputy Grand Master.

The report on Foreign Correspondence, by Bro. R. S. Burns, is quite voluminous, containing a vast amount of valuable information.

M∴ W∴ Bro. James Connor was elected Grand Master, and R∴ W∴ Bro. R. S. Burns, Grand Secretary.

TENNESSEE.

This Grand ☐ met in annual communication at Nashville, Oct. 4th, 1868. M∴ W∴ Grand Master Joseph M. Anderson, presiding.

Two hundred and seventy-three chartered and twenty-seven U. D. ☐ were represented. The aggregate membership of the State is 15,790, and the work of the year was: Initiated, 2,060; passed, 1,182; raised, 1,900.

This from the Grand Master's address:

"The growth of our order is rapid, and the principles of Freemasonry are doing much by their wide-spread influence to soften the asperities of life, and promote good fellowship among men throughout this broad land.

The uninitiated may not feel and see this, but we know that there is an under-current of good in the land, fed and directed by the prayers and sympathies of millions of hearts; and do we not feel gratefully proud that we can number ourselves with these hearts, if we are worthily enrolled with them, when we hear murmured thanks of those to whom relief has been given? May we not render thanksgiving and praise to Almighty God, whose Spirit has inclined our hearts to unite ourselves in a common brotherhood?

"Our numbers and resources are vast. Our banners swell in every breeze that sweeps the continent, and the army of self-sacrificing and zealous men, engaged in doing the deeds of charity and beneficence, excite our admiration, and suggest that as a part of that host we all, individually and collectively, have committed to us a sacred trust.

"But the magnitude of that army is well calculated to excite apprehension. May not our numbers be too great? Are not our ☐ too numerous, and our membership too great? I think I have placed an average estimate upon the goodness and virtue of mankind, and am of the opinion that a very small proportion of men are fit to become Masons, or have the ability to live up to its requirements."

From the conclusion of a not long but well-written report on Foreign Correspondence, we clip as follows:

"It is pleasing to see that under the care of a merciful Providence and an all-wise Ruler, the order continues to advance in harmony and prosperity. The only fear that we can express is, that too many men are being made Masons. It is becoming fashionable, like church-going, and persons are getting anxious for initiation, not influenced by a desire of knowledge, but for idle show, and because it is respectable. And these brethren, be they ever so moral, do little good to the craft; they burden it with drones who serve to diminish the honey stored in the hive, but never bring any to it; and when the winter of trouble comes, they sneak out to leave the few workers all the labor. There are too many vain men who pride themselves on their dignified titles, and showy regalia, and so-called Masonic jewelry, and who care no farther for the institution. There are men who have not the intellect to grasp, nor the education to understand, our sacred mysteries. There are many who are glib enough with their tongues, but alas! their heart is far away. Too many such are found among us; let us see that there are no more. Let us raise higher the standard of our membership; let us labor to vitalize our principles, and let the earnest and intelligent members of our body be its teachers and controllers, and not the martinets and puppies, who believe that they and they only understand matters—'they are the world, and wisdom dies with them.' Let us bear this in mind, and adopt the watch-cry of Missouri: 'More morals and less numbers.' Think of the deep solemnity of our own obligations, and cry aloud against the evils which are demoralizing the order. Let us all try and force this moral reform on ourselves, and the community will believe in our purity, they will see it is not all boasting, and will endeavor to follow and be guided by us. Let there be no such thing as a profane Mason—a poor worm who would dare to tamper with that unutterable name before which every knee should bow. Away with the drunken Mason—poor, unfortunate victim of self and its love! Out with the liquor-dealing Mason, the purveyor of woes and sorrows for others, he who is cursed in holy writ for giving his neighbor drink! No more Masonic debauchees or whoremongers, stepping from the ☐ meeting to the brothel, or stealing into the bower of peace and pouring venomous poison on domestic bliss! No more gambling, lying, loafing, cowardly Masons! No more false-hearted friends, hollow pretenders, hypocritical religionists! Let us all try, at least, to be pure, and show the good that is in us, for an example to others. Thank God, Tennessee and Tennessee Masons have the true stuff in them! Brothers, let us use it, and so live that we may all meet again yonder in the glories of the temple where light perpetual reigns, and join in the anthem of endless praise to the divine Architect, and perpetual fraternity of the blessed!

"The great truths and precepts upon which our order is founded, are the civilization of the times in which we live. We are called on to better the race, to do our best to bring about that period when Masonic charity shall prevail, when all doubt and disunion shall cease, and the world will appreciate and know the blessings of universal brotherhood."

M∴ W∴ Bro. Jonathan S. Dawson was elected Grand Master, and R∴ W∴ Bro. John Frizzell, Grand Secretary.

TEXAS.

This Grand ☐ met in annual communication at Houston, June 14th, 1868, M∴ W∴ Grand Master Peter W. Gray, presiding.

Two hundred and sixty-five ☐ were represented, with an aggregate membership of 10,506. The work of the year was: Initiated, 875; passed, 728; raised, 725.

The Grand Master's address is confined mostly to home matters.

The committee on Foreign Correspondence review briefly the proceedings of thirty-seven Grand ☐.

M∴ W∴ Bro. Philip C. Tucker was elected Grand Master, and R∴ W∴ Bro. Geo. H. Bringhurst, Grand Secretary.

VERMONT.

This Grand ☐ met in annual communication at St. Johnsbury, June 10th, 1868, M∴ W∴ Grand Master Leverett B. Englesby, presiding.

Seventy-three chartered and seven U. D. ☐ were represented. No statistics reported.

The Grand Master's address is devoted to local matters only.

The committee on Foreign Correspondence review the proceedings of twenty-three Grand ☐.

M∴ W∴ Bro. George M. Hall was elected Grand Master, and R∴ W∴ Bro. Henry Clark, Grand Secretary.

VIRGINIA.

This Grand □ met in annual communication at Richmond, December 14, 1868, M∴ W∴ Grand Master William Terry, presiding.

No statistics given.

The Grand Master's address is devoted principally to matters relating to the Grand □ of West Virginia.

There is no report from the committee on Foreign Correspondence.

M∴ W∴ Bro. William Terry was elected Grand Master, and R∴ W∴ Bro. John Dove, Grand Secretary.

WASHINGTON TERRITORY.

This Grand □ met in annual communication at Olympia, September 17, 1868, R∴ W∴ Deputy Grand Master E. A. Light, presiding. Eleven chartered and one U. D. □ represented. Total membership 348. The work of the year was: Initiated, 38; passed, 28; raised, 25.

The Grand Master's address relates solely to home matters.

No report by the committee on Foreign Correspondence.

M∴ W∴ Bro. Benj. E. Lombard was elected Grand Master, and R∴ W∴ Bro. Thomas M. Reed, Grand Secretary.

WEST VIRGINIA.

This Grand □ met in annual communication at Wheeling, November 10, 1868, M∴ W∴ Grand Master Wm. J. Bates, presiding. Thirty □ were represented. Total membership, 1,590. The work of the year was: Initiated, 307; passed, 246; raised, 230.

The Grand Master's address is devoted to matters relative to the relations of this Grand □ and that of Virginia.

Committee on Foreign Correspondence review the proceedings of thirty-five Grand □, including Colorado.

M∴ W∴ Bro. William J. Bates was elected Grand Master, and R∴ W∴ Bro. Thomas H. Logan, Grand Secretary.

WISCONSIN.

This Grand □ met in annual communication at Milwaukee, June 9th, 1868, M∴ W∴ Grand Master Harlow Pease, presiding.

One hundred and four chartered and four U. D. □ represented. Total membership 7,713. Work of the year: Initiated, 1,284; passed, 1,099; raised, 1,073.

The Grand Master's address is of local interest only.

The report of the committee on Foreign Correspondence is short and to the point.

M∴ W∴ Bro. Harlow Pease was elected Grand Master, and R∴ W∴ Bro. Wm. T. Palmer, Grand Secretary.

All of which is respectfully submitted.

HAL SAYR, *Chairman.*

CONSTITUTION

M. W. GRAND LODGE OF COLORADO.

WHEREAS, Every Grand □ posseses the inherent power to form a Constitution, as the fundamental law of its Masonic action, and to enact such By-Laws from time to time, as it may deem necessary for its own government, and to make such rules and prescribe such regulations for the administration of its subordinate □ as will insure the prosperity thereof, and promote the general good of Masonry ; and,

WHEREAS, Every Grand □ is the true representative of all the fraternity in communication therewith, and is, in that behalf, an absolute and independent body, with supreme legislative authority. *Provided, always,* That the ancient landmarks of the order be held inviolate ; therefore, upon these principles, which have never been disputed, the Grand □ of Colorado does hereby ordain, establish and promulgate the following Constitution and By-Laws for its future government, and does make and prescribe the following rules and regulations for the government of the ⊡ under its jurisdiction.

ARTICLE I.

This Grand □ shall forever hereafter be known by the name and style of the Most Ancient and Honorable Fraternity of Free and Accepted Masons of Colorado.

ARTICLE II.

The Grand □ shall consist of a Grand Master, Deputy Grand Master, Senior Grand Warden, Junior Grand Warden, Grand Treasurer, Grand Secretary, Grand Chaplain, Grand

45

Orator, Grand Lecturer, Grand Marshal, Senior Grand Deacon, Junior Grand Deacon, and Grand Tyler, with such other officers as it may, from time to time, create, together with the Masters and Wardens, or their proxies, duly constituted, of the chartered ▱ under its jurisdiction, and such Past Grand Masters and Past Deputy Grand Masters as shall be present, and are members of a subordinate ▱.

ARTICLE III.

The Grand ▱ shall hold a stated communication at least once in every two years, at such time and in such place as may be designated in its By-Laws.

ARTICLE IV.

The Grand ▱ shall not be opened, nor shall any business be transacted therein, unless there be present a representative from at least three of the chartered ▱; but a smaller number may meet and adjourn from day to day, until a constitutional quorum shall attend.

ARTICLE V.

The officers of the Grand ▱ shall be styled and take rank as follows:

The Most Worshipful Grand Master.
The Right Worshipful Deputy Grand Master.
The Right Worshipful Senior Grand Warden.
The Right Worshipful Junior Grand Warden.
The Right Worshipful Grand Treasurer.
The Right Worshipful Grand Secretary.
The Right Worshipful Grand Chaplain.
The Right Worshipful Grand Orator.
The Right Worshipful Grand Lecturer.
The Right Worshipful Grand Marshal.
The Worshipful Senior Grand Deacon.
The Worshipful Junior Grand Deacon.
The Grand Tyler.

ARTICLE VI.

No brother shall be eligible to the office of Grand Master,

Deputy Grand Master, or Grand Warden, who has not been duly elected, installed, and presided over a subordinate ▭.

ARTICLE VII.

At each stated communication of the Grand ▭, there shall be elected by ballot, from among the brethren who are at the time constitutionally eligible to seats therein, a Grand Master, a Deputy Grand Master, a Senior Grand Warden, a Junior Grand Warden, a Grand Treasurer, and a Grand Secretary; all other Grand Officers shall be appointed by the Grand Master, with the advice and consent of the Grand ▭.

ARTICLE VIII.

No Grand Officer shall officiate in the station to which he is elected until he has been legally installed.

ARTICLE IX.

The Most Worshipful Grand Master has the right to convene the Grand ▭ in special Grand Communication on any emergency which in his judgment may require it. He has the power, at his discretion, to assemble any subordinate ▭, and preside therein, inspect its work, and require a strict conformity to the constitutional rules and regulations of the order. For good cause, he may suspend the functions of any such ▭ until the ensuing stated communication of the Grand ▭. It is his prerogative to make Masons at sight, and for this purpose, may summon to his assistance such brethren as he may deem necessary. He has the command of every other Grand Officer touching the duties and ministrations of their several offices, and may call on any and all of them at any time, for advice and assistance, on all business relative to the craft.

ARTICLE X.

In case of the death, absence, or inability of the Grand Master, the powers and duties of his station for all regular and necessary purposes shall, for the time being, devolve upon the Deputy Grand Master, Senior Grand Warden, or Junior Grand Warden, in the order here enumerated.

ARTICLE XI.

No dispensation shall be granted for constituting a new ▭, except upon the petition of eight Master Masons, one of whom must be a Past Master, and the recommendation of the chartered ▭ nearest the location of the new ▭, vouching for the moral character and Masonic qualifications of the petitioners.

ARTICLE XII.

No warrant or dispensation for the institution of a new ▭ shall be granted for a less sum than twenty-five dollars, twenty dollars additional for the charter; and no charter shall be issued to any new ▭ which has not worked under dispensation a sufficient length of time, and which shall not have regularly conferred the degrees of Entered Apprentice, Fellowcraft and Master Mason.

ARTICLE XIII.

No charter or dispensation for creating new ▱ shall be granted to any person or persons whomsoever, residing out of the Territory (or State), if within the jurisdiction of any other constitutional Grand ▭.

ARTICLE XIV.

The Grand ▭ has original and exclusive jurisdiction over all subjects of Masonic legislation, and appellate jurisdiction, from the decisions of the subordinate ▱; and its enactments and decisions upon all questions shall be the supreme Masonic law of the Territory (or State). It shall prescribe such rules and regulations for the government of the subordinate ▱, as will, in its arbitrament, conduce to the welfare, prosperity and happiness of the craft, and may require from them such dues and fees as will, at all times, discharge the engagements of the Grand ▭.

ARTICLE XV.

The Book of Constitutions hereunto attached, this Grand ▭ does recognize and adopt as the fundamental laws, rules and regulations for the government of Masons; and declares that it should be frequently read and perused by Masters and other craftsmen, as well within the subordinate ⊡ as thereout, to the end that none may be ignorant of the excellent principles and precepts it inculcates.

ARTICLE XVI.

This Constitution may be altered or amended in the following manner only: The proposed alteration or amendment must be made in writing, at some stated communication. The Grand Master shall put the question upon its adoption, and if concurred in by a vote of three-fourths of the members present, it shall, from thenceforth, be considered as a part and parcel of this Constitution.

BY-LAWS.

SECTION 1. The Annual Communications of the Grand ▭ shall be held on the last Tuesday of September in each year, alternately, at the city of Denver and Central City.

ELIGIBILITY.

SEC. 2. No brother shall be eligible to either of the offices of Grand or Deputy Grand Master, Senior or Junior Grand Warden, unless he shall have passed the Chair in some regular ▭.

SEC. 3. No member shall be eligible to any office in this Grand ▭, who is not a member of a subordinate ▭ in this jurisdiction.

PROXIES.

SEC. 4. Whenever the Master or Wardens of a ▭ cannot attend in person, the ▭ shall appoint some member or members of said ▭ to act in his or their stead, at the last Regular Communication preceding the annual session of the Grand ▭.

ANNUAL RETURNS.

SEC. 5. Every ▭, subordinate to this Grand ▭, shall, at least ten days prior to the first day of each Annual Grand Communication, pay to the Grand Secretary for the use of the Grand ▭, the sum of one dollar and fifty cents for each Master Mason belonging to their ▭ at the time of making the annual return. And no representative of any ▭ shall be entitled to a seat in the Grand ▭ until the dues of his ▭ are paid, and the Grand Secretary's receipt therefor produced. And in case of the neglect or refusal of any ▭ to pay its annual dues at the time herein specified, on or before the next Annual Communication of the Grand ▭, such ▭ may be stricken from the books of the Grand ▭, and their warrant or charter considered null and void; but on proper application to the Grand ▭, making full returns and paying of all dues, such ▭ may be restored to its former rank and privileges.

SEC. 6. No ▭ shall be required to pay dues for non-contributing members who shall have permanently removed without the jurisdiction of this Grand ▭.

LEAVE OF ABSENCE.

SEC. 7. No brother, after having taken his seat as a member, shall be permitted to leave without obtaining permission of the Grand Master.

COMMITTEES—THEIR DUTIES.

SEC. 8. At each Annual Communication of the Grand ▭, as soon as practicable after its organization, the Grand Master shall appoint the following committees:

1. A committee on Credentials, to consist of three members, whose duty it shall be to examine the credentials of all Masons claiming the right of membership, and report their names and Masonic connection to the Grand ▭.

2. A committee to examine visiting brethren, to consist of three members, whose duty it shall be to examine all visitors not properly vouched for, and report their respective names, address and Masonic connection to the Grand ▭.

3. A committee on Returns and Work of ▭ U. D., on Chartered ▭, and on Petitions, consisting of three members, whose duty it shall be to examine the By-Laws, records of work and the returns of ▭ U. D., and to make report to the Grand ▭ if or not, in their opinion, charters should be granted to such ▭; to examine the returns of proceedings and work of chartered ▭; to examine all petitions for new ▭ U. D., for changes of location or for change of name, and report on the same to the Grand ▭.

4. A committee on Appeals and Grievances, consisting of three members, whose duty it shall be to examine and report upon all appeals, memorials and petitions in relation to any

matter of complaint within this jurisdiction, which shall come before the Grand ▢.

5. A committee on Finance, Mileage and Per Diem, consisting of three members, whose duty it shall be to examine and report on all accounts and financial matters to them referred, and to make a full report before the close of each Annual Grand Communication, of the financial condition of the Grand ▢; also to ascertain the distance necessarily traveled by each officer and representative entitled to mileage and per diem, and report the same to the Grand ▢.

SEC. 9. Before the close of each Annual Communication of the Grand ▢, the Grand Master shall appoint standing committees for the ensuing Masonic year, as follows, viz:

1. On Masonic Correspondence, to consist of three members, whose duty it shall be to examine the correspondence and documents from other Grand 🏛 in correspondence with this Grand ▢, and report at each Annual Communication whatever may seem of sufficient importance and interest to demand its attention or action.

2. On Masonic Jurisprudence, to consist of three members; whose duty it shall be to examine and report upon all questions, documents and papers requiring investigation and decision upon points of Masonic law, and to make report upon the same.

SEC. 10. The Grand Officers, members of the committees on Masonic Correspondence and Masonic Jurisprudence, and the representative highest in rank from each ▢ under this jurisdiction, shall be allowed twelve and one-half cents per mile, going and returning, for every mile traveled from his place of residence, computed by the necessarily traveled route, and two dollars per day for each day's actual attendance at the Grand ▢: *Provided*, No one shall draw mileage both as a Grand Officer and representative.

🏛 UNDER DISPENSATION.

SEC. 11. No dispensation shall be granted by the Grand Master or by the Grand ▢ for the formation of a new ▢, but

46

upon the petition of eight known and approved Master Masons, in which their first Master and Wardens shall be nominated; said petition shall set forth the name of the county and place, also that the petitioners have procured a suitable room, with convenient ante-rooms, for the practice of Masonic rites, and that the material in their town and neighborhood is sufficient to sustain a healthy and reputable ▭, which shall be accompanied by a recommendation from the ▭ nearest the place in which the new ▭ is to be holden, certifying to the truth of the statements contained in said petition, and that the brother named for Master is qualified to open and close a ▭, and to confer the three degrees.

SEC. 12. There shall be paid for every dispensation for a new ▭, the sum of forty dollars; for every charter, the sum of twenty dollars; and the further sum, in addition, of two dollars, to be paid to the Grand Secretary; which said sums, respectively, shall be paid before the delivery of the dispensation or charter. The seal of the Grand ▭ shall be affixed to every charter without additional charge.

SEC. 13. No charter shall issue to a ▭ under dispensation, until it shall have conferred the degrees of Entered Apprentice, Fellowcraft, and Master Mason, in manner and form as prescribed by the rules and regulations of the Grand ▭.

SPECIAL DISPENSATIONS.

SEC. 14. There shall be paid into the hands of the Grand Master the sum of five dollars for every dispensation granted to confer any degree or degrees in less than the usual time specified in the By-Laws or regulations of this Grand ▭, to be paid, in all cases, before the dispensation is issued; also, the sum of two dollars for every special dispensation for any other purpose.

NON-AFFILIATED MASONS.

SEC. 15. Jurisdiction and discipline shall be exercised over non-affiliated Masons by the oldest ▭, only, in cities or places where two or more ▭ may be situated.

EXPULSIONS, SUSPENSIONS, RESTORATIONS, AND REJEC-
TIONS.

SEC. 16. Notices of expulsions, suspensions and rejections, shall be given in the following manner: When any brother shall be suspended or expelled, or any candidate for initiation shall be rejected by any ☐, immediate notice thereof shall be sent to each ☐ in this jurisdiction. All expulsions and suspensions shall also be published with the proceedings of the Grand ☐. No member shall be permitted to make any expulsion or suspension public, or to communicate the same to any person not a Mason, except by a resolution to make public by the ☐ from which the brother has been suspended or expelled, and which shall also be reported to the Grand Secretary.

SEC. 17. All appeals from any subordinate ☐ shall be in writing, and left with the Grand Secretary, and the appellant shall give the other party reasonable notice thereof; and in case the decision of any ☐ suspending or expelling a brother, shall be reversed by the Grand ☐, such brother shall be restored to all his rights and privileges as a member of the order.

SEC. 18. In all cases of the suspension or expulsion of a member, two thirds of the members present shall be required, and in all cases of the restoration of a Mason, suspended by any ☐ under the jurisdiction of this Grand ☐, the same majority shall be required. No expelled Mason shall be restored to the privileges of Masony except by a vote of the Grand ☐, and such restoration shall not reinstate him in membership in the ☐ from which he was expelled, without the unanimous consent of the members thereof.

SEC. 19. No ☐ acting under the jurisdiction of this Grand ☐, shall knowingly receive any candidate in any of the degrees of Masonry, who has been rejected by any other ☐, within twelve months after such rejection, without first receiving the unanimous consent of the ☐ that rejected him.

GRAND TREASURER—HIS DUTIES.

SEC. 20. The Grand Treasurer shall have charge of all the funds, property, securities and vouchers of the Grand ☐; and it shall be his duty to attend all Grand Communications, and report the condition of the finances of the Grand □; and finally, to pay or deliver over to his successor in office, or such other person or persons as the Grand □ may appoint, all the funds, property, securities, vouchers, records, and books belonging to the Grand □.

GRAND SECRETARY—HIS DUTIES.

SEC. 21. The Grand Secretary shall attend at all Regular and Special Communications of the Grand □, and duly record its proceedings, and shall receive and accurately account for, and promptly pay or deliver over to the Grand Treasurer all the funds and property of the Grand □, from whatever source, taking his receipt for the same. He shall keep a record of the returns made by subordinate ⊡, receive and preserve all petitions, applications, appeals, and other documents; sign, certify to, and duly seal all instruments of writing emanating from the Grand □; conduct the correspondence of the Grand □, under the direction of the Grand Master, and report annually to the several Grand ⊡ in correspondence with this Grand □, the names of Grand Officers elected. He shall, at each Annual Grand Communication, make a report to the Grand □ of moneys received and paid over to the Grand Treasurer, of failure or want of punctuality on the part of subordinate ⊡ in paying dues and making proper returns, and of such other matters as, in his judgment, may require the action of the Grand □. He shall, in due time, previous to each Annual Grand Communication, furnish each subordinate □ with blank returns, with such instructions in regard to them as the rules and regulations of the Grand □ may require. He shall cause the Constitution, By-Laws, regulations and binding resolutions of this Grand □ to be published annually, with the proceedings of the Grand □.

OTHER OFFICERS—THEIR DUTIES.

SEC. 22. The Grand Chaplain shall attend the communications of the Grand □ and perform religious services.

The Grand Marshal shall proclaim the Grand Officers at their installation, introduce the representatives of foreign

Grand ⌑ and distinguished visiting brethren, and conduct processions of the Grand ⌑.

The Grand Standard Bearer shall take charge of the Grand Standard of the order, in processions and public ceremonies.

The Grand Sword Bearer shall carry the sword in procession, and perform such other duties as by ancient usage pertain to his office.

The Grand Stewards shall have immediate superintendence, under the direction of the Junior Grand Warden, in the provisions to be made on all festive occasions.

The Grand Pursuivant shall communicate with the Grand Tyler, announce all applicants for admission by their Masonic address, names and connection, and take charge of the jewels and clothing.

The Grand Deacons shall perform the duties incident to their respective offices.

The Grand Tyler shall guard the door of the Grand ⌑ on the outside, report all persons claiming admission, and see that none enter but such as are duly authorized and properly clothed.

The Grand Tyler shall have all the rights and be entitled to all the honors of other Grand Officers, except the right to vote.

UNLAWFUL LECTURES.

SEC. 23. The delivery or teaching of any Masonic lectures, not authorized, or which have not received the sanction of the Grand ⌑, or of its lawful authority, is forbidden.

SEC. 24. On all questions arising in the Grand ⌑, the elected Grand Officers, together with such Past Grand Masters and Past Deputy Grand Masters as may be present, and are members thereof, shall each be entitled to one vote; and the Master and Wardens of each subordinate ⌑, or their regularly constituted proxies, shall each be entitled to one vote; but in no case whatsoever, shall a member, by virtue of any proxy or authority, cast more than three votes.

BY-LAWS PERTAINING TO LODGES.

INDIVIDUAL □—THEIR DUTIES.

SEC. 25. All □ subordinate to this Grand □ shall, immediately after each annual election by such □, report to the Grand Secretary the names of the Master, Wardens, and Secretary-elect.

SEC. 26. Upon the demise of any □ within the jurisdiction of this Grand □, the Secretary and Treasurer of the □ shall, within three months thereafter, transmit to the Grand Secretary all the books, papers, jewels, furniture, funds, and other property, or evidence thereof, of the □ so demised.

SEC. 27. No elections for officers shall take place in a □ U. D., but all vacancies shall be filled by appointment by the Worshipful Master.

PETITIONS FOR INITIATION OR MEMBERSHIP.

SEC. 28. Subordinate □ are instructed not to act upon any petition, either for initiation or membership, unless the same shall have lain over one lunar month.

SEC. 29. Subordinate □ shall not receive a petition for initiation from an applicant who lives nearer to another □ than the one he petitions, without first obtaining the unanimous consent of the other □, at a regular meeting.

SEC. 30. After a petition is regularly received by a subordinate □, and entered upon its minutes, it shall not be withdrawn.

SEC. 31. The subordinate □ under the jurisdiction of this Grand □, are instructed not to initiate any candidate who has not resided in the jurisdiction of this Grand □ twelve calendar months before such application be made.

CONFERRING DEGREES.

SEC. 32. No subordinate □ in this jurisdiction shall confer the degrees upon any candidate, unless he be a perfect man, having no maim or defect in his body that may render him incapable of learning the art and becoming perfect in the degrees.

SEC. 33. No subordinate ▭ in this jurisdiction shall confer any of the degrees on non-resident citizens without the consent of the proper jurisdiction first had and obtained.

SEC. 34. No ▭ working under the jurisdiction of this Grand ▭, shall be allowed to do any work out of the regular order, unless it be by dispensation from the Grand Master; and any ▭ working under such dispensation, shall return the same to the Grand Master.

SEC. 35. A petition from the ▭ to the M∴ W∴ Grand Master, praying for a special dispensation to confer degrees, shall set forth, fully and clearly, the emergency.

SEC. 36. Advancement to the degrees may be stayed at any time, for good reasons, by the ▭ or the Master.

SEC. 37. No candidate shall receive more than one degree on the same day without dispensation from the Grand Master, nor unless he has passed a satisfactory examination in open ▭, on that degree, nor shall any ▭ confer the first section of the first, second or third degree, on more than one candidate at the same time.

BALLOTING.

SEC. 38. No ballot shall be spread, except at a regular communication, unless by special dispensation.

SEC. 39. In balloting for candidates, all members of the ▭ present shall vote, for, according to an old regulation, " no man can be entered a brother in any particular ▭, or admitted to be a member thereof, without the unanimous consent of all the members of that ▭, then present when the candidate is proposed." No Mason shall be required, by the Master or ▭, to give his reasons for the vote he has deposited, for the very secrecy of the ballot is intended to secure the independence and irresponsibility to the ▭ of the voter.

SEC. 40. The ballot shall be spread for each degree, and shall be unanimous. A unanimous ballot for each of the three degrees should be understood literally, and should be the same in each, and unanimous in all, upon the moral, intellectual and Masonic qualifications of the applicant. But in cases where the report of the committee to whom the petition is referred be unfavorable, the report shall not be considered a rejection, and the ballot shall be spread.

SEC. 41. After the ballot has been taken and duly examined, first by the Wardens, and finally by the Master, the result shall be declared by the Master, unless only one negative vote appears, in which case the Master may order the second trial of the ballot, which shall in all cases be final, nor can it be set aside by the □, Master, Grand Master, or even the Grand □.

FEES.

SEC. 42. No □ shall confer the three degrees for a less sum than thirty dollars, to be paid in advance.

RIGHTS OF WARDENS.

SEC. 43. ⌷ shall not open or call to labor unless the Master or one of the Wardens be present.

SEC. 44. Wardens may preside and confer degrees in the absence of the Master.

DIMITS.

SEC. 45. It is contrary to, and inconsistent with, the ancient usages and precepts of our order to withdraw from a subordinate □, or to reside in the neighborhood of a subordinate □ without becoming a member thereof.

SEC. 46. A masonic dimit dates from the □ record, when the same was granted, and membership ceases with said date.

CHARTERS.

SEC. 47. It is not in the power of a majority of the members of a subordinate □ to surrender the charter of said □ so long as seven Master Masons, members thereof, continue to work under said charter, according to the ancient landmarks of Masonry.

SEC. 48. Whenever the charter of a □ shall be destroyed by fire, or any other manner, or shall be stolen or surreptitiously taken and detained, or become so defaced as to be unfit for use, without the fault of the □ or Master, it shall be lawful for the Grand Master to order another charter to be issued to such □, which charter shall set forth the names of the members and officers named in the charter so lost, detained or destroyed, the Grand Communication at which it was granted, the names of the Grand Officers attached thereto, and the circumstances of its loss, destruction or detention, and shall be signed by the Grand Master, and attested by the Grand Secretary under his hand and the seal of the Grand □, without fee.

TRIALS.

Sec. 49. All trials for Masonic offenses in ▣ under the jurisdiction of this Grand □, shall be as follows: A regular charge in writing, specifying the nature of the offense, and signed by the accuser, shall be delivered to the Secretary, who shall read it at the next Regular Communication. And it shall be the duty of the Secretary to give due and timely notice to the accused of the time, place and manner of the trial, who shall be entitled to a copy of the charges, and to ample time and opportunity to prepare his defense.

Sec. 50. All Masonic trials shall be in the □ of the highest degree to which the accused has attained, in which the examination of witnesses shall take place, in the presence of both the accused and the accuser, who shall have the right to be present at all examinations of witnesses, in or out of the □, and to propose such relevant questions as they may desire.

Sec. 51. After the trial is concluded, the accused and the accuser shall be requested to retire, and, in case the trial has been in a □ of Entered Apprentices or Fellowcrafts, the □ shall then be opened on the third degree, for no decision shall be made for or against a brother, after regular trial, except in a Master Mason's □, in which the question of guilty or not guilty shall be put by the Master, in which all the members present shall be required to vote, and of which two-thirds shall be in the affirmative, or the accused shall be declared not guilty.

Sec. 52. If the verdict is guilty, the Master or presiding offi-

47

cer shall put the question as to the amount of punishment, beginning with the highest and ending with the lowest Masonic punishment herein provided. The vote on the nature of the punishment may be taken by show of hands, and decided by a two-thirds vote of the members present.

SEC. 53. If the residence of the accused is not known, or if, upon due summons, he refuses or neglects to attend, a □ may proceed to a trial without his presence.

SEC. 54. The witnesses in all Masonic trials, whether Masons or not, shall be persons who have the use of their reason, and such religious belief as to feel the obligations of an oath, and who have not been convicted of any infamous crime.

SEC. 55. The testimony of Masons shall be taken in □ or in committee; that of competent persons not Masons by a committee, on oath, administered by a competent legal officer, and may be by affidavit.

SEC. 56. A subordinate □ should not suspend a member for non-payment of dues, without written notice and fair trial.

PUNISHMENTS.

SEC. 57. The Masonic punishment which may and shall be inflicted by the Grand □ and its subordinates for unmasonic conduct, shall be either reprimand, definite or indefinite suspension, or expulsion from all the rights and privileges of Masonry.

SEC. 58. A reprimand may be either private or public, but shall not be given except by a majority vote of the members present, nor until the offender has had due notice and an opportunity for explanation or excuse, nor by any one but the acting Master, in the manner and form he may deem proper, to the offender in private, or in open □ from his appropriate station.

SEC. 59. When a Mason is expelled from a □, he is thereby expelled from all the rights and privileges of Masonry.

APPEALS—RESTORATIONS.

SEC. 60. All Masons have the right to appeal from the decisions of subordinate ▭ to the Grand □, in which case the

▢ shall furnish the Grand ▢ and the appellant with an attested copy of its proceedings on the trial, and such testimony in its possession as he may require for his defense.

SEC. 61. An application to reinstate an expelled Mason, must, in all cases, be accompanied with a recommendation from the ▢ by which the brother was expelled: *Provided*, such ▢ be still in existence.

SEC. 62. Restoration, after definite suspension by a ▢, shall take place at the expiration of the time specified in the sentence.

SEC. 63. Restoration, after indefinite suspension by a ▢, shall be by the action of such ▢ at a regular meeting, after due notice, and by a two-thirds vote of the members present.

SUMMONS.

SEC. 64. A summons issued by a subordinate ▢, or the Worshipful Master thereof, must be written or printed, and under the seal of the ▢.

SEC. 65. Any summons issued as aforesaid, need not contain any other matter, except the requisition to attend the ▢ issuing the same, or the Master thereof, when required.

SEC. 66. Every Master Mason is bound to attend before the ▢, at the meeting of the ▢ so requiring him, on being summoned or notified.

SEC. 67. Any member of a subordinate ▢ is subject to the discipline thereof, excepting only the Worshipful Master.

AMENDMENTS.

SEC. 68. No alterations or amendments shall take place in these By-Laws except by a two-thirds vote of the members present.

RULES OF ORDER

FOR CONDUCTING

BUSINESS OF GRAND LODGE.

---

1. The Most Worshipful Grand Master shall take the chair every day precisely at the hour to which the Grand ▭ shall have adjourned on the preceding day, when the journal shall be read, to the end that any mistake or improper entries may be corrected.

2. During the hours of business the members are required to keep their seats and observe strict order and decorum; and no member shall leave the hall without leave, or absent himself from the service of the Grand ▭ unless he has permission, or be sick and unable to attend.

3. No member shall be permitted to speak more than twice upon any subject, unless it is merely to explain, without permission from the Grand ▭. If any member is twice called to order at a meeting for transgressing these rules, and is guilty of a third offense of the same nature, the presiding officer shall peremptorily order him to leave the Grand ▭; and he may further be amenable to reprimand, suspension or expulsion, as the Grand ▭ shall deem proper.

4. When a question is put, it shall be the duty of every member present to vote, unless, for good cause, the Grand ▭ may excuse him; but no member shall vote upon any question in the event of which he is personally interested.

5. No motion shall be entertained until it is seconded; and there shall no debate be had thereon, until it is stated by the Chair.

6. Every motion shall be reduced to writing, with the name of the mover indorsed thereon, if the Chair or the Grand Secretary desire it.

7. When a question is under debate, no motion shall be received but to lay on the table, to commit, to amend, or to postpone indefinitely, which several motions shall have precedence in the order in which they are here arranged.

8. Any member may call for the division of a question, which shall be divided if it comprehends questions so distinct that one being taken away the rest may stand entire for the decision of the Grand ▭. A motion to strike out and insert shall be deemed indivisible.

9. When a motion has been once made and carried in the affirmative or negative, it shall be in order for any member of the majority to move for a reconsideration thereof.

10. All questions shall be propounded in the order in which they were moved, except in filling up blanks, when the largest sum and longest time shall be put first.

11. No report shall be received from any of the committees of the Grand ▭, unless the same be reduced to writing, and signed by at least a majority of the members thereof.

12. No committee shall sit during the sitting of the Grand ▭, without special leave.

13. These rules of order may be altered, added to, or abrogated, at any meeting of the Grand ▭, two-thirds of the members present concurring therin.

STANDING RESOLUTIONS

OF THE

M. W. GRAND LODGE OF COLORADO.

Resolved, That it shall be the duty of the Grand Lecturer, under the direction of the Grand Master, to visit the several ⌸ in this jurisdiction, and instruct them in the work and lectures, and any ▢ requesting his services shall pay for the same.

November, 1862.

Resolved, That if any subordinate ▢, under the jurisdiction of the M∴ W∴ Grand ▢ of Colorado, shall fail to meet, for six successive months, their charter shall be declared forfeited.

November, 1862.

Resolved, That no ▢ under the jurisdiction of this Grand ▢ shall admit to membership any brother who shall be exempt from any of the Masonic duties, obligations and privileges required by the Constitution, regulations and landmarks of the order.

November, 1863.

Resolved, That non-affiliated Masons shall be required to pay Grand ▢ dues, or not be permitted to visit any of the subordinate ⌸ in this jurisdiction more than twice.

November, 1863.

Resolved, That, from and after this communication of the Grand ▢ of Colorado, it shall not be lawful for the ⌸ under its jurisdiction to hold communications on the Sabbath day, for any purpose whatever, except to attend the funeral of a member thereof, or of a brother Master Mason.

November, 1863.

Resolved, That no subordinate ▢ under this jurisdiction shall grant a dimit to any one of its members, except for the purpose of affiliating with some other ▢, or about to remove out of the jurisdiction of this Grand ▢.

November, 1863.

Resolved, That it shall be the duty of the Grand Lecturer, under the direction of the Grand Master, to visit the several ⊟ in this jurisdiction, and instruct them in the work and lectures; and the Grand Lecturer, visiting any subordinate ▢ under the direction of the M∴ W∴ Grand Master, shall receive the same compensation as the highest representative of any subordinate ▢ attending the Grand ▢, to be paid by the ▢ requiring his services.

November, 1863.

Resolved, That when a petition has been rejected for initiation in any ▢ in this jurisdiction, the applicant shall not be allowed to petition the same ▢ in a less time than six months, nor any other ▢ in this jurisdiction, in a less time than one year.

November, 1865.

Resolved, That it shall be, and is hereby made, the imperative duty of the subordinate ⊟ in this jurisdiction to restrain, as far as possible, the Masonic crime of intemperance by trial and suspension, or expulsion, as the case may require, and for the faithful performance of that duty, the said subordinate ⊟ will be held accountable to this Grand ▢.

November, 1865.

Resolved, That this Grand ▢ requires all ⊟ under dispensation to pay a fee of one dollar and fifty cents for each Mason raised.

October, 1866.

Resolved, That it is the sense of this Grand ▢ that a member of a subordinate ▢ may, by a vote of the ▢, be stricken from the roll of membership for arrearages in dues for the space of one year.

October, 1866.

Resolved, That in all elections in Grand □ and subordinate ⌷ no person shall be declared elected, unless he shall have received a majority vote of all the members present.

October, 1867.

Resolved, That no subordinate □ shall hereafter allow its hall, or place of holding Masonic meetings, to be used for dances or other amusements, after it shall be dedicated for Masonic purposes.

October, 1867.

Resolved, That it is at variance with the spirit of Masonry to make nominations for officers in Grand or subordinate ⌷, and the practice is hereby prohibited in this Grand □ jurisdiction.

October, 1867.

Resloved, That no □ in this jurisdiction shall knowingly hereafter recognize as a Mason any citizen of Colorado who shall hereafter be made a Mason outside of the jurisdiction of this Grand □, during his citizenship, unless by permission of the □ in whose jurisdiction he resided.

October, 1868.

Resolved, That the Worshipful Master and Wardens representing the several subordinate ⌷ in this Grand □ be instructed to wear their jewel of office of their respective ⌷ in all future attendance upon this body.

October, 1868.

Resolved, That it is the sense of this Grand □ that whenever the admission of a visiting brother is objected to by a member of a subordinate □ within this jurisdiction, the Master shall refuse to admit such visiting brother.

September, 1869.

Resolved, That all subordinate ⌷ within the jurisdiction of this Grand □ be instructed not to receive a petition for affiliation from any brother holding membership outside of this jurisdiction, unless accompanied by a dimit or a certificate of good standing from the ☐ of which the petitioner was last a member.

September, 1869.

Resolved, That the Grand Secretary be authorized to collect a fee of one dollar for each certificate of standing issued to members of defunct ☐, and a like sum for each other certificate, not otherwise provided for, given by him under the seal of the Grand ☐, and that the amounts so received be paid into the library fund.

September, 1869.

———

FORM OF CERTIFICATE

OF A ☐ CONSENTING TO THE FORMATION OF A NEW ☐ AND RECOMMENDING THE PETITIONERS.

To the M∴ W∴ Grand Master of Masons in the Territory of. Colorado :

This is to certify, that at a regular meeting of ———— ☐, No. ——, held on the —— day of ————, A. D. 18 , A. L. 58 , the petition of brethren —— ————, —— ————, —— ————, —— ————, —— ————, —— ————, and —— ————, to form and open a new ☐ at ————————, county of ————, Colorado, was presented; and thereupon it was

Resolved, That the matters and things set forth in said petition are true, and that the same be recommended to the M∴ W∴ Grand Master for approval.

Attest: A. B., *Master.*

· C. D., *Secretary.*

[SEAL.]

48

FORM OF PETITION FOR A NEW ▢.

To the M∴ W∴ Grand Master of the Grand ▢ of Colorado:

We, the undersigned Master Masons in good standing, having the prosperity of the craft at heart, are anxious to exert our best endeavors to promote and diffuse the genuine principles of Freemasonry; and, that fuller opportunity for the same may be afforded us, are desirous of forming a new ▢, to be named ————.

The brother named herein for Master is able to open and close a ▢ in the three degrees, and to confer the three degrees of Masonry, according to the usual forms practiced within this jurisdiction.

We also have procured a suitable and safe room, wherein to practice Masonic rites, with convenient ante-rooms connected with the same.

The material in the town where the said ▢ is proposed to be located is amply sufficient to sustain a healthy and reputable ▢.

We, therefore, with the approbation and recommendation of ———————— ▢, No. ———, which is the nearest ▢ to our place of residence, (or is the oldest ▢ in our place of residence), respectfully pray for a dispensation empowering us to meet as a regular ▢, at ——————————————, in the county of ————————, there to discharge the duties of Freemasonry in a constitutional manner, agreeably to the original forms of the order, and the Laws of the Grand ▢. We do nominate and recommend Bro. A. B. to be the first Master; Bro. C. D. to be the first Senior Warden, and Bro. E. F. to be the first Junior Warden of said ▢.

The prayer of this petition being granted, we promise a strict obedience to the commands of the Grand Master, and to the laws and regulations of the Grand ▢.

———— ————, A. D. 18 , A. L. 58 .

(This petition must be signed by eight well known and approved Master Masons.)

INDEX.

ND - #0020 - 150223 - C0 - 229/152/22 [24] - CB - 9780332919652 - Gloss Lamination